THE ROUTINES OF
DECISION MAKING

THE ROUTINES OF DECISION MAKING

Edited by

Tilmann Betsch
Susanne Haberstroh
University of Erfurt

Psychology Press
Taylor & Francis Group
NEW YORK AND HOVE

First published by
Lawrence Erlbaum Associates, Inc., Publishers
10 Industrial Avenue
Mahwah, New Jersey 07430

This edition published 2012 by Psychology Press

Psychology Press   Psychology Press
Taylor & Francis Group   Taylor & Francis Group
711 Third Avenue   27 Church Road, Hove
New York, NY 10017   East Sussex BN3 2FA

Psychology Press is an imprint of the Taylor & Francis Group, an informa business

First issued in paperback 2012

Cover design by Kathryn Houghtaling Lacey

Library of Congress Cataloging-in-Publication Data

The routines of decision making / edited by Tilmann Betsch, Susanne Haberstroh.
    p. cm.
    Includes bibliographical references and indexes.
    ISBN 0-8058-4613-1 (alk. paper)
    1. Decision making. 2. Experience. 3. Decision making—Research. I. Betsch, Tilmann.
II. Haberstroh, Susanne.

HD30.23.R68 2004
003'.56—dc22   2004046474
                                                        CIP

ISBN13: 978-0-8058-4613-3 hardback
ISBN13: 978-0-415-65273-5 paperback

Contents

Preface

Over the course of a lifetime, human beings make countless decisions, most of which are repeated decisions. In repetitive decision making, individuals can rely on their prior knowledge and experiences. Experience helps the decision makers cope with the complexity of the real world. Consider, for instance, product decisions: Malls, catalogue companies, Internet auctions, and other types of markets offer consumers a virtually infinite set of possibilities to satisfy their needs. Fortunately, adult decision makers already know a lot about groceries, clothes, household devices, computers, TVs, or automobiles. They already hold preferences for certain brands, they can rely on advice from friends and consumer magazines, and, most important, they have a huge repertoire of behavioral routines.

Development of routines allows decision makers to maintain mastery of the situation (Athay & Darley, 1981). Once a behavioral solution to a decision problem has been learned and stored in memory, individuals can use this knowledge when they reencounter the same kind of problem. Under situational and processing constraints, routinization enables individuals to quickly arrive at a decision.

Memory and learning processes have been largely neglected in psychological decision research (Weber, Goldstein, & Busemeyer, 1991). Other disciplines, such as economic game theory and behavioral economics, devoted much more attention to the relationship among prior behavior, learning, and decision making (Foxall, 2003; Harsanyi, 1967/1968; Nash, 1951; Selten, 1965; for recent developments, see e.g., Erev & Roth, 1998). By contrast, cognitive psychologists primarily studied decision making in one-shot, novel situations. Until the late 1980s, studies on recurrent decisions were rarely documented in the judgment and decision-making literature. Significant reviews and textbooks of that time did not consider the role routines play in decision making (e.g., Abelson & Levi, 1985; Baron, 1988; Payne, Bettman, & Johnson, 1992). It was not until the 1990s that research on recurrent, experienced-based decision making began to accumulate.

The goal of this book is to provide the reader with a comprehensive overview of theory, methodology, and basic and applied research in this emerging field of psychology. We invited scholars from different subdisciplines, including experimental, social, consumer, organizational, and applied psychology, to contribute to the volume. As a leading theme, all contributions consider the relation between prior experience and decision making. The authors have different theoretical backgrounds, employ different strategies in their research, and focus on different aspects of the problem. We hope that the volume stimulates exchange and cross-fertilization among fields and helps pave the way toward an integrative approach on experience, routines, and decision making.

In the following, we briefly consider the origins of the neglect of prior experience and routines in psychological decision research. Thereafter, we sketch out early attempts of theoretical integration. Then we briefly review essential empirical results stemming mostly from the past decade. Finally, we give an overview of the chapters.

ORIGINS OF NEGLECTING ROUTINES: THE SIMILARITY TRAP

Empirical sciences rely on observations to develop and test their theories. Thus, the theoretical and phenomenological levels are necessarily intertwined. The physical surface of appearances can do much to mold the shape of scientific theories. Often principles of similarity guide early stages of explanation. The similarity between phenomena invites the conclusion that they share joint properties, are brought forth by similar processes, or even represent a causal relationship. However, relying on similarity may yield invalid concepts of reality. In their seminal work on judgmental heuristics, Tversky and Kahneman (1983) showed that the similarity between an event and a category or mental model could cause serious fallacies in judgment.

Even professional scientists are prone to being led astray by phenomenological similarity and dissimilarity. In early chemical theory, for example, combustion and corrosion were assumed to involve different chemical processes. The physical appearance of these reactions is different indeed. Combustion (e.g., the burning of carbon) involves a rapid chemical reaction accompanied by the generation of heat, sound, and light. In contrast, corrosion (e.g., the rusting of iron) is a comparatively slow reaction that lacks dramatic side effects. In accordance with the phenomenological distinction, chemists in the 17th century proposed different theories to account for burning and rusting. Today we know that both reactions, although they appear to be distinct on the phenomenological level, belong to the same broad class of chemical reactions involving the transfer of oxygen.

Reliance on phenomenological similarity as a guiding principle for theory development has been hindering progress in many other areas of scholarly research. It manifests itself in narrow definitions of fields and in separation between peer communities in which scientific exchange takes place. Each camp attempts to model only an exclusive set of findings and neglects the evidence obtained in neighboring fields. As a consequence, scientists accumulate local theories of narrow scope for phenomena that look different on the surface, but might reflect identical underlying processes. At this stage of scientific progress, the advocates of integration must face a rivalry or even open dispute between camps in which each one resists claiming an emergent property of its subject of study. It seems that this is the point where we currently stand in decision research.

Scientific communities such as the Society for Judgment and Decision Making (JDM) and the European Association of Decision Making (EADM) host a couple of camps that differ with regard to their historical origins, theoretical pre-assumptions, and interests in phenomena and research methodology. One year after the Millennium, a special issue of the *Journal of Behavioral Decision Making* (Vol. 15, No. 5) provided a forum for the dispute among subdisciplines by focusing on one as a target—the Naturalistic Decision Making (NDM) group. NDM was initiated by a conference in 1989 and is strongly associated with the work by Gary Klein (Klein, 1989, 1999; Klein, Orasanu, Calderwood, & Zsambock, 1993; Zsambok & Klein, 1997). In a nutshell, NDM can be considered "an attempt to understand how people make decisions in real world contexts that are meaningful and familiar to them" (Lipshitz, Klein, Orasanu, & Salas, 2001, p. 332). This approach opposes both the methodology and theoretical pre-assumptions of classical judgment and decision-making research, which is rooted in utility theory. In the debate between NDM and utility theorists, it becomes apparent that many of the opponents' arguments originate from the dissimilarity of the phenomena to be studied in mutual domains.

Scholars of utility theory have been focusing on waging problems resembling those described by Blaise Pascal in his ingenious reflections on rational choice (Pascal, 1670/1966). Waging is a slow and cold process that involves conscious deliberation. Utility theorists commonly study deliberative decisions by help of the so-called *gambling paradigm* (Goldstein & Hogarth, 1997). In the gambling paradigm, individuals are confronted with a novel and well-structured decision problem. The problem is comprised of a set of alternatives, which lead to a limited number of outcomes. The experimenter gives the utility values and probabilities of these outcomes. Decision making in such problems involves the deliberative evaluation of stated utilities and risks and the application of a decision rule resting on an integration of utilities and subjective probabilities.

In contrast, NDM researchers focus on routine decision making. Decisions are studied in the field where experts—such as fire-ground commanders, surgeons, or aircraft pilots—make numerous high-stakes decisions under severe contextual constraints. Because these choices must occur quickly, they are not usually accompanied by time-consuming deliberation. Rather they seem to be borne out from intuition, which capitalizes on a huge arsenal of routines, learned preferences, and expectations.

At first glance, deliberative and routine decision making may seem to be as distinct from one another as corrosion and combustion. The dissimilarity of these phenomena seems to justify the separation between different subdisciplines in decision research. The debate between NDM and classical decision researchers has been initiated only recently and is currently in the limelight. However, the problem of separation in decision research is much older. It has its origins in the schism between behaviorism and cognitive psychology in the 20th century. The fall of behaviorism in the 1950s was accompanied by a shift of the vision of man. Cognitive psychologists began to view humans as naive scientists who process information in a quasirational fashion. In accordance with this perspective, cognitive theories often borrowed on extensional models of information processing from other sciences such as mathematics, statistics, and cybernetics. The foundation of psychological decision research falls into this period of time. Edwards (1954), Savage (1954), and others suggested using principles of rationality and probability theory to describe human decision making.

Thereafter, decision making was studied in two separate fields using different methodologies. Learning psychologists studied recurrent choices and principles of routinization from the perspective of association theory. They commonly employed conditioning procedures in the laboratory using animals as subjects. Meanwhile cognitive psychologists studied one-shot decision making within the framework of rational choice theory. They commonly relied on variants of the gambling paradigm, which confronts human subjects with novel decision problems. Both groups pursued their lines of research over decades without any substantial cross-fertilization.

EARLY THEORETICAL ATTEMPTS
OF INTEGRATION

Unlike mainstream decision research, some early attempts were made to delineate integrative theories of decision making. Examples are the conflict model (Janis & Mann, 1977) and the contingency model (Beach & Mitchell,

1978). Both models reflect the conviction that decision makers rarely tend to maximize expected utility in their choices, but rather seek to achieve satisfying outcomes. Bound by situational and processing constraints, individuals were assumed to employ shortcut strategies or heuristics to arrive at their decision. These basic assumptions reflect Herbert Simon's concept of bounded rationality (Simon, 1967, 1982). Subsequently, the results accumulated in the heuristics-and-biases program at that time (Kahneman, Slovic, & Tversky, 1982).

The conflict model assumes that decisions are anchored on prior choices (routines) (Janis & Mann, 1977). Prior choices are assumed to be repeated in the future unless they are uncontested. If the context signals that routine maintenance might produce malevolent consequences, decision makers will employ different shortcut versions of the expected-utility rule to determine whether they should maintain or deviate from their routine. The contingency model also adopts a multiple strategy perspective. Beach and Mitchell (1978) proposed that decision making starts with the selection of decision strategy. Strategy selection is assumed to be contingent on a number of contextual and personal factors, such as time constraints and motivation. The individual's repertoire of decision strategies contains analytic rules—for instance, the expected-utility rule and nonanalytic ones, such as a "habit." A habit can be considered a rule stating to choose the behavior that was beneficial in the past (the routine).

At the same time, the topic of routines was investigated in another area of cognitive decision research. In social psychology,[1] Triandis (1977) and Bentler and Speckart (1979) extended the model of reasoned action (Fishbein & Ajzen, 1974) by including a habit component. The model of reasoned action proposes that behavioral choices are guided by attitudes and social norms. Attitudes are thought to reflect the linear aggregation of beliefs and evaluations of a behavior's outcomes. As such the attitude concept dovetails with the concept of expected utility. Bentler and Speckart (1979), however, assumed that reason could be overruled by routines. Employing a structural equation approach, they showed that the predictive power of the Fishbein–Ajzen model could be increased if one included the frequency of prior behavior as a predictor variable. The most comprehensive refinement of the Fishbein–Ajzen model was put forward by Triandis (1977), who explicitly spelled out the interdependence between routines and deliberatively formed intentions on choice. The major assumption of his model states that the impact of intentions on choice decreases as a reciprocal

---

[1]The interplay between prior knowledge and new evidence has also been addressed by a wide range of social judgment theories (e.g., Higgins, Rholes, & Jones, 1977; Kruglanski & Webster, 1996; Srull & Wyer, 1989). It is beyond the scope of this introductory chapter to discuss this literature. In the present review, we concentrate on those approaches that deal with preferential decision making or behavioral choice.

function of habit strength. Habit strength is assumed to correlate positively with behavior repetition. Moreover, the model considers a number of other variables, such as physiological arousal, affect, and context factors. Decision research, both in social and cognitive psychology, was also influenced by Abelson's work on scripted processing (Abelson, 1976). In decision making, scripts may serve as if–then rules connecting implementation of a routine with antecedent conditions.

Unfortunately, the initial impact of these integrative approaches on decision research was marginal at best. It took the field more than another decade until cognitive psychologists started to systematically study the routines of decision making in real-life settings and in the lab. This movement independently arose in the early 1990s in different camps of decision research. As already stated, a band of researchers had started to observe routine decisions of experts in natural contexts, the beginning of the NDM research program (e.g., Klein, 1989). Consumer researchers began to investigate the effects of prior purchases and brand loyalty on subsequent decisions (e.g., Muthukrishnan, 1995). In social psychology, research on habits celebrated its renaissance (e.g., Verplanken, Aarts, van Knippenberg, & van Knippenberg, 1994). In laboratory decision research, the first attempts were made to experimentally manipulate routine strength and assess its impact on deliberative decision making (Betsch, Fiedler, & Brinkmann, 1998).

When this movement began, it was considered a revolution (Beach & Potter, 1992), which has not yet reached its climax. Today we observe that research on routinized decision making has an increasing impact on the field, but it is still far away from tackling the dominion of models of calculated decision making. The same is true for other areas such as social psychology. Recently, Verplanken and Aarts (1999) noted that "habit" is still not an entry in textbooks and reviews of social psychology in general and attitude research in particular. Recently, in a review paper on the role of habits in the attitude–behavior relation, Icek Ajzen (2002) claimed that consideration of prior behavior would not be necessary to explain and predict behavior.

In the next section, we briefly review the evidence on the role of routines in decision making. We show that understanding how humans make decisions is not possible without acknowledging the role of routines.

ROUTINES AND DECISION MAKING: A REVIEW OF THE EVIDENCE

Recurrent decision making involves feedback learning. In most cases, the behavior's consequences indicate whether one has made a good or bad choice. Thus, experience helps the decision maker discern good and bad alternatives. Once a good or satisfying solution to a decision problem has been formulated, it can be added to the routine repertoire. Therefore, decision makers who are confronted with familiar decision problems can capitalize on their behavioral knowledge. They become aware of potential solutions on recognition of the situation (Klein, 1999). In contrast, individuals facing a novel decision problem are ignorant in the beginning (otherwise these problems would not have been novel to them). They must search for behavioral candidates, evaluate the consequences of these behaviors, and apply some sort of decision rule to identify a promising solution. As such, experience makes an important difference: Recurrent decisions are anchored on learned solutions or routines, whereas novel decisions are not. As we see later, routines systematically influence each step of the decision process.

ROUTINES AND THE GENERATION OF BEHAVIORAL ALTERNATIVES

After encountering a decision problem, individuals first have to identify a set of eligible behaviors. In classical decision research, especially in gambling studies, the experimenter determines the behavioral alternatives; the individual does not need to search for alternatives because they are already part of the stimulus material. As a consequence of this research strategy, we know very little about how decision makers generate options in novel situations (Johnson & Raab, 2003).

In contrast, in recurrent decision making, alternatives are generated automatically. This is not to say that *all* alternatives are automatically generated, but at least routines are automatically activated from memory when a familiar decision problem is recognized (Aarts & Dijksterhuis, 2000; Klein, 1989). The automatic activation of routines may involve simple stimulus–response mechanisms (Triandis, 1977) or perhaps more complex processes, such as pattern matching, which rests on parallel processing of multiple cues (Klein, 1989). Not surprisingly, routine activation is facilitated by all factors that increase accessibility in memory (e.g., frequency of repetition). With increasing repetition, routines can freeze into habits. When a routine has become a habit, the entire process from behavior recognition to implementation can be performed automatically (Hull, 1943; James, 1890; Ouelette & Wood, 1998; Ronis, Yates, & Kirscht, 1988).

ROUTINES AND THE SEARCH FOR INFORMATION

Routines impact on the individual's search for information before a choice is made. First of all, routines may generally decrease the need for consideration of new information because the decision maker already knows of a promising alternative. Accordingly, strong routine individuals are prone to collect less information and use less elaborate search strategies than weak routine individuals (Aarts, Verplanken, & van Knippenberg, 1997; Verplanken, Aarts, & van Knippenberg, 1997). Moreover, routine decision makers are susceptible to confirmation biases when searching through the problem space (Betsch, Haberstroh, Glöckner, Haar, & Fiedler, 2001, Exp. 2). If the situation appears highly similar to those under which the routine has been established, individuals tend to focus on confirmatory information and avoid consideration of evidence that challenges the routine. However, even subtle context cues, which reduce the degree of perceived similarity between prior and current situations, can prevent routine decision makers from confirmation biases (Betsch et al., 2001, Exp. 2). As such, the ease of recognition of a decision situation strongly influences processing of new evidence. Therefore, and as Klein (1989) noted, experts are flexible in their choices especially if significant contextual changes occur.

ROUTINES AND THE APPRAISAL OF EVIDENCE

Routines not only influence how individuals search for information, but also how they appraise the encoded evidence. Although research on appraisal processes in routinized decision making is still in its infancy, there are a few studies available underlining that routines can decrease the relative weight of evidence contradicting routine choice. Individuals are especially likely to attenuate contradicting evidence if cognitive capacities are constrained (Betsch, Brinkmann, Fiedler, & Breining, 1999; Betsch et al., 1998). Processing constraints, however, are not a necessary condition for the occurrence of attenuation effects. Even if decision makers have enough time and capacity, they tend to discard unfavorable evidence if their routines are strong. Accordingly, Betsch and colleagues (2001, Exp. 1) found that strong routine participants maintained their routines despite new evidence, whereas weak routine participants did not.

It is important to stress that these attenuation effects occurred independently from the search strategy people employed. In one study, Betsch and colleagues (1999) led participants to maximize choice frequency for one out of three alternatives in a series of recurrent multi-attribute decision tasks. One week after routine acquisition, participants returned to the lab to complete another set of decision tasks containing the previously preferred alternative. Each task required participants to actively search for information prior to making a decision. Participants' information search was traced by using a variant of the "mouselab" paradigm (Johnson, Payne, Schkade, & Bettman, 1986). With increasing time pressure, participants switched from compensatory to noncompensatory strategies of information acquisition. This change in strategy was expected based on the literature on adaptive decision making (Payne, Bettman, & Johnson, 1993). In anticipation of this result, the authors arranged the outcomes in such a fashion that the retrieved information would challenge the routine alternative and favor alternative choices. Consequently, changes in information search led participants to detect evidence that contested the routine alternative. Nevertheless, with increasing time pressure, participants tended to maintain their routines. This finding indicates that routine decision makers may discount disconfirming evidence especially under the presence of situational constraints (see also Betsch et al., 1998).

Attenuation effects, however, are not limited to constrained situations. With increasing repetition of routine choices in the past, the likelihood that attenuation effects will occur in unconstrained situations increases. In a series of studies, Betsch and colleagues manipulated the strength of routines in participants making recurrent decisions in a microworld simulation (Betsch, Glöckner, & Haberstroh, 2000; Betsch et al., 2001). In these simulations, participants could buy forecasts from a market research institute before making trading decisions. From the learning phase of the experiment, participants knew that these forecasts were highly reliable (80% hit rate). As a matter of a fact, they relied on the forecasts during the initial phase of the study. However, with increasing repetition of a routine choice, they tended to neglect the forecasts as if they suggested pursuing alternative courses of action.

Altogether these studies demonstrate that routines can yield conservatism in decision making. Clearly, these effects cannot be attributed to deficits in information search or encoding. However, the processes underlying these attenuation effects are not yet well understood. Specifically, the present evidence does not allow us to decide whether routinized decision makers attenuate the validity, probability, importance, or value of the evidence they had considered before they made their choices.

ROUTINES AND THE IMPLEMENTATION OF BEHAVIOR

In the previous sections, we reviewed several findings indicating that routinized decision makers are apt to maintain their routine even in the light of new evidence that suggests deviation from prior choice patterns. Nevertheless, under certain circumstances, individuals may decide to depart from a routine. For instance, if a routine behavior repeatedly produces negative outcomes, one may eventually decide to quit the routine and pursue another course of action in the future. Such deviation intentions do not guarantee, however, that the decision maker will actually implement the divergent course of action. Several studies have shown that routines can influence future behavior independent from intentions (e.g., Bagozzi, 1981; Beck & Ajzen, 1991; Bentler & Speckart, 1979; Fredricks & Dosset, 1983; Landis, Triandis, & Adamopoulus, 1978; Mittal, 1988; Montano & Taplin, 1991; Orbell, Blair, Sherlock, & Conner, 2001; Ouelette & Wood, 1998; Sheeran & Orbell, 1999; Verplanken, Aarts, van Knippenberg, & Moonen, 1998).

Psychologists have been interested in the dynamics of routine deviation for a long time. Over a century ago, Hugo Münsterberg (1889–1892) reported a number of observations obtained from self-studies. All involved deviation from everyday routines. For instance, one day, Münsterberg decided to quit with his routine of leaving his office through a door leading to the hallway. His new intention was, instead, to leave his office through a different door that led to his secretary's room. To his annoyance, he subsequently found himself trying to use the hallway door several times. About 30 years later, Georg Schwarz, a student of Kurt Lewin, began to study the implementation of deviation decisions in the laboratory (Schwarz, 1927, 1933). In his case studies, he provided the first empirical demonstration of counterintentional routine choice. He termed this phenomenon *relapse error* ("Rückfallfehler," Schwarz, 1927, p. 125). More recently, relapse errors have been referred to as *action slips* (Reason, 1992) or implementation slips during relearning (Heckhausen & Beckmann, 1990). The susceptibility to relapse errors increases with enhanced routine strength (e.g., Bentler & Speckart, 1979; Norman & Shallice, 1986). However, routines need not be frozen into habits to produce relapse errors. Even low rates of routine repetition can produce counterintentional effects. Empirical evidence indicates that when the implementation phase is constrained by time pressure, individuals were unable to deviate from their prior routine in over 70% of their choices (Betsch, Haberstroh, Molter, & Glöckner, 2004).

FURTHER FINDINGS

The activation of routines from memory affects motivation. Recently, it has been shown that attainment means can activate the goals they typically serve (Shah & Kruglanski, 2003). Accordingly, activation of routines may evoke a tendency to maintain them because they activate the goals they had promoted in the past. Moreover, the valence of a routine may increase with the number of experiences (Muthukrishnan, 1995). Consequently, a routine choice may seem to be more attractive than novel alternatives even if they dominate the routine. This can cause a status quo bias (i.e., a tendency to keep with prior courses of action instead of changing to better alternatives). The status quo bias is a robust finding and has been documented relatively early in research on repeated decision making (e.g., Samuelson & Zeckhauser, 1988). These biases do not require frequent choice repetition; even single choices can have motivational effects on subsequent decisions. A famous example is the endowment effect (Thaler, 1980). The valence of a good increases when it becomes part of a person's endowment. After having purchased a product, participants are reluctant to trade it in for an equivalent amount of money (Beggan, 1992; Kahneman, Knetsch, & Thaler, 1991). Furthermore, choice repetition strengthens the endowment effect, although choice repetition is not necessarily a condition to increase an object's value. Evaluation also increases with mere duration of ownership (Strahilevitz & Loewenstein, 1998).

EXPLAINING ROUTINE EFFECTS IN DECISION MAKING

In a recent article, Betsch and colleagues reviewed theories of preferential decision making and applied them to explain and predict several routine effects (Betsch, Haberstroh, & Höhle, 2002). It turned out that the arsenal of cognitive decision theories as a whole allows us to derive post hoc explanations for many routine effects with the help of a few auxiliary assumptions. As such, the pessimistic view that routines are beyond the scope of decision theory is not justified. Unfortunately, only a few theories are able to make clear-cut a priori predictions about how routines influence decision making. In particular, decision theories have great difficulties to cover the processes by which prior behavior impacts information search and appraisal of new information. Remarkably, the Triandis (1977) model—one of the earliest integrative approaches to routinized decision making—reveals the highest extent of predictive power. The a priori predictions derived from this model converge with a substantial amount of the evidence. Specifically, the Triandis model accounts for the influences of routines on behavior generation and choice implementation. It also predicts that the impact of counterevidence on the routine would decrease with increasing routine repetition. However, the impact of routines on information search and the moderating influences of context factors, such as time pressure and novelty of the situation, are not predicted by the model.

In summary, we need to create integrative models to understand the dynamics of routine decision making. The present volume was inspired by the notion that it is worthwhile to pursue an integrated decision science. The next section gives an overview of the contributions to this volume.

OVERVIEW OF THE CHAPTERS

The chapters are ordered in four parts. The first part comprises theoretical frameworks and models that link prior experience, behavioral routines, and subsequent decision making. The second part contains essential empirical results on experienced-based decision making obtained from laboratory research with nonexpert participants. It also addresses issues of methodology in research on routine decision making. The third part focuses on applied research in such domains as aviation, firefighting, sports, and consumer decision making. Finally, the fourth part presents techniques as to how routine decision making can be taught to experts.

PART I: UNDERSTANDING AND MODELING
THE ROUTINES OF DECISION MAKING

Joseph G. Johnson and Jerome R. Busemeyer (chap. 1) put forward a general model of decision making called *rule-based decision field theory*. The authors introduce a computational model of transitions among decision strategies that is capable of accounting for several of the routine effects discussed herein. Richard P. Bagozzi and Utpal M. Dholakia (chap. 2) provide a broad theoretical framework of goal setting and goal striving. Within this framework, they analyze the role of prior experience and routines on decision making (goal setting) and the implementation of choices (goal striving). Tilmann Betsch (chap. 3) introduces an affect-based approach to routinized decision making called *preference theory*. He applies preference theory to predict conditions under which experienced deciders maintain or deviate from their routines. Robin M. Hogarth (chap. 4) provides a framework for integrating two systems of thought—the tacit or intuitive and the deliberate or analytic system. He discusses the conditions under which intuition resulting from prior learning yields accuracy or biases in judgment and decision making. Peter Sedlmeier (chap. 5) also considers the transition between learning and subsequent intuitions in judgment and decision making. He shows how PASS, an associative learning model, can be applied to understand how intuitions evolve from prior learning. David M. Sanbonmatsu, Kort C. Prince, Sam Vanous, and Steven S. Posavac (chap. 6) focus on the role of attitudes in routinized decision making. Their framework represents an attempt to integrate the research on the attitude–behavior relation from social psychology and behavioral decision-making research from cognitive psychology.

PART II: THE ROUTINES OF DECISION MAKING:
BASIC RESEARCH

Nigel Harvey and Ilan Fischer (chap. 7) examine the conditions under which outcome feedback affects subsequent performance in five different types of judgment and decision making: multiple cue probability learning, advice taking, confidence judgment, probability estimation, and dynamic decision making. Frank R. Kardes, A. V. Muthukrishnan, and Vladimir Pashkevich (chap. 8) discuss the effects of experience and motivation on judgment and choice. Based on a review of the literature, they spell out a few conditions under which routines and motivation decrease decision accuracy. Helmut Jungermann and Katrin Fischer (chap. 9) present results from research on advice giving and taking (i.e., a type of situation under which a nonroutinized decision maker has to rely on the routines of another). They show that this informational asymmetry systematically evokes different decision strategies in advisors and clients. Torsten Reimer, Anne-Louise Bornstein, and Klaus Opwis (chap. 10) report results from studies on group decision making and problem solving. They demonstrate that routines of the group members can systematically impair group performance in a transfer task. Herbert Bless and Eric R. Igou (chap. 11) focus on the conditions determining when decision makers rely on prior knowledge or new evidence in judgment and decision making. They review empirical evidence indicating that individuals are more likely to rely on their prior knowledge when they are in a positive mood state. Susanne Haberstroh, Tilmann Betsch, Andreas Glöckner, Thomas Haar, and Anja Stiller (chap. 12) introduce a microworld simulation (COMMERCE) to study routines and decision making in the laboratory. They review the results from a couple of studies using COMMERCE as a research tool. Bas Verplanken, Vemund Myrbakk, and Erik Rudi (chap. 13) focus on automatic routines or habits. After a brief overview of essential research in the area of habitual decision making, the authors evaluate different techniques to measure habits.

PART III: THE ROUTINES OF DECISION MAKING: APPLIED RESEARCH

James Shanteau, Brian M. Friel, Rickey R. Thomas, and John Raacke (chap. 14) present a longitudinal study on the development of expertise in a professional air traffic control simulation. They introduce the Cochran–Weiss–Shanteau (CWS) measure of expertise, which indexes consistency and discrimination of the individual's responses to different decision situations. Mary M. Omodei, Jim McLennan, and Alexander J. Wearing (chap. 15) study routinized decision making in experienced firemen under natural conditions. They describe nonreactive methods for data collection in real-world environments that are characterized by high stakes, time pressure, and complexity. Michaela Wänke and Malte Friese (chap. 16) review research from the literature on consumer decision making. Focusing on the case of brand loyalty, they discuss how prior experience with a brand impacts on information search and appraisal of new product information. Henning Plessner (chap. 17) reviews the literature of referee decisions in sports. From a social cognition perspective, he analyzes the conditions under which referee decisions are biased or profit from the expert's prior experience and routines.

PART IV: EDUCATING THE ROUTINES OF DECISION MAKING

Karol G. Ross, James W. Lussier, and Gary Klein (chap. 18) describe how decision skills can be trained in experts (e.g., in battlefield commanders who already possess a huge repertoire of routines). The trainings are embedded in their theoretical framework—the recognition-primed decision model. David W. Glasspool and John Fox (chap. 19) present the domino model as a cognitive framework for understanding routine decision making. They show how this framework can be applied in aiding and educating practical decisions in health care settings. Finally, in chapter 20, we summarize the contributions to this book. We discuss current themes, advances in research and theorizing, and speculate on directions for future research.

ACKNOWLEDGMENTS

The book is partly based on the contributions to a conference on "Experience-Based Decision Making" held at the University of Heidelberg, Germany, in 2001. The conference was generously sponsored by the German Science Foundation (Deutsche Forschungsgemeinschaft) via the national research grant SFB 504, "Rationality Concepts and Economic Modeling." We gratefully acknowledge this financial support.

REFERENCES

Aarts, H., & Dijksterhuis, A. (2000). Habits as knowledge structures: Automaticity in goal-directed behavior. *Journal of Personality and Social Psychology, 78*, 53–63.

Aarts, H., Verplanken, B., & van Knippenberg, A. (1997). Habit and information use in travel mode choices. *Acta Psychologica, 96*, 1–14.

Abelson, R. P. (1976). Script processing in attitude formation and decision making. In J. S. Carroll & J. W. Payne (Eds.), *Cognition and social behavior* (pp. 33–45). Hillsdale, NJ: Lawrence Erlbaum Associates.

Abelson, R. P., & Levi, A. (1985). Decision making and decision theory. In G. Lindzey & E. Aronson (Eds.), *Handbook of social psychology* (Vol. 1, pp. 231–309). New York: Random House.

Ajzen, I. (2002). Residual effects of past on later behavior: Habituation and the reasoned action perspectives. *Personality and Social Psychology Review, 6*, 107–122.

Athay, M., & Darley, J. M. (1981). Toward an interaction-centered theory of personality. In N. Cantor & J. F. Kihlstrom (Eds.), *Personality, cognition and social interaction* (pp. 55–83). Hillsdale, NJ: Lawrence Erlbaum Associates.

Bagozzi, R. P. (1981). Attitudes, intentions, and behavior: A test of some key hypotheses. *Journal of Personality and Social Psychology, 41,* 607–627.

Baron, J. (1988). *Thinking and deciding.* Cambridge: Cambridge University Press.

Beach, L. R., & Mitchell, T. R. (1978). A contingency model for the selection of decision strategies. *Academy Management Review, 3,* 439–449.

Beach, L. R., & Potter, R. E. (1992). The pre-choice screening of options. *Acta Psychologica, 81,* 115–126.

Beck, L., & Ajzen, I. (1991). Predicting dishonest actions using the theory of planned behavior. *Journal of Research in Personality, 25,* 285–301.

Beggan, J. K. (1992). On the social nature of nonsocial perception: The mere ownership effect. *Journal of Personality and Social Psychology, 62,* 229–237.

Bentler, P. M., & Speckart, G. (1979). Models of attitude–behavior relations. *Psychological Review, 86,* 452–464.

Betsch, T., Brinkmann, B. J., Fiedler, K., & Breining, K. (1999). When prior knowledge overrules new evidence: Adaptive use of decision strategies and the role of behavioral routines. *Swiss Journal of Psychology, 58,* 151–160.

Betsch, T., Fiedler, K., & Brinkmann, B. J. (1998). Behavioral routines in decision making: The effects of novelty in task presentation and time pressure on routine maintenance and deviation. *European Journal of Social Psychology, 28,* 861–878.

Betsch, T., Glöckner, A., & Haberstroh, S. (2000). COMMERCE—A micro-world simulation to study routine maintenance and deviation in repeated decision making. *Methods of Psychological Research, 5*(2), online.

Betsch, T., Haberstroh, S., Glöckner, A., Haar, T., & Fiedler, K. (2001). The effects of routine strength on adaptation and information search in recurrent decision making. *Organizational Behavior and Human Decision Processes, 84,* 23–53.

Betsch, T., Haberstroh, S., & Höhle, C. (2002). Explaining routinized decision making—a review of theories and models. *Theory and Psychology, 12,* 453–488.

Betsch, T., Haberstroh, S., Molter, B., & Glöckner, A. (2004). Oops—I did it again: When prior knowledge overrules intentions. *Organizational Behavior and Human Decision Processes, 93,* 62–74.

Edwards, W. (1954). The theory of decision making. *Psychological Bulletin, 51,* 380–417.

Erev, I., & Roth, A. (1998). Predicting how people play games: Reinforcement learning in games with unique mixed strategy equilibrium. *American Economic Review, 88,* 848–881.

Fishbein, M., & Ajzen, I. (1974). Attitudes towards objects as predictors of single and multiple behavioral criteria. *Psychological Review, 81,* 59–74.

Foxall, G. R. (2003). The behavior analysis of consumer choice: An introduction to the special issue. *Journal of Economic Psychology, 24,* 581–588.

Fredricks, A. J., & Dosset, D. L. (1983). Attitude–behavior relations: A comparison of the Fishbein–Ajzen and the Bentler–Speckart models. *Journal of Personality and Social Psychology, 45,* 501–512.

Goldstein, W. M., & Hogarth, R. W. (1997). *Research on judgment and decision making: Currents, connections and controversies.* Cambridge: Cambridge University Press.

Harsanyi, J. C. (1967/1968). Games with incomplete information played by "Bayesian Players." *Management Science, 14,* 159–182, 320–334, 486–502.

Heckhausen, H., & Beckmann, J. (1990). Intentional action and action slips. *Psychological Review, 97,* 36–48.

Higgins, E. T., Rholes, W. S., & Jones, C.R. (1977). Category accessibility and impression formation. *Journal of Experimental Social Psychology, 13,* 141–154.

Hull, C.L. (1943). *Principles of behavior.* New York: Appleton-Century-Crofts.

James, W. (1890). *The principles of psychology* (Vol. 1). New York: Dover.

Janis, I. L., & Mann, L. (1977). *Decision making: A psychological analysis of conflict, choice, and commitment.* New York: The Free Press.

Johnson, E. J., Payne, J. W., Schkade, D. A., & Bettman, J. R. (1986). *Monitoring information processing and decisions: The mouselab system.* Unpublished manuscript, Center for Decision Studies, Fuqua School of Business, Duke University.

Johnson, J., & Raab, M. (2003). Take the first: Option generation and resulting choices. *Organizational Behavior and Human Decision Processes, 91,* 215–229.

Kahneman, D., Knetsch, J. L., & Thaler, R. (1991). Anomalies: The endowment effect, loss aversion and status quo bias. *Journal of Economic Perspectives, 5,* 193–206.

Kahneman, D., Slovic, P., & Tversky, A. (Eds.). (1982). *Judgment under uncertainty: Heuristics and biases.* Cambridge: Cambridge University Press.

Klein, G. A. (1989). Recognition-primed decisions. *Advances in Man-Machine System Research, 5,* 47–92.

Klein, G. A. (1999). *Sources of power. How people make decisions.* Cambridge, MA: MIT Press.

Klein, G. A., Orasanu, J., Calderwood, R., & Zsambock, C. E. (1993). *Decision making in action: Models and methods.* Norwood, NJ: Ablex.

Kruglanski, A. W., & Webster, D. M. (1996). Motivated closing of the mind: "Seizing" and "freezing." *Psychological Review, 103,* 263–283.

Landis, D., Triandis, H. C., & Adamopoulos, J. (1978). Habit and behavioral intentions as predictors of social behavior. *The Journal of Social Psychology, 106,* 227–237.

Lipshitz, R., Klein, G., Orasanu, J., & Salas, E. (2001). Taking stock of naturalistic decision making. *Journal of Behavioral Decision Making, 14,* 331–352.

Mittal, B. (1988). Achieving higher seat belt usage: The role of habit in bridging the attitude-behavior gap. *Journal of Applied Social Psychology, 18,* 993–1016.

Montano, D. E., & Taplin, S. H. (1991). A test of an expanded theory of reasoned action to predict mammography participation. *Social Science and Medicine, 32,* 733–741.

Münsterberg, H. (1889–1892). *Beiträge zur experimentellen Psychologie* [Contributions to experimental psychology]. Freiburg: Mohr.

Muthukrishnan, A. V. (1995). Decision ambiguity and incumbent brand advantage. *Journal of Consumer Research, 15,* 1–18.

Nash, J. F. (1951). Non-cooperative games. *Annals of Mathematics, 54,* 286–295.

Norman, D. A., & Shallice, T. (1986). Attention to action: Willed and automatic control of behavior. In P. J. Davidson, G. E. Schwarts, & D. Shapiro (Eds.), *Consciousness and self-regulation. Advances in research and theory* (Vol. 4, pp. 1–18). New York: Plenum.

Orbell, S., Blair, C., Sherlock, K., & Conner, M. (2001). The theory of planned behavior and ecstasy use: Roles for habit and perceived control over taking versus obtaining substances. *Journal of Applied Social Psychology, 31,* 31–47.

Ouelette, J. A., & Wood, W. (1998). Habit and intention in everyday life: The multiple processes by which past behavior predicts future behavior. *Psychological Bulletin, 124,* 54–74.

Pascal, B. (1670/1966). *Pensées.* London: Penguin.

Payne, J. W., Bettman, J. R., & Johnson, E. J. (1992). Behavioral decision research: A constructive processing perspective. *Annual Review of Psychology, 43,* 87–131.

Payne, J. W., Bettman, J. R., & Johnson, E. J. (1993). *The adaptive decision maker.* Cambridge: Cambridge University Press.

Reason, J. (1992). *Human error.* Cambridge: Cambridge University Press.

Ronis, D. L., Yates, J. F., & Kirscht, J. P. (1988). Attitudes, decisions and habits as determinants of repeated behavior. In A. R. Pratkanis, S. J. Breckler, & A. G. Greenwald (Eds.), *Attitude structure and function* (pp. 213–239). Hillsdale, NJ: Lawrence Erlbaum Associates.

Samuelson, W., & Zeckhauser, R. (1988). Status quo bias in decision making. *Journal of Risk and Uncertainty, 1,* 7–59.

Savage, L. J. (1954). *The foundation of statistics.* New York: Wiley.

Schwarz, G. (1927). Über Rückfälligkeit bei Umgewöhnung: 1. Teil: Rückfalltendenz und Verwechselungsgefahr [On lapses during habit change: Part 1: Tendency towards relapses and problems of confusion]. *Psychologische Forschung, 9*, 86–158.

Schwarz, G. (1933). Über Rückfälligkeit bei Umgewöhnung: 2. Teil: Über Handlungsganzheiten und ihre Bedeutung für die Rückfälligkeit [On lapses during habit change: Part 2: On the meanings of whole action units for the likelihood of relapses]. *Psychologische Forschung, 18*, 143–190.

Selten, R. (1965). Spieltheoretische Behandlung eines Oligopolmodells mit Nachfrageträgheit [A game-theoretic approach to oligopol models with inert demand]. *Zeitschrift für die gesamte Staatswissenschaft, 121*, 301–324, 667–689.

Shah, J. Y., & Kruglanski, A. W. (2003). When opportunity knocks: Bottom-up priming of goals by means and its effects on self-regulation. *Journal of Personality and Social Psychology, 84*, 1109–1122.

Sheeran, P., & Orbell, S. (1999). Implementation intentions and repeated behaviour. Augmenting the predictive validity of the theory of planned behaviour. *European Journal of Social Psychology, 29*, 349–369.

Simon, H. A. (1967). Motivational and emotional controls of cognition. *Psychological Review, 74*, 29–39.

Simon, H. A. (1982). *Models of bounded rationality*. Cambridge, MA: MIT Press.

Srull, T. K., & Wyer, R. S., Jr. (1989). Person memory and judgment. *Psychological Review, 96*, 58–83.

Strahilevitz, M. A., & Loewenstein, G. (1998). The effect of ownership history on the valuation of objects. *Journal of Consumer Research, 25*, 276–289.

Thaler, R. (1980). Toward a positive theory of consumer choice. *Journal of Economic Behavior and Organization, 1*, 39–60.

Triandis, H. C. (1977). *Interpersonal behavior*. Monterey, CA: Brooks/Cole.

Tversky, A., & Kahneman, D. (1983). Extensional versus intuitive reasoning: The conjunction fallacy in probability judgment. *Psychological Review, 90*, 293–315.

Verplanken, B., & Aarts, H. (1999). Habit, attitude, and planned behavior: Is habit an empty construct or an interesting case of goal-directed automaticity? In W. Stroebe & M. Hewstone (Eds.), *European review of social psychology* (Vol. 10, pp. 101–134). Chichester: Wiley.

Verplanken, B., Aarts, H., & van Knippenberg, A. (1997). Habit, information acquisition, and the process of making travel mode choice. *European Journal of Social Psychology, 27*, 539–560.

Verplanken, B., Aarts, H., van Knippenberg, A., & Moonen, A. (1998). Habits versus planned behavior: A field experiment. *British Journal of Social Psychology, 37*, 111–128.

Verplanken, B., Aarts, H., van Knippenberg, A., & van Knippenberg, C. (1994). Attitude versus general habit: Antecedents of travel mode choice. *Journal of Applied Social Psychology, 24*, 285–300.

Weber, E. U., Goldstein, W. M., & Busemeyer, J. R. (1991). Beyond strategies: Implications of memory representation and memory processes for models of judgment and decision. In E. Hockley & S. Lewandowsky (Eds.), *Relating theory and data: Essays on human memory in honor of Bennet B. Murdock* (pp. 75–100). Hillsdale, NJ: Lawrence Erlbaum Associates.

Zsambok, C. E., & Klein, G. (1997). *Naturalistic decision making*. Mahwah, NJ: Lawrence Erlbaum Associates.

—Tilmann Betsch
Susanne Haberstroh

List of Contributors

Richard P. Bagozzi
J. Hugh Liedtke Professor of Management
Jesse H. Jones Graduate School of
  Management
Professor of Psychology
Psychology Department
Rice University
Houston, TX 77005-1892
USA

Tilmann Betsch
University of Erfurt
Department of Psychology
Nordhäuser Str. 63
99089 Erfurt
Germany

Herbert Bless
Mikrosoziologie und Sozialpsychologie
Fakultät für Sozialwissenschaft
Universität Mannheim
68163 Mannheim
Germany

Anne-Louise Bornstein
Department of Psychology
University of Basel
Missionsstrasse 62A
4055 Basel
Switzerland

Jerome Busemeyer
Department of Psychology
Indiana University, Bloomington
1101 E. 10th Street
Bloomington, IN 47405
USA

Paul Dholakia
Assistant Professor of Management
Rice University
329 Jones Hall - MS 531
6100 Main Street
Houston, TX 77005-1892
USA

Ilan Fischer
Department of Behavioral Sciences
Ben Gurion University of the Negev
Be'er Sheva 84105
Israel

Katrin Fischer
Institut für Psychologie und
  Arbeitswissenschaft
Technische Universität Berlin
Franklinstr. 5-7
10587 Berlin
Germany

John Fox
Advanced Computation Laboratory
Cancer research UK
61 Lincoln's Inn Fields
London WC2A 3PX
UK

Nigel Harvey
Department of Psychology
University College London
Gower Street
London WC1E 6BT
UK

Brian M. Friel
Department of Psychology, Bluemont
Hall 492
Kansas State University
1100 Mid-Campus Dr
Manhattan, KS 66506-5302
USA

Robin M. Hogarth
ICREA Research Professor
Universitat Pompeu Fabra
Department of Economics & Business
Ramon Trias Fargas, 25-27
08005 Barcelona
Spain

Malte Friese
Psychologisches Institut
Universität Heidelberg
Hauptstr. 47- 51
69117 Heidelberg
Germany

Eric R. Igou
Mikrosoziologie und Sozialpsychologie
Universität Mannheim
Seminargebäude A 5
68131 Mannheim
Germany

David W. Glasspool
Advanced Computation Laboratory
Cancer research UK
61 Lincoln's Inn Fields
London WC2A 3PX
UK

Joseph G. Johnson
Department of Psychology
Indiana University, Bloomington
1101 E. 10th Street
Bloomington, IN 47405
USA

Andreas Glöckner
Deutsche Lufthansa AG
Führungskräfteentwicklung, FRA PU/E
Lufthansa Basis
60546 Frankfurt
Germany

Helmut Jungermann
Institut für Psychologie und
Arbeitswissenschaft
Technische Universität Berlin
Franklinstr. 5-7
10587 Berlin
Germany

Thomas Haar
University of Heidelberg
Psychological Institute
Hauptstr. 47- 51
69117 Heidelberg
Germany

Frank R. Kardes
College of Business
University of Cincinnati
Cincinnati, OH 45221-0145
USA

Susanne Haberstroh
University of Erfurt
Department of Psychology
Nordhäuser Str. 63
99089 Erfurt
Germany

Gary Klein
Klein Associates Inc
1750 Commerce Center Blvd. North
Fairborn, OH 45324
USA

James W. Lussier
U.S. Army Research Institute for the
  Behavioral and Social Sciences
2423 Morande Street
Fort Knox, KY 40121
USA

Jim McLennan
Complex Decision Making Research Group
School of Psychological Science
La Trobe University
Bundoora, Vic, 3083
Australia

A. V. Muthukrishnan
Department of Marketing
School of Business and Management
Hong Kong University of Science and
  Technology
Kowloon, Hong Kong

Vemund Myrbakk
University of Tromsø
Department of Psychology
NO- 9037 Tromsø
Norway

Mary M. Omodei
Complex Decision Making Research Group
School of Psychological Science
La Trobe University
Bundoora, Vic, 3083
Australia

Klaus Opwis
Department of Psychology
University of Basel
Missionsstrasse 62A
4055 Basel
Switzerland

Vladimir Pashkevich
College of Business
University of Cincinnati
Cincinnati, OH 45221-0145
USA

Henning Plessner
University of Heidelberg
Psychological Institute
Hauptstrasse 47- 51
69117 Heidelberg
Germany

Steven S. Posavac
Simon Graduate School of Business
University of Rochester
Rochester, NY 14627
USA

Kort C. Prince
University of Utah
Department of Psychology
380 S 1530 E Rm 502
Salt Lake City, UT 84112-0251
USA

John Raacke
Department of Psychology, Bluemont Hall 492
Kansas State University
1100 Mid-Campus Dr
Manhattan, KS 66506-5302
USA

Torsten Reimer
Center for Adaptive Behavior and Cognition
Max Planck Institute for Human Develop-
  ment
Lentzeallee 94
14195 Berlin
Germany

Karol G. Ross
Klein Associates Inc
10901 133rd Circle North
Champlin, MN 55316
USA

Erik Rudi
University of Tromsø
Department of Psychology
NO-9037 Tromsø
Norway

David M. Sanbonmatsu
University of Utah
Department of Psychology
380 S 1530 E Rm 502
Salt Lake City, UT 84112-0251
USA

Peter Sedlmeier
Chemnitz University of Technology
Department of Psychology
09107 Chemnitz
Germany

James Shanteau
Department of Psychology, Bluemont Hall 492
Kansas State University, 1100 Mid-Campus Dr
Manhattan, KS 66506-5302
USA

Anja Stiller
University of Heidelberg
Psychological Institute
Hauptstr. 47- 51
69117 Heidelberg
Germany

Rickey J. Thomas
Department of Psychology, Bluemont Hall 492
Kansas State University, 1100 Mid-Campus Dr
Manhattan, KS 66506-5302
USA

Sam Vanous
University of Utah
Department of Psychology
380 S 1530 E Rm 502
Salt Lake City, UT 84112-0251
USA

Bas Verplanken
University of Tromsø
Department of Psychology
NO-9037 Tromsø
Norway

Michaela Wänke
Institut für Psychologie
Universität Basel
Missionsstr. 62a
4055 Basel
Switzerland

Alexander Wearing
Department of Psychology
University of Melbourne
Parkville, Vic, 3052
Australia

UNDERSTANDING AND MODELING THE ROUTINES OF DECISION MAKING

1

Rule-Based Decision Field Theory: A Dynamic Computational Model of Transitions Among Decision-Making Strategies

Joseph G. Johnson
Jerome R. Busemeyer
Indiana University

Heading down the highway of life, we are faced with many decisions. There are different types of decisions that we must make as well. For example, when planning for a vacation, someone may make a detailed, logical analysis concerning where to go. Along the way, he may then use simple rules to decide when and where to stop and which specific routes to take, depending on incidental factors such as traffic. It is important to understand how these various decision domains are differently perceived and processed. On the one hand, under novel decision-making conditions, there is no prior experience to guide the decision-making process. In this case, how does one select the appropriate strategy? On the other hand, under repetitive decision-making conditions, there is a long history of experience. In this case, are some decisions truly automatic in the sense that they require no deliberation? In this chapter, we address the issue of how decision processes transit from more controlled or deliberative strategies, to simple decision rules, and finally to automatic or routine strategies. We attempt to answer these questions by developing a dynamic, computational model of decision making.

Questions about strategy use have been treated in several different lines of decision-making research. Largely, a distinction arises in terms of when and why deliberative processing (characterized generally here as calculated, resource-consuming processing) versus rule-based processing (heuristic, efficient) best describes decision-making behavior. Some propose behavior within one task is guided by an initial phase of quick rule-based processing, followed by a more deliberative choice among the narrowed choice alternatives (e.g., Svenson, 1979). Others claim that different strategies are used depending on accuracy–effort trade-offs (e.g., Beach & Mitchell, 1978; Payne, Bettman, & Johnson, 1993). That is, simple rules provide results that are good enough for trivial decisions, but more cognitive resources are required for more important decisions. Another view is that efficient heuristics are adapted to specialized environments where they work well (Gigerenzer, Todd, & the ABC Research Group, 1999).

Repeated exposure to a task may lead to the development of routines that may replace more deliberative processes in guiding behavior (Betsch, Haberstroh, Glöckner, Haar, & Fiedler, 2001; Haberstroh, Betsch, Glöckner, Haar, & Stiller, chap. 12, this volume). Betsch, Haberstroh, and Höhle (2002) identified some characteristics of these routines of decision making, as well as how they might be incorporated in various models. However, of the literatures mentioned, only Betsch (chap. 3, this volume) attempted to specify a model for decision making that describes exactly when each strategy might be used or how the use of rules and individual habits develop over time. In this chapter, we propose an alternative approach based on a sequential sampling framework to capture this behavior. First, we briefly review important contributions to the understanding of the behavior we are treating in the chapter. Then we provide a computational model to describe transitions from deliberative to rule-based processing, with simulations that illustrate the broad range of phenomena to which the theory can be applied.

FROM RUMINATION TO ROUTINES

Cognitive psychologists have long been interested in the development of cognitive skills from experience. For example, Shiffrin and Schneider (1977) proposed ways to distinguish between automatic and controlled processes, and they presented evidence to support the differences between these two processes. Anderson's ACT-R model (e.g., Anderson & Lebiere, 1998) assumes that problem-solving strategies begin with slow, declarative processes that change with experience into faster procedural routines. Logan (1988) proposed a model of skill learning that is composed of a mixture of rule-based processes and exemplar memory retrieval. In Logan's model, individuals begin using the slower rule-based processing, but with experience they tend to switch to a faster process that simply relies on memory retrieval.

Routine decision making is also an important feature of the naturalistic decision-making program (refer to Omodei, McLennan, & Wearing, chap. 15, this volume; Ross, Lussier, & Klein, chap. 18, this volume; Shanteau, Friel, &

Raacke, chap. 14, this volume; see Lipshitz, Klein, Orasanu, & Salas, 2001, and the associated commentaries for a program review). This research studies the performance of experts in their natural environments, giving a different insight into the use of specific strategies, rules, and so on. Klein's (1999) Recognition Primed Decision (RPD) model, for example, suggests successful decisions during training result in efficient generation of similar future decisions. This approach contributes understanding of experience-based decision making. Along similar lines, Ben-Zur (1998) suggested a distinction among comprehensive, dimension-wise processing; low-effort heuristics; and "compound pattern matching." The latter is perceived as an automatic application of similar rules to matching environments. For example, when our traveler thoughtlessly applies the rule, "Rest for ten minutes, every two hours," he is hardly performing any explicit calculations of the probability he will fall asleep while driving or the relative utility of the time spent resting versus driving on. Rather, when in the situation "driving long distance," this resting rule is a good match (e.g., has performed safely in the past) and is simply applied. Connolly (1999) proposed that when a situation is faced repeatedly, then a "trial-and-error" strategy, coupled with the appropriate feedback, can eventually result in good and efficient decision-making strategies (see also Harvey & Fischer, chap. 7, this volume; Hogarth, chap. 4, this volume). However, this requires minimal environmental changes or application of rules to restricted environments. Otherwise, if the environment changes sufficiently, previous feedback may no longer be reliable.

Betsch et al. (2002) provided the most comprehensive review of the way these approaches and many others may apply to studying routine decision behavior. In particular, they suggested how different models could be specified to incorporate the use of routines. We present next a model that accomplishes not only this, but can describe the dynamic evolution of these routines as well. In fact our model belongs to a class identified by Betsch et al. (2002) as criterion-dependent choice models. Furthermore, they provide a summary of qualitative patterns associated with the use of routines, which is helpful in initial empirical evaluation of the model. Before presenting the theory, it is helpful to use a concrete example decision problem to introduce the main concepts.

EXAMPLE DECISION TASK

Imagine that a new regional sales manager has just moved from California to the midwest, and her job entails daily travel among several locations within her area. During these trips, she must decide how fast she is going to drive on a main highway, reflecting on whether she will get a speeding ticket. If the speed limit is 55 mph, then assume her options are to drive 60,

65, or 70 mph. Associated with each option is a monetary cost of receiving a ticket and a gain in terms of time if no ticket is received. To ease discussion, assume that we can formulate a common metric for the possible outcomes—perhaps she translates the "driving time saved" for each option into what she thinks it is worth to her, so she can construct a table of her subjective values (Table 1.1) for each option (rows) for each possible outcome (columns). For example, being caught driving 60 mph in a 55 mph zone results in a $50 fine, and each 5 mph greater costs an additional $25 in our manager's state—the first column of Table 1.1. Furthermore, suppose possible outcomes (column headings of Table 1.1) are that the police ticket those driving above either 60, 65, or 70 mph, or they do not give a ticket regardless of speed (e.g., they are not patrolling). If the police give a speeding ticket for those driving 70 mph or faster, and she only drives 65 mph, she will get the time benefit of arriving at her client's office rather than the cost of a speeding ticket. This time benefit is translated into $90 in the example, and the second row of Table 1.1 shows that she also gains this if the police are not ticketing. In contrast, the first two cells of the second row in Table 1.1 illustrate the $75 fine she will have to pay if the police ticket at 60 or 65 mph. Note finally that if the sales manager is running late, there is an added benefit of excessive speeding at 70 mph to avoid delaying and annoying a client; this translates into $300 subjectively, found in the last cell of the last row in Table 1.1.

The probabilities of the outcomes depend on several factors, including whether our manager is running late, traffic conditions, and weather conditions. To be specific, suppose the traffic is bad 25% of the time and the probabilities of the police giving tickets depend on this as follows: The police ticket at 60 mph only in heavy traffic with a probability of 0.40, ticket at 65 mph only in heavy traffic with a probability of 0.60, and ticket at 70 mph with a probability of 0.25 in any traffic. Suppose our manager was informed about the probabilities of the outcomes from some friends who had been living in the area for a long time. To be specific, she has learned that the probability of receiving a ticket at 60, 65, and 70 mph are 0.10, 0.15, and 0.25, respectively, and there is a 0.50 chance she will not get a ticket at any speed. Furthermore, 20% of the time our manager is running late, in which

TABLE 1.1
Table of Values for Example Problem

	Ticket at 60	Ticket at 65	Ticket at 70	No Ticket Not Late	No Ticket Late
Drive 60	−50	30	30	30	30
Drive 65	−75	−75	90	90	90
Drive 70	−100	−100	−100	150	300

case there is an added benefit to excessive speeding (if she is not ticketed and thus arrives on time). Finally, assume the weather is poor 10% of the time.

In the past, when our sales manager lived in California, she used a simple rule to determine how fast to drive depending on whether she was running late, the amount of traffic, and the weather: "If I'm running late, go 15 mph over the speed limit; if there is heavy traffic and bad weather, drive only 5 mph over; if there is light traffic and good weather, drive 15 mph over; otherwise drive 10 mph over in all other cases." So she is faced with three options (driving speed), each with different outcomes (time gains, monetary losses) and different probabilities of occurrence. Furthermore, she must use this information to make a decision, either by careful deliberation of her expected gains from each option or by using the rules she thinks may apply. We can adopt this scenario within the computational process model provided next.

RDFT: A DYNAMIC MODEL OF DECISION STRATEGY EVOLUTION

We model the decision process by using a sequential sampling mechanism that has proved successful in previous applications to decision making (Böckenholt, Albert, Aschenbrenner, & Schmalhofer, 1991; Busemeyer & Townsend, 1993; Diederich, 1997; Roe, Busemeyer, & Townsend, 2001) and other cognitive domains (e.g., Nosofsky & Palmeri, 1997; Link & Heath, 1975; Ratcliff, 1978). The framework used in this chapter is an extension of multi-alternative decision field theory (MDFT; Roe et al., 2001). The new feature of this extension is that it allows for the application of any number of rules that may be applicable in an environment.

Assume that in a repetitive decision task, there are different options described on different attributes. The first few encounters with a task may require deliberative processing of the options using only attribute information, according to the original version of MDFT. Based on repeated experience, simple rules may become applicable that result in successful decisions. In this case, the decision maker attends either to the values of the attributes for each option or the advice provided by a rule. The preference for each option accumulates over time, but now on the basis of either attribute value information or advice from a rule.[1] Once preference for an option is strong enough to pass a threshold, it is chosen. Subsequent feedback associated with the outcome affects whether the rule process resulted

---

[1]We thank Dr. Jun Zhang for suggesting this idea to us. This idea also appears in earlier work by Danny Oppenheimer.

in a good or poor choice, and this feedback forms the basis for rule learning. If the environment changes, the earlier rules may no longer suffice, and the deliberative process may resume again.

The original version of MDFT provides us with a means to understand our manager's driving decisions if she only attends to attributes. That is, while she is deliberating about how fast to drive, her attention shifts to thinking about each possible outcome (the police ticket at 60, 65, or 70 mph, or not at all), where the probability of attention to an attribute at each moment is equal to the probability (of occurrence) of each outcome. Only the values of the attended attribute (outcome) are considered at any moment, but for all alternatives. On this attribute, she considers the relative advantage that each option has—if she is thinking about being ticketed at 65 mph, the option "60 mph" looks relatively the best because it is the only option with a positive outcome for this event. Thus, whenever she is thinking about receiving a ticket at 65 mph, the manager will perceive the option "60 mph" most favorably. This evaluation, or valence, is integrated with the previous preference state to form a new preference state. Preferences continue to evolve in this manner as attention shifts from one attribute to another over time.

To determine when a choice is made, we must introduce some method for terminating this deliberation process. Specifically, the sales manager must determine at some point that she has deliberated enough and a decision should be made. A threshold parameter, θ, is used here, as in general random walk and counter models (Townsend & Ashby, 1983). When the preference for an alternative exceeds this threshold—when the sales manager has collected enough information and evaluations favoring a particular alternative—the alternative is chosen and no further processing of the task information is assumed. The personal characteristics of the sales manager may influence how great the preference for any option must be before choosing it—impulsive individuals may exhibit lower thresholds than more careful and deliberative individuals. Regardless of the magnitude of the threshold, the accumulation of preference for each option is driven toward this decision boundary by oscillations in momentary attention during a decision task.

Now we assume that a set of rules is available. In this case, at each moment in time, the sales manager may attend to her rules in addition to attribute values. A rule is represented by a set of columns, where each column provides advice favoring one alternative over other alternatives. The environmental cues given by the current situation determine the column of a rule to which attention is applied. If a specific condition is present, then one of the columns of the rule is selected for advice. For example, the previously described if-then rule used by our hypothetical manager could be represented as:

$$\mathbf{X} = \begin{pmatrix} y & 0 & 0 \\ 0 & y & 0 \\ 0 & 0 & y \end{pmatrix}$$

Rule $\mathbf{X}$ = if(traffic, bad weather, ~late) then apply $\mathbf{X}_1$
if(traffic, ~bad weather, ~late) then apply $\mathbf{X}_2$
if(late) then apply $\mathbf{X}_3$
if(~traffic, ~bad weather, ~late) then apply $\mathbf{X}_3$
if(~traffic, bad weather, ~late) apply $\mathbf{X}_2$

Attending to a rule at a particular moment in time thus changes the valences for options, in the same way as attending to a specific attribute. If the advice of the rule is sufficiently strong (i.e., $y = \theta$), then a decision is reached as soon as the rule is applied. That is, if there is heavy traffic and bad weather and she is not running late, then the manager uses the first column of the rule matrix, and the change in valence for the first option is $+\theta$, which results in immediate choice of the first option.

A rule as a whole gains (or loses) strength based on its performance. If the rule is applied and the manager consistently gets speeding tickets, she will use the rule less; if she does not get tickets, she will use the rule more. This is operationalized by changing the probability of thinking about the rule—its attention weight.

Formal Theory

Now we present a formal version of Rule Based Decision Field Theory (RDFT). This extension introduces two levels of dynamics: a short time scale, indexed by t, representing the deliberation process within a single choice; and a longer time scale, indexed by n, representing the learning process based on the outcomes across choices. Momentary fluctuations in how to approach any single instance of a decision task is a result of the deliberation process occurring in time t. This intratask or short-term scale is usually thought of as lasting moments or minutes. Evolution of decision rules is a result of the reinforcement experienced after each decision. This takes place on another time scale in terms of periods, n. This intertask or long-term scale can take place over learning trials spanning minutes, days, weeks, or a lifetime. The current model is unique in its capability of making predictions for both types of time scales.

First, let us apply the original RDFT model (Eqs. 1–3a in Fig. 1.1) to represent a deliberative analysis of the choice options. The sequential sampling mechanism assumes that at each point in time during deliberation the attention weights $\mathbf{W}(t)$ select only a single attribute j, which focuses on the

$$\mathbf{V}(t) = \mathbf{CM}(n)\mathbf{W}(t) \qquad (1)$$

$$\mathbf{P}(t) = \mathbf{SP}(t-1) + \mathbf{V}(t) \qquad (2)$$

$$\mathbf{w}_1 = \lfloor \ldots \; w_j \; \ldots \rfloor \qquad (3a)$$

$$\mathbf{w}_2 = [\ldots \; \Pr(\text{rule } i) \; \ldots] \qquad (3b)$$

$$\mathbf{w}(n) = [\alpha \cdot \mathbf{w}_1 \mid \mathbf{w}_2] = E_n(\mathbf{W}(t)) \qquad (3c)$$

$$\mathbf{M}(n) = [\mathbf{M} \mid \mathbf{X}(n)] \qquad (4)$$

$$\Pr(\text{rule } i) = \frac{s_{i,n}}{\sum_i s_{i,n} + K} \qquad (5)$$

$$s_{i,0} = \Delta \qquad (6a)$$

$$s_{i,n} = \beta \cdot s_{i,n-1} + F_{i,n} \qquad (6b)$$

$$F_{i,n} = \begin{cases} \Delta \cdot r & \text{if } i \text{ successful at } n-1 \\ 0 & \text{if } i \text{ not used at } n-1 \\ -\Delta \cdot p & \text{if } i \text{ unsuccessful at } n-1 \end{cases} \qquad (7)$$

$$\alpha = 1 - \sum \Pr(\text{rule } i) \qquad (8)$$

where:

$\mathbf{S}$	=	feedback matrix	constant elements determine updating degree/manner
$\mathbf{C}$	=	contrast matrix	computes relative (across alternatives) valences
$\mathbf{M}$	=	value matrix	attribute values for all alternatives
$\mathbf{W}(t)$	=	weight matrix	the attention weights at each moment t
w_j	=	attribute weight	probability of attending to attribute j
θ	=	choice threshold	necessary strength for termination and choice
$\mathbf{M}(n)$	=	attribute/rule matrix	attributes and rules concatenated
$\mathbf{X}(n)$	=	rule implementation	adjustment of preference values by rules;
$s_{i,n}$	=	rule strength	success of rule i in period n
K	=	rule dominance	determines preference for rules over attributes
Δ	=	step size	weights impact of feedback to rules (learning rate)
β	=	success weight	weights impact of previous rule success (memory)
r	=	reinforcement strength	feedback strength of successful outcome (reward)
p	=	punishment strength	feedback strength of unsuccessful outcome (punishment)
α	=	attribute attention	probability that an attribute (not rule) is used
t	=	time	short-term dynamics
n	=	period	long-term dynamics

FIG. 1.1. Equations and parameters of the RDFT model.

values of a single attribute from $\mathbf{M}$ (i.e., $W_j(t) = 1$, $W_k(t) = 0$, for all $k \neq j$). The momentary valence, $V_i(t)$, for an alternative is the advantage of an alternative relative to all others on this processed attribute (see Eq. 1). The default form of the contrast matrix $\mathbf{C}$ that performs this comparison is such that the diagonal elements, $c_{xx} = 1$, and the off-diagonal elements, $c_{xy} = -1/(m-1)$, where m is the number of alternatives. Adding this valence to some degraded (by $\mathbf{S}$) trace of the previous preference state results (see Eq. 2) in the momentary preference vector, $\mathbf{P}(t)$, containing as elements the preference values for all alternatives. With three options (and rather good memory for previous states), these two matrixes become:[2]

$$\mathbf{C} = \begin{bmatrix} 1 & \frac{-1}{2} & \frac{-1}{2} \\ \frac{-1}{2} & 1 & \frac{-1}{2} \\ \frac{-1}{2} & \frac{-1}{2} & 1 \end{bmatrix} \qquad \mathbf{S} = \begin{bmatrix} 0.95 & 0 & 0 \\ 0 & 0.95 & 0 \\ 0 & 0 & 0.95 \end{bmatrix}$$

Rules are introduced now, in addition to attributes ($\mathbf{M}$). The rules are represented in a matrix denoted $\mathbf{X}(n)$, where the values within each column of $\mathbf{X}(n)$ represent the advice of a rule for each alternative. Essentially, the columns in $\mathbf{X}(n)$ contain the assessment of the relevant alternative according to the hypothesized rule: element $x_{ab}(n)$ = the preference for alternative a if rule b is used in period n. For example, an expected value rule could be formed in one column of $\mathbf{X}(n)$ by setting each row value equal to the expected value of the corresponding alternative. As another example, a lexicographic rule could be formed in another column of $\mathbf{X}(n)$ by assigning a large positive value to the row corresponding to the alternative that is best on the most important attribute and setting all other rows to zero. The rules can be easily accommodated in the MDFT model by concatenating the two value matrixes, $\mathbf{M}$ and $\mathbf{X}(n)$, forming $\mathbf{M}(n)$ and using it in place of $\mathbf{M}$ in the MDFT model just described (see Eq. 4 in Fig. 1.1). With this RDFT representation, rules (of any sort) are treated like attributes, in that they have some chance of being used at each point in time over the deliberation process.

The probability of using each rule is specified in the weight vector, just as weights exist for attributes (w_j). In general, the subjective success probability (Eq. 3b) for each rule is concatenated with attribute weights (Eq. 3a) to form $\mathbf{w}(n)$ (Eq. 3c). The probability of using attributes rather than rules, α, is redistributed among the original terms from $\mathbf{w}_1$. This "leftover probability" is equal to the difference between one and the sum of success probabilities across rules. In other words, because the elements of $\mathbf{w}(n)$ must sum to one, the rule success probabilities are determined first, and the remainder from one is portioned among the relative attribute weights from $\mathbf{w}_1$. Although it may seem precedence is given to rules, in the sense that they are "allotted probability" first, the parameter K in Eq. 5 (see Fig. 1.1) allows for control of how much attention is afforded to the rule relative to attribute processing. The actual derivation of the subjective success probability for each rule is explained next.

---

[2]In Roe et al. (2001), it is important to allow the off-diagonal elements of $\mathbf{S}$ to be nonzero to account for a wide range of robust empirical phenomena; the form used here is to simplify exposition.

The rule learning process borrows from earlier ideas presented in Busemeyer and Myung (1992). After each repetitive decision, the strength $(s_{i,n})$ for each rule i is updated (Eqs. 6 and 7 in Fig. 1.1). The first time a decision is encountered, $n = 0$, potential rules are assigned some marginal strength of use, $s_{i,0} = \Delta_0$. Those rules that are not relevant to a task—such as driving rules for grocery shopping—would be modeled with $\Delta_0 = 0$, effectively isolating only the rules that fit with a particular task. If a rule is applied, then the next time a decision is encountered in a similar environment, the value of success for each rule is updated by Eqs. 6 and 7, and this update is controlled by feedback parameters that represent the salience of reward (r) or punishment (p) produced by using the rule (if any), as well as memory of the past success of the rule (β). There are obvious implications of the values and signs of these and other parameters, some of which are covered in the later simulations. The default form shown for the feedback function, F_n, that relates these parameters also has implications. In particular, the current function reinforces only rules that were *used* the last time period, ignoring rules that may have specified a successful outcome, but were *not employed*. Practice is an essential component in the model, guiding the evolution of successful rules. In fact, there is nothing that restricts the model from incorporating probability learning, as well, for the events in the example. The weight vector, $\mathbf{w}(n)$, that is specified for each decision period could be updated using simple learning models to derive all w_j from experience. Although this adds further parameters, it could prove useful. We refrain from this treatment for sake of simplicity in the current chapter, and we assume in simulations that the probabilities are (roughly) known.

Rules Versus Habits

Habitual behavior can be distinguished from rule-based decision making in that rules require significant information-processing resources (attention to relevant environmental cues, logical checks for the appropriate pattern of conditions), whereas habits are automatic reactions that require little or no information-processing resources (Verplanken, Myrbakk, & Rudi, chap. 13, this volume). Although habitual behavior is not the focus of this chapter, it is useful to point out how this type of behavior can be accommodated by RDFT. The main mechanism for modeling habitual behavior is through the initial preference state that is retrieved before the deliberation process even begins. We consider this initial preference vector as a representation of the preference of each alternative based on memory retrieval to a decision situation. In other words, the elements of $\mathbf{P}(0) = \mathbf{z}$, z_x for $x = 1$ to m, are the initial habits that, if they exceed the decision threshold, could be implemented with no further deliberative processing. Other momentary and historical influences could also adjust the initial preference matrix from the default of $\mathbf{P}(0) = \emptyset$, incorporating effects such as sustained marketing, extensive past experience, or immediate goals. J. Johnson (2003) showed the model's capability of providing parameter interpretations for these and other individual, environmental, and task factors. In our example, perhaps our driver has recently acquired a few speeding tickets, which could introduce an initial bias against the 70 mph option in $\mathbf{z}$.

Summary

This is considered our model representation of routinized decision behavior. Note how our model incorporates points from other approaches mentioned in the introductory review. In particular, it allows the possible implementation of different strategies and rules in a common framework (e.g., Payne et al., 1993); the emergence of "expert" use of efficient routines in stable environments (e.g., Betsch et al., 2002; Klein, 1999) and the gradual learning of these skills (e.g., Connolly, 1999); and, finally, the adaptation of efficient heuristics for particular environments (e.g., Gigerenzer et al., 1999). In speaking of applicable rules and strategies, we should note that the precise formulation of these is extraneous to the model. That is, as long as any decision pattern—whether it be if-then, heuristic, or analytic (cf. Ben-Zur, 1998)—can be formalized in the mathematical framework by assigning a preference value to each alternative, it can be thought of as a strategy or rule in the current context. This is indeed a rather modest assumption, but the implications are large: By assigning any decision rules and applying the model to a particular environment, it is possible to observe the evolution of successful rules in a process-oriented manner. The following section provides our first application of such an idea.

IMPLICATIONS: PHENOMENA, THEORETICAL PREDICTIONS, AND SIMULATIONS

The phenomena outlined by Betsch et al. (2002) provide a means for a first analysis of the efficacy of the present model. Table 1.2 contains some of these phenomena, as well as the proposed explanations provided by the model (see Betsch et al., 2002, for further details and references to empirical support for specific effects). For example, consider the points related to routine strength. Intuitively, as routines are repeated, it seems the likelihood with which they are implemented should increase, in turn decreasing the depth and elaborateness of information search. However, none of the models outlined by Betsch et al. (2002) is able to account for all of these effects. Table 1.2 provides a theoretical description of how RDFT explains these effects, as well as how the mathematical model (Fig. 1.1) formally re-

TABLE 1.2

Some Representative Behavioral Characteristics, and How They Are
Modeled by RDFT Theoretically (T) and Mathematically (M)

Power law (Anderson, Fincham, & Douglass, 1999)
   T: Gradual learning and asymptote of rules over time
   M: Use of the updating equation (6)
Routine effects (Betsch, Haberstroh, & Höhle, 2002)
1. Identification of selection problem causes routine activation from memory.
   T: Specification of rules for each task application
   M: $\mathbf{X}(n)$ into $\mathbf{M}(n)$
2. Recognition of selection problem can directly evoke selection of routine behavior.
   T: Strict adherence to rules or formalizing initial (habitual) preferences
   M: $y = \theta$, or by allowing dynamics in, e.g., $\mathbf{P}(0) = \mathbf{z} = \mathbf{X}$
3. Routine strength matters: the higher the frequency of prior behavior repetition, the
   higher the likelihood of immediate selection of the routine behavior.
   T: Rule use increases with successful prior use
   M: Increases in use may increase s_i (if successful), increasing $\Pr(\text{use } i)$.
4. Depth of information search decreases with increasing routine strength.
   T: Prior success of rules decreases attribute-wise search
   M: Increase in any s_i decreases α, which decreases $\Pr(\text{use attributes})$.
5. Elaborateness of search strategies decreases with increasing routine strength.
   T: Prior success of rules decreases use of multiple attributes
   M: Increase in any s_i decreases α, which decreases $\Pr(\text{use attributes})$.

---

produces the effects. The simulations described next explore the ability of RDFT to predict and capture these trends. Consider our example of the regional sales manager, who is constantly traveling along a state highway between her field offices. We continue with the assumptions made earlier in the simulations that follow. In particular, we use the environment outlined previously, with the aforementioned options, outcomes, probabilities, and associated gains/losses. The simulations then show the postulated evolution in her decision behavior over time.

Baseline Model Parameters

For the simulation, the value matrix $\mathbf{M}$ of the decision maker was set equal to the values shown in Table 1.1 after normalizing them. The weight matrix is defined by the event probabilities described in the "Example Decision Task" section: $\mathbf{w}_1' = [.10\ .15\ .25\ .40\ .10]$. The if-then rules that our decision maker uses were also described earlier (Rule $\mathbf{X}$ described in the previous section).

The remaining parameters, which are not determined by the environment, were independently manipulated to test separate hypotheses. The "default" values—at which the corresponding parameter was held constant if not manipulated—for the remaining parameters were: $\beta = 0.99$, representing excellent memory for the success rate of the rule at the previous period; $\theta = 1$ for all alternatives, which is a moderately low level of overall preference necessary to make a choice; $K = 10$, which determines how much a rule (or rules) must succeed before it tends to be used half of the time; $\Delta = 1$, representing the impact of the payoffs on the rules; and $y = .9$, used to control the influence of the rule on the choice. The default level implies strong, but not strict, adherence to the rule so that it does not always immediately terminate deliberation with a choice on use.

Simulations With a Single Rule

With the parameter specification and formulation given, we conducted 1,000 replications of simulations with 200 trials each in MATLAB. In our simulations, each trial represents a new (successive) encounter of the decision (speed determination) problem. The results of the simulation from the first 200 days the sales manager drives in this environment are summarized as follows. The probability of rule use increases monotonically with an asymptote of approximately 0.60 after 70 to 120 trials, and choice probabilities eventually reach 0.05, 0.25, and 0.70 for the 60, 65, and 70 mph options, respectively. Also the deliberation time decreased with increasing probability of rule use, beginning around 20 time units on the average and eventually reaching an asymptote at less than 5 time units.

How should changes in the various model parameters affect this baseline result? First, consider manipulations of the feedback parameter β. Due to the small (normalized) values of the simulation, even small decreases in β, to 0.98 or 0.97, greatly reduced the probability of rule use, decreasing the asymptote to around 0.5, increasing the time to reach this asymptote, and increasing the noise at all points. This indicates the importance of memory for feedback in determining rule use.

Increasing the step size, $\Delta > 1$, raises the asymptote slightly, and these large steps increase the possibility of noise in deliberation time on later trials—after asymptote, a negative outcome can cause a large decline in the probability of rule use, and attribute processing may again prevail. With a small step size, this is not probabilistically likely. Although using smaller steps, $\Delta < 1$, slows the learning and achievement of asymptote, this affects the slope of the learning curve on later trials, not the general trend (shape).

Decreases in y, adherence to the rule, do not seem to have a dramatic effect on the baseline results. The results are somewhat noisier, and rule use asymptote comes slightly later. Even if a rule only assigns one fifth of the threshold value to the relevant option, if the rule receives repeated attention it will make the decision regardless. This does imply, however, a minimum decision time of $1/y$.

Finally, consider the model parameter K. This parameter has direct interpretability and impact by adjusting the strength necessary for rules to become more probable of receiving attention than attributes. In our situation, with one rule, equal probability of rule or attribute processing occurs when the rule's success is equal to K. Increasing K, therefore, increases the amount of success the rule must accumulate to be probabilistically favored, which was confirmed in simulations of $K = 20, 25, 30,$ and 50. In fact, when $K > 25$, the rule was almost never favored even after 200 learning trials.

Simulations With Two Competing Rules in a Changing Environment

The second set of simulations was intended to examine the effects of environmental changes that occur midway during the simulation. Specifically, once the rule had been learned in the environment given in the first simulations, what sort of generalization to new environments would we see? If the environment changed such that the rule was no longer beneficial, would we observe its extinction? We attempted to perform initial tests of this hypothesis with modified simulations. After 200 days in the midwest, the sales manager reads about the following changes in the speed enforcement policy of the police. First, there has been the addition of a "reckless driving fine" of $30 for those who are caught speeding at 15 mph over the speed limit. Second, a larger police force now means increased probability of getting a ticket when there is light traffic. The resulting effects, decreasing the first three columns in the last row of **M** by 30 and an increase in Pr(ticket | light traffic) from 0.25 to 0.5, were used in a second set of MATLAB simulations of 1,000 replications with the default parameters.

Another important characteristic of these simulations was the presence of a second new rule that could compete with the first rule. The new rule implies that our manager should simply follow the flow of traffic, which would imply a constant speed of 60 mph. This new rule (social rule), which always selects column $\mathbf{X}_1$, was included in simulations with the original rule (personal rule), both with the same initial success rate Δ. For the first 200 of 500 trials, these rules were applied exactly as before. The updated success and probability of rule use after Trial 200 was retained in Trial 201 to see how the rules performed in the new environment. The new policy, with modified punishment values and event probabilities, was used for the last 300 trials, as were revised subjective probability estimates. That is, the sales manager was aware on Trial 201 that the new policy was in effect, and her subjective probabilities ($\mathbf{w}_1$) shifted accordingly.

The results of this simulation provide a reasonable representation of a response to the new environment (see Fig. 1.2). Toward the end of the first 200 trials, the personal rule was favored, although its use declined some-

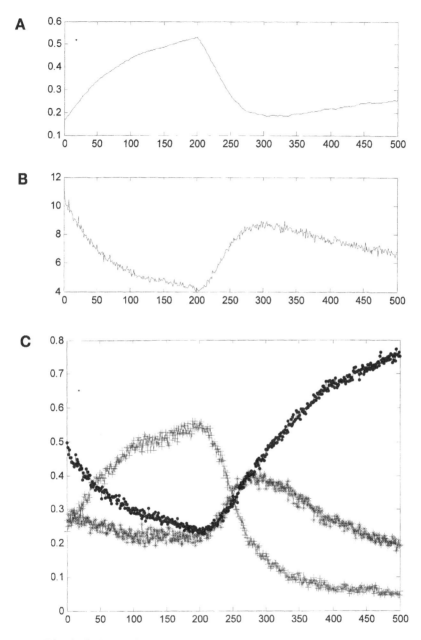

FIG. 1.2. Evolution of decision behavior for second simulation. The dynamics of (a) probability of rule use, (b) deliberation time t, and (c) choice probabilities as a function of period n over 500 trials are shown, averaged over 1,000 replications. The environment changes after Trial 200, where attribute processing is used instead of the personal rule until the social rule succeeds enough to guide choice. In (c), dark crosses represent 70 mph, light stars represent 65 mph, and black dots represent 60 mph choices.

what due to the competition from the social rule. This can be inferred from the slight decrease in probability of rule use, coupled with comparison of the success rates for the personal (s_P = 13.8) versus social (s_S = 1.1) rules, and the evolution of choices that indicates more use of the personal rule (Fig. 1.2c).

In the new environment, Trials 201 to 500, the personal rule is no longer favored due to the punishments (and increased chance thereof) of the new environment. As rule use declines and deliberative processing resumes (Fig. 1.2a), choices shift from 70 mph to 65 mph in accord with the expected value of the deliberative RDFT process (Fig. 1.2c). Furthermore, the time to make a decision slows down as a result (Fig. 1.2b).

Ultimately, the social rule begins to gain success (s = 3.5 for the social vs. s = 0.35 for the personal rule) and subsequent use: The choice dynamics show increases in the social choice, 60 mph, with an increase in rule use and decreases in deliberation time. The social rule is slow to gain success in overcoming its (relatively) poor performance in the first environment, although lower tendencies for attribute processing (decreasing K) could also speed the acquisition of the social rule. Thus, RDFT accurately portrays scenarios where evolution and extinction of multiple rules can occur in addition to deliberative processing depending on the environment.

RDFT can capture the transitions in the types of decision strategies used in different settings. The simulations provided encouraging results considering the artificiality of the current example. Yet there is nothing that prevents analysis of nontrivial decisions using experiments and real environments, which remain avenues for future research. Also, by using the RDFT framework, various other decision rules could be formalized and compared. For example, the strategies covered by Payne et al. (1993), the heuristics studied by Gigerenzer et al. (1999), or still other rules could be implemented by simply computing the necessary elements of the rule matrix.

CONCLUSION

This chapter has shown how computational modeling techniques can be applied to a new domain of inquiry: transitions from deliberative to routine decision making. The model introduced, RDFT, offers a psychologically plausible account of this dynamic behavior, and it includes consideration of individual and environmental factors. For example, it shows how the evolution of rule-based or even automatic behavior can occur in experienced domains (e.g., Betsch, 2002; Klein, 1999). Furthermore, by formulating various decision strategies as rules in RDFT, various choice models can now be compared dynamically, perhaps using an effort–accuracy metric for success per Payne et al. (1993). Yet it can still represent deliberative compensatory processing using a sequential sampling mechanism (Roe et al., 2001). Finally, dynamic predictions can be derived on two time scales, representing both the momentary fluctuations in behavior and the evolution of task-dependent strategies. Although the current chapter leaves many interesting open questions, it provides a comprehensive framework for traveling down those roads.

REFERENCES

Anderson, J. R., Fincham, J. M., & Douglass, S. (1999). Practice and retention: A unifying analysis. *Journal of Experimental Psychology: Learning, Memory, & Cognition, 25*(5), 1120–1136.

Anderson, J. R., & Lebiere, C. (1998). *The atomic components of thought.* Mahwah, NJ: Lawrence Erlbaum Associates.

Beach, R. L., & Mitchell, R. M. (1978). A contingency model for the selection of decision strategies. *Academy of Management Review, 3*, 439–449.

Ben-Zur, H. (1998). Dimensions and patterns in decision-making models and the controlled/automatic distinction in human information processing. *European Journal of Cognitive Psychology, 10*(2), 171–189.

Betsch, T., Haberstroh, S., Glöckner, A., Haar, T., & Fiedler, K. (2001). The effects of routine strength on information acquisition and adaptation in recurrent decision making. *Organizational Behavior and Human Decision Processes, 84*, 23–53.

Betsch, T., Haberstroh, S., & Höhle, C. (2002). Explaining routinized decision making: A review of theories. *Theory and Psychology, 12*(4), 453–488.

Böckenholt, U., Albert, D., Aschenbrenner, M., & Schmalhofer, F. (1991). The effects of attractiveness, dominance, and attribute differences on information acquisition in multiattribute binary choice. *Organizational Behavior & Human Decision Processes, 49*(2), 258–281.

Busemeyer, J. R., & Myung, I. J. (1992). An adaptive approach to human decision making: Learning theory, decision theory, human performance. *Journal of Experimental Psychology: General, 121*(2), 177–194.

Busemeyer, J. R., & Townsend, J. T. (1993). Decision field theory: A dynamic-cognitive approach to decision making in an uncertain environment. *Psychological Review, 100*, 432–459.

Connolly, T. (1999). Action as a fast and frugal heuristic. *Minds & Machines, 9*(4), 479–496.

Diederich, A. (1997). Dynamic stochastic models for decision making under time constraints. *Journal of Mathematical Psychology, 41*, 260–274.

Gigerenzer, G., Todd, P. M., & the ABC Research Group. (1999). *Simple heuristics that make us smart.* Oxford: Oxford University Press.

Johnson, J. G. (2003). Incorporating motivation, individual differences, and other psychological variables in utility-based choice models. *Utility Theory and Applications, Dipartimento di Matematica applicata Bruno de Finetti, Università di Trieste (Italy), Pubblicazione, 7*, 123–142.

Klein, G. (1999). *Sources of power: How people make decisions.* Cambridge, MA: MIT Press.

Link, S. W., & Heath, R. A. (1975). A sequential theory of psychological discrimination. *Psychometrika, 40*, 77–111.

Lipshitz, R., Klein, G., Orasanu, J., & Salas, E. (2001). Taking stock of naturalistic decision making. *Journal of Behavioral Decision Making, 14*, 331–352.

Logan, G. D. (1988). Toward an instance theory of automatization. *Psychological Review, 95*(4), 492–527.

Nosofsky, R. M., & Palmeri, T. J. (1997). An exemplar-based random walk model of speeded classification. *Psychological Review, 104,* 266–300.

Payne, J. W., Bettman, J. R., & Johnson, E. J. (1993). *The adaptive decision maker.* Cambridge, England: Cambridge University Press.

Ratcliff, R. (1978). A theory of memory retrieval. *Psychological Review, 85,* 59–108.

Roe, R. M., Busemeyer, J. R., & Townsend, J. T. (2001). Multi-alternative decision field theory: A dynamic connectionist model of decision-making. *Psychological Review, 108,* 370–392.

Shiffrin, R. M., & Schneider, W. (1977). Controlled and automatic human information processing: II. Perceptual learning, automatic attending, and a general theory. *Psychological Review, 84,* 127–190.

Svenson, O. (1979). Process descriptions of decision making. *Organizational Behavior & Human Decision Processes, 23*(1), 86–112.

Townsend, J. T., & Ashby, F. G. (1983). *Stochastic modeling of elementary psychological processes.* Cambridge, England: Cambridge University Press.

2

Three Roles of Past Experience in Goal Setting and Goal Striving

Richard P. Bagozzi
Utpal M. Dholakia
Rice University

Many behaviors are goal-directed and effortful in the sense that goals are first consciously chosen by the decision maker and then attaining the chosen goal is not straightforward, but rather involves substantial effort to pursue after it has been chosen. Studying or weight-control regimens, childrearing tasks, business- or work-related projects, and planful shopping expeditions are all examples of such effortful goal-directed behaviors. Under such conditions, past experience influences the process by which decisions are reached and enacted by individuals in many ways: through cognitive (memory-related and evaluative), motivational, and volitional means. In this chapter, we consider these different influences of past experience, summarizing what is known as well as highlighting interesting opportunities for future research.

In understanding these roles of past experience in goal-directed behavior, it is useful to first make and elaborate on the conceptual distinction between processes of goal setting and those of goal striving (Bagozzi, 1992; Bagozzi & Dholakia, 1999; Gollwitzer, 1996; Oettingen & Gollwitzer, 2001). With this objective, we first discuss a theoretical framework elaborating on the processes of goal setting and goal striving. We then consider the different ways in which past experience influences these processes of decision makers.

A FRAMEWORK OF GOAL SETTING AND GOAL STRIVING PROCESSES

Goal-directed behavior can be conceived as beginning with goal setting, which involves decision-making processes where the decision maker addresses two broad questions: *"What are the goals I can pursue? Why do I want to or not want to pursue them?"* (Bagozzi, Bergami, & Leone, 2003; Bagozzi & Edwards, 1998). In answering the first question, goal alternatives may be activated either externally, such as when the environment presents opportunities or imposes imperatives on the decision maker, or internally, such as when the individual constructs a goal schema or chooses from among self-generated alternatives. Many times, some or all of these goal alternatives may have been pursued and attained by the decision maker in the past, such as buying gifts for friends and family members every holiday season or planning a vacation every summer. At other times, they may be entirely novel for the decision maker. Our emphasis in this chapter is mostly on goals that have been previously pursued by the decision maker.

During goal setting, the decision maker evaluates the desirability and feasibility of available goal alternatives. Depending on the characteristics of the task, such as the number of alternatives to be considered, importance of the outcome, and so on, the decision maker may use analytical strategies or simple heuristics, which behavioral decision theorists have studied extensively, in this evaluation process (see Yates, 1990; Payne, Bettman, & Johnson, 1993, for reviews). The decision maker's cognitive orientation at this time is characterized by openness to new information and evaluation, whereby utilities of the different alternatives are compared, attention is given to all available choices, and information is processed more objectively. Social psychologists call this a *deliberative mindset* (Gollwitzer & Bayer, 1999).

It is useful to note here that such a conceptualization of goal setting is consistent with an expectancy-value approach to decision making. As such, goal alternatives in our framework correspond to what behavioral decision scientists refer to as options or choice alternatives; desirability to the utility or value of a particular option; feasibility to the weight of the utility such as probability, expectancy, belief, importance, and so on; and goal intention to the outcome of the decision process (i.e., making the choice; see also Dholakia & Bagozzi, 2002).

Moreover, this decision-making process, imbued with a certain degree of effort and confidence, is motivating by itself in that it musters regulatory strength and facilitates subsequent goal pursuit and enactment of actions (Bagozzi, Dholakia, & Basuroy, 2003; Dholakia & Bagozzi, 2002). The process culminates in a goal intention, which is characterized by the decision maker's self-commitment to achieve the chosen goal. The formation of the goal intention implies that the individual has chosen a particular goal and made it binding in the sense that it is accompanied by a sense of determination or obligation to attain it.

Goal setting processes as construed here may be of three different types (Bagozzi & Dholakia, 1999; Oettingen & Gollwitzer, 2001). First, for many activities where the decision maker has extensive experience, and those performed on a regular basis, the desire for a particular goal may be activated more or less automatically through responses to learned cues, and the decision maker engages in little conscious processing in selecting or enacting goals (e.g., repetitive ordering and paying for food at a fast-food restaurant). This might be labeled as *habitual goal-directed behavior* (e.g., Ouellette & Wood, 1998; Wood, Quinn, & Kashy, 2002).

In contrast to a learned response, a second way in which goal setting occurs and is followed through, at least minimally, is through the activation of an impulse. By definition, impulsive acts do not entail prior deliberation or planning, but they rather involve some awakening of a need or desire that quickly transforms into a goal to be achieved through purposive, instrumental actions. Cognitive psychologists have referred to such goal setting as "intentions in action" to reflect this quick transformation (Kvavilashvili & Ellis, 1996). The chosen goal is then enacted or resisted with little or no deliberation depending on whether it is viewed as harmonious or incompatible with other long-term goals and plans of the decision maker, and whether any incompatible desire can be resisted successfully (Dholakia, Bagozzi, & Nataraajan, 2004). The enactment process in the case of impulsive acts is typically automatic, unconscious, or, on occasion, minimally conscious. In our view, an important difference between habitual and impulsive behaviors stems from the role played by self-regulation in their occurrence or nonoccurrence. Whereas the enactment of habitual behaviors involves few, if any, aspects of self-regulation, individuals may seek to regulate their impulses more actively (Dholakia & Bagozzi, 2003a, 2003b). As such, both may be viewed as goal-directed.

The third type of goal setting is more clearly volitional and elaborate in nature. As shown in the framework of Fig. 2.1, in this case, goal setting occurs volitionally through a more or less formal decision-making process, and it concludes with the formation of a goal intention. The decision maker figuratively answers the question, "What is it for which I strive?" Goal intentions may be targeted either at specific behaviors as end performances by themselves (e.g., "I intend to call my grandmother this evening") or toward particular outcomes to be achieved through the execution of a series of instrumental actions (e.g., "I intend to adopt a healthier lifestyle by exercising regularly and monitoring what and how much I eat").

Once formed, goal intentions result in the consideration and formation of a second type of volition involving decision making called the *implementation intention* (Gollwitzer, 1996; Heckhausen & Gollwitzer, 1987). The implementation intention refers to a person's intention to enact a goal-directed behavior given that a future contingency occurs: "I intend to do X when situation Y is encountered" (Gollwitzer, 1996, p. 292). At this point, the decision maker moves from goal setting to goal striving, which has been characterized by action psychologists as the "crossing of the Rubicon" (e.g.,

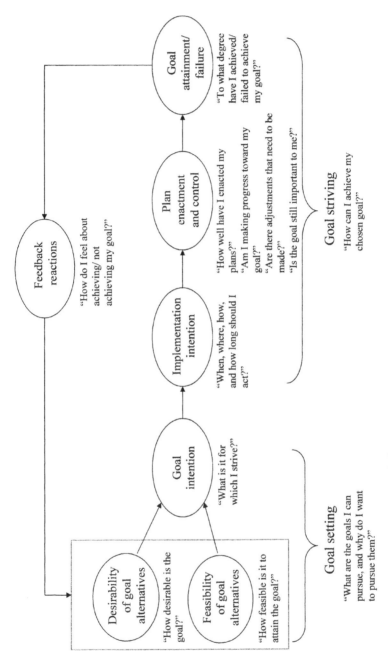

FIG. 2.1. A theoretical framework of goal setting and goal striving.

Goal attainment/ failure

"To what degree have I achieved/ failed to achieve my goal?"

Plan enactment and control

"How well have I enacted my plans?"
"Am I making progress toward my goal?"
"Are there adjustments that need to be made?"
"Is the goal still important to me?"

Goal striving

"How can I achieve my chosen goal?"

Feedback reactions

"How do I feel about achieving/not achieving my goal?"

Implementation intention

"When, where, how, and how long should I act?"

Goal intention

"What is it for which I strive?"

Desirability of goal alternatives

"How desirable is the goal?"

Feasibility of goal alternatives

"How feasible is it to attain the goal?"

Goal setting

"What are the goals I can pursue, and why do I want to pursue them?"

Gollwitzer, 1996; Heckhausen, 1991), in that the decision maker's cognitive orientation and motivational functioning are different in the two stages. The transition from goal intention to implementation intention is typically governed by a desire to perform an instrumental act (not shown in Fig. 2.1), where goal intentions are integrated or combined with such criteria as attitudes, anticipated emotions, subjective norms, social identity, and perceived behavioral control (e.g., Bagozzi et al., 2003; Bagozzi & Dholakia, 2002).

In the "implementation intention" stage, the decision maker selects a plan of action, presumably from alternative means available, by considering and finalizing details regarding when, where, how, and how long to perform goal-directed action in the service of goal attainment. The general question of "How can I achieve my goal?" is addressed through the formation of a specific action plan. Thus, decision making may be viewed as occurring at two levels in the framework shown in Fig. 2.1: first at the level of goals, and second at the level of action plans to achieve those goals.

Research has shown that the implementation intention serves many useful purposes in goal striving (Bagozzi & Edwards, 2000; Brandstätter, Langfelder, & Gollwitzer, 2001; Gollwitzer, 1999; Sheeran & Orbell, 1999; but also see Betsch et al., 2003, for a different view). First, it facilitates the initiation of goal-directed behavior by creating a perceptual readiness for and guiding the decision maker's attention toward available opportunities for enacting the decision. Second, it fosters an inflated sense of optimism and an orientation to act—referred to as an "implemental mindset" (Gollwitzer, 1996)—dispelling any lingering doubts about the chosen goal. Third, it may also help reduce the conflict arising from other alternative action courses. Fourth, it initiates choice and action by integrating self-efficacy, instrumental beliefs, and affect toward the means of goal striving in the face of impediments to action and goal achievement (Bagozzi & Edwards, 2000). Finally, it also supports the progress of initiated goal pursuits by mobilizing effort in the face of difficulties and warding off any distractions that might occur (Brandstätter et al., 2001). If disruptions to goal-directed actions do occur at some point, it enables undelayed resumption of actions afterward.

The actual execution of the plan occurs in the fourth stage, labeled as "plan enactment and control" in Fig. 2.1. In many cases, this may occur after a considerable amount of time has elapsed and when the proper opportunity has arrived. Often the decision maker has a limited window of opportunity during which to enact the behaviors necessary for goal attainment. We have referred to such actions as "short-fuse behaviors" (Dholakia & Bagozzi, 2003a, 2003b). During this fourth stage, *prospective memory* (i.e., memory for future actions and *plan monitoring* (i.e., evaluating progress of plan execution and making necessary adjustments) are both important. The decision maker addresses four questions during plan enactment and control: "Am I making adequate progress toward my goal?" "How well have I enacted my plans?" "Are there adjustments that need to be made?" and "Is this goal still important to me?" The implementation intentions are enacted (or modified or abandoned) at this stage.

The fifth stage in our framework, "goal attainment/failure," involves a final comparison of the outcome achieved with a standard or reference value, and the determination of whether to maintain or increase efforts at goal pursuit or disengage from further efforts (e.g., Carver & Scheier, 1998). Past experiences play an important role in creating the reference value used by the decision maker in this process. In this stage, the decision maker figuratively asks, "To what degree have I achieved/failed to achieve my ends, and should I continue on with or terminate goal striving?"

Finally, after this evaluation, the discrepancy between the decision maker's goal and its achievement is appraised, and emotional responses are generated in the sixth "feedback reactions" stage (e.g., Bagozzi, Baumgartner, & Pieters, 1998). The question considered here is: "How do I feel about achieving/not achieving my goal?" Emotional and rational reactions to goal attainment/failure ultimately update the decision maker's knowledge structure about goals, motivation to pursue this and other goals in the future, and other learning about planning, means, implementation, and environmental conditions.

THREE ROLES OF PAST EXPERIENCE IN GOAL SETTING AND GOAL STRIVING

The influence of past experience on goal setting and goal striving processes may be described in at least three conceptually distinct ways. At the simplest level, past experience may be viewed as a *statistical control*, substituting for all the consistency-producing variables not considered explicitly in the framework. However, treating past experience in this manner does not provide much insight into how it may actually influence goal setting and goal striving, or the consequences of this influence. A second view suggests that past experience should be treated as a *predictor* of future goal-directed behavior. According to this conceptualization, including past experience in a predictive model of goal-directed behavior attenuates the predictive power of other antecedents, whereas past experience becomes a significant predictor. Here, too, the researcher's interest may lie more in studying the other variables in the framework and their influence on behavior, rather than on an in-depth understanding of past experience's workings.

The third view is different from the first two in that it accords greater importance and pays more attention to the past experience construct and how it produces its effects. It posits that past experience cannot only predict, but actually influences goal-directed behavior through different mechanisms. It suggests that the decision maker's past experience serves as the basis for predecision information processing during goal setting, as well as for plan selection, prospective memory, self-regulation, action initiation, and execution during goal striving. In other words, past experience is integral to how the entire goal setting and goal striving process plays out and its outcome. We discuss each of these three conceptualizations in greater detail next.

Role 1: "Past Experience Is a Control for Future Goal-Directed Behavior"

In this first conceptualization, past experience simply "controls for" the unmeasured effects of all the variables not included in the theoretical framework, and which produce consistent choices of goals and action plans across different occasions. Such variables might include personality characteristics of the decision maker, motivating variables such as task importance, task difficulty, or time pressure, and situational attributes common to the goal-directed behavior from one time to the next. Here past experience essentially serves as a content-free statistical control.

In our theoretical framework, past experience with a goal would function as a control for goal intention formation, whereas past experience with an action plan would serve as a control for implementation intention formation and enactment. Such an approach allows the researcher to estimate the unique influence of antecedent constructs (such as specific decision-making strategies, attitudes, subjective norms, etc.) on consequent constructs such as intentions, plan monitoring, behavior, and so on in the theoretical framework, and it has been widely used by social psychologists (e.g., Albarracín et al., 2001; Ouellette & Wood, 1998; see Ajzen, 2002, for a recent review). In a sense, this conceptualization represents the least informative characterization of past experience's influence.

Role 2: "Past Experience Predicts Future Goal-Directed Behavior"

According to this second conceptualization, past experience serves as a proxy for expedited decision making during goal setting (see also Haberstroh, Betsch, Glöckner, Haar, & Stiller, chap. 12, this volume) and for *habit*—defined as learned sequences of actions that become automatic responses when the decision maker encounters certain situations (e.g., Aarts & Dijksterhuis, 2000; Verplanken, Aarts, & van Knippenberg, 1997; Verplanken, Myrbakk, & Rudi, chap. 13, this volume)—and influences goal-directed behavior directly. This view is consistent with the large body of findings in the attitude theory literature, which show that when past behavior is included in models predicting future behavior, it is often a significant direct predictor and frequently attenuates the mediating influence of attitudes and behavioral intentions (e.g., Bagozzi, 1981; Bentler & Speckart, 1979; Triandis, 1980). The degree of influence of past experience is greater to the extent that the context in which the goal-directed behavior occurs is stable from one occasion to the next and is also governed by how frequently the behavior has been performed in the past by the decision maker (e.g., Bagozzi & Warshaw, 1990).

Such an influence of past experience applies to both goal setting and goal striving processes, and in general it implies that with greater past experience the processes leading to goal-directed behavior become less elaborate. The goal selection as well as the actions to be performed become automatic, and they come to be executed with reduced (and with sufficient repetition, without *any*) mediation of goal and implementation intentions (cf. Ronis, Yates, & Kirscht, 1989; see also Harvey & Fischer, chap. 7, this volume; Ross, Lussier, & Klein, chap. 18, this volume). When the decision maker has to make a particular goal or means selection, he or she may simply activate the stored reasons for attaining the goal or acting automatically, assuming that the reasons from the past apply again in the present as well (e.g., Bagozzi, 1982). Consistent with this view, Verplanken et al. (1997) found that those who were strongly habituated to use a particular mode of travel engaged in lesser predecisional information search and used less elaborate choice strategies relative to those who were weakly or not so habituated. This view suggests that past experience may provide a heuristic basis for goal setting and goal striving by itself, substituting for goal intention and implementation intention (Albarracín & Wyer, 2000).

The effect of past experience on action may become accentuated when intentions are uncertain or ill formed (Bagozzi & Yi, 1989). For example, this may occur when the time for performance of a goal-directed behavior is too remote for a person to have crystallized plans. Here the person will be likely to report his or her behavioral expectation rather than an intention when responding to an intention query, and past experience may predict action better than intention per se.

In studying goal setting, psychologists make the distinction between decision-making processes that are reflective and those that are reflexive (Bargh & Chartrand, 1999; Betsch et al., 2001; Oettingen & Gollwitzer, 2001). Whereas reflective goal setting involves deliberative processes of goal selection, reflexive goal setting is more akin to the impulsive and habitual modes described before. Past experience is especially pertinent for reflexive goal setting, where strong mental links are formed between the cognitive representation of situations and the goals that the decision maker chronically pursues within them (Bargh & Chartrand, 1999). Because of repeated, frequent, and consistent coactivation in the past, a goal may be activated automatically when the decision maker encounters a particular situation. This habit-activated goal then guides behavior, bypassing the deliberative processes of decision making. It is useful to note here that for any given goal, repeated reflexive and presumably successful decision making morphs into more reflexive processes over time, as the decision maker relies more and more on past experience and expends less effort in the goal setting process (Bargh, 1990).

Further, goals, whether reflectively or reflexively chosen, may evoke and activate a habitual plan of action (Aarts & Dijksterhuis, 2000; Verplanken et al., chap. 13, this volume). This is because, when the goal has been chosen before and the decision maker has selected the same means to achieve it, and done so successfully, the instrumental actions enacted come to be associated with this goal over time. The association between the goal and the means is manifested as a habit. Habits have been viewed by social psychologists to be hierarchical mental representations in which the activation of a goal leads to the activation of one or more associated behaviors, lower in the abstraction hierarchy, automatically and immediately (Aarts & Dijksterhuis, 2000; Wood et al., 2002).

Whereas relatively little empirical research has examined this issue, habits for specific actions may be viewed as similar in representation and function to implementation intentions in many ways (Verplanken & Faes, 1999; Verplanken et al., chap. 13, this volume). Both habits and implementation intentions encode specific behavioral responses to certain cues in the environment to be activated automatically at the opportune time. In both cases, the control of behavior is transferred from the decision maker to the environment. Moreover, just like implementation intentions, habits foster closed-mindedness—steering the decision maker's attention toward one course of action to the exclusion of other possibilities. It is also likely that habits may yield many of the same volitional benefits (such as illusory optimism, warding off distractions, etc.) during goal striving that implementation intentions do, but more research is needed to study this possibility.

In most cases, habits are formed due to the repeated and successful execution of implementation intentions. There are also some interesting differences between the two constructs. One important difference between the two is this: Whereas implementation intentions entail volitional planning before and monitoring during their execution, habits form and are used through the repeated enactment of the same actions and require little cognitive effort. Implementation intentions also involve detailed evaluation afterward and influence feedback reactions to a greater extent relative to habits.

Finally, goals pursued through habitual courses are either attained or not attained by the decision maker. Environmental conditions or the failure to enact habitual behaviors correctly may result in nonattainment of a goal. Whereas researchers have focused on studying the consequences of non-attainment for nonhabitual actions (e.g., Bandura, 1997; Chartrand, 1999), relatively little is known about conditions where habitual actions result in nonattainment of goals. It would be useful to study both the consequences of failure on the decision maker's emotional reactions and perceptions of self-efficacy (cf. Bandura, 1997), and also the durability of habits under such conditions. More specifically, understanding when and how the habit is maintained versus broken is very useful.

In summary, in this second prediction-oriented view of past experience, it is implicitly assumed that past experience represents the instigator for a form of goal-directed automatic behavior that is consciously executed, based on linkages of particular goals to known specific desired or undesired outcomes *through* particular courses of action that are instrumental in attaining those outcomes. A conscious awareness that these goals have been attained or actions enacted successfully in the past is what distinguishes such goal-directed behavior from that which is mindless, such as reflexive movements (Verplanken et al., 1997). It is useful to note here that past experience may be operationalized similarly in both Roles 1 and 2, but it is the conceptualization of its importance and function that is crucially different in the two cases.

Role 3: "Past Experience Influences Future Goal-Directed Behavior"

In this third role, past experience influences specific processes of goal setting and goal striving. According to this conceptualization, past experience may form one important basis for both information processing during goal setting, as well as facilitating prospective memory and action initiation during goal striving. Contrary to the passive views in the first two cases, here past experience is seen as actively influencing processes of goal setting, prospective memory, and goal striving, each of which is considered in detail next.

Early efforts to disentangle the nature of past behavior effects on decision making were done by Bagozzi and Warshaw (1990), who partitioned experience into frequency and recency effects. The former occurs when attitudes and expectancies are dependent on self-perception processes of past action or else past frequency of experience is a proxy for stored scripts. The latter happens when biases akin to availability or anchoring/adjustment processes color judgments of expectations of success or self-efficacy in goal-directed decision making.

Influence of Past Experience on the Goal Setting Process. Past experience with goals may influence the goal setting process in at least three ways (see also Harvey & Fischer, chap. 7, this volume; Ross et al., chap. 18, this volume). First, as noted before, past experience may make the process with which goals are chosen less elaborate. With increasing experience, goals may be chosen with little effort as the alternatives to be considered, the criteria to be used in the evaluation, and the decision rules applied to the information all become readily available to the decision maker from previous occasions. Behavioral decision researchers have studied this issue extensively using "routines" to describe such choices (e.g., Betsch, Haberstroh, & Höhle, 2002).

With repeated enactment, goal setting may become largely automatic and be performed with minimal effort and little conscious control. It is important to note, however, that this does not imply that the same goal will necessarily be chosen every time. The decision maker may choose the same goal as the last time or may choose from some predefined set of goal alternatives using a meta-evaluative decision rule. For example, for the sake of a need or preplanned decision for variety, a consumer may implement switching strategies in his or her ongoing purchase patterns (e.g., "I went to McDonald's last time, so I plan to go to Burger King this time").

A second way in which past experience may influence goal setting is through influencing the valences of the specific goal alternatives under consideration. A large body of research by behavioral decision scientists on the endowment effect and the status quo bias (Kahneman, Knetsch, & Thaler, 1991; Samuelson & Zeckhauser, 1988) is interesting in this regard (an overview of similar results can be found in Haberstroh et al., chap. 12, this volume; Kardes, Muthukrishnan, & Pashkevich, chap. 8, this volume). The endowment effect posits that the value of an object or experience increases once it becomes part of an individual's possession. Similarly, the status quo bias refers to the decision maker's preference for a current choice or course of action relative to other more attractive alternatives. For goal-directed behavior, attaining a particular goal in the past is analogous to its becoming part of the decision maker's endowment or being the status quo alternative. This would imply that goals chosen and attained in the past may be evaluated in a rosier light, and they may become more likely to be chosen again when compared with competing alternatives that have never been attained before. Moreover, such effects may occur even after controlling for the desirability and feasibility of the alternatives.

A third possibility is that, with past experience, the criteria used by the decision maker during goal selection change. In general, when evaluating goals, decision makers conceive of feasibility as subordinate to desirability (Sagristano, Trope, & Liberman, 2002). In other words, feasibility is only considered once desirability of an alternative has been established. On considering past experience explicitly, it is possible that for easier goals, knowing from before that feasibility is very high, the decision maker may focus predominantly on desirability considerations. Nevertheless, for difficult goals, past experience may shift the decision maker's emphasis away from desirability and toward feasibility considerations.

Emerging research from the temporal construal theory has the potential to inform this issue further. This theory proposes that individuals use more abstract mental models, or higher level construals, to represent information about distant future events than information about near future events (Trope & Liberman, 2001). Building on this distinction, research has shown that feasibility is more influential when choice is imminent, but desirability is more influential when goal choice is far off (Liberman & Trope, 1998; see also Sanbonmatsu, Prince, Vanous, & Posavac, chap. 6, this volume).

Studying how past experience influences the predictions of temporal construal theory may yield interesting insights. For instance, it is possible that the outcome of the past experience may moderate these main effects of desirability and feasibility (i.e., the effects would be as expected in the case of previous goal success, but reversed for previous goal failure with feasibility playing a more important role at a distant time, and desirability becoming more relevant later on).

Past Experience and Prospective Memory. As noted before, prospective memory pertains to memory for future actions (Kvavilashvili & Ellis, 1996) and plays an important role in goal-directed behavior, especially where there is a considerable gap between implementation intention formation and action enactment, and when actions to attain a goal are short-fuse (i.e., they must be remembered and enacted within a small window of opportunity; Dholakia & Bagozzi, 2003a, 2003b). In such cases, the encoding, retention, and retrieval of the implementation intention all involve processes of prospective memory. Here encoding refers to the content of the implementation intentions formed and stored by the decision maker, retention refers to the length of the delay between intention formation and the time of action enactment, and retrieval pertains to successfully and accurately remembering the contents of the implementation intentions at the right time and executing actions accordingly. Relatively little research has examined the role of prospective memory in goal setting and goal striving processes. Consequently, we highlight some interesting research opportunities for social and decision scientists interested in studying how past experience may influence prospective memory for goal-directed actions.

Past experience may play a salient role during all of the prospective memory processes noted earlier. First, it is possible that actively thinking about previous acts (e.g., when, where, how, and how long I did action X) may promote encoding (i.e., decision making, and implementation intention formation for the future performance of the action). Second, this active thinking about past action may also enhance retention of the implementation intention during the time delay, reducing the possibility of forgetting the intention. Further, it is also useful to consider whether, how, and under what conditions remembering the past performance of one act (action X, say) influences the implementation intention formation and prospective memory for another act (action Y, say).

Third, emerging research on memory for actions shows that retrieving self-performed actions from the past is relatively effortless and similar in process to recognition memory for retrospective tasks (Guynn, McDaniel, & Einstein, 2001; Zimmer & Cohen, 2001). This similarity implies that remembering the past performance of an act may initiate and/or promote (i.e., work as a cue for) the retrieval of prospective memory and the performance of the planned act in the future. Here the retrieval of past experience may result in the recognition that the behavior has to be performed again in the future, in turn enhancing the retrieval of the implementation intention. Such a mechanism might be mediated by the explicit consideration of past recency and frequency of acting, where the decision maker interprets the meaning of past acting.

Memory research shows that recognition memory is a function of recency relative to frequency, which in turn determines familiarity (Guynn et al., 2001). A high level of familiarity then leads to the consideration of the underlying reasons, which in turn trigger a memory search for the prospective implementation intentions. Comparing this mechanism to the habit-driven processes described before may yield interesting findings. For instance, consider the case where the decision maker feels that she was to do something but cannot recall what it was. This awareness may be driven by the recency and frequency of the past behavior, and it may then stimulate a search process and/or increase the perceptual readiness for a cue, thereby increasing the chances of performing the behavior at the appropriate time. In contrast, habit-driven processing would predict that the decision maker would mindlessly react to an environmental cue in performing behavior. We believe that understanding the conditions under which each of these processes operates is of great value. Similarly, the recency and frequency of past behaviors may also serve as positive or negative reasons for acting during goal setting or when selecting action plans.

Finally, considering prospective memory processes also brings attention to goal-directed behaviors involving standing or long-standing goal intentions, such as maintenance actions: actions to maintain relationships, health, possessions, and so on. For instance, at a certain point in time, seeing an advertisement for toothpaste may remind the decision maker that he or she has not been to the dentist in a long time. This in turn may prompt an appointment for a check-up. In this case, a cue leads to the recall of *a gap in time* since the last performance of the act, and it motivates goal-directed behavior. These possibilities all warrant more research attention and promise a better understanding of how past experience influences memory-based cognitive processing during goal-directed behavior.

Counterintentional Habits and Goal Striving. So far we have considered goals where past experience is compatible with and supports future goal-directed behavior. Another interesting possibility is when a particular goal and action course conflicts with entrenched habits of the decision maker (Betsch et al., 2004; see also Verplanken et al., chap. 13, this volume). This may occur when a heavy smoker chooses to quit smoking, a person accustomed to buying unhealthy calorie-laden foods opts for a healthier lifestyle, or a person commuting to work and accustomed to driving alone decides to car-pool instead. Verplanken and Faes (1999) referred to such habits as *counterintentional habits,* and they noted that in such cases "implementation intentions and counterintentional habits may constitute opposite forces, which are will-based and experience-based, respectively" (p. 595). In a study of healthy eating, these authors found that participants forming a specific implementation plan regarding how and when to perform goal-directed behavior were more successful than those without such a plan. Yet the effects of implementation intentions and counterintentional habits on the goal-directed behavior were independent of each other (see also Betsch et al., 2004).

Several interesting issues regarding the role and effects of counterintentional habits in goal striving are worth considering. The first question pertains to the outcome of the goal pursuit process: What determines the decision maker's goal-directed behavior in this case? On the one hand, by creating relatively chronic contingencies between situational cues and habitual action responses, counterintentional habits favor the usually enacted (and now disfavored) course of action. On the other hand, by identifying and elaborating on a different objective, perhaps of long-term benefit such as better health, the goal and implementation intentions favor the opposite course. In such cases, Verplanken and Faes (1999) suggested that "habits or implementation intentions may win this battle to the extent that there has been extensive previous repetition of behavior or that a strong motivation to achieve a goal is present, respectively" (p. 595).

This raises the question of what motivational intensity implies in the case of habit and implementation intention, and how to compare one to the other. In defining habit strength, researchers have mostly used the frequency with which the behavior was performed in the past given a particular situation (Aarts & Dijksterhuis, 2000; Hull, 1943). Although this is certainly an important determinant, the role of other habit attributes in determining strength deserves attention. It can be argued that recency (how recently the habitual behavior was performed last), stability or consistency (the extent to which the situation invokes the same rather than some other behavior), and the *importance* of the goal outcome to the decision maker may all contribute to the habit strength and help determine the effort that the decision maker will need to break the counterintentional habit. Similarly, the differences in efficacy and process between automatic and nonautomatic routine actions also need to be studied (Betsch et al., 2003).

For the implementation intention, motivational intensity may be determined by the degree of behavioral desire of the decision maker (Bagozzi et al., 2003). Such a desire represents the motivational impetus of the decision-making process regarding the means to be used and serves to integrate a series of emotional, cognitive, self-perception, and social appraisals of the decision maker prior to implementation intention formation.

Second, the role of self-regulation—altering one incipient behavioral pattern and replacing it with another so as to prevent or inhibit dominant responses (Baumeister, 2002)—deserves more attention. Kuhl (1984) identified seven different strategies that decision makers may use to promote goal striving in accordance with the implementation intention, but little research has examined how and to what extent such strategies are used to break counterintentional habits.

Finally, the role of task framing in breaking counterintentional habits is also interesting. It is possible that implementation intentions framed as "to enact new behaviors" (e.g., to jog 1 mile every day) may be more effective than those framed as "to resist habitual behaviors" (e.g., to stop eating dessert after dinner). Some of our research examining the experience and resistance of incompatible desires by consumers suggests that this might be the case (Dholakia et al., 2002). We defined incompatible desires as those that conflict with long-term goals, resources, and contingencies of the decision maker. In a study of consumers experiencing such desires, we found that persons who framed their task as *approaching* the goal of resistance and used *approach-congruent* self-regulation strategies were more successful in resisting incompatible desires, compared with those who framed it as *avoiding* the incompatible temptation and used *avoidance-congruent* strategies.

CONCLUSION

Because most goal-directed actions of decision makers have some precedent, the past experience plays an important and multifaceted role in goal-directed behavior. At the simplest level, past experience may be conceptualized as a content-free statistical control to take into account all excluded variables in a model of goal-directed behavior. In a second role, it may be viewed as a predictor of future behavior, serving to account for the role of habitual processes in goal setting and goal striving. In a third role, it may be viewed as influencing goal-directed behavior through memory-related, eval-uation-related, and motivation-related mechanisms. Incorporating past ex-perience in this third role in our framework of goal setting and goal striving provides interesting insights and raises important questions regarding such topics as how desirability and feasibility are considered by decision makers in goal setting, the role of prospective memory processes in plan enact-ment and control, and the role of self-regulation in breaking counterin-tentional habits. Building on its rich history, considering the roles of past experience in goal-directed behavior is likely to continue raising interesting and important questions and stimulate psychological research.

REFERENCES

Aarts, H., & Dijksterhuis, A. (2000). Habits as knowledge structures: Automaticity in goal-directed behavior. *Journal of Personality and Social Psychology, 78*(1), 53–63.

Ajzen, I. (2002). Residual effects of past on later behavior: Habituation and reasoned action per-spectives. *Personality and Social Psychology Review, 6*, 107–122.

Albarracín, D., Johnson, B. T., Fishbein, M., & Muellerleile, P. A. (2001). Theories of reasoned ac-tion and planned behavior as models of condom use: A meta-analysis. *Psychological Bulletin, 127*(1), 142–161.

Albarracín, D., & Wyer, R. S. (2000). The cognitive impact of past behavior: Influences on beliefs, attitudes, and future behavioral decisions. *Journal of Personality and Social Psychology, 79*(1), 5–22.

Bagozzi, R. P. (1981). Attitudes, intentions, and behavior: A test of some key hypotheses. *Journal of Personality and Social Psychology, 41*, 607–627.

Bagozzi, R. P. (1982). A field investigation of causal relations among cognitions, affect, intentions, and behavior. *Journal of Marketing Research, 19*, 562–584.

Bagozzi, R. P. (1992). The self-regulation of attitudes, intentions, and behavior. *Social Psychology Quarterly, 55*, 178–204.

Bagozzi, R. P., Baumgartner, H., & Pieters, R. (1998). Goal-directed emotions. *Cognition and Emo-tion, 12*, 1–26.

Bagozzi, R. P., Bergami, M., & Leone, L. (2003). Hierarchical representation of motives in goal-setting. *Journal of Applied Psychology, 88*, 915–943.

Bagozzi, R. P., & Dholakia, U. M. (1999). Goal setting and goal striving in consumer behavior. *Jour-nal of Marketing, 63*, 19–32.

Bagozzi, R. P., & Dholakia, U. M. (2002). Intentional social action in virtual communities. *Journal of Interactive Marketing, 16*, 2–21.

Bagozzi, R. P., Dholakia, U. M., & Basuroy, S. (2003). How effortful decisions get enacted: The mo-tivating role of decision processes, desires, and anticipated emotions. *Journal of Behavioral Decision Making, 16*, 273–295.

Bagozzi, R. P., & Edwards, E. A. (1998). Goal setting and goal pursuit in the regulation of body weight. *Psychology and Health, 13*, 593–621.

Bagozzi, R. P., & Edwards, E. A. (2000). Goal-striving and the implementation of goal intentions in the regulation of body weight. *Psychology and Health, 15*, 255–270.

Bagozzi, R. P., & Warshaw, P. R. (1990). Trying to consume. *Journal of Consumer Research, 17*, 127–140.

Bagozzi, R. P., & Yi, Y. (1989). The degree of intention formation as a moderator of the attitude-behavior relationship. *Social Psychology Quarterly, 52*, 266–279.

Bandura, A. (1997). *Self-efficacy.* New York: Freeman.

Bargh, J. A. (1990). Auto-motives: Preconscious determinants of thought and behaviour. In E. T. Higgins & R. M. Sorrentino (Eds.), *Handbook of motivation and cognition: Foundations of social behavior* (Vol. 2, pp. 93–130). New York: Guilford.

Bargh, J. A., & Chartrand, T. L. (1999). The unbearable automaticity of being. *American Psychologist, 54*(7), 462–479.

Baumeister, R. F. (2002). Yielding to temptation: Self-control failure, impulsive purchasing, and consumer behavior. *Journal of Consumer Research, 28*(4), 670–676.

Bentler, P. M., & Speckart, G. (1979). Models of attitude-behavior relations. *Psychological Review, 86*, 452–454.

Betsch, T., Haberstroh, S., Glöckner, A., Haar, T., & Fiedler, K. (2001). The effects of routine strength on adaptation and information search in recurrent decision making. *Organizational Behavior and Human Decision Processes, 84*, 23–53.

Betsch, T., Haberstroh, S., Glöckner, A., & Molter, B. (2004). Oops—I did it again: When prior knowledge overrules intentions. *Organizational Behavior and Human Decision Processes, 93*, 62–79.

Betsch, T., Haberstroh, S., & Höhle, C. (2002). Explaining routinized decision making: A review of theories and models. *Theory and Psychology, 12*, 453–488.

Brandstätter, V., Langfelder, A., & Gollwitzer, P. M. (2001). Implementation intentions and efficient action initiation. *Journal of Personality and Social Psychology, 81*, 946–960.

Carver, C. S., & Scheier, M. F. (1998). *On the self-regulation of behavior.* Cambridge, England: Cambridge University Press.

Chartrand, T. L. (1999). *Consequences of automatic motivation for mood, self-efficacy, and subsequent performance.* Unpublished doctoral dissertation, New York University.

Dholakia, U. M., & Bagozzi, R. P. (2002). Mustering motivation to enact decisions: How decision process characteristics influence goal realization. *Journal of Behavioral Decision Making, 15*, 167–188.

Dholakia, U. M., & Bagozzi, R. P. (2003a). *The role of desires in sequential impulsive choices.* Manuscript submitted for publication.

Dholakia, U. M., & Bagozzi, R. P. (2003b). As time goes by: How goal and implementation intentions influence enactment of short-fuse behaviors. *Journal of Applied Social Psychology, 33*(5), 889–922.

Dholakia, U. M., Bagozzi, R. P., & Nataraajan, R. (2004). *How people experience and control incompatible desires: The role of regulatory focus.* Manuscript submitted for publication.

Gollwitzer, P. M. (1996). The volitional benefits of planning. In P. M. Gollwitzer & J. A. Bargh (Eds.), *The psychology of action. Linking cognition and motivation to behaviour* (pp. 287–312). New York: Guilford.

Gollwitzer, P. M. (1999). Implementation intentions: Strong effects of simple plans. *American Psychologist, 54*, 493–503.

Gollwitzer, P. M., & Bayer, U. (1999). Deliberative versus implemental mindsets in the control of action. In S. Chaiken & Y. Trope (Eds.), *Dual-process theories in social psychology* (pp. 403–422). New York: Guilford.

Guynn, M. J., McDaniel, M. A., & Einstein, G. O. (2001). Remembering to perform actions: A different type of memory? In H. D. Zimmer, R. L. Cohen, M. J. Guynn, J. Engelkamp, R. Kormi-Nouri, & M. A. Foley (Eds.), *Memory for action: A distinct form of episodic memory?* (pp. 25–48). Oxford: Oxford University Press.

Heckhausen, H. (1991). *Motivation and action.* New York: Springer-Verlag.

Heckhausen, H., & Gollwitzer, P. M. (1987). Thought contents and cognitive functioning in motivational versus volitional states of mind. *Motivation and Emotion, 11*, 101–120.

Hull, C. L. (1943). *Principles of behavior: An introduction to behavior theory.* New York: Appleton-Century-Crofts.

Kahneman, D., Knetsch, J. L., & Thaler, R. (1991). The endowment effect, loss aversion, and status quo bias. *Journal of Economic Perspectives, 5*(1), 193–206.

Kuhl, J. (1984). Motivational aspects of achievement motivation and learned helplessness: Toward a comprehensive theory of action control. In B. A. Maher & W. B. Maher (Eds.), *Progress in experimental personality research* (Vol. 13, pp. 99–171). New York: Academic Press.

Kvavilashvili, L., & Ellis, J. (1996). Varieties of intention: Some distinctions and classifications. In M. Brandimonte, G. O. Einstein, & M. A. McDaniel (Eds.), *Prospective memory: Theory and applications* (pp. 23–52). Mahwah, NJ: Lawrence Erlbaum Associates.

Liberman, N., & Trope, Y. (1998). The role of feasibility and desirability considerations in near and distant future decisions: A test of Temporal Construal Theory. *Journal of Personality and Social Psychology, 75*, 5–18.

Oettingen, G., & Gollwitzer, P. M. (2001). Goal setting and goal striving. In A. Tesser & N. Schwarz (Eds.), *Blackwell handbook of social psychology: Intraindividual processes* (pp. 328–347). Oxford: Blackwell.

Ouellette, J. A., & Wood, W. (1998). Habit and intention in everyday life: The multiple processes by which past behavior predicts future behavior. *Psychological Bulletin, 124*(1), 54–74.

Payne, J. W., Bettman, J. R., & Johnson E. J. (1993). *The adaptive decision maker.* New York: Cambridge University Press.

Ronis, D. L., Yates, J. F., & Kirscht, J. P. (1989). Attitudes, decisions, and habits as determinants of repeated behavior. In A. R. Pratkanis, S. J. Breckler, & A. G. Greenwald (Eds.), *Attitude structure and function* (pp. 213–239). Hillsdale, NJ: Lawrence Erlbaum Associates.

Sagristano, M. D., Trope, Y., & Liberman, N. (2002). Time-dependent gambling: Odds now, money later. *Journal of Experimental Psychology: General, 131*(3), 364–376.

Samuelson, W., & Zeckhauser, R. (1988). Status quo bias in decision making. *Journal of Risk and Uncertainty, 1*, 7–59.

Sheeran, P., & Orbell, S. (1999). Implementation intentions and repeated behavior: Augmenting the predictive validity of the theory of planned behavior. *European Journal of Social Psychology, 29*, 344–369.

Triandis, H. C. (1980). Values, attitudes, and interpersonal behavior. In H. E. Howe, Jr., & M. M. Page (Eds.), *Nebraska symposium on motivation, 1979* (pp. 195–259). Lincoln, NE: University of Nebraska Press.

Trope, Y., & Liberman, N. (2001). *Temporal construal.* Working Paper, New York University.

Verplanken, B., Aarts, H., & van Knippenberg, A. (1997). Habit, information acquisition, and the process of making travel mode choices. *European Journal of Social Psychology, 27*, 539–560.

Verplanken, B., & Faes, S. (1999). Goal intentions, bad habits, and effects of forming implementation intentions for healthy eating. *European Journal of Social Psychology, 29*, 591–604.

Wood, W., Quinn, J. M., & Kashy, D. A. (2002). Habits in everyday life: Thought, emotion, and action. *Journal of Personality and Social Psychology, 83*, 1281–1297.

Yates, F. J. (1990). *Judgment and decision making.* Englewood Cliffs, NJ: Prentice-Hall.

Zimmer, H. D., & Cohen, R. L. (2001). Remembering actions: A specific type of memory? In H. D. Zimmer, R. L. Cohen, M. J. Guynn, J. Engelkamp, R. Kormi-Nouri, & M. A. Foley (Eds.), *Memory for action: A distinct form of episodic memory?* (pp. 3–24). Oxford: Oxford University Press.

3

Preference Theory:
An Affect-Based Approach
to Recurrent Decision Making

Tilmann Betsch
University of Erfurt, Germany

In this chapter, I introduce a theory of decision making that emphasizes the fundamental importance of routines and affect in choice. In classical decision theories, neither routine nor affect has played a key role for a long time. Decision researchers almost exclusively focused on new decisions and thus neglected the importance of prior behavior. This neglect was at least partly caused by the dominance of the *gambling paradigm*—a research paradigm in which participants are asked to choose among artificial monetary lotteries. Values and probabilities in these problems are stated by the researcher. Prior experience rarely applies to such gambling problems. Most of the biases and anomalies that fill the textbooks were identified by studies using this research paradigm (see Goldstein & Hogarth, 1997, for an overview). Not surprisingly, decision theories were primarily designed to account for decision making in novel situations rather than to explain and predict everyday decisions involving experience and routines.

Although this shortcoming has been recognized and lamented earlier (Abelson & Levi, 1985; Janis & Mann, 1977; Triandis, 1977), research on prior behavior and decision making did not accumulate until the late 1990s (see Betsch & Haberstroh, chap. 20, this volume; Betsch et al., 2002; Verplanken & Aarts, 1999; Zsambok & Klein, 1997, for overviews). A considerable number of studies was conducted in naturalistic settings with expert decision makers (e.g., Lipshitz et al., 2001). There are also attempts, however, to manipulate behavioral knowledge such as the strength of routines in the laboratory (e.g., Betsch, Haberstroh et al., 2001). To date, there is ample evidence indicating that prior behavioral knowledge in general, and routines in particular, systematically impact deliberate decision making.

A similar development can be witnessed with regard to affect. Although affect has always played a key role in other areas of psychology, the majority of decision researchers focused on the cognitive side of choice (Busemeyer et al., 1995). In 1994, Antonio Damasio, a neurologist, published a book that challenged the cognitive approach to decision making. Damasio reported evidence indicating that damage to the ventromedial frontal cortices substantially impairs the patients' ability to make rational decisions. Most important, the cognitive abilities of those patients were perfectly intact, whereas the affective abilities were not. Specifically, anticipation of choice consequences did not evoke positive or negative feelings in the patients. Those and other findings encouraged decision researchers to study the impact of affect on decisions (e.g., Finucane et al., 2000; Mellers et al., 1999; Van der Plight et al., 1998). New models and theoretical frameworks emerged. Paul Slovic and colleagues (2003), for example, suggested that many mundane decisions and a couple of effects obtained in the laboratory (e.g., preference reversals, evaluability effects) can be attributed to the work of a simple affect heuristic. Robin Hogarth (2001; chap. 4, this volume) recently developed a framework to explain the role of feelings and intuition in decision making.

The theory to be presented next extends this line of theorizing. Preference theory assumes that most of our decisions center on our prior behavioral knowledge and particularly on our routines. Moreover, it postulates that decision making is primarily guided by the affective reactions that are elicited by the alternatives under consideration. Before I introduce preference theory, I briefly define the key concepts of the theory—routine and affect.

ROUTINES

We use the term *routine* to refer to a learned behavioral solution b, which comes to mind when a decision problem p is encountered by the individual. The representation of a decision problem p consists of goals or desires (e.g., "I'm hungry, I want to get something spicy to eat") and typical context features (e.g., "It is lunch time and I am at the office"). Goals and context features provide the antecedent conditions for choice. They call for action and define what should be achieved in a given type of situation (cf. Bagozzi & Dholakia, chap. 2, this volume). The routine is the behavior (e.g., "go to the Chinese restaurant"), which, by virtue of past experience, is known to serve the goals embedded in the particular type of situation. Routines can differ with regard to the strength they are associated with p in memory. One important factor that affects this association is repetition frequency. In our research, my colleagues and I have exclusively focused on nonautomatic routines (Betsch et al., 1998, 1999, 2000, 2001, 2004). If a routine is frequently repeated, however, it can become automatic (i.e., the behavior can be automatically instantiated on recognition of the decision problem). Automatic routines are commonly called *habits* (Bryan & Harter, 1899; James, 1890/1950; Ouellette & Wood, 1998; Ronis et al., 1988; Verplanken, Myrbakk, & Rudi, chap. 13, this volume; Verplanken & Aarts, 1999).

AFFECT

The term *affect* refers to the hedonic quality of experience—the positive and negative feelings evoked by a stimulus in the individual. Affective responses need no inferences (Zajonc, 1980). They are the first reactions that automatically arise when a (familiar) stimulus exceeds the threshold of consciousness (Wundt, 1907). Affect requires direct experience. To a substantial part, the affective reactions vis-à-vis a behavioral alternative reflect the prior experiences with that behavior. In such, the affective orientation toward a behavior is the product of the continuous work of associative learning (Triandis, 1977). There are good reasons to assume that affect should be conceptualized at least as a two-dimensional construct (Carver, 2001) involving two independent dimension for positive and negative feelings. Accordingly, a behavior can evoke positive and negative affective responses in the individual at the same time (Cacioppo, Gardner, & Berntson, 1997). Brain research supports this notion. Positive and negative affective reactions are accompanied by electrophysiological activity in different areas of the brain (George et al., 1995). There is also empirical evidence indicating that positive and negative reactions can evolve and change independently (e.g., Goldstein & Strube, 1994). The concept of affect does not imply high activation (Carver, 2001). Consideration of behavioral alternatives, especially of our routines, will probably not always evoke "hot" affective reactions in the individual. Sometimes this might be the case if one imagines spending the night with one's beloved partner, attending one's favorite opera, or opening a bottle of the best wine from the cellar. Regularly, however, the affective reactions toward an eligible behavior will manifest in moderate feelings of liking or disliking.

THEORY

Preference theory provides an affect-based framework to understand recurrent decision making. Its major tenets are summarized in six assumptions, which I introduce hereafter. The process of decision making is depicted in Fig. 3.1. The present outline of the theory consists of four parts. The first

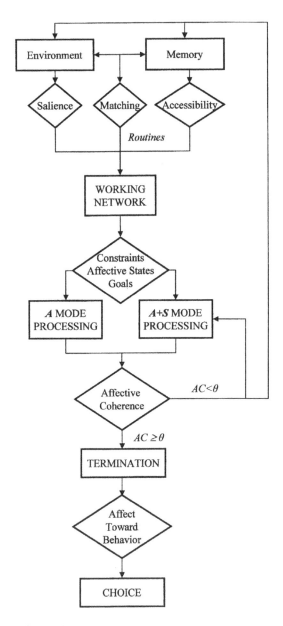

FIG. 3.1. Preference theory—The process of decision making.

part concerns the representation of prior knowledge and new evidence in a temporary working network. In the second part, I introduce a dual-process model for predicting the mechanisms of information processing before a decision is made (autonomous [A] mode, supervisor [S] mode). In the third part, I put forward a rule for termination of the decision process that rests on affective coherence. Finally, in the fourth part, I introduce an affect-based rule for choice.

Formation of Temporary Working Network

This section concerns the first stage of the decision process—the selection and representation of information after a decision problem has been encountered. Specifically, it deals with the transition of information from long-term memory and the environment into a temporary working network. The information contained in this hypothetical network provides the input for the decision. Consideration of memory processes has not been pervasive in classical decision research (Weber, Goldstein, & Busemeyer, 1991). They are of fundamental importance, however, if one considers routinized decision making that capitalizes on prior experience.

Cognitive Components. Preference theory borrows on a connectionist metaphor to describe how pieces of input information are represented in working memory. Accordingly, the representation of a decision problem (goals, antecedent conditions), behavioral alternatives (routines, other alternatives), evaluations (cognitive representations of "goodness" or "badness"), beliefs, and other kinds of information altogether form a temporary working network. The links between the units are assumed to represent the learned relations among them. For example, an exhibitory link between a behavior and a goal symbolizes goal promotion, whereas an inhibitory link represents goal obstruction (e.g., Thagard & Millgram, 1995). The network metaphor is further illustrated in the section on affect.

The input for the working network is provided by the environment and long-term memory (see Fig. 3.1). Preference theory assumes that three mechanisms drive the formation of the working network. One rests on the principle of *matching*; the others rest on the principles of *salience* and *accessibility*. Information that is salient in the environment or currently accessible in memory is automatically fed into the working network regardless of whether it is applicable to the decision problem. In contrast, the matching process involves directed memory search and selection of applicable information. The key assumption is that, whenever a decision problem arises, the system searches in long-term memory for applicable routines. In the previous section, I defined a *routine* as a learned behavioral solution b to a decision problem p. The activation of a particular routine from the behavioral repertoire depends on the match between the previously encountered type of decision problem, p_{old}, and the current decision problem, p_{new}. When the match or degree of similarity between p_{old} and p_{new} exceeds a threshold of acceptability, the appropriate routine is fed into the working network. The postulates put forward so far are summarized in the following.

Assumption 1. Whenever a decision problem p_{new} is encountered, the memory is searched for representations of a similar decision problem p_{old}. If the match between p_{new} and p_{old} exceeds a threshold of acceptability, the appropriate routine is fed into a temporary working network and is linked to the other pieces of information that are salient in the environment or currently available from memory.

Affect. A number of models converge in assuming that the identification or recognition of a behavioral rule, script, or policy can be sufficient as a condition to instigate the implementation of a behavioral routine (Aarts & Dijksterhuis, 2000; Abelson, 1981; Beach, 1990; Goldstein & Gigerenzer, 2002; Klein, 1999; Ross, Lussier, & Klein, chap. 18, this volume; Verplanken, Myrbakk, & Rudi, chap. 13, this volume). Preference theory, in contrast, assumes that decision making is primarily determined by the affective reactions toward the behavior under consideration and not merely by recognition. I put forward affect-based rules for termination of the decision process and for choice in Assumptions 5 and 6 (see also Fig. 3.1). In this section, I focus on how affect shapes the representation of a decision problem.

Consider the case that a routine or any other "old" behavioral alternative is loaded into the working network. Preference theory posits that it will immediately evoke affective reactions depending on the nodes in the network to which it is associated. To a considerable degree, these affective reactions depend on the goals contained in the working network. The affective reactions vis-à-vis a goal are assumed to reflect the entire stream of prior goal-relevant experiences or feedback a person has made with this particular behavior (cf. Harvey & Fischer, chap. 7, this volume). Specifically, any instance of goal promotion will increase or consolidate the disposition that the behavior will evoke positive affective reactions when it is activated from memory together with the goal. Instances of goal obstruction, in turn, increase or consolidate the disposition for the elicitation of negative affective reactions. In such, the affective system registers the hedonic quality of behavioral alternatives. The resulting affective orientation or attitude toward a behavior establishes the crucial link between past experience and future decisions (Betsch, Hoffmann, Hoffrage, & Plessner, 2003; Betsch, Plessner, & Schallies, in press; Betsch, Plessner, Schwieren, & Gütig, 2001; see also Sanbonmatsu, Prince, Vanous, & Posavac, chap. 6, this volume).

Taken together, preference theory posits that past experience is mainly conveyed by affect in decision making.

The affective reactions toward a behavior not only reflect the goals to which the behavior is tied, but also other pieces of information contained in the working network. As an example, consider the following situation. It is lunchtime and you are at your office. You are hungry, but you do not wish to spend much money on food. This particular combination of antecedent conditions (lunchtime, being at the office) and goals (get something tasty to eat, save money) activates your routine from memory (e.g., to go to the Chinese restaurant). Activation of the routine is accompanied by the elicitation of positive affective reactions, reflecting your goal-relevant experiences with this behavior in the past (you had many tasty meals at this place, meals were never expensive). Now assume a nasty colleague (who knows about your restaurant preferences) comes into your office to inform you that he found a cockroach in his meal the last time he had been to the Chinese restaurant. Associating your routine with such a disgusting event might spoil your positive feelings toward your routine (cf. Rozin & Royzman, 2001). The example illustrates that the concert of affective reactions toward a behavior can be conceived as a joint function of the history of prior goal promotion and obstruction on the one hand, and of other pieces of currently accessible information.

Assumption 2. The pattern of affective reactions evoked by a behavior reflects the entire set of prior experiences (promotion and obstruction) with regard to the activated goals, and the affective reactions evoked by the other constituents to which it is tied in the working network.

PROCESSING NETWORK INFORMATION

A temporary working network contains cognitive components, such as representations of goals, context conditions, evaluations, and behaviors, and affective components, which represent the feelings toward the behavioral alternatives. Preference theory assumes that the information contained in the working network can be processed in two different ways before a decision is made. First, the activation of the nodes in the working network can be changed. Second, the structure of the network can be changed. Structural changes involve adding new information and altering the relations between the constituents (formally represented by the weights of the links between the nodes). Both kinds of changes influence the pattern of affective reactions toward the behaviors. I first delineate the operation of the modes. Thereafter, I introduce the factors that trigger mode selection.

A Mode: Autonomous Change of Activation

Autonomous or A-mode processing is assumed to be the default strategy in decision making. The A mode is on set whenever a working network for a decision problem is formed. A-mode operation does not require deliberative supervision, and it cannot be terminated by volitional verdict. It requires only a minimum of mental resources. A single process characterizes this mode–activation change. Under A-mode operation, the structure of the working network (number of nodes or nodes relations) remains stable and provides the constraints under which the activations of the nodes evolve. The activation of a node within the network depends on the activation it receives from the other nodes. If two nodes are symmetrically connected, activation of one node will yield activation of the other if the connection is excitatory (positively weighted connection). Conversely, in the case of an inhibitory linkage (negative weight), activation of one node will lead to deactivation of the other. A positive or excitatory link reflects a facilitative relation among nodes (promotion, compatibility, causation, confirmation, etc.), whereas a negative or inhibitory link reflects a nonfacilitative relation (obstruction, incompatibility, inhibition, negation, etc.).

For illustration, let us return to the restaurant example. Assume that your colleague suggests to lunch at the Sushi Bar after he has told you about the cockroach incident. You know that the Sushi Bar offers delicious meals. However, they are very expensive. A hypothetical network for the resulting decision problem is depicted in Fig. 3.2. It contains five types of

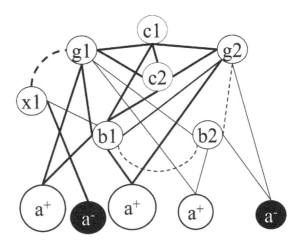

FIG. 3.2. Example of a hypothetical working network containing two behavioral alternatives (b1, b2), two goals (g1, g2), antecedent conditions (c1, c2), and another piece of information (x1). These cognitive representations are linked to positive (a⁺) and negative (a⁻) affective reactions. Links between nodes can be exhibitory (solid lines) or inhibitory (dotted lines).

nodes, goals (g_i), antecedent conditions (c_i), behaviors (b_i), other cognitions (x_i), and affective reactions (a^+, a^-). Specifically, it contains the two goals "get something tasty to eat" ($g1$) and "save money" ($g1$); the antecedent conditions "lunchtime" ($c1$) and "being at the office" ($c2$); the routine behavior "have lunch at the Chinese Restaurant" ($b1$) and the alternative "have lunch at the Sushi Bar" ($b2$); the "cockroach incident" ($x1$); and a number of affective reactions (a^+, a^-).

Relations among nodes are expressed by solid and dotted lines, which represent exhibitory and inhibitory associations, respectively. Formally, the strength of associations can be expressed by weights. For the sake of simplicity, the exhibit merely shows bold lines indicating strong associations and thin lines indicating weak associations. The routine ($b1$) holds strong exhibitory relations with the antecedent conditions ($c1$, $c2$), the two goals ($g1$, $g2$), and positive affective reactions. The strength of these exhibitory relations reflects prior associative learning. Moreover, the affective reactions are comparatively strong (big circles). This reflects the continuous registration of the hedonic quality of instances of goal promotion in the past.[1] The new piece of information ($x1$) holds inhibitory link to the first goal ($g1$) and evokes a negative affective reaction (e.g., disgust). Note that the routine and negative affect are not directly connected. This reflects the assumption that a direct association between a behavior and an affective reaction requires prior associative learning (you never had a cockroach in your meal at the Chinese restaurant before). The alternative ($b2$) holds weaker associations with the goals and affective reactions that reflect a smaller sample of prior learning compared with the routine behavior. Nevertheless, positive affect vis-à-vis the hedonic goal ($g1$) is strong (meals were delicious when you attended the Sushi Bar). The inhibitory link between $b1$ and $g2$ reflects goal obstruction. Specifically, meals at the Sushi Bar were awfully expensive. The two alternatives ($b1$, $b2$) are negatively connected because they are mutually exclusive behaviors (you cannot have lunch at the same time in two different restaurants).

The resulting activation of a node in the network is assumed to be a function of all the inputs (activations, deactivations) it receives from the other nodes. The level of a node's activation can be seen as the solution to the constraints represented by the links. The process of dynamic activation adjustment, or *parallel constraint satisfaction* as it is often termed (e.g., Read, Vanman, & Miller, 1997), involves continuous activation change. It is possible, although not necessary, that the nodes' activations eventually reach stable (asymptotic) values and the process of passing and updating activa-

---

[1]My coworkers and I provided evidence that implicit registration of hedonic experiences follows a summation principle. We termed the resulting hypothetical knowledge structure *value account* (e.g., Betsch, Plessner, Schwieren, & Gütig, 2001).

tions can be stopped. Several possible activation functions have been suggested modeling the process of activation updating in a connectionist network (e.g., McClelland & Rumelhart, 1986; Smith, 1996; Thagard, 1989). Thagard and Millgram (1995) recently provided a computational implementation to model activation change in decision networks. Because such formal models have been fruitfully applied to a variety of domains of judgment (e.g., Kunda & Thagard, 1996; Shultz & Lepper, 1996), I do not attempt to add another.

The activation of a node reflects the properties of the entire network because the nodes in the working network are interconnected and pass activations among each other. Consequently, the experienced intensity of an affective reaction toward a behavior is a function of the entire information contained in the working network. In such, affective reactions tuned by A-mode operation indicate the valence of a behavior by taking prior experiences, new evidence, and the complex structure of relations among all nodes into account. A-mode operation does not change the structure of the network. It neither adds nor eliminates nodes (e.g., goals, behaviors, affective reactions), nor does it change relations or, to put it in technical terms, the weights among the nodes. What it does is accentuate the relative importance of a node within the concert of the others by changing its activation.

In such, A-mode operation is conservative and context-sensitive at the same time. It is conservative because it leaves the structure of the network unchanged. In other words, the weights on the links representing the relations among nodes serve as constraints to the decision process. These relations primarily reflect associative learning from prior behavioral episodes. A-mode operation conserves prior experience. In contrast, the A mode is sensitive to the particular situation. All pieces of information that constitute the temporary working network will affect the relative importance of each other. Therefore, there is some latitude for changes in preferences or goal hierarchies. These changes manifest themselves in changes in activation. The latitude of activation change, however, is constrained by the learned relations expressed by the weights on the links among nodes.

Consider the hypothetical working network depicted in Fig. 3.2 again. Apparently, the routine behavior (b1) holds more exhibitory relations to other nodes than the alternative behavior (b2). Moreover, most of these links are stronger than the associations between the alternative and the other nodes. Therefore, under A-mode processing, the routine's activation will increase. As a consequence, the activation of the positive affective reactions associated with the routine will also increase despite the fact that the disgusting incident has been associated with the routine. This means that under A-mode processing, the new information (x1) can be expected to only have a weak influence on the activation of affective reactions toward the routine. In this example, A-mode processing is likely to decrease the impact of new information on choice and accentuate the impact of prior knowledge.

S Mode: Supervised Structural Change

Supervised or S-mode processing can change both the activation and structure of the network. On the phenomenological level, the S mode is characterized by attention, deliberation, and mental control. A decision maker can focus on a specific information contained in the working network and evaluate the desirability and probability of its consequences with respect to a certain goal. Such mental activity can result in specific changes to the network. First, mere focusing causes amplification of a node's activation. Second, new nodes can be added to the network, for instance, as a result of inference processes or active search for information in memory or the environment. Third, a decision maker can deliberatively change the relations among nodes in the network. For example, consideration of new evidence might result in changes of prior beliefs about a behavior's feasibility. Such changes can be modeled by tuning the weights of the links among nodes. A positively weighted connection between a goal and a behavior (indicating goal promotion) can be changed toward the negative direction to represent goal obstruction.

Assume you start pondering about the restaurant problem (Fig. 3.2). Presumably, your attention might be absorbed by the disgusting cockroach incident. Merely focusing on this piece of information will increase its activation and, thus, its relative importance in the working network. You might also start to assess the validity of the evidence. Assume that the Chinese restaurant has always been a clean place and your colleague is a known joker. In this case, you might conclude that the cockroach story was not true and, therefore, should not be considered in the decision. This conclusion changes the structure of the network. In technical terms, the weights on the link between the incident (x1) and the hedonic goal (g1), and on the link between the incident and the routine behavior (b1), will decrease. This reduces the impact of the new evidence on the decision. The opposite might happen if you believe that your colleague is an honest and a serious person. As a consequence, the weights on the associations between the incident and the connected nodes will increase in strength. Moreover, the positive weight between the routine (b1) and the hedonic goal (g1) might be changed to a negative weight. This would represent your conviction that you are unable to enjoy any kind of meal in a restaurant that hosts cockroaches. In this case, the relative influence of the piece of evidence on the decision will increase substantially.

Preference theory assumes that changes of weights caused by S-mode operations are transient and require cognitive control to last. The rationale behind this proposition is that the relations between nodes are developed within a slow learning system that obeys the rules of associative and feedback learning (cf. Sedlmeier, chap. 5, this volume). For instance, the learned relation between a goal and a behavior largely reflects the individual's reinforcement history. Although such learned relations can be temporarily altered by virtue of deliberation, lasting changes require feedback about the consequences of the behavior (see also Hogarth, chap. 4, this volume). When S-mode operation causes changes to the original relations among nodes, S-mode control is necessary to conserve these changes during the decision process. It does not suffice, however, that the S mode is on-set. Additionally, the focus of attention has to be placed on the changed part of the network. These processes consume cognitive resources. Consequently, distraction, emergence of constraints, or withdrawal of cognitive resources increase the likelihood that the weight of the changed links approximates their prior values. The propositions about A-mode and S-mode processing are summarized in the third assumption.

Assumption 3. Under A-mode operation, the activations of the nodes in the working network are automatically changed contingent on the constraints imposed by the network structure. Structural changes (adding information, changing relations among nodes) require S-mode operation. In the absence of S-mode control, changed relations tend to reach their prior state.

Mode Selection

Preference theory assumes that A-mode processing is automatically instigated whenever a decision problem arises. In such, the A mode provides the default strategy for decision making. Most important, the rules for termination and choice are handled by the A mode. Thus, decisions can be reached without S-mode operation. These are the decisions that appear to be automatic. However, decisions can be supervised and influenced by deliberative or reflective mental operations. The point in time at which the focus of attention is shifted toward the information contained in the working network is called S-mode onset. Subsequent S-mode processing will not cause off-set of the A mode. Preference theory assumes that the S mode can only work in concert with the A mode and never alone.

What are the determinants of S-mode on-set? Preference theory posits that the likelihood of S-mode on-set is a function of three classes of factors—*capacity constraints, affect,* and *activation of deliberation goals* (see Fig. 3.1). Deliberative or reflective activities consume a greater amount of cognitive resources than automatic processes. Therefore, variables that reduce the available amount of cognitive resources should obstruct on-set and operation of the S mode. Many of those variables have been identified in the literature—for instance, time pressure (Svenson & Maule, 1993; Wright, 1974), resource consumption by other tasks (Stager & Zufelt, 1972), high arousal (Easterbrook, 1959), fatigue (Christensen-Szalanski, 1978), or intoxication (MacDonald, Zanna, & Fong, 1995; Steele & Josephs, 1990).

Preference theory assumes that affect is not only the crucial determinant of choice, but is also a key determinant of processing style. Everything else being equal, S-mode on-set is assumed to become more likely according to the extent that the representation of the current decision problem is accompanied by negative affect. Negative affect signals failure, threat, or danger. In such, affect is assumed to bear an informative function of what is currently at stake in a decision (Oatley & Johnson-Laird, 1987; Simon, 1967; see also Bless & Igou, chap. 11, this volume). Preference theory posits that negative affect provokes S-mode operation.

There is another important aspect of affect. Preference theory assumes that S-mode on-set depends on the degree of affective coherence (AC) produced by the working network. The concept of AC is spelled out in the next section. Basically, AC is a property of the pattern of affective reactions evoked by the representation of a decision problem. High AC reflects, for instance, absence of decisional conflict. Conversely, low AC reflects the lack of dominance or presence of decisional conflict. Low AC or incoherence is assumed to instigate S-mode on-set (see Fig. 3.1).

The last factor—activation of deliberation goals—is a trivial, although important, one. In the case a deliberation goal has been recently activated, subsequent decisions are more likely to be made under S-mode control than otherwise. Deliberation goals can be set up intentionally—for example, by self-instruction or compliance with task requirements. Owing to suboptimal outcomes of prior decisions, an individual might decide to think more carefully in subsequent decisions. The activation of deliberation goals may also vary as a function of individual differences. It has been suggested, for instance, that people may differ in their need for cognition (Cohen, Stotland, & Wolfe, 1955) or validity (Kruglanski & Webster, 1996). Accordingly, people with a high need for cognition or validity may supervise their decisions more frequently. The propositions regarding mode selection are summarized in the fourth assumption.

Assumption 4. The information contained in the working network will always be processed in the A mode. The likelihood that the S mode will additionally be on-set increases to the extent that capacity constraints are low, negative affect is high, affective coherence is low, and deliberation goals are activated.

TERMINATION OF THE DECISION PROCESS

Preference theory postulates that termination of information processing depends on the level of affective coherence (AC). AC is a property of the pattern of affective reactions that are evoked by the cognitive representation of the decision problem (see bottom layer in Fig. 3.2). If AC in the network exceeds a critical threshold (θ_{AC}), the decision process is terminated and the decision rule (see next paragraph) is applied. The level of the subjective threshold, θ_{AC}, may depend on several factors, such as the subjective importance of the decision problem or the time available for the decision. Preference theory assumes that θ_{AC} will be lowered when time pressure increases.

The AC evoked by a decision problem at a particular point in time is assumed to be a joint function of the affective coherence *within* the behaviors (ACW) and the affective coherence between the behaviors included in the working network (ACB):

$$AC = f\ [\Sigma ACW_i,\ ACB]$$

ACW_i reflects the inside structure of affective reactions toward a particular alternative *i*. Affective reactions with common polarity are assumed to cohere (positive–positive; negative–negative), whereas affective reactions with divergent polarity (positive–negative) are assumed to be incoherent. Accordingly, an option that primarily evokes one type of reaction (positive or negative) is considered to be affectively coherent. Conversely, emotional ambiguity (positive and negative affective reactions at the same time) decreases the affective coherence of an option. For example, the alternative b2 in Fig. 3.2 is low in ACW because it simultaneously evokes positive and negative affective reactions at the same time.

ACB reflects the affective difference between the alternatives. ACB is high if alternatives clearly differ with regard to their net affect A. The net affect toward a behavior *i* equals the sum of affective reactions a_j, which are directly associated with the behavior. Each affective reaction is weighted by its current level of activation w_j in the network:

$$A_i = \Sigma\ a_{ij} w_j$$

Recall that the level of activation is produced by A-mode processing, which involves passing of activation through the network. In such, the current activation of an affective reaction mirrors the properties of the entire working network. High ACB indicates a dominance relation between behaviors. This means that the eligible behaviors are distinct with regard to their mutual net affect. Low ACB indicates similarity. Accordingly, the behaviors hold similar net-affect values.

In an ideal decision situation, overall AC is high. Such a situation is characterized by dominance (one behavior clearly dominates the others, high ACB) and absence of ambiguity (each behavior evokes primarily positive or primarily negative reactions, high ACW). Under high AC, the decision process can be quickly terminated, and the most promising candidate can be selected. Therefore, the system seeks to achieve and maintain a level of AC beyond an acceptability threshold. These propositions are summarized in the fifth assumption.

Assumption 5. If affective coherence, AC, exceeds a critical threshold, θ_{AC}, processing of the information in the working network is terminated. The likelihood that AC exceeds θ_{AC} increases to the extent that (a) the net-affect values, A_i, differentiate between the behaviors (ACB), (b) the affective reactions within each behavior are similar or unambiguous (ACW), and (c) time and processing constraints cause lowering of θ_{AC}. The processing system tends to achieve and maintain AC beyond θ_{AC}.

CHOICE AND ATTITUDE TOWARD THE BEHAVIOR

After predecisional processing of the network has been terminated, the decision rule can be applied. Preference theory posits only one decision rule. It exclusively rests on the assessment of the affective reactions and not an assessment of cognitive elements such as evaluations and beliefs. Only the behavior that evokes the highest net-affect A is considered. If the alternatives involve positive outcomes, it is the behavior with the highest positive net affect. In the case that behaviors involve negative outcomes (avoidance decisions), it is the behavior with least negative net affect. The net affect of the behavior, A_i, is compared against an acceptability threshold, θ_A. If it exceeds the threshold, the behavior is chosen. The attitude toward the behavior is assumed to be a joint function of its net affect and the affective coherence of all the behaviors included in the working network. Accordingly, the attitude toward the behavior i increases in favorability with increasing A_i and increasing AC.

Assumption 6. After information processing has been terminated, the behavior with the highest net-affect A is chosen if it exceeds an acceptability threshold θ_A. The attitude toward the behavior is a joint function of the behavior's net affect A and the affective coherence AC.

In the next section, I use preference theory to account for a major class of phenomena in recurrent decision making. We know from an increasing number of studies that decision makers are sometimes conservative in their choices, neglect new evidence, and stick to their routines. However, there is also evidence for the opposite case. Sometimes people neglect prior success rates of behaviors, follow new evidence, and instantly deviate from their routines. I show that preference theory is capable of predicting the conditions under which people maintain or deviate from their routines.

EMPIRICAL EVIDENCE

Sometimes decision making is a strenuous affair. It consumes time and cognitive effort to wage the pros and cons of behavioral alternatives. The costs of deliberation can be effectively reduced through routinization (Athay & Darley, 1981). Learning a repertoire of routines enables the actor to quickly respond to recurrent choice situations. Indeed, it is an adaptive strategy to maintain a routine as long as the context remains stable and the consequences of the behavior meet the individual's goals. However, the context can change as personal goals change. Changes in the world can alter the contingencies between behaviors and outcomes. If the routine stops to promote the goals of the actor, it would be maladaptive to further maintain the routine.

A general theory of decision making has to be capable of predicting the conditions under which decision makers maintain or deviate from their routines. In this section, I consider four types of routine-decision situations that differ with regard to problem recognition and the presence of counterevidence to the routine: status quo (problem recognition, absence of counterevidence), conflict (problem recognition, presence of counterevidence), challenge (imperfect problem recognition, presence of counterevidence), and doubt (imperfect problem recognition, absence of counterevidence). These types cover a wide range of settings under which researchers have been studying routinized decision making. I also briefly consider novel decision situations for which routines are not available. On the basis of the six assumptions introduced previously, I delineate how preference theory accounts for decision making in these situations. I substantiate the predictions by empirical evidence stemming mostly from our own research on routinized decision making.

As we see, routines can produce both conservatism and base-rate neglect in preferential decision making depending on the interaction among recognition of the situation, presence of counterevidence, and processing style. Throughout the book, the reader can find discussions of other routine effects that, for the sake of brevity, cannot be considered here (cf. Betsch & Haberstroh, chap. 20, this volume; Haberstroh, Betsch, Glöckner,

Haar, & Stiller, chap. 12, this volume; Johnson & Busemeyer, chap. 1, this volume; Reimer, Bornstein, & Opwis, chap. 10, this volume; Wänke & Friese, chap. 16, this volume).

Status Quo: Problem Recognition and Absence of Counterevidence

Obviously, there are some trivial conditions encouraging people to repeat prior choices. If the decision context remains stable and the routine is steadfastly reinforced by instances of goal promotion, we commonly find that routines are immediately maintained on recognition of the situation (Ouellette & Wood, 1998; Ronis, Yates, & Kirscht, 1988). This finding is in line with theories of learning (e.g., Davis, Staddon, Machado, & Palmer, 1993; Hull, 1943), attitude-behavior models (e.g., Fazio, 1990; Triandis, 1977), and an increasing number of theories of recurrent decision making (e.g., Betsch, Haberstroh, & Höhle, 2002; Johnson & Busemeyer, chap. 1, this volume; Klein, 1999; Pennington & Hastie, 1992; Ross, Lussier, & Klein, chap. 18, this volume; Verplanken, Myrbakk, & Rudi, chap. 13, this volume).

Preference theory also accounts for status quo decision making. According to Assumption 1 (A1), routine activation is triggered by a matching process. Recurrent decision problems of the present type are characterized by a stable combination of salient cues. Therefore, they match the internal representation of the antecedents of the decision problem. Hence, stable problems directly and unambiguously activate the routine from memory. Preference theory further posits (A2) that the slow learning system registers the entire history of those behavioral consequences pertaining to the goals pursued by the actor. The personal history of goal promotion and obstruction is conveyed by the affective system. A routine that has been repeatedly and reliably reinforced by goal achievement in the past will primarily evoke positive and not negative affective reactions. Consequently, the affective reactions toward those routines are highly coherent (*ACW*, see A5). Additionally, we can expect that routines evoke highly positive net affect especially if they had been frequently and successfully repeated in the past (A2). The affective lead of such a routine is not challenged in a status quo situation. Hence, the overall pattern of affective reactions in the working network favors the routine. The absence or extremely low level of affective incoherence allows the system to finish information processing very quickly. Thus, information processing and choice do not require S-mode operation (A3, A4). The entire process of decision making can be performed in the A mode. Therefore, preference theory predicts instant routine choice (conservatism) in status quo situations unless explicit deliberation goals have been activated before (A4).

Challenge: Perfect Problem Recognition
and Presence of Counterevidence

Assume a decision maker recognizes a familiar decision problem (perfect match between p_{new} and p_{old}). As a consequence, the routine (and only the routine) is activated from memory (A1). Further assume that after problem recognition, new evidence is encountered that challenges the adequacy of the routine. As an illustration, consider our restaurant example (Fig. 3.2). The stable features of the recurrent situation (being at the office, lunchtime) and the same combination of personal goals (have a tasty meal, save money, etc.) activate the person's routine (Chinese restaurant) from memory. Thereafter, an additional piece of information is encoded that evokes unfavorable affective reactions (colleague says he found a cockroach in his Chinese meal).

Preference theory predicts that challenge of a routine after problem recognition provokes a tendency in individuals to neglect or underweight new evidence and maintain their routine. Problem match immediately activates the routine alternative and instigates a favorable pattern of affective reactions toward the routine (A1). If information is processed in the A mode, the structure of prior associations remains stable and is not influenced by new evidence (A3). New information can only contribute to the decision process by changing the activations of associated nodes in the network. The relative influence of new evidence under A-mode operation depends on the strength or consolidation of the routine complex (goals, antecedents, routine, and learned affective reactions) in the network. The stronger the bonds among goals, affective reactions, and the routine, the less likely it is that a new piece of information can prevent the system to reach an acceptable level of affective coherence that allows the system to terminate the decision process and choose the routine (A5, A6).

Under S-mode operation, however, prior relations can be (temporarily) altered, and, thus, the impact of new information can increase substantially (A3). Nevertheless, preference theory predicts that individuals tend to stick to their routine even when they walk the deliberative route to choice. Recall that the S mode is assumed to always be accompanied by background operation of the A mode (A4; see also Fig. 3.1). As already noted, problem match allows the A mode to quickly identify a choice candidate because affective coherence in the network is generally high. Therefore, changes to the structure of the system bear the threat of decreasing affective coherence in the network. Preference theory, however, assumes that decision makers are motivated to seek and maintain a high level of affective coherence (A5). As a consequence, individuals are likely to downplay the importance, reliability, or probability of challenging evidence and search for pieces of information confirming their routine. This tendency should increase with increasing routine strength (e.g., prior repetition frequency) because initial affective coherence and the affective lead of the routine in the network reflect the prior success rate of the routine (A2).

Taken together, preference theory predicts a general tendency toward conservatism and evidence neglect in challenge situations. Under S-mode operation, it additionally predicts a tendency toward confirmatory or biased processing of new information. Hence, the decision maker in our restaurant example might question the validity of the colleague's report ("found a cockroach in the meal"), rather than change her belief in the adequacy of her routine.

These predictions are in line with recent findings from laboratory research on routinized decision making. In one study (Betsch, Brinkmann, Fiedler, & Breining, 1999), my colleagues and I trained participants to prefer a certain choice (routine) over a couple of recurrent decision trials. Prior to each decision, participants looked up relevant information in a choice by attribute matrix. Movements in the matrix were tracked by using a variant of the Mouselab procedure introduced by Johnson and colleagues (1986). Time pressure was varied as an independent variable to constrain S-mode processing. After the learning trials, the entries in the pay-off matrix were altered so that the routine was dominated by other alternatives. Although participants looked up information that challenged the routine, they maintained the routine under severe time limits. This finding supports the prediction that people are conservative in their choices in challenge situations.

In another study, we examined how the level of routine strength affects information acquisition in deliberative decision making (Betsch, Haberstroh, et al., 2001, Exp. 2). First, participants were trained to prefer a certain choice alternative either 15 or 30 times on average over a series of recurrent decision trials (induction of weak and strong routines). In a second phase of the study, half of the participants were confronted with a highly similar description of another decision problem (high problem match), whereas the others received an unfamiliar description of the problem (low problem match; for results, see next section). We found evidence for a confirmation bias in subsequent information search when problem match was high. Moreover, confirmation biases almost vanished in weak routine participants—a finding that additionally supports Assumption 2, stating that affect toward the routine reflects the entire learning history.

Conflict: Imperfect Problem Recognition and Challenging Evidence

Unfamiliar aspects of the task can decrease perceived problem match if they are salient or activated from memory when a decision problem is encountered. A challenging piece of evidence can also impair problem recognition if it is simultaneously encoded. Under impaired recognition, it is un-likely that a learned solution can be immediately identified. Hence, the search in long-term memory may become more intense. Moreover, the acceptance threshold for matching candidates may be lowered. As a consequence, the likelihood increases that multiple behavioral candidates will be loaded into the working network. If the working network contains multiple candidates from the repertoire of learned behaviors, the level of affective coherence in the network is likely to be lower in comparison to a perfect match situation.

What happens in a decision situation that involves (a) imperfect problem match, and (b) new evidence that challenges the routine? Preference theory assumes that the likelihood of routine maintenance depends on the mode of processing. Under A-mode processing (e.g., due to time constraints), preference theory predicts that routinized decision makers are still likely to maintain their routine. This tendency should increase as a function of routine strength. Conversely, it predicts that individuals tend to deviate from their routine if information is processed in the S mode. In other words, preference theory predicts conservatism or evidence neglect under A-mode processing and base-rate neglect under S-mode processing.

If information in the network can only be processed in the A mode, preference theory generally predicts that the relative influence of contradicting evidence is weak (A3). Therefore, the routine with the highest net affect is chosen as soon as an acceptable level of affective coherence is achieved. In a conflict situation, the level of affective coherence is likely to decrease because other behavioral candidates are contained in the working network. A-mode processing can yield an increase in affective coherence by changing the activations of the nodes (under the constraint that the weights between links are kept stable; see A3). However, activation change may fail to bring out a level of affective coherence exceeding the acceptability threshold (1). Now there are two possibilities. Either the threshold is lowered or the S mode is on-set. If time and cognitive constraints prevent the system from operating in the S mode, the threshold is lowered (A5). Such a change of the criterion again leads to routine maintenance.

Next, consider the case that the situation allows for S-mode operation. In the previous paragraph, I argued that new information is neglected or down weighted under S-mode operation. Recall, however, that in the previous type of situation (challenge), affective coherence was high from the moment the network was built. Hence, affective coherence had to be merely maintained rather than achieved. Conversely, in conflict situations, the pattern of affective reactions is generally less coherent. Thus, the system attempts to increase affective coherence, rather than bolster the network structure against change. Therefore, conflict situations leave greater latitude for change especially if other behavioral candidates are already contained in the working network. Consequently, new pieces of evidence, favoring alternative courses of action, can have a substantial impact on decisions in conflict situations. Prior associations among the routine, its affective reactions, and the goals can be down weighted to achieve affective coherence. In effect of such changes, other behavioral candidates may eventually dominate the routine. Taken together, in conflict situations, the impact of new counterevidence increases under S-mode operation. Thus, individuals are more likely to deviate rather than maintain their routines when they process conflicting information in a deliberative fashion.

In one of our own studies, we manipulated the degree of problem match in routine decision making (Betsch, Fiedler, & Brinkmann, 1998). Prior to the critical decision task, participants received additional evidence, indicating that the demands of the task were altered. This information should challenge the individual's confidence in her routine. Prior to the critical choice task, participants learned to prefer a certain travel route in a trucking game simulation. After learning the routine, half of the participants were exposed to a slightly altered visual presentation of the decision problem on the computer screen, whereas for the other half, the pictorial format was the same as in the learning trials. Altering the depiction of the problem should reduce the actual match between the current appearance of the problem and the representation stored in memory. Recall that under imperfect problem match, preference theory predicts a tendency toward routine choice under A-mode processing and a tendency toward routine deviation under S-mode processing. To induce differential modes of processing, we varied time pressure as the second independent variable. The results converge with the predictions derived from preference theory. Under time pressure, the majority of participants maintained the routine even when the problem's visual presentation was altered. Conversely, without time pressure and when the problem was perceived as being novel, the majority of participants deviated from the routine.

In another study described earlier (Betsch, Haberstroh et al., 2001, Exp. 2), my colleagues and I varied the perceived novelty of the decision task and examined information acquisition in routine decision makers. There were no time constraints so that participants were able to carefully consider new evidence (S-mode operation in all participants). When the presentation of the decision problem slightly deviated from prior trials, participants focused on those pieces of new evidence that challenged their routine choice. In accordance with this information, participants were more likely to deviate from their routine than those individuals who received a familiar problem representation. Most interesting, we found this pattern of information search and choice when routines were strong. This indicates that a strong routine does not necessarily entail evidence neglect and conservatism in choice. As predicted by preference theory, S-mode operation allows the individual to instantly adapt to changes in the information. Instant adaptation, however, requires as a prerequisite that problem match is less than perfect.

Doubt: Imperfect Problem Recognition and Absence of Counterevidence

Under A-mode operation, preference theory again predicts a tendency toward routine maintenance in choice. As pointed out throughout this chapter, this tendency primarily reflects prior learning and, hence, the strength of routines. The stronger a routine is tied to affective reactions and goals (reflecting its reinforcement history), the higher the probability that individuals will maintain their routine under A-mode processing. Both termination of the decision process and choice depend on the pattern of affective reactions in the network. The stronger the routine is, the more positive and coherent reactions it will evoke. The absence of counterevidence further helps in achieving a sufficient level of affective coherence by adjusting the activation of nodes in the network (A3). Otherwise the level of the threshold is lowered. Hence, preference theory predicts conservatism in doubt situations if information is processed in the A mode only.

S-mode processing is a necessary condition for routine deviation in doubt situations. In a conflict situation as described in the previous section, new evidence advises individuals to quit with their routine. In doubt situations, however, the picture is less clear. Therefore, a general choice tendency cannot be predicted without considering the informational architecture of the particular situation beforehand. Similar to conflict situations, inclusion of other candidates in the working network can decrease affective coherence below threshold. If this is the case, individuals will seek and analyze new information in an unbiased fashion. Depending on the evidence available, they may subsequently realize that a new course of action provides a more promising mean to achieve their goals than the routine.

Novel Decision Problems

Preference theory has been designed as a general account of decision making. Thus, it can also be applied to novel decision problems. The major tenet of the theory holds that decisions are guided by the affective reactions toward the behavioral alternatives. Therefore, one has to distinguish between the surface and depth structure of a decision problem. For illustration, consider the gambling paradigm employed in the vast majority of research in the area of judgment and decision making. The stated values and probabilities of the lotteries constitute the surface structure of the problem. After being encoded, they are subjectively represented by the cognitive nodes in the individual's working network. This kind of evaluative and probabilistic knowledge, however, does not directly guide the decision. According to preference theory, the cognitive nodes can only indirectly impact choice. This indirect influence depends on the number and strength of the associations among the cognitive nodes contained in the working network and the affective system. The pattern of affective reactions constitutes the depth structure of a problem representation. According to preference theory, it is necessary to consider the affective consequences of a problem to understand and predict choices in novel decision situations.

A recent re-interpretation of several decision anomalies by Slovic, Finucane, Peters, and MacGregor (2003) underlined the great explanatory potential of an affect-based approach to novel decisions. These authors account for several empirical findings such as preference reversals between pricing and choice (Slovic, 1995), risk perception (Finucane et al., 2000), evaluability effects (Hsee, 1996), and the less-is-better effect (Hsee, 1998). Slovic and colleagues assumed that individuals often rely on an affect heuristic in their decisions. The affect-heuristic approach, however, is not yet sufficiently elaborated on a theoretical level. In a nutshell, the affect heuristic states that individuals sometimes rely on their affective reactions toward the alternatives when they make a decision. In contrast, preference theory provides a more radical and elaborated theoretical approach to affect-based decision making. The scientific study of affect-based decision making is just at its beginning. The set of assumptions put forward in this chapter should stimulate future research and, thus, might help increase our understanding of the role of affect in choice.

CONCLUDING COMMENTS

On several occasions, my colleagues and I analyzed to what extent existing theories of decision making are capable of accounting for the dynamics of recurrent choice (e.g., Betsch, Haberstroh, & Höhle, 2002). Indeed there are some theories available that explicitly address the role of prior behavior in decision making. Promising examples are Bentler and Speckart's (1979) model of attitude–behavior relation, the recognition-primed decision model (Klein, 1999), and Triandis' (1977) model of attitude–behavior relation. However, neither of these models, nor any other theory of decision making, was able to cover the entire process of routinized decision making. Most important, all models failed to predict information search, evaluation of criteria, and the influence of context variables on routinized making. As a consequence, we could not identify any theory in our review that was capable of predicting under which conditions individuals will maintain or deviate from a routine (cf. Betsch, Haberstroh, & Höhle, 2002, p. 481).

The literature reveals that routinized decision makers are sometimes conservative in their choices. They neglect counterevidence and might even actively avoid the consideration of promising alternatives. As a consequence, they stick with their routines even if they are obviously inadequate in the given situation. However, there is also evidence indicating a converse tendency in choice. Sometimes even strong routine individuals are highly sensitive to new evidence and instantly quit with their routines. From a Bayesian point of view, those individuals underweigh or even neglect the prior base rate of successful routine implementation.

In this chapter, I introduced an affect-based theory of decision making. The previous section showed that preference theory can account for both conservatism and base-rate neglect in recurrent decision making. The prior discussion revealed that decision making in experienced individuals reflects a complex interaction of a bunch of factors, including problem recognition, new evidence, processing style, and routine strength. Preference theory is capable of capturing these factors and predicting their interaction. In such, preference theory exceeds prior theories with regard to predictive power. Having said this, I am pleased to note that theorists are currently increasing their efforts to model recurrent decision making. The chapter by Johnson and Busemeyer (chap. 1, this volume) provides an excellent example. Elaborating on decision field theory (Busemeyer & Townsend, 1993), these authors delineate a formal model of recurrent choice. Throughout the book, the reader will find other fascinating attempts to advance our understanding of routinized decision making. Subsequent research has to decide about the fate of these models.

REFERENCES

Aarts, H., & Dijksterhuis, A. (2000). Habits as knowledge structures: Automaticity in goal-directed behavior. *Journal of Personality and Social Psychology, 78*, 53–63.

Abelson, R. P. (1981). Psychological status of the script concept. *American Psychologist, 36*, 715–729.

Abelson, R. P., & Levi, A. (1985). Decision making and decision theory. In G. Lindzey & E. Aronson (Eds.), *Handbook of social psychology* (Vol. 1, pp. 231–309). New York: Random House.

Athay, M., & Darley, J. M. (1981). Toward an interaction-centered theory of personality. In N. Cantor & J. F. Kihlstrom (Eds.), *Personality, cognition and social interaction* (pp. 55–83). Hillsdale, NJ: Lawrence Erlbaum Associates.

Beach, L. R. (1990). *Image theory: Decision making in personal and organizational contexts.* New York: Wiley.

Bentler, P. M., & Speckart, G. (1979). Models of attitude-behavior relations. *Psychological Review, 86*, 452–464.

Betsch, T., Brinkmann, J., Fiedler, K., & Breining, K. (1999). When prior knowledge overrules new evidence: Adaptive use of decision strategies and the role of behavioral routines. *Swiss Journal of Psychology, 58*, 151–160.

Betsch, T., Fiedler, K., & Brinkmann, B. J. (1998). Behavioral routines in decision making: The effects of novelty in task presentation and time pressure on routine maintenance and deviation. *European Journal of Social Psychology, 28,* 861–878.

Betsch, T., Glöckner, A., & Haberstroh, S. (2000). COMMERCE—A micro-world simulation to study routine maintenance and deviation in repeated decision making. *Methods of Psychological Research, 5*(2), 73–93.

Betsch, T., Haberstroh, S., Molter, B., & Glöckner, A. (2004). Oops—I did it again: When prior knowledge overrules intentions. *Organizational Behavior and Human Decision Processes, 93,* 62–74.

Betsch, T., Haberstroh, S., Glöckner, A., Haar, T., & Fiedler, K. (2001). The effects of routine strength on adaptation and information search in recurrent decision making. *Organizational Behavior and Human Decision Processes, 84,* 23–53.

Betsch, T., Haberstroh, S., & Höhle, C. (2002). Explaining routinized decision making—a review of theories and models. *Theory and Psychology, 12,* 453–488.

Betsch, T., Hoffmann, K., Hoffrage, U., & Plessner, H. (2003). Intuition beyond recognition: When less familiar events are liked more. *Experimental Psychology, 50,* 49–54.

Betsch, T., Plessner, H., & Schallies, E. (in press). The value-account model of attitude formation. In G. R. Maio & G. Haddock (Eds.), *Theoretical perspectives on attitudes in the 21st century—the Gregynog Symposium.* Hove: Psychology Press.

Betsch, T., Plessner, H., Schwieren, C., & Gütig, R. (2001). I like it but I don't know why: A value-account approach to implicit attitude formation. *Personality and Social Psychology Bulletin, 27,* 242–253.

Busemeyer, J., Hastie, R., & Medin, D. L. (Eds.). (1995). *Decision making from a cognitive perspective.* San Diego: Academic Press.

Busemeyer, J. R., & Townsend, J. T. (1993). Decision field theory: A dynamic-cognitive approach to decision making in an uncertain environment. *Psychological Review, 100,* 432–459.

Bryan, W. L., & Harter, N. (1899). Studies on the telegraphic language. *Psychological Review, 6,* 345–375.

Cacioppo, J. T., Gardner, W. L., & Berntson, G. G. (1997). Beyond bipolar conceptualizations and measures: The case of attitudes and evaluative space. *Personality and Social Psychology Review, 1,* 3–25.

Carver, C. S. (2001). Affect and the functional bases of behavior: On the dimensional structure of affective experience. *Personality and Social Psychology Review, 5,* 345–356.

Christensen-Szalanski, J. (1978). Problem solving strategies: A selection mechanism, some implications and some data. *Organizational Behavior and Human Performance, 22,* 307–323.

Cohen, A., Stotland, E., & Wolfe, D. (1955). An experimental investigation of need for cognition. *Journal of Abnormal and Social Psychology, 51,* 291–294.

Davis, D. G. S., Staddon, J. E. R., Machado, A., & Palmer, R. G. (1993). The process of recurrent choice. *Psychological Review, 100,* 320–341.

Easterbrook, J. A. (1959). The effect of emotion on cue utilization and the organization of behavior. *Psychological Review, 66,* 183–201.

Fazio, R. H. (1990). Multiple processes by which attitudes guide behavior: The MODE model as an integrative framework. *Advances in Experimental Social Psychology, 23,* 75–109.

Finucane, M. L., Alhakami, A., Slovic, P., & Johnson, S. M. (2000). The affect heuristic in judgments of risks and benefits. *Journal of Behavioral Decision Making, 13,* 1–17.

George, M. S., Ketter, T. A., Parekh, P. I., Horwitz, B., Herscovitch, P., & Post, R. M. (1995). Brain activity during transient sadness and happiness in healthy women. *American Journal of Psychiatry, 152,* 341–351.

Goldstein, D. G., & Gigerenzer, G. (2002). Models of ecological rationality: The recognition heuristic. *Psychological Review, 109,* 75–90.

Goldstein, M. D., & Strube, M. J. (1994). Independence revisited: The relation between positive and negative affect in naturalistic setting. *Personality and Social Psychology Bulletin, 20,* 57–64.

Goldstein, W. M., & Hogarth, R. M. (1997). Judgment and decision research: Some historical context. In W. M. Goldstein & R. M. Hogarth (Eds.), *Research on judgment and decision making: Currents, connections and controversies* (pp. 3–65). Cambridge: Cambridge University Press.

Hogarth, R. M. (2001). *Educating intuition*. Chicago: University of Chicago Press.

Hsee, C. K. (1996). The evaluability hypothesis: An explanation for preference reversals between joint and separate evaluations of alternatives. *Journal of Organizational Behavior and Human Decision Processes, 67*, 242–257.

Hsee, C. K. (1998). Less is better: When low-value options are values more highly than high-value options. *Journal of Behavioral Decision Making, 11*, 107–121.

Hull, C. L. (1943). *Principles of behavior*. New York: Appleton-Century-Crofts.

James, W. (1890/1950). *The principles of psychology* (Vol. 1). New York: Dover.

Janis, I. L., & Mann, L. (1977). *Decision making: A psychological analysis of conflict, choice, and commitment*. New York: The Free Press.

Johnson, E. J., Payne, J. W., Schkade, D. A., & Bettman, J. R. (1986). *Monitoring information processing and decisions: The mouselab system*. Unpublished manuscript, Center for Decision Studies, Fuqua School of Business, Duke University.

Klein, G. (1999). *Sources of power. How people make decisions*. Cambridge, MA: MIT Press.

Kruglanski, A. W., & Webster, D. M. (1996). Motivated closing of the mind: "Seizing" and "freezing." *Psychological Review, 103*, 263–283.

Kunda, Z., & Thagard, P. (1996). Forming impressions from stereotypes, traits, and behaviors: A parallel-constraint-satisfaction theory. *Psychological Review, 103*, 284–308.

Lipshitz, R., Klein, G., Orasanu, J., & Salas, E. (2001). Taking stock of naturalistic decision making. *Journal of Behavioral Decision Making, 14*, 331–352.

MacDonald, T. K., Zanna, M. P., & Fong, G. T. (1995). Decision making in altered states: Effects of alcohol on attitudes toward drinking and driving. *Journal of Personality and Social Psychology, 68*, 973–985.

McClelland, J. L., & Rumelhart, D. E. (Eds.). (1986). *Parallel distributed processing. Explorations in the microstructure of cognition: Vol. 2. Psychological and biological models*. Cambridge, MA: MIT Press/Bradford.

Mellers, B., Schwartz, A., & Ritov, I. (1999). Emotion-based choice. *Journal of Experimental Psychology: General, 128*, 332–345.

Oatley, K., & Johnson-Laird, P. N. (1987). Towards a cognitive theory of emotions. *Cognition and Emotion, 1*, 29–50.

Ouellette, J. A., & Wood, W. (1998). Habit and intention in everyday life: The multiple processes by which past behavior predicts future behavior. *Psychological Bulletin, 124*, 54–74.

Pennington, N., & Hastie, R. (1992). Explaining the evidence: Tests of the story model for juror decision making. *Journal of Personality and Social Psychology, 62*, 189–206.

Read, S. J., Vanman, E. J., & Miller, L. C. (1997). Connectionism, parallel constraint satisfaction, and Gestalt principles: (Re)Introducing cognitive dynamics to social psychology. *Personality and Social Psychology Review, 1*, 26–53.

Ronis, D. L., Yates, J. F., & Kirscht, J. P. (1988). Attitudes, decisions and habits as determinants of repeated behavior. In A. R. Pratkanis, S. J. Breckler, & A. G. Greenwald (Eds.), *Attitude structure and function* (pp. 213–239). Hillsdale, NJ: Lawrence Erlbaum Associates.

Rozin, P., & Royzman, E. B. (2001). Negativity bias, negativity dominance, and contagion. *Personality and Social Psychology Review, 5*, 296–320.

Shultz, T. R., & Lepper, M. R. (1996). Cognitive dissonance reduction as constraint satisfaction. *Psychological Review, 103*, 219–240.

Simon, H. A. (1967). Motivational and emotional controls of cognition. *Psychological Review, 74*, 29–39.

Slovic, P. (1995). The construction of preference. *American Psychologist, 50*, 364–371.

Slovic, P., Finucane, M., Peters, E., & MacGregor, D. G. (2003). The affect heuristic. In T. Gilovich, D. Griffin, & D. Kahneman (Eds.), *Intuitive judgment: Heuristics and biases* (pp. 397–420). Cambridge: Cambridge University Press.

Smith, E. R. (1996). What do connectionism and social psychology offer each other? *Journal of Personality and Social Psychology, 70,* 893–912.

Stager, P., & Zufelt, K. (1972). Dual-task method in determining load differences. *Journal of Experimental Psychology, 94,* 113–115.

Steele, C. M., & Josephs, R. A. (1990). Alcohol myopia: Its prized and dangerous effects. *American Psychologist, 45,* 921–933.

Svenson, O., & Maule, A. J. (1993). *Time pressure and stress in human judgment and decision making.* New York: Plenum.

Thagard, P. (1989). Explanatory coherence. *Behavioral and Brain Sciences, 12,* 435–467.

Thagard, P., & Millgram, E. (1995). Inference to the best plan; A coherence theory of decision. In A. Ram & D. B. Leake (Eds.), *Goal driven learning* (pp. 439–454). Cambridge, MA: MIT Press.

Triandis, H. C. (1977). *Interpersonal behavior.* Monterey, CA: Brooks/Cole.

Van der Plight, J., Zeelenberg, M., van Dijk, W., de Vries, N. K., & Richard, R. (1998). Affect, attitudes and decisions: Let's be more specific. In W. Stroebe & M. Hewstone (Eds.), *European review of social psychology* (Vol. 8, pp. 33–66). Chichester: Wiley.

Verplanken, B., & Aarts, H. (1999). Habit, attitude, and planned behavior: Is habit an empty construct or an interesting case of goal-directed automaticity? In W. Stroebe & M. Hewstone (Eds.), *European review of social psychology* (Vol. 10, pp. 101–134). Chichester: Wiley.

Weber, E. U., Goldstein, W. M., & Busemeyer, J. R. (1991). Beyond strategies: Implications of memory representation and memory processes for models of judgment and decision making. In W. E. Hockley & S. Lewandowsky (Eds.), *Relating theory and data: Essays on human memory in honor of Bennet B. Murdock* (pp. 75–100). Hillsdale, NJ: Lawrence Erlbaum Associates.

Wright, P. (1974). The harassed decision maker: Time pressures, distractions and the use of evidence. *Journal of Applied Psychology, 59,* 555–561.

Wundt, W. (1907). *Outlines of psychology.* Leipzig: Wilhelm Engelmann.

Zajonc, R. B. (1980). Feeling and thinking: Preferences need no inferences. *American Psychologist, 35,* 151–175.

Zsambok, C. E., & Klein, G. (1997). *Naturalistic decision making.* Mahwah, NJ: Lawrence Erlbaum Associates.

4

Deciding Analytically or Trusting Your Intuition? The Advantages and Disadvantages of Analytic and Intuitive Thought

Robin M. Hogarth
ICREA and Pompeu Fabra University

The idea that decision making involves distinctive analytic and intuitive components resonates with everyday experience. It has also been discussed across at least two millennia. Recently, the distinctive natures of intuitive and analytic thought have been the subject of much psychological research, with many theorists postulating so-called *dual models* of thought.

Accepting this dichotomy, a natural question centers on whether one form of thinking is more valid (however defined) than the other. It is tempting to think that analytic thought must be better. After all, much education involves teaching people to think more analytically. Yet there is much anecdotal evidence supporting the use of intuition (as well as much that does not). However, what should people do when they find that their analysis contradicts their intuitions?

The purpose of this chapter is to illuminate this question. I first define *intuition* and *analysis* within the context of a dual-process model, where I distinguish between *tacit* and *deliberate* systems of thought. I next present a framework for understanding how these systems work in tandem. I assume that stimuli are first filtered by a *preconscious* processor, and that much thought takes place outside of cognitive awareness. The tacit system is always involved in making judgments and choices, but can be subject to control by the deliberate system. I further stress the role of tacit learning and how the environment affects the subsequent validity of tacit responses (see also Sedlmeier, chap. 5, this volume). In *kind* learning environments, people receive accurate and timely feedback. In *wicked* learning environments, feedback is lacking or misleading, and people can acquire inaccurate responses.

I next make some general comments about the relative validities of the tacit and deliberate systems prior to reviewing studies that have *directly* contrasted the relative validities of the two systems on the *same* tasks. This leads to identifying the underlying trade-off. Whereas the tacit system can be subject to bias, using the deliberate system appropriately requires knowledge of the "correct rule" as well as making no errors in execution. Assuming that the latter is a function of the analytical complexity of tasks, I present a framework illustrating the nature of this trade-off (i.e., bias [in implicit, tacit responses] vs. analytical complexity [when using the deliberate mode]).

Finally, whether tacit or deliberate processes are more valid than the other is not the critical issue. Rather, this is to make *valid* responses in which both systems are implicated. However, whereas much has been done to develop analytical abilities, intuition has received little attention. The payoff from understanding the relative strengths of analysis and intuition lies in identifying ways to educate the latter (cf. Hogarth, 2001).

DUAL SYSTEMS OF THOUGHT:
THE TACIT AND THE DELIBERATE

Several areas of psychology acknowledge that people process information in two quite different ways: cognitive psychology (see Bruner, 1986; Hasher & Zacks, 1979, 1984; Schneider & Shiffrin, 1977; Shiffrin & Schneider, 1977; Sloman, 1996); personality (see Epstein, 1994); social psychology (see the extensive volume edited by Chaiken & Trope, 1999), as well as attitude research (see Sanbonmatsu, Prince, & Vanous, chap. 6, this volume; Wilson, Lindsey, & Schooler, 2000); judgment and decision making (see Hammond, 1996; Kahneman & Frederick, 2002; Stanovich & West, 1998); and neuropsychology (see Ochsner & Lieberman, 2001). Although differences exist between dualities proposed by different scholars, most agree that the systems differ by the presence or absence of cognitive effort. I call these systems the *deliberate* and *tacit* (Hogarth, 2001).

The deliberate system involves explicit reasoning. It is mainly rule-governed, precise, and capable of abstract thought. The tacit system is triggered to operate automatically. It is sensitive to context and operates speedily providing approximate responses, typically without conscious awareness. It often involves feelings and emotions.

Using an iceberg metaphor, tacit thought lies below the surface (of consciousness), and our access to it is severely limited; deliberate thought lies above the surface and can be made explicit. There is also much more activity below the surface than above it. Many tacit responses are genetic in origin (cf. Seligman, 1970, on *preparedness*.) However, learning is also critical. Responses that are initially acquired through the deliberate system can become automated and move to the tacit system.

The tacit–deliberate distinction helps define what are commonly known as *intuition* and *analysis*. Specifically, "the essence of intuition or intuitive responses is that *they are reached with little apparent effort, and typically without conscious awareness. They involve little or no conscious deliberation*" (Hogarth, 2001, p. 14; italics original). Intuitive responses are therefore outputs of the tacit system. Analysis is the domain of the deliberate system.

A FRAMEWORK FOR INTEGRATING THE TWO SYSTEMS OF THOUGHT

Figure 4.1 illustrates the interconnections between the tacit and deliberate systems (see also Hogarth, 2001, chap. 6). Boxes with heavy lines indicate the deliberate system; boxes with dotted lines indicate the tacit system. Actions and outcomes, the two right-hand boxes (numbers 5 and 6), denote events that can be observed by (in principle) both the organism and third parties.

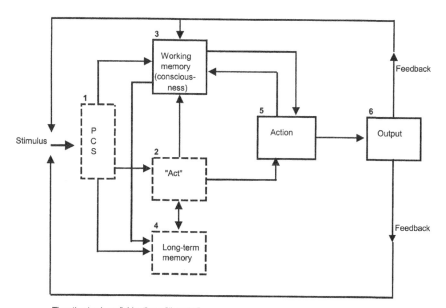

The stimulus is an "object" or a "thought."
PCS = preconscious screen.
The dotted lines indicate functions of the tacit system.

FIG. 4.1. The deliberate and tacit systems (from Hogarth, 2001).

The diagram illustrates how the tacit and deliberate systems interact in the processing of a stimulus (shown on the left of the diagram). The stimulus can take several forms: It can be external to the organism (e.g., something that is seen or heard), it can be internal (e.g., a thought triggers other thoughts), and so on. A key assumption is that all stimuli are first processed *preconsciously* (by the preconscious screen—Box 1). Consider three types of cases.

In the first case, information about stimuli are recorded without conscious awareness and stored for possible future use. This lies at the heart of tacit learning (see e.g., Hasher & Zacks, 1979, 1984).

In the second case, actions are taken automatically and bypass consciousness. Thus, people are only aware of actions after their occurrence (i.e., the link from Box 1 to Box 5 does not involve Box 3). Consider reactions to fear-inducing stimuli. You hear a noise and find that you have already moved to avoid danger before realizing what it is. Thus, outcomes are used to make sense—at a conscious level—of what we have just done—at a subconscious level (see e.g., Bargh & Chartrand, 1999). More generally, this case also accounts for many priming phenomena as well as effects of mood, which can divert attention at subconscious levels (see also Bless & Igou, chap. 11, this volume).

In the third case—of deliberate actions—consciousness plays an important role. People use the deliberate system to produce specific actions. Consider reading or deciding explicitly to do something. Moreover, the deliberate system can overrule outputs of the tacit system provided action has not already taken place. For example, we can overrule suggestions of our own angry feelings. (Imagine another motorist has taken advantage of you and stolen "your" parking space.) People can also create intentions in consciousness and decide when to delegate to automatic processes. Consider driving a car. Typically, we decide where we want to go and then delegate many functions to automatic processing. However, we maintain sufficient attention to be able to assume control when necessary.

Attention is limited. Thus, because the deliberate system consumes limited resources, it is used sparingly. It is allocated to tasks that are deemed important, but can be switched as needed. It is rarely "shut down" completely and has a monitoring function. In most cases, the tacit system is our "default," and the deliberate system is invoked when either the tacit system cannot handle the task or we make a conscious decision (e.g., planning what to do). At any time, however, both the tacit and deliberate operate together.

Whereas cognitive processes occur inside the head and are unobservable, actions and outputs (Boxes 5 and 6) occur, for the most part, in the environment and are observable. Indeed the interpretation of automatic actions often takes place after the fact (as noted earlier). This is indicated in Fig. 4.1 by the arrow that leads from action (Box 5) to consciousness or working memory (Box 3).

Feedback from the environment occurs because actions (Box 5) lead to outcomes (Box 6). For example, you turn the steering wheel while driving and the car adjusts direction. For most small actions, feedback is immediate and impacts both consciousness (Box 3) and long-term memory (Box 4). Observed feedback also becomes a stimulus that is subsequently processed by the preconscious screen (Box 1). Thus, whereas its effect on working memory (Box 3) can be direct (when paying specific attention), its effect on long-term memory is mediated by the preconscious screen.

Finally, actions can affect the environment and create their own feedback. Thus, the feedback from action (Box 6) becomes the next stimulus to be processed by the preconscious screen (Box 1). For instance, the fact that a smile at a person was reciprocated can affect your sense that the person likes you. However, had you not smiled in the first place, failing to observe the person smile could automatically lead to inferring less attraction. (For elaboration of the interplay between affect-based choices and experience with outcomes, see also Betsch, chap. 3, this volume).

THE ROLE OF LEARNING

In Hogarth (2001), I noted that tacit learning can take place in environments that are *kind* or *wicked*. Kind and wicked environments are distinguished by the degree to which people receive accurate feedback. In kind environments, people receive timely and veridical feedback; in wicked environments, they do not. This distinction follows the analysis of learning situations developed by Einhorn and Hogarth (1978), which showed that, even in simple tasks, feedback can be distorted by many factors, including the actions that people take. For example, the fact that you take a particular action can prevent you from learning about outcomes associated with the actions you did not take. (For a more detailed discussion of the role of feedback, see Harvey & Fischer, chap. 7, this volume).

The key point is that the accuracy and timeliness of feedback affects the quality of the intuitions we acquire through tacit learning processes. You cannot learn from feedback you do not receive, and some feedback may simply act to increase confidence in erroneous beliefs (Einhorn & Hogarth, 1978). Thus, the quality of intuition is highly dependent on whether it was acquired in kind or wicked environments (see also Kardes, Muthukrishnan, & Pashkevich, chap. 8, this volume).

ON THE RELATIVE VALIDITIES OF TACIT AND DELIBERATE THOUGHT: SOME GENERAL COMMENTS

Recent decades have witnessed much interest in whether people are "good" or "bad" at making judgments and decisions. Several explanations have been offered. Some emphasize the role of individual variables such as experience and training (e.g., Klein, 1998; Ross, Lussier, & Klein, chap. 18, this volume). Others involve the role of incentives (cf. Camerer & Hogarth, 1999), problem formats (e.g., using frequencies instead of probabilities, Gigerenzer & Hoffrage, 1995; whether tasks are continuous or discrete, Hogarth 1981), as well as whether people respond analytically as opposed to intuitively (Stanovich & West, 1998).

Rather than considering this literature within the context of two systems that can produce different responses—"good" characterizing one system and "bad" the other—a more fruitful approach is to specify the relative advantages and disadvantages of both systems.

Consider the following thought experiment. You are at the checkout counter of your local supermarket. To assess your bill, you rely on a deliberate process. You let the clerk calculate the amount with an adding machine. As you are preparing to pay, the clerk announces the total—$2,376.53. You are astounded. In fact you had already implicitly estimated that your bill would be around $100. Surely, there must be an error?

This situation illustrates several points. First, although a deliberate process was used to estimate the bill, you still made a tacit estimation. In other words, we do not seem able to suppress the tacit response system.

Second, tacit and deliberate processes rely on different kinds of information. To appreciate this, consider how to model the deliberate and tacit processes involved is estimating your bill. The deliberate process can be represented by a formula,

$$\text{Grocery bill} = \sum_i \beta_i x_i, \ i = 1,\dots\dots k. \tag{1}$$

where the x_is represent the prices of the k items purchased and, in this case, the β_is are all equal to 1.

The deliberate approach requires: (a) identifying and defining the variables (the products); (b) defining relevant measures for the variables (the prices); and (c) determining a rule for aggregating the information from the preceding step (arithmetic). Note that deliberate thought requires using information that is not contained in the triggering stimulus—here, the rules of arithmetic.

This example shows both the strengths and weaknesses of the deliberate process. If you define the appropriate variables and measures and use the "right formula" correctly, your solution will match the criterion. However, success depends on executing *all* of these steps correctly.

Now consider how one might model the tacit process. This could be described by an anchoring-and-adjustment process, where the person adjusts the typical bill by a variable capturing "how full" the shopping cart is relative to usual:

$$\text{Tacit estimate of grocery bill} = \alpha \cdot z \qquad (2)$$

where z represents the typical bill and α indicates the estimate of how full the shopping cart is (relative to its usual level). There are several noteworthy features of this process. First, it is simple to execute (i.e., "fast and frugal"; Gigerenzer, Todd et al., 1999). Second, it uses a variable that is correlated with the criterion (i.e., grocery bills are correlated with the levels of goods in shopping carts). Third, although the estimate is based on only part of the information potentially available (the level of goods), this acts as a surrogate for the total. In addition, there is no need to access additional information such as the rules of arithmetic.

In this case, the tacit response is quite effective. However, this depends on the fact that the stimulus that triggered the response (i.e., the level of goods) is a good predictor of the criterion. Alternatively, imagine having bought an unusually expensive mix of products such that the level of goods is a biased estimator of total cost.

EVIDENCE ON THE RELATIVE VALIDITIES OF TACIT AND DELIBERATE RESPONSES

As noted earlier, there is much evidence that people process information in two distinctive modes. Moreover, whether the person engages primarily in tacit or deliberate processing depends heavily on the nature of the triggering stimulus as perceived by the individual. For example, although people may not remember the specific stimuli that triggered attitudes toward specific objects, their spontaneous judgments are quite accurate in reflecting the sum of their experiences (Betsch, Plessner, Schwieren, & Gütig, 2001). However, an issue addressed by relatively few studies is the specification of *when, faced by the same triggering stimulus*, it is tacit or deliberate processes that produce more *valid* responses in decision making.

To date, the most complete study of this issue was conducted by Hammond, Hamm, Grassia, and Pearson (1987). They emphasized that most studies have used *indirect* means to assess the adequacy of decision making—typically by comparing decisions with external criteria deemed to be "correct"—for example, the implications of probability theory (e.g., Kahneman, Slovic, & Tversky, 1982; Tversky & Kahneman, 1983), the axioms of expected utility theory (e.g., Kahneman & Tversky, 1979), or empirically based criteria (see e.g., Dawes, Faust, & Meehl, 1989).

To address the issue of concern here, therefore, comparisons between tacit and deliberate (or intuitive and analytic) processes need to be *direct*. Facing the same stimuli, do people make decisions that are more valid when they use tacit as opposed to deliberate processes or vice versa?

Hammond et al. made both theoretical and empirical contributions. At the theoretical level, they postulated the existence of a continuum of cognitive styles, on the one hand, and a continuum of task characteristics, on the other. Cognition is assumed to vary from *intuitive* to *analytic* with intermediate or mixed styles labeled *quasirational*. Similarly, tasks can be defined by characteristics that induce intuitive as opposed to analytic thinking or vice versa. Their central hypothesis was that performance would be affected by the degree of match between task and mode of cognition on their respective continua. Thus, tasks with intuition-inducing characteristics are better handled in intuitive mode, and those with analytic-inducing characteristics are better handled in analytic mode. Empirically, in tasks that required experienced highway engineers to judge the safety of highways (based on different presentations of the same information and requiring the explicit use of different modes of thought), their hypotheses were confirmed.

Other studies have also used direct tests. Wilson and Schooler (1991) investigated the effect of introspection, in the form of providing explicit reasons, on the quality of choice. The question posed was whether people are better off trusting their initial feelings or taking time to reason deliberately.

Wilson and Schooler made the point that people cannot always explain why they have certain preferences. That is, many preferences simply reflect often passive interactions with the environment and are not easy to justify on reflection. For example, Betsch, Fiedler, and Brinkmann (1998) demonstrated how time pressure can trigger people's routine responses even when deviating from routine is in their interest. However, in many choice situations, there are also salient and plausible reasons that people recognize as being relevant, which, if they think explicitly, may come to mind. The question is whether thinking explicitly about such reasons changes people's preferences for the better.

In studies of preferences, it is problematic to establish what is or is not "good." Wilson and Schooler studied students' preferences for brands of strawberry jam and college courses and, for both types of stimuli, used expert opinions as the criterion of "goodness." Results show that introspection—or making reasons explicit—led to inferior decisions relative to control subjects who had not engaged in introspection. According to Wilson and Schooler, thinking about the choice led the experimental subjects to consider inappropriate reasons. Thus, had they not spent time in thinking, they would have responded in similar fashion to controls whose initial preferences were closer to the experts' opinions. In a further study, two groups of students evaluated several posters and were allowed to choose one to take home. One group was asked to introspect explicitly about their evaluations; the other was not. About 3 weeks later, the second group was found to be more satisfied with their choices (Wilson, Lisle, Schooler, Hodges, Klaaren, & LaFleur, 1993).

Although studies such as these have been cited as examples of how intuition may be superior to analysis, care should be taken in generalizing. First, what the studies show is that deliberation changes expressed preferences if subjects are unaware of the origins of those preferences (see also Wilson et al., 1993). However, other studies have shown that when people are aware of such origins, these are less likely to be changed by thinking about reasons (Wilson, Kraft, & Dunn, 1989).

Second, decision aids that force people to be explicit about reasons for their decisions heighten satisfaction in choices relative to control groups without such aids (Kmett, Arkes, & Jones, 1999). Similarly, several studies in judgmental forecasting have examined the validity of "decomposition" methods, in which people split the prediction task into subtasks, make judgments about the parts, and then aggregate the different judgments. Decomposition methods prove more accurate than directly estimating the outcome (MacGregor, 2002).

Third, McMackin and Slovic (2000) both replicated Wilson and Schooler's results and emphasized the importance of understanding the joint effects of types of task and cognition emphasized by Hammond et al. (1987). Specifically, McMackin and Slovic asked two groups of subjects to make judgments in two tasks: assessing how much people would like advertisements (an "intuitive" task), and estimating uncertain facts such as the length of the Amazon River (an "analytical" task). One group of subjects was just asked to answer the questions; the other was explicitly instructed to provide reasons for their answers. Results show that, for the intuitive task (advertisements), providing reasons had a negative effect on performance, thereby replicating Wilson and Schooler. In contrast, generating reasons had a positive effect on performance in the uncertain facts task. Thus, McMackin and Slovic also replicated the results of Hammond et al. (1987) involving the interaction of type of cognition with type of task (i.e., "intuition" was seen to be more valid in an "intuitive" task and "analysis" in an "analytic" task).

Fourth, there is much evidence that verbalizing thoughts leads to more deliberate thinking and cuts off access to tacit processes (Schooler, Ohlsson, & Brooks, 1993). What needs to be made clearer, however, is whether and when this leads to "better" outcomes (Schooler & Dougal, 1999). For example, when subjects engaged in problem solving are asked to verbalize their thoughts, this has deleterious effects on problems that require "insightful" solutions, although not on more analytical problems. Similarly, recognition memory is highly dependent on the tacit system and can be less accurate if people are asked to make explicit use of the deliberate system through verbalization (Schooler & Engster-Schooler, 1990).

INTUITION (TACIT THOUGHT) OR ANALYSIS (DELIBERATION)?

To summarize, tacit thought is based on part of the information present in the triggering stimulus, and its accuracy depends on the extent to which this leads to biased responses. Tacit thought typically involves approximate answers. Thus, even when a series of tacit responses might be unbiased (in a statistical sense), specific responses will involve some error. In deliberate thought, accuracy depends on whether the person knows and is able to apply the "correct formula." Unlike errors from tacit responses, errors in deliberate thought tend to have an "all or nothing" quality. (Recall the example of the checkout counter.) Let us now examine the trade-off between errors involved in the two kinds of thought.

Of course, there are many cases in which tacit responses are biased, but where such biases are functional (e.g., reactions to potential sources of danger). Ignoring these kinds of cases, bias in tacit decisions will reflect the conditions in which response tendencies have been learned. Were these acquired in *kind* or *wicked* learning environments? Similarly, is there bias in the information on which tacit responses are based?

In deliberate thought, what is the probability that the person will know and apply the appropriate "formula" correctly? Two factors are critical. One is how the problem is presented (i.e., does this invite use of the appropriate formula?). The second (possibly related to the first) is the complexity of the problem as presented. In the following, I assume that the probability that a person knows and applies the appropriate formula correctly is a monotonic function of the *analytical complexity* of the task. In other words, the greater the complexity a task exhibits in analytical terms (as measured, e.g., by the number of variables, types of functions, weighting schemes, etc.), the less likely it is that a person will both know the appropriate formula and apply it correctly. (Individuals vary, of course, in the extent to which they perceive tasks as analytically complex.)

Consider, for example, the experiment of McMackin and Slovic (2000) described earlier. From an analytical viewpoint, it is difficult to judge whether people will like an advertisement. (What are the appropriate variables and how should they be measured and combined?) Thus, an intuitive judgment based perhaps on how much the people just liked the advertisement would be a more valid response (assuming no significant bias). Similarly, when asked the length of the Amazon River, a first intuitive response could be biased by different sources of information. (What were the last distances in your mind?) Thus, thinking through different explicit reasons would not be difficult analytically and could help improve the accuracy of the response.

Figure 4.2 explores the trade-off between bias in tacit (intuitive) thought and the effects of analytical complexity in deliberate thought (analysis). It shows how the differential accuracy of the two modes varies when tasks are characterized by the extent to which they (a) induce different levels of bias in tacit thought, and (b) vary in analytical complexity. To simplify, I have considered three levels of each variable and thus nine types of situation. Bias is characterized as being "large," "medium," and "small/zero"; analytical complexity is said to be "easy," "moderate," or "hard." For the moment, I ignore individual differences.

Consider Cell 1, where bias is large, but the level of analytical complexity is easy. Here deliberation is likely to be more accurate than tacit thought. An example is provided by the Müller–Lyer illusion. A tacit judgment suggests that one line is larger than the other. However, the deliberate use of a ruler can demonstrate that both lines are equal.

However, note that as analytical complexity increases, the differential accuracy between the two types of thought is predicted to decrease. In Cell

	Analytical complexity		
	Easy	**Moderate**	**Hard**
Large	1 D > T	2 D > T	3 ?
Medium	4 D > T	5 D ~ T	6 T > D
Small/zero	7 D = T	8 T > D	9 T > D

Bias and error implied by tacit processes

D > T means deliberate thought more accurate than tacit
D ~ T means deliberate and tacit thought approximately equally accurate
D = T means deliberate and tacit thought equally accurate
T > D means tacit thought more accurate than deliberate

FIG. 4.2.   The relative accuracy of tacit and deliberate thought.

2—with moderate analytical complexity—deliberation is still preferable to tacit thought. (Imagine other optical illusions where people cannot resolve uncertainty by using a simple analytical device.)

In Cell 3—when analytical complexity becomes hard—it is not clear whether the errors of deliberate or tacit processes would be greater. Consider, for example, a person making a complicated investment but lacking relevant experience. The person could be biased by misleading prior experience and also lack the analytical ability to make the appropriate deliberate decision. However, it is not clear which error would be greater.

The interaction between bias and analytical complexity is most clearly illustrated in Cells 4, 5, and 6, where bias is maintained at a "medium" level. When analytical complexity is easy, deliberate thought should be preferred to tacit. For example, consider a simple base-rate task such as the "engineer-lawyer" problem (Kahneman & Tversky, 1973). This is not analytically complex (for most people), and even approximate use of the correct formula will be more accurate than the prototypical tacit response. However, as analytical complexity increases, tacit processes become progressively more accurate in a relative sense (Cells 5 and 6; i.e., the increasing probability of making errors in analysis eventually outweighs the bias and error inherent in tacit responses).

Finally, consider Cells 7, 8, and 9, where the bias from tacit thought is insignificant. For tasks that are easy in analytical complexity (Cell 7), there should be no difference in accuracy between deliberate and tacit responses. Consider adding two numbers explicitly (e.g., 2 + 2 = 4) or simply recognizing the pattern that the sum of two numbers makes (e.g., 4 can be "seen" to result from 0 and 4, 1 and 3, and 2 and 2). However, for moderate and hard levels of analytical complexity (Cells 8 and 9), tacit process responses are predicted to be more accurate. For example, when people are asked to judge frequencies spontaneously, they are quite accurate at doing so. However, if they think explicitly about this task, their judgments can be biased by the availability of exemplars (Haberstroh & Betsch, 2001).

Similarly, many areas of expertise depend on perceptual processes and use of the recognition heuristic for tasks that are difficult to analyze (Goldstein & Gigerenzer, 2002; see also Plessner, chap. 17, this volume; Ross, Lussier, & Klein, chap. 18, this volume). Presumably, these tasks fall in Cells 7, 8, and 9 as would the everyday ("nonexpert") use of our perceptual processes for a wide range of tasks. These can vary from discriminating between real and simulated phenomena from filmstrips (see Hogarth, 2001, chap. 4) or predicting teaching ability based on "thin slices" of behavior (short video clips; Ambady & Rosenthal, 1993).

The purpose of Fig. 4.2 is to provide a framework for considering the conditions under which tacit (intuitive) or deliberate (analytic) thought is likely to be more valid. In summary, deliberate thought is predicted to be more accurate than tacit thought in Cells 1, 2, and 4; intuitive thought is predicted to be more accurate than deliberate thought in Cells 6, 8, and 9; no differences are predicted in Cell 7; differences in Cell 5 will be small; and no predictions seem possible for Cell 3. Whereas this framework has not been empirically tested as such, it provides a means for classifying and thinking about studies that have been reported in the literature. Finally, one aspect not explicitly addressed here is the role of individual differences. Clearly people vary in their susceptibility to bias in tacit thought (depending on their learning history), and certainly expertise affects the extent to which people perceive tasks as analytically complex. Thus, the framework could also be adapted to predict when and where people with differential experience in specific domains would be better advised to trust their "analysis" or "intuition."

TOWARD MORE VALID JUDGMENTS AND DECISIONS

As this chapter shows, attempts to define the circumstances under which tacit (intuitive) or deliberate (analytic) judgments and decisions are likely to be more accurate raise a host of interesting issues. On the one hand, it is necessary to have a holistic view of how tacit and deliberate processes interact. On the other hand, one also needs to specify much of the minute details of each system. By looking at the operation of both systems in tandem, one is struck by senses of both complexity and efficacy. The human system is complex, but it is also effective at handling a wide variety of different cognitive tasks.

Although effective, we know that the human cognitive system is not perfect in the sense that people's judgments and decisions still involve errors that cannot be attributed merely to random events in the environment. An important issue, therefore, is how to help people achieve their goals by making fewer errors; indeed a large part of our educational system is dedicated toward this objective. As educators, we spend much time teaching analytic methods designed to help people hone their capacity for deliberate thought. It could also be argued that when such reasoning is assimilated, people can learn to use some tools of analysis in tacit fashion. However, what is not done is to train people explicitly in how to develop their capacity for intuitive thought.

In Hogarth (2001, chaps. 6, 7, & 8), I provide a framework and many suggestions as to how people can develop their intuitive skills. Central to these ideas is the notion that our tacit systems are constantly honing our responses to the feedback we receive in the environments in which we operate (recall the prior discussion on *kind* and *wicked* learning environments).

Thus, selecting appropriate learning environments and monitoring the kinds of feedback that we receive must rank high on the conditions that foster the acquisition of good intuitions. In addition, I believe that people need to be more aware of how often they allow themselves to take decisions automatically as opposed to exercising greater cognitive control (as elegantly discussed by Langer, 1989).

In the scientific study of decision making, there is undoubtedly a bias toward studying processes underlying *important* decisions. Yet it can be argued that it is the aggregate effects of *small* decisions that are more important for the ultimate quality of our lives. Moreover, many of these decisions reflect tacitly acquired routines and habits that escape our conscious control (cf. Betsch, Haberstroh, Glöckner, Haar, & Fiedler, 2001; Verplanken, Myrbakk, & Rudi, chap. 13, this volume). Greater awareness of the dual nature of thought can, by itself, lead to better use of our limited cognitive resources.

ACKNOWLEDGMENT

Robin M. Hogarth is ICREA Research Professor at Universitat Pompeu Fabra, Barcelona, Spain. This research was financed partially by grants from the Spanish Ministerio de Ciencia y Tecnología and CREI. I thank Susanne Haberstroh for an illuminating critique of an earlier version of this chapter.

REFERENCES

Ambady, N., & Rosenthal, R. (1993). Half a minute: Predicting teacher evaluations from thin slices of nonverbal behavior and physical attractiveness. *Journal of Personality and Social Psychology, 64*, 431–441.

Bargh, J. A., & Chartrand, T. L. (1999). The unbearable automaticity of being. *American Psychologist, 54*, 462–479.

Betsch, T., Fiedler, K., & Brinkmann, J. (1998). Behavioral routines in decision making: The effects of novelty in task presentation and time pressure on routine maintenance and deviation. *European Journal of Social Psychology, 28*, 861–878.

Betsch, T., Haberstroh, S., Glöckner, A., Haar, T., & Fiedler, K. (2001). The effects of routine strength on adaptation and information search in recurrent decision making. *Organizational Behavior and Human Decision Processes, 84*, 23–53.

Betsch, T., Plessner, H., Schwieren, C., & Gütig, R. (2001). I like it but I don't know why: A value-account approach to implicit attitude formation. *Personality and Social Psychology Bulletin, 27*, 242–253.

Bruner, J. (1986). *Actual minds, possible worlds*. Cambridge, MA: Harvard University Press.

Camerer, C. F., & Hogarth, R. M. (1999). The effects of financial incentives in experiments: A review and capital-labor-production framework. *Journal of Risk and Uncertainty, 19*, 7–42.

Chaiken, S., & Trope, Y. (Eds.). (1999). *Dual-process theories in social psychology*. New York: Guilford.

Dawes, R. M., Faust, D., & Meehl, P. E. (1989). Clinical versus actuarial judgment. *Science, 243*, 1668–1674.

Einhorn, H. J., & Hogarth, R. M. (1978). Confidence in judgment: Persistence of the illusion of validity. *Psychological Review, 85*, 395–416.

Epstein, S. (1994). Integration of the cognitive and the psychodynamic unconscious. *American Psychologist, 49*, 709–724.

Gigerenzer, G., & Hoffrage, U. (1995). How to improve Bayesian reasoning without instruction: Frequency formats. *Psychological Review, 102*, 684–704.

Gigerenzer, G., Todd, P. M., & the ABC Research Group. (1999). *Simple heuristics that make us smart.* New York: Oxford University Press.

Goldstein, D. G., & Gigerenzer, G. (2002). Models of ecological rationality: The recognition heuristic. *Psychological Review, 109*(1), 75–90.

Haberstroh, S., & Betsch, T. (2001). Online strategies versus memory-based strategies in frequency estimation. In P. Sedlmeier & T. Betsch (Eds.), *Frequency processing and cognition* (pp. 205–220). Oxford, England: Oxford University Press.

Hammond, K. R. (1996). *Human judgment and social policy: Irreducible uncertainty, inevitable error, unavoidable injustice.* New York: Oxford University Press.

Hammond, K. R., Hamm, R. M., Grassia, J., & Pearson, T. (1987). Direct comparison of the efficacy of intuitive and analytical cognition in expert judgment. *IEEE Transactions on Systems, Man, and Cybernetics, 17*, 753–770.

Hasher, L., & Zacks, R. T. (1979). Automatic and effortful processes in memory. *Journal of Experimental Psychology: General, 108*, 356–358.

Hasher, L., & Zacks, R. T. (1984). Automatic processing of fundamental information: The case of frequency of occurrence. *American Psychologist, 39*, 1372–1388.

Hogarth, R. M. (1981). Beyond discrete biases: Functional and dysfunctional consequences of judgmental heuristics. *Psychological Bulletin, 90*, 197–217.

Hogarth, R. M. (2001). *Educating intuition.* Chicago, IL: The University of Chicago Press.

Kahneman, D., & Frederick, S. (2002). Representativeness revisited: Attribute substitution in intuitive judgment. In T. Gilovich, D. Griffin, & D. Kahneman (Eds.), *The psychology of intuitive judgment: Heuristics and biases* (pp. 49–81). New York: Cambridge University Press.

Kahneman, D., Slovic, P., & Tversky, A. (Eds.). (1982). *Judgment under uncertainty: Heuristics and biases.* New York: Cambridge University Press.

Kahneman, D., & Tversky, A. (1973). On the psychology of prediction. *Psychological Review, 80*, 237–251.

Kahneman, D., & Tversky, A (1979). Prospect theory: An analysis of decision under risk. *Econometrica, 47*, 263–291.

Klein, G. (1998). *Sources of power: How people make decisions.* Cambridge, MA: MIT Press.

Kmett, C. A., Arkes, H. R., & Jones, S. K. (1999). The influence of decision aids on high school students' satisfaction with their college choice decision. *Personality and Social Psychology Bulletin, 25*, 1293–1301.

Langer, E. J. (1989). *Mindfulness.* Reading, MA: Perseus.

MacGregor, D. G. (2001). Decomposition for judgmental forecasting and estimation. In J. Scott Armstrong (Ed.), *Principles of forecasting: A handbook for researchers and practitioners* (pp. 107–123). Boston, MA: Kluwer Academic.

McMackin, J., & Slovic, P. (2000). When does explicit justification impair decision making? *Journal of Applied Cognitive Psychology, 14*, 527–541.

Ochsner, K. N., & Lieberman, M. D. (2001). The emergence of social cognitive neuroscience. *American Psychologist, 56*, 717–734.

Schneider, W., & Shiffrin, R. M. (1977). Controlled and automatic human information processing: I. Detection, search, and attention. *Psychological Review, 84*, 1–66.

Schooler, J. W., & Dougal, S. (1999). The symbiosis of subjective and experimental approaches to intuition. *Journal of Consciousness Studies, 6*, 280–287.

Schooler, J. W., & Engster-Schooler, T. Y. (1990). Verbal overshadowing of visual memories: Some things are better left unsaid. *Cognitive Psychology, 22*, 36–71.

Schooler, J. W., Ohlsson, S., & Brooks, K. (1993). Thoughts beyond words: When language overshadows insight. *Journal of Experimental Psychology: General, 122*, 166–183.

Seligman, M. E. P. (1970). On the generality of laws of learning. *Psychological Review, 77*, 406–418.

Shiffrin, R. M., & Schneider, W. (1977). Controlled and automatic human information processing: II. Perceptual learning, automatic attending, and a general theory. *Psychological Review, 84*, 127–190.

Sloman, S. A. (1996). The empirical case for two systems of reasoning. *Psychological Bulletin, 119*, 3–22.

Stanovich, K. E., & West, R. F. (1998). Individual differences in rational thought. *Journal of Experimental Psychology: General, 127*, 161–188.

Tversky, A., & Kahneman, D. (1983). Extensional versus intuitive reasoning: The conjunction fallacy in probability judgment. *Psychological Review, 90*, 293–315.

Wilson, T. D., Kraft, D., & Dunn, D. S. (1989). The disruptive effects of explaining attitudes: The moderating effect of knowledge about the attitude object. *Journal of Experimental Social Psychology, 25*, 379–400.

Wilson, T. D., Lindsey, S., & Schooler, T. Y. (2000). A model of dual attitudes. *Psychological Review, 107*(1), 101–126.

Wilson, T. D., Lisle, D. J., Schooler, J. W., Hodges, S. D., Klaaren, K. J., & LaFleur, S. J. (1993). Introspecting about reasons can reduce post-choice satisfaction. *Personality and Social Psychology Bulletin, 19*, 331–339.

Wilson, T. D., & Schooler, J. W. (1991). Thinking too much: Introspection can reduce the quality of preferences and decisions. *Journal of Personality and Social Psychology, 60*, 181–192.

5

From Associations to Intuitive Judgment and Decision Making: Implicitly Learning From Experience

Peter Sedlmeier
Chemnitz University of Technology

The areas of judgment and decision making, on the one hand, and learning theory, on the other hand, peacefully coexist in psychology without much contact, as if the one had nothing to do with the other. Textbooks on judgment and decision making usually treat judgmental preferences and processes without reference to their origins. This neglect is especially unfortunate in the case of decisions that are made largely intuitively and without explicit deliberations because if one can reconstruct the origin of intuitive decision making, one possesses the key to understanding and modifying behavior of this kind. Intuitive decision making plays a dominant role in routinized decisions (e.g., Betsch, Fiedler, & Brinkmann, 1998; Betsch, Haberstroh, & Hoehle, 2002; Ericsson & Lehman, 1996; Haberstroh et al., chap. 12, this volume; Norman, 1998; Patel, Arocha, & Kaufman, 1999). The broad thesis of this chapter is that much of the intuitive basis of decision making can be traced back to some kind of associative learning, thus postulating an important connection between decision making and learning theory. Herein, I concentrate on computational models of associative learning. I first discuss in more detail specific cases from our own work on frequency-related judgments, and then I try to make the argument more general: Many kinds of decisions may be almost entirely based on intuitive knowledge that is acquired by associative learning.

FROM ASSOCIATIONS TO INTUITIONS

According to Hogarth (2001), who provided an illuminating overview of the literature on intuition, intuitive responses are "reached with little apparent effort, and typically without conscious awareness. They involve little or no conscious deliberation" (p. 14).[1] Hogarth (2001; chap. 4, this volume) arrived at the conclusion that intuitions are (largely) based on learning from experience, but he was not explicit on the mechanisms that transform experiences into intuitions. This chapter suggests such a mechanism (associative learning), shows how it can explain frequency-related judgments and decisions, and explores the mechanism's explanatory scope.

One may regard James' (1890) definition as the first attempt to give an explicit account on how intuitive responses come about: "Objects once experienced together tend to become associated in the imagination, so that when any one of them is thought of, the others are likely to be thought of also, in the same order of sequence or coexistence as before" (p. 561). Associative learning theory had its first heyday when behaviorism reigned, but in its initial form suffered from theoretical shortcomings concerning several learning phenomena and issues of knowledge representation (e.g., Baars, 1986; Chomsky, 1959; Minsky & Papert, 1969). Largely beginning with the publication of the parallel distributed processing books (McClelland & Rumelhart, 1986; Rumelhart & McClelland, 1986), associative learning theory in its new computational form became popular again. In its present version—known under such labels as *connectionism* or (artificial) *neural networks*—it is able to explain how memory representations arise, how serial behavior can be modeled, and even how rules might be represented in memory (e.g., Elman, Bates, Johnson, Karmiloff-Smith, Parisi, & Plunkett, 1996). Learning in a neural network is implicit and automatic. It creates or modifies (part of) an associative memory that can be seen as intuitive knowledge or a collection of intuitions. These intuitions in turn are the basis for intuitive responses—that is, judgments and decisions that are reached with little apparent effort and little or no conscious deliberation (see Hogarth's earlier definition).

If one accepts the assumption that intuitions largely arise as the result of experience-based learning, then most kinds of intuitive judgments and decisions, and therefore many kinds of routinized decisions, are related to frequencies. Why? Because, exceptions notwithstanding (see e.g., Garcia, 1990), experience is nothing but the result of having been repeatedly ex-

---

[1]Hogarth seems to try out an experiment on the reader with this definition. He repeated it verbatim several times throughout the book, which might eventually make that definition an intuitive response when one is prompted with the word *intuition*—at least this is what PASS, the associative learning model introduced later, would predict.

posed to events (henceforth, events stand for both objects and events)—that is, to frequencies of events. From the role that routinized decision making plays in everyday life, one would expect a large research effort to explain how intuitive judgments and decisions come about. However, to date, the connection between learning—especially implicit or associative learning, on the one hand, and judgment and decision making, on the other hand—has not received much attention. This chapter is an attempt to change this state of affairs.

COMPUTATIONAL MODELS OF ASSOCIATIVE LEARNING

There exists a huge variety of computational models of associative learning differing in system architectures—that is, the way relevant aspects are represented in memory and in the learning rules used. In almost all current computational models of associative learning, events are represented by a collection of features that define that event. Computational models of associative learning can be distinguished in several ways. To understand the way the model we used in our research—the PASS model—works, it is useful to briefly consider two such distinctions—exemplar versus prototype models—and models that exploit contingencies versus models that rely on contiguities.

Exemplar Versus Prototype Models

The simplest learning rule one can probably think of is just to store one specific event or exemplar after the other. One may wonder whether this process should be called associative learning at all. In such models, whose architecture basically consists of an ever-growing matrix of memory traces (consisting of lists of features or feature vectors), associations are created at retrieval by computing some function of the similarity of the memory traces to a given memory prompt. Such models are often called *multiple trace* or *exemplar models* (e.g., Estes, 1986; Hintzman, 1986). Exemplar models are quite widespread in research on category learning and frequency estimation (e.g., Dougherty & Franco-Watkins, 2002; Hintzman, 1988), but play only a minor role in more complex intuitive judgments (see Fiedler, 1996, for an exception).

Such judgments are the realm of another class of models termed *prototype models* (e.g., Smith & Medin, 1981). This term is commonly used as a synonym to *neural network model* or *connectionist model*. In contrast to exemplar models, the architecture of the memory does not change (i.e., grow) as new information arrives. Instead the associations or connection weights between the contents of memory (e.g., the features used to define events) are modified after every new input to the model. The kind of modification depends on the learning rule. This learning rule may exploit the difference between the model's response and the actual event in the case of contingencies and try to optimize its responses by modifying the associations accordingly; or it may react on the pattern of the input (i.e., modify the associations according to feature contiguities).

Contingency Versus Contiguity Models

Usually associative learning is seen as the learning of contingencies between two events (e.g., turning a switch and the lighting up of a lamp). The event "turning a switch" is predictive for the event "lamp lights up." This example may be seen as a causal contingency (unless there are power problems or problems with the equipment). However, contingencies can also be of a noncausal type—that is, two events that occur concurrently, such as seeing a trumpet and hearing the sound it produces. One could, for instance, consider the sight and sound of a trumpet as one combined event, which would be defined exclusively by the contiguity of the features present. Shanks (1995) called these two types of contingencies *causal* and *structural* predictive relationships, respectively.

Contingency learning in causal relationships (either in a strong or probabilistic sense) implies a modification of the associations that optimizes the prediction from the cause (e.g., "switch turned") to the effect (e.g., "light on"). This is usually achieved within neural network models by comparing the prediction against the teaching input—that is, the "true solution"—and by using the discrepancy between the predicted event and the actual (true) event to modify the associations. Such a piece of additional information is not necessary to learn contiguities. The association between the features that define an event (e.g., the sound and sight of a trumpet played) can be learned in several ways by neural networks (see Sedlmeier, 1999, for a detailed discussion). For instance, a simple way of contiguity learning consists of directly modifying the associations among all features of an event. If two features are both present, the association between them increases and otherwise it decreases.

In many situations in everyday life, there are no clear contingencies, and there is not even an explicit structural predictive relationship, but just events (collections of features) that occur one after the other. There is no difference between such simple events and structural relationships: Every event can be seen as a structural predictive relationship between the features that constitute the event. In the next paragraph, it is shown that the information contained in the contiguity of features of an event is already sufficient to develop a memory representation that allows intuitive frequency judgments and judgments of confidence, and that may be seen as the basis for routinized decisions.

ASSOCIATIVE LEARNING AND FREQUENCY-RELATED JUDGMENTS

The basic input to associative learning is repeatedly occurring events. Therefore, it seems to be the natural basis for all kinds of frequency-related judgments. An overview of the literature reveals that intuitive frequency judgments, especially judgments of relative frequency, are quite accurate if the encoding process is not biased in any systematic way (Sedlmeier, Betsch, & Renkewitz, 2002; Zacks & Hasher, 2002). However, frequency judgments can be severely biased by deliberations or explicit memory search at the time of retrieval of frequency information or when a "wrong" sample is collected from memory (Fiedler, 2002; Schwarz & Wänke, 2002). Deliberate processes are not covered by the model introduced next. This model can, however, explain both accurate frequency judgments and judgments that are biased due to special conditions at encoding.

The PASS Model

The PASS (Probability ASSociator) model was initially developed to cover both judgments of relative frequency and judgments of probability (for more details, see Sedlmeier, 1999, 2002). It consists of an associative learning mechanism, termed FEN (frequency encoding network), that relies on the learning of the contiguities between features and the CA module (cognitive algorithms module) that acts as an interface between the task (e.g., a frequency or confidence judgment) and FEN. The CA module contains procedures that act on FEN's activations, which are elicited by a prompt. A prompt is represented in the same way as the input to FEN: a featural description of an event. FEN's activation is just the sum of the activity in FEN's (output) nodes elicited by the prompt. FEN does not stand for a specific kind of neural network. In fact all kinds of neural networks whose learning process (i.e., the modification of associations) is not restricted by external teaching inputs (the "true" solutions) should work. To date, we have tried several architectures and learning rules and have found quite comparable results (Köhlers & Sedlmeier, 2001). We have also verified that learning algorithms that employ feedback by way of teaching input do not work. We see this independence from specific assumptions about architecture and learning rules (except the one mentioned earlier) as a strength of the model rather than a weakness because it shows that the relationship between associative learning and frequency estimation is robust. Many, but not all, of the following frequency-related judgments can be modeled by exemplar models as well, but for want of space these models are not discussed here (for a discussion of possible shortcomings of exemplar in comparison to prototype models, see Sedlmeier, 1999; Smith, 2002).

Frequency Estimates: Adequate and Biased

How does PASS produce frequency estimates? Basically, it uses its memory contents to produce "intuitive responses"—that is, activations when prompted with an event. To produce relative frequency estimates, it follows the definition of relative frequency. For instance, if PASS were presented several apples and oranges and it was to estimate the relative frequency of oranges, it would produce an activation for the prompt "orange" and then divide that activation by the sum of activations for "oranges" and "apples" (for details, see Sedlmeier, 2002). For judgments of absolute frequency, an additional piece of information from outside the model (in its current version) is necessary that provides an absolute frequency equivalent to a given activation. For instance, if the information were that PASS' activation of 0.4 corresponds to 8 oranges, an activation of 0.55 would mean that PASS' estimate of the number of oranges was 11.

As already mentioned, intuitive frequency judgments are rather accurate (e.g., Zacks & Hasher, 2002). This should, for instance, include intuitive estimates of the relative frequency with which letters occur in the first as compared with other positions in words (e.g., whether the letter "r" is more likely to occur in the first or the third position in the English language). Interestingly, this rather remote task can be found in many textbooks in cognitive psychology as an example of biases in frequency judgments. This is due to Tversky and Kahneman's (1973) finding that the majority of their participants judged a collection of letters that actually are more frequent in the third position to occur more frequently in the first position of English words. Despite the popularity of this result, there is no single published replication, with the exception of a largely ignored one-page article that could not replicate the original result (White, 1991). On the contrary, Yaniv and Hogarth (1993) found their participants to be very sensitive to the frequencies with which letters appear in different positions in English words.

To clarify the issue, we ran three attempts to replicate the original results (Sedlmeier, Hertwig, & Gigerenzer, 1998). In each of the three replications, we found results that followed the actual relative frequencies well, although the relative frequency estimates were somewhat "regressed" (high values were under- and low values were overestimated). This is exactly what PASS (then ELF) predicts. Participants, when asked how they had gone about this task, often remarked that they did not really have any idea about the relative frequencies, but relied on their feeling—that is, they made intuitive judgments.[2]

Intuitions can be biased if the memory representation does not correctly mirror the true state of affairs. When would PASS predict biased intuitive knowledge, and therefore biased judgments? We explored three such cases: changes of relative frequencies over time, different levels of attention at encoding, and degree of association across stimuli.

Time Course. A frequent assumption for statistical prediction is that things do not change over time. Obviously, this assumption often does not hold: The number of problems per day with a piece of computer hardware may increase over time or the relative frequency of positive conversations may decrease during a certain period in a relationship. What impact on estimates does it have if relative frequencies change over time? PASS predicts a kind of recency effect: This is also what our participants showed. They were repeatedly presented symbols on the left and right sides of a computer screen. At the end of the sequence, they were asked to estimate the relative frequency with which each of the symbols had occurred on the left side. The total relative frequency with which a symbol occurred on the left side was held constant, but locally the relative frequency either increased or decreased over presentations. Participants overestimated the total relative frequency when it increased over time, and they underestimated it when it decreased as predicted by the model (Sedlmeier, 1999).

Attention at Encoding. PASS captures the level of attention directed at an event at encoding by a transient adjustment of its learning parameter. Higher attention, expressed by an increased value for the learning parameter, leads to a more pronounced increase of the associations between the features that define an event. So if an event or stimulus is given a higher amount of attention as compared with an event that was encoded equally often, PASS predicts higher frequency judgments for the former due to the stronger modifications of associations. According to the PASS model, these

---

[2]There are at least two possible explanations for the discrepant results: First, Tversky and Kahneman's (1973) participants had to compare first and third position. However, the number of letters in the first position in English words is higher than the number of letters in third position in English words (because there are one- and two-letter words that do not have a third letter). This could have led to an overestimation of the number of letters in the first position in their study, but not in ours, because we had participants compare letters in the first and second positions for the German language. In German, there are no one-letter words, and therefore the numbers of letters in the first and second position are equal. Another possible cause for the discrepancy could be that participants in the original experiment did not rely on their intuitive knowledge of letter frequencies (as apparently was generally the case in our studies), but on deliberate processes such as explicitly searching for words with letters in the respective positions. It seems, however, that explicit or deliberate judgment strategies often result in less exact frequency estimates than intuitive judgments (Haberstroh & Betsch, 2002).

modifications should not depend on whether the amount of attention is varied externally or internally. This prediction was confirmed in several experiments (Sedlmeier, Renkewitz, & Brunstein, 2003). To vary the amount of attention externally, the saliency of words presented on a computer screen was varied by changing fonts and background colors. For an internal variation of the amount of attention, male and female surnames were used: Participants were asked to pay attention to surnames of the specified gender (e.g., only girls) and to pay special attention to some of those names (e.g., to "Mary" and "Susan"). With identical numbers of presentation, frequency estimates for salient words and specified people were generally higher than for nonsalient words and nonspecified people, respectively.

Preexisting Associations. The basis for PASS' predictions are the associations between the features contained in memory. The strength of these associations is influenced by how often the features occur together—that is, how often an event occurs. Most often an event will not reoccur exactly in the same way it occurred earlier, but even then the associations between most features that define the (prototypical) event will be strengthened. This is a general principle: The higher the general association between an event that has already been encoded and a newly encoded event, the higher the chance that at least some of the associations between the features present in the original event are strengthened by the other event. As a consequence, the more highly associated events have been encoded lately, the more the frequency estimate for a given event increases.[3] PASS predicts that when encoded in a context of highly associated words, target words are judged to be more numerous than when the context words are not strongly associated. Moreover, the model predicts that the estimates for associated words are less exact than for nonassociated words: For a given presentation frequency, the variance of predicted frequency judgments is higher for associated than for nonassociated words (this may be taken to express uncertainty due to a higher chance of mixing up different words). These predictions were corroborated in several experiments that varied the amount of association between words that were presented in a stimulus list (Renkewitz, Sedlmeier, Wettler, & Seidensticker, 2003).

Judgments of Association

The last paragraph described the impact of associations on frequency judgments. Yet associative memory should also allow us to predict associative

---

[3]Note that associations between events also increase when these events do not occur strictly concurrently, but are active in the short-term memory at the same time. For instance, this is the case in reading (see also next paragraph). Therefore, high association does not necessarily mean high similarity.

responses per se. A prototypical example is the free-associative response—that is, the word that immediately comes to one's mind when one is given a stimulus word. Common intuitive responses of this kind are *moon* when one hears *sun* or *day* when one hears *night*. How do such associations arise? As already mentioned, for the PASS model it does not make a difference whether it encodes events one by one or whether it encodes several events together that constitute a structurally contingent relationship. An ordered list of words (e.g., a sentence) can be seen as such a relationship. In the PASS model, it is assumed that reading or listening to spoken text is equivalent to moving an attentional window of a certain size (e.g., seven words) along a text. PASS treats time in a discrete way, moving the attentional window one word forward per time step, and modifies the associations between the words in the memory after every step. We had PASS build up an associative memory in this way by having it "read" the text from a large machine-readable text corpus. This learning process created a memory that can account well for people's free associative responses (Sedlmeier, Wettler, & Seidensticker, 2003).[4] Free associations have been found to play an important role in more complex kinds of judgments as, for instance, in sales promotion: When customers can choose among different products that have comparable quality, they tend to base their choices on intuitive impressions—that is, their free associations that are evoked by the message contained in advertisements (Wettler, 2002; Wettler & Rapp, 1993).

Confidence Increases With Sample Size: The Size-Confidence Intuition

The repeated encoding of events naturally leads to samples. Samples, in turn, allow judgments about aggregates such as proportions. An important aspect of such judgments (e.g., "I guess that 45% of the delegates will vote for candidate A") is the confidence with which one should make them. According to sampling theory, one should be more confident in proportions from larger than from smaller samples. One does not need formal statistics, however, to arrive at this conclusion. Just from observation, one can learn that in a random sample estimates of averages or proportions tend to increase in their accuracy as the size of the sample increases—a rule often called the *empirical law of large numbers*. A survey of the literature revealed that people apparently have an intuition that conforms to this empirical rule (Sedlmeier & Gigerenzer, 1997, 2000).[5] Such an intuition leads people to

---

[4]Although it seems natural to explain judgments of association by the common occurrence of words, the dominant explanation since the 1970s is one that relies on elaborate symbolic processes (see Sedlmeier et al., 2003).

[5]Such a conclusion may come as a surprise to the reader who is familiar with the results reported in the heuristics and biases tradition (e.g., Kahneman & Tversky, 1972). However, it turns

immediately say "poll with 100" when asked whether they would trust more in the result of an opinion poll with 50 persons or one with 100 persons, or whether it would make no difference. How can PASS explain this size-confidence intuition?

PASS uses the variance across the output units' activations as an index for confidence: The higher the variance, the higher the confidence. The rationale for using the variance of these activations is that the more specialized the pattern of activations is (i.e., the higher the variance of the activations is) for a given event, the more exactly this event is represented in memory. A more exact representation, in turn, is taken as a basis for more confidence in a judgment involving this event. PASS' variance of output unit activations exhibits the same pattern as found in people's confidence judgments: It tends to increase with increasing sample size, thus exhibiting the size-confidence intuition (Sedlmeier, 1998, 1999). Note that there is no additional mechanism involved: The variation of output activations is just a by-product of the learning process. However, that confidence increases with sample size or, in other words, practice or experience, does not mean that higher confidence always means higher accuracy. Depending on the kind of judgment task, the size-confidence intuition might also lead to high confidence in wrong judgments and decisions (see Harvey & Fischer, chap. 7, this volume).

Other Kinds of Frequency-Related Intuitive Judgments

Meanwhile computational models of associative learning (that all rely exclusively on some kind of frequency information) can explain a wide range of cognitive behavior (e.g., McLeod, Plunkett, & Rolls, 1998). These include intuitive judgments about category membership (e.g., "Is that furry thing over there a dog or a cat?"), grammaticality of sentences (e.g., Cleeremans & McClelland, 1991; Elman, 1990, 1993), causal judgments (e.g., Lober & Shanks, 2000), risky choice (Bechara, Damasio, Tranel, & Damasio, 1997; March, 1996), and social judgments (Read & Miller, 1998), among many others. One could say that all these kinds of implicitly learned memory contents that build the basis for intuitive judgments arise as a side effect of be-

---

out that the "sample-size literature" has dealt with two quite different types of problems—one type asking about means or proportions calculated from a single sample (e.g., about the probability that the proportion of male births on 1 day in a hospital is higher than 60%) and the other basically asking about the variance of empirical sampling distributions (e.g., the number of days in a year in which more than 60% of babies born are males). The former we termed *frequency distribution task* and the latter *sampling distribution task* (Sedlmeier, 1998; Sedlmeier & Gigerenzer, 1997). The empirical law of large numbers and the PASS model only apply to frequency distribution tasks. Sampling distribution tasks seem to defy the intuition of lay people, and their solution needs deliberative thinking.

ing repeatedly exposed to objects or events and of using a simple (implicit) learning rule that creates and modifies associations between events or between the features that constitute them.

FROM INTUITIVE JUDGMENTS TO ROUTINIZED DECISIONS

In the last few paragraphs, I discussed several kinds of frequency-related judgments that might be directly related to associative learning. It is difficult to draw a clear line between what one should regard as a judgment and what might be considered a decision. Some of the kinds of frequency-related judgments discussed could be seen as (largely unconscious) decisions (e.g., to say "60%" when asked about the relative frequency with which an event occurred, to say "day" when one hears "night," or to judge a sentence as grammatically wrong). Other judgments might become the basis for decisions. For instance, I might base a decision about which student to offer a research assistantship on my intuitive impression of how often this student made intelligent remarks in class. I could decide about which of two specialists to consult with my back problems by relying on the amount of confidence I have in their skills, and the confidence might in turn have arisen as the result of how often I happened to listen to positive remarks about the two physicians.

However, the relationship between associative strength and decisions seems to be more direct. Since the pioneering work of Zajonc (1968), it has been shown again and again that originally neutral stimuli gain in positive valence by mere repetitive exposure (see Bornstein, 1989, for overview). This effect is often attributed to perceptual fluency (e.g., Bornstein & D'Agostino, 1994). In the PASS model, perceptual fluency is captured by a higher degree of association between the features that define an event: The more frequently an event is encoded, the higher the associative response to that event. Thus, if we assume that associative strength covaries with valence (in the absence of qualifying additional information) and leads to preferences, we should expect these preferences and the routinized decisions based thereon to be more stable the more often the action corresponding to that decision (which qualifies as a complex event in the PASS model) is executed. An example of a strong routine may be exhibited by the driver who turns right at a crossing at which she has turned right for years, although the route has been changed recently. If (more or less automatic) preferential behavior is based on the strength of an associative response, as postulated here, one should expect more resistance to changing a routine the more often this routine is performed. This is what Betsch et al. (2001) observed in studies that systematically manipulated the frequency of routinized decision making using a microworld simulation called COMMERCE (Haberstroh, Betsch, Glöckner, Haar, & Stiller, chap. 12, this volume).

Admittedly, the previous brief sketch is not much more than a first attempt to fill the theoretical gap between associative learning and decision theory. In the remainder of the chapter, I advance some arguments for why it is worthwhile to put more effort into studying the relationship between learning and decision making.

WHY STUDY THE RELATIONSHIP BETWEEN LEARNING AND DECISION MAKING?

As already mentioned, routinized decisions make up the bulk of our daily decision behavior, and most of these decisions are probably of an intuitive nature. It is therefore highly desirable to learn more about the intuitive basis for decision making. This is important from both theoretical and practical perspectives.

Theoretical Perspective: Integrating the Implicit

Intuitive judgments, even within the same domain, have been found to be both sound (e.g., Kaiser, Proffitt, & Anderson, 1985; Peterson & Beach, 1967) and quite biased (e.g., Kaiser, Jonides, & Alexander, 1986; Kahneman, Slovic, & Tversky, 1982). Therefore, a conclusion from this state of affairs should be that it does not contribute much to theoretical progress to search for examples of sound or biased intuitive judgments (one always will find some). Instead one should look for how specific intuitions come about and which conditions trigger which kind of intuitive behavior. The PASS model introduced earlier may be seen as a module in such a model that explains how intuitive judgments and decisions arise (for additional components of routinized decision making and their interactions with intuitive mechanisms, see Betsch, chap. 3, this volume; Hogarth, chap. 4, this volume). To achieve a fuller understanding of our decision processes, it may be worthwhile to use computational models in the exploration of the relationship between intuitive and deliberate judgments and their connections to different forms of learning. Computational models have the benefit of making theories more precise (imprecise computational models do not run), and their use could have beneficial effects on theories of nonroutinized decision making as well.

Practical Perspective: Improving Intuition

A further advantage of examining intuitive judgment from the perspective of learning theory is a practical aspect: the potential for the improvement of our intuitive decision-making behavior by some kind of relearning or by making proper use of the results of learning. If our intuitions can be both valid and invalid, this suggests two ways to improve judgment and decision making: educate the invalid intuitions and exploit the valid ones.

Educating Intuition. If intuitions are learned from experience, a biased or "wicked" environment leads to invalid intuitions. This is what Hogarth (2001) suggested in his book *Educating Intuition.* He mostly dealt with causal predictive relationships and argued that proper feedback is essential for learning proper intuitions. In some environments, the problem is that some events do not occur at all and therefore cannot be used for learning a proper intuition. Consider one of Hogarth's (2001) examples: The part-time waitress, Anna, has built an impression that well-dressed customers give larger tips than badly dressed customers. Because Anna is usually under time pressure, she allocates more attention to the well-dressed customers (and gets larger tips from them). It could be, however, that it is not the dress, but the amount of attention that makes the difference, but Anna might never find out. So how can one educate intuitions? Hogarth suggested seven guidelines that involve several kinds of deliberate actions (e.g., active choice of the environment) and the use of information contained in emotions as guides for the learning process. His suggestions culminate in the seventh guideline, which proposes to make scientific method intuitive. Intuitions should definitely be educated whenever necessary, but sometimes it might suffice to rely on valid intuitions that are already there.

Exploiting Valid Intuitions. Instead of adapting intuitions to the environment (i.e., educating them), one may think about adapting the environment to existing intuitions. Norman (1988, 1993) gave numerous examples for how the design of everyday things elicits either valid or invalid intuitive responses. For instance, the way a handle is fixed on a door invites us to either pull the door or to push it. For a large variety of man-made products, Norman offered valuable advice for designers on how these products should be made so that people intuitively make the right decisions—that is, use the products correctly. Exploitation of valid intuitions is not restricted to the design of products, but also applies to the solution of logical or mathematical problems (e.g., Fischbein, 1994; Zhang, 1997).

A specific case in point is statistical reasoning. Recall that, according to the PASS model, there should be valid intuitions about relative frequencies, probabilities (derived from relative frequencies), and the impact of sample size on the confidence one should have about proportions. However, these intuitions are strongly connected to the format in which events are encountered: Events have to be encoded separately, either in reality or in the imagination (for recent evidence that it works with imagination alone, see Mazzoni & Memon, 2003). If the PASS model is correct, these valid intuitions should work better if statistical information is presented in terms of frequencies of events instead of in terms of the conventional probability information. Although other kinds of intuitions might also be involved in statistical reasoning (e.g., Fiedler, Brinkmann, Betsch, & Wild, 2000), the superiority of frequency format over probability format has been found consistently in studies on statistical problem solving (e.g., Gigerenzer & Hoffrage, 1995; Hertwig & Gigerenzer, 1999). The superiority of frequency formats has also been exploited in computerized training programs for statistical reasoning: Training regimes that used frequency format lead to much higher learning effects than comparable ones that relied on probability format (Sedlmeier, 1997, 2000; Sedlmeier & Gigerenzer, 2001). Also the size-confidence intuition, which refers to a proportion calculated from a sample, has been successfully used in training to solve difficult problems about sampling distributions—that is, the distribution of these proportions or means (Sedlmeier, 1998, 1999; see also Footnote 5). The optimized training programs are meanwhile tested and used in German high schools (Sedlmeier & Köhlers, 2001; Wassner, Martignon, & Sedlmeier, 2002) and may hopefully result in improving some people's decision making under uncertainty.

CONCLUSION

In this chapter, I wanted to show that there is a theoretically and practically relevant relationship between associative learning and intuitive judgment and decision making. This relationship was illustrated with frequency-related judgments and possible decisions based thereon. I do not argue that all of associative learning eventually leads to decisions, nor is it the case that all decisions arise from associative learning. Nonetheless, I argue that associative learning plays an important role in explaining how a considerable part of routinized decision making works. Putting more effort into exploring the relationship among learning, judgment, and decision making should benefit the areas of learning theory and decision research.

ACKNOWLEDGMENT

Thanks to Johannes Hönekopp, Frank Renkewitz, and the editors for their very useful feedback on an earlier version of this chapter.

REFERENCES

Baars, B. J. (1986). *The cognitive revolution in psychology.* New York: Guilford.
Bechara, A., Damasio, H., Tranel, D., & Damasio, A. R. (1997). Deciding advantageously before knowing the advantageous strategy. *Science, 275,* 1293–1295.

Betsch, T., Fiedler, K., & Brinkmann, J. (1998). Behavioral routines in decision making: The effects of novelty in task presentation and time pressure on routine maintenance and deviation. *European Journal of Social Psychology, 28*, 861–878.

Betsch, T., Haberstroh, S., Glöckner, A., Haar, T., & Fiedler, K. (2001). The effects of routine strength on adaptation and information search in recurrent decision making. *Organizational Behavior and Human Decision Processes, 84*, 23–53.

Betsch, T., Haberstroh, S., & Hoehle, C. (2002). Explaining and predicting routinized decision making: A review of theories. *Theory and Psychology, 12*, 453–488.

Bornstein, R. F. (1989). Exposure and affect: Overview and meta-analysis of research, 1968–1987. *Psychological Bulletin, 106*, 265–289.

Bornstein, R. F., & D'Agostino, P. R. (1994). The attribution and discounting of perceptual fluency: Preliminary tests of a perceptual fluency/attributional model of the mere exposure effect. *Social Cognition, 12*, 103–128.

Chomsky, N. (1959). Review of Skinner's *Verbal behavior. Language, 35*, 26–58.

Cleeremans, A., & McClelland, J. L. (1991). Learning the structure of event sequences. *Journal of Experimental Psychology: General, 120*, 235–253.

Dougherty, M. R. P., & Franco-Watkins, A. (2002). A memory models approach to frequency and probability judgment: Applications of Minerva 2 and Minerva-DM. In P. Sedlmeier & T. Betsch (Eds.), *Etc. Frequency processing and cognition* (pp. 121–136). Oxford: Oxford University Press.

Elman, J. L. (1990). Finding structure in time. *Cognitive Science, 14*, 179–212.

Elman, J. L. (1993). Learning and development in neural networks: The importance of starting small. *Cognition, 48*, 71–99.

Elman, J. L., Bates, E. A., Johnson, M. H., Karmiloff-Smith, A., Parisi, D., & Plunkett, K. (1996). *Rethinking innateness: A connectionist perspective on development*. Cambridge, MA: MIT Press.

Ericsson, K. A., & Lehman, A. C. (1996). Expert and exceptional performance: Evidence of maximal adaption to task constraints. *Annual Review of Psychology, 47*, 273–305.

Estes, W. K. (1986). Array models for category learning. *Cognitive Psychology, 18*, 500–549.

Fiedler, K. (1996). Explaining and simulating judgment biases as an aggregation phenomenon in probabilistic, multiple-cue environments. *Psychological Review, 103*, 193–214.

Fiedler, K. (2002). Frequency judgments and retrieval structures: Splitting, zooming, and merging the units of the empirical world. In P. Sedlmeier & T. Betsch (Eds.), *Etc. Frequency processing and cognition* (pp. 67–88). Oxford: Oxford University Press.

Fiedler, K., Brinkmann, B., Betsch, T., & Wild, B. (2000). A sampling approach to biases in conditional probability judgments: Beyond base rate neglect and statistical format. *Journal of Experimental Psychology: General, 129*, 399–418.

Fischbein, E. (1994). The interaction between the formal, the algorithmic, and the intuitive components in a mathematical activity. In R. Biehler, R. W. Scholz, R. Strässer, & B. Winkelmann (Eds.), *Didactics of mathematics as a scientific discipline* (pp. 231–245). Dordrecht: Kluwer.

Garcia, J. (1990). Learning without memory. *Journal of Cognitive Neuroscience, 2*, 287–305.

Gigerenzer, G., & Hoffrage, U. (1995). How to improve Bayesian reasoning without instruction: Frequency formats. *Psychological Review, 102*, 684–704.

Haberstroh, S., & Betsch, T. (2002). Online strategies versus memory-based strategies in frequency estimation. In P. Sedlmeier & T. Betsch (Eds.), *Etc. Frequency processing and cognition* (pp. 205–220). Oxford: Oxford University Press.

Hertwig, R., & Gigerenzer, G. (1999). The "conjunction fallacy" revisited: How intelligent inferences look like reasoning errors. *Journal of Behavioral Decision Making, 12*, 275–305.

Hintzman, D. L. (1986). "Schema abstraction" in a multiple-trace memory model. *Psychological Review, 93*, 411–428.

Hintzman, D. L. (1988). Judgments of frequency and recognition memory in a multiple-trace memory model. *Psychological Review, 95*, 528–551.

Hogarth, R. (2001). *Educating intuition*. Chicago: The University of Chicago Press.

James, W. (1890). *The principles of psychology*. New York: Dover.

Kahneman, D., Slovic, P., & Tversky, A. (Eds.). (1982). *Judgment under uncertainty: Heuristics and biases.* New York: Cambridge University Press.

Kahneman, D., & Tversky, A. (1972). Subjective probability: A judgment of representativeness. *Cognitive Psychology, 3,* 430–454.

Kaiser, M. K., Jonides, J., & Alexander, J. (1986). Intuitive reasoning about abstract and familiar physics problems. *Memory and Cognition, 14,* 308–312.

Kaiser, M. K., Proffitt, D. R., & Anderson, K. (1985). Judgments of natural and anomalous trajectories in the presence and absence of motion. *Journal of Experimental Psychology: Learning, Memory, and Cognition, 11,* 795–803.

Köhlers, D., & Sedlmeier, P. (2001). [Simulating frequency judgments: A comparison of several neural-network models]. Unpublished raw data.

Lober, K., & Shanks, D. R. (2000). Is causal induction based on causal power? Critique of Cheng (1997). *Psychological Review, 107,* 195–212.

March, J. G. (1996). Learning to be risk averse. *Psychological Review, 103,* 309–319.

Mazzoni, G., & Memon, A. (2003). Imagination can create false autobiographical memories. *Psychological Science, 14,* 186–188.

McClelland, J. L., & Rumelhart, D. (Eds.). (1986). *Parallel distributed processing: Vol. II.* Cambridge, MA: MIT Press.

McLeod, P., Plunkett, K., & Rolls, E. T. (1998). *Introduction to connectionist modelling of cognitive processes.* Oxford: Oxford University Press.

Minsky, M. L., & Papert, S. A. (1969). *Perceptions: An introduction to computational geometry.* Cambridge, MA: MIT Press.

Norman, D. A. (1988). *The design of everyday things.* New York: Doubleday.

Norman, D. A. (1993). *Things that make us smart.* Reading, MA: Addison-Wesley.

Patel, V. L., Arocha, J. F., & Kaufman, D. R. (1999). Medical cognition. In F. T. Durso (Ed.), *Handbook of applied cognition* (pp. 663–693). Chichester: Wiley.

Peterson, C. R., & Beach, L. R. (1967). Man as an intuitive statistician. *Psychological Bulletin, 68,* 29–46.

Read, S. J., & Miller, L. C. (Eds.). (1998). *Connectionist models of social reasoning and social behavior.* Mahwah, NJ: Lawrence Erlbaum Associates.

Renkewitz, F., Sedlmeier, P., Wettler, M., & Seidensticker, P. (2003). [The impact of the association of context words on frequency estimates]. Unpublished raw data.

Rumelhart, D. E., & McClelland, J. L. (Eds.). (1986). *Parallel distributed processing: Vol. I.* Cambridge, MA: MIT Press.

Schwarz, N., & Wänke, M. (2002). Experiential and contextual heuristics in frequency judgment: Ease of recall and response scales. In P. Sedlmeier & T. Betsch (Eds.), *Etc. Frequency processing and cognition* (pp. 89–108). Oxford: Oxford University Press.

Sedlmeier, P. (1997). BasicBayes: A tutor system for simple Bayesian inference. *Behavior Research Methods, Instruments, & Computers, 29,* 328–336.

Sedlmeier, P. (1998). The distribution matters: Two types of sample-size tasks. *Journal of Behavioral Decision Making, 11,* 281–301.

Sedlmeier, P. (1999). *Improving statistical reasoning: Theoretical models and practical implications.* Mahwah, NJ: Lawrence Erlbaum Associates.

Sedlmeier, P. (2000). How to improve statistical thinking: Choose the task representation wisely and learn by doing. *Instructional Science, 28,* 227–262.

Sedlmeier, P. (2002). Associative learning and frequency judgments: The PASS model. In P. Sedlmeier & T. Betsch (Eds.), *Etc. Frequency processing and cognition* (pp. 137–152). Oxford: Oxford University Press.

Sedlmeier, P., Betsch, T., & Renkewitz, F. (2002). Frequency processing and cognition: Introduction and overview. In P. Sedlmeier & T. Betsch (Eds.), *Etc. Frequency processing and cognition* (pp. 1–17). Oxford: Oxford University Press.

Sedlmeier, P., & Gigerenzer, G. (1997). Intuitions about sample size: The empirical law of large numbers? *Journal of Behavioral Decision Making, 10*, 33–51.

Sedlmeier, P., & Gigerenzer, G. (2000). Was Bernoulli wrong? On intuitions about sample size. *Journal of Behavioral Decision Making, 13*, 133–139.

Sedlmeier, P., & Gigerenzer, G. (2001). Teaching Bayesian reasoning in less than two hours. *Journal of Experimental Psychology: General, 130*, 380–400.

Sedlmeier, P., Hertwig, R., & Gigerenzer, G. (1998). Are judgments of the positional frequencies of letters systematically biased due to availability? *Journal of Experimental Psychology: Learning, Memory, and Cognition, 24*, 754–770.

Sedlmeier, P., & Köhlers, D. (2001). *Wahrscheinlichkeiten im Alltag: Statistik ohne Formeln* (with training program on CD). Braunschweig: Westermann.

Sedlmeier, P., Renkewitz, F., & Brunstein, A. (2003). *Attentional processes at encoding and frequency estimation*. Unpublished manuscript, Chemnitz University of Technology.

Sedlmeier, P., Wettler, M., & Seidensticker, P. (2003). *Why do we associate "woman" when we hear "man"? A computational model of associative responses based on co-occurrences of words in large text corpora*. Manuscript submitted for publication.

Shanks, D. R. (1995). *The psychology of associative learning*. Cambridge, England: Cambridge University Press.

Smith, E. E., & Medin, D. L. (1981). *Categories and concepts*. Cambridge, MA: Harvard University Press.

Smith, J. D. (2002). Exemplar theory's predicted typicality gradient can be tested and disconfirmed. *Psychological Science, 13*, 437–442.

Tversky, A., & Kahneman, D. (1973). Availability: A heuristic for judging frequency and probability. *Cognitive Psychology, 4*, 207–232.

Wassner, C., Martignon, L., & Sedlmeier, P. (2002). Die Bedentung der Darbietungsform für das alltagsorien-tierte Lehren von Stochastik [The importance of representational format for teaching everyday-life statistics]. *Zeitschrift für Pädagogik, 45 (Beiheft)*, 35–50.

Wettler, M. (2002). Free word associations and the frequency of co-occurrence in language use. In P. Sedlmeier & T. Betsch (Eds.), *Etc. Frequency processing and cognition* (pp. 271–284). Oxford: Oxford University Press.

Wettler, M., & Rapp, R. (1993). Associative text analysis of advertisements. *Marketing and Research Today, 21*, 241–246.

White, P. A. (1991). Availability heuristic and judgements of letter frequency. *Perceptual and Motor Skills, 72*, 34.

Yaniv, I., & Hogarth, R. M. (1993). Judgmental versus statistical prediction: Information asymmetry and combination rules. *Psychological Science, 4*, 58–62.

Zacks, R. T., & Hasher, L. (2002). Frequency processing: A twenty-five year perspective. In P. Sedlmeier & T. Betsch (Eds.), *Etc. Frequency processing and cognition* (pp. 21–36). Oxford: Oxford University Press.

Zajonc, R. B. (1968). Attitudinal effects of mere exposure. *Journal of Personality and Social Psychology Monograph Supplement, 9*, 1–27.

Zhang, J. (1997). The nature of external representations in problem solving. *Cognitive Science, 21*, 179–217.

6

The Multiple Roles of Attitudes in Decision Making

David M. Sanbonmatsu
Kort C. Prince
Sam Vanous
University of Utah

Steven S. Posavac
University of Rochester

An examination of the literature on decision making reveals a surprising neglect of the attitude construct. Although the evaluative processes that are fundamental to choice have been a basic staple of attitudes research for decades, this enormous body of work is commonly ignored in discussions of decision making. Decision theorists infrequently make references to predictive models of attitudes and behavior such as information integration theory (e.g., Anderson, 1974) and the theory of reasoned action (e.g., Ajzen & Fishbein, 1980). More significantly, research on the basic processes through which attitudes guide behavior and decisions are rarely considered in theories of choice. Generally, attitudes are not even conceived to play a role in most accounts of how decisions are made. We suggest that the neglect of attitudes theory reflects more the narrow scope of most scientific endeavor (see Kruglanski, 2001) and the lack of familiarity with the attitudes literature more than the lack of an important role of attitudes in decision making.

In this chapter, we present our conceptualization of the multiple roles of attitudes in appraisal and choice. Our framework draws from work on both the attitude-behavior relation and decision making and, thus, represents an integration of the two literatures. The chapter begins with a definition of attitudes. This is followed by a discussion of the role of attitudes in appraisal and the multiple processes through which attitudes guide choice. We suggest that attitudes influence decisions not only by guiding the evaluation of choice options, but also by guiding the assessment of goals and appraisals of the situation. However, we emphasize that attitudes do not operate alone; rather they influence choice in conjunction with routines and other decision-relevant representations. As a consequence, the effect of attitudes is often dependent on the activation of these constructs. The chapter moves on to examine the codevelopment and functionality of global attitudes and routines. We then discuss the conditions under which attitudes influence decisions and behavior. Finally, the chapter closes with arguments for linking research on attitudes with theory on choice.

WHAT IS AN ATTITUDE?

Attitudes are the feelings and evaluations associated with a representation of an object in memory (for related definitions, see Fazio, 1990; Oskamp, 1977; Petty & Cacioppo, 1981; Zanna & Rempel, 1988). An attitude object is basically anything that can be discriminated by a perceiver (Eagly, 1992). Thus, attitudes are the stored evaluations of or feelings toward persons, objects, events, situations, routines, instructions, goals, positions, ideas, behaviors, and issues. Attitudes take a variety of different forms. They may be relatively "hot" affect or "cold" cognitive evaluations (Fazio, Sanbonmatsu, Powell, & Kardes, 1986). They may be stored in explicit memory or implicit memory (e.g., Betsch, Plessner, Schwieren, & Gütig, 2001; Greenwald & Banaji, 1995). Moreover, they are housed in different levels of the neural substratum (Cacioppo & Tassinary, 1989). Finally, different attitudes toward the same object may co-exist and vary in their evaluative implications (e.g., Cacioppo, Gardner, & Berntson, 1997; Thompson, Zanna, & Griffin, 1995; Wilson, Lindsey, & Schooler, 2000).

Attitudes differ from attitudinal beliefs, which are subjective knowledge of the evaluative qualities, attributes, or relations of an attitude object. Attitudinal beliefs take the form of propositions such as "porcupines have sharp quills" or "Corona beer tastes great." Note that by definition, these evaluative qualities, attributes, or relations are attitude objects toward which there exists an attitude. For example, a person may have an aversion to sharp quills and positive feelings about great taste in memory.

The overlap between decision and attitudes theory is most apparent in the structural models that have been developed (e.g., Anderson, 1974; Fishbein, 1963; Kahneman & Tversky, 1979; Savage, 1954; Von Neumann & Morgenstern, 1947). For example, expectancy value models define an attitude as the sum of the values associated with the attributes of an attitude object and the expectations that the object has the attributes (e.g., Fishbein, 1963). When the attitude object is behavior, the attitude is a function of the values associated with the behavioral consequences and the expectation of those consequences. Similarly, the subjective utility of a behavior is defined as the sum of the subjective utilities and perceived probabilities of the associated outcomes (e.g., Savage, 1954). Thus, models in both fields posit the assessment of a choice option to be a function of the valuations of the outcome's perceived attributes or outcomes and the subjective probabilities or weights of the attributes or outcomes.

HOW DO ATTITUDES GUIDE DECISIONS?

One of the most fundamental tasks performed by mental systems is evaluation or appraisal (e.g., Katz, 1960; Lazarus, 1966; Zajonc, 1980). The mind continually sizes up situations, response options, outcomes, and other attitude objects for the opportunities they afford or the threats they entail. These appraisals play a central role in decision making and behavior by serving as an impetus to action—that is, by prompting the selection and implementation of particular approach or avoidance options.

Decision making is often characterized by a two-step process involving the (a) perception and appraisal of the situation, and (b) generation, evaluation, and selection of choice options. Attitudes are the stored evaluations or feelings that guide these assessments or appraisals. Following Katz (1960) and other functional theorists (e.g., Shavitt, 1990), we suggest that attitudes enable individuals to size up objects for the opportunities or threats they afford. By guiding assessments of the situation and evaluations of choice options, attitudes determine choice. Moreover, as we discuss later, attitudes further influence decisions by guiding the appraisal of goals. In this sense, attitudes are the stored motivation that guide the selection and evaluation of alternatives.

ATTITUDES GUIDE APPRAISALS THROUGH A VARIETY OF PROCESSES

The evaluation of decision options and other attitude objects is guided by attitudes through a variety of different processes or mechanisms. Of course for an attitude to guide an appraisal, it must be activated from memory. Research indicates that, in some instances, attitudes are activated automatically on observation of the attitude object (Bargh, Chaiken, Govender, & Pratto, 1992; Fazio, Sanbonmatsu, Powell, & Kardes, 1986), making the process of appraising an object or response option relatively effortless. However, in other instances, a global attitude may not be accessible or even available in memory. Consequently, the search for relevant attitudes and the formation of an evaluation must be more deliberate or controlled.

The appraisal of an object or response option may also be either global attitude-based or feature-based (Fazio, 1990; Fiske & Pavelchak, 1986; Sanbonmatsu & Fazio, 1990). Often strong and accessible global attitudes toward an object exist in memory that serve as the basis for an assessment (Lynch, Marmorstein, & Weigold, 1988; Sanbonmatsu & Fazio, 1990; Sanbonmatsu, Kardes, & Gibson, 1991). However, when a global attitude toward an object or choice option is not accessible or available, featured-based processing must occur in which specific information about the features or qualities of an object is acquired or accessed and integrated. Decision theorists, of course, have identified a number of different feature-based processes or rules that are used to assess and compare choice options or routines (see Einhorn & Hogarth, 1981; Payne, Bettman, & Johnson, 1993; Slovic, Lichtenstein, & Fischhoff, 1985). In some instances, the salient attributes, qualities, exemplars, and outcomes associated with an alternative are evaluated and integrated singularly to form an overall assessment (Savage, 1954; Von Neumann & Morgenstern, 1947). Alternatively, the features or outcomes of a choice option may be compared with those of alternatives using one of a number of comparative rules such as elimination by aspects (Tversky, 1972; see also McGuire, 1985) or a lexicographic strategy (Fishburn, 1974; Gigerenzer et al., 1999). In these noncompensatory feature-based processes, the assessment of different outcomes or options is based on a comparison of individual features rather than on a comparison of holistic evaluations that are inferred from the features (e.g., Payne, 1976; Russo & Dosher, 1983). The type of processing that occurs is important, of course, because preferences and choices can vary markedly as a function of the rule that is employed.

The appraisals and preferences that are derived through these feature-based processes are momentary constructions that do not necessarily reflect a person's chronic inclination toward an attitude object (e.g., Kahneman & Miller, 1986; Tversky, Sattath, & Slovic, 1988; Wilson, Dunn, Kraft, & Lisle, 1989; Zanna & Rempel, 1988). In many instances, responses are based on highly limited information because of processing constraints. Moreover, they are often skewed by select beliefs and external cues (e.g., Chaiken & Baldwin, 1981; Tesser, 1978; Wood, 1982) and thus are highly context specific and episodic.

Some theorists might consider these feature-based processes to be nonattitudinal. In particular, subjective utility assessments and other integrative processes might be seen as entirely based on beliefs rather than attitudes. For example, the integration of information about price, appearance, and gas mileage to form an overall evaluation of an automobile may be seen as wholly belief-based. However, all feature-based assessments are thought to involve an integration of the valuations as well as the perceived probabilities or weights of the attributes, or outcomes. We suggest that these momentary valuations are based on attitudes toward the features. Thus, it is consumers' specific attitudes about price, appearance, and gas mileage that are integrated along with weighting beliefs to form an overall assessment of an automobile.

Attitude-behavior researchers, like decision theorists (e.g., Payne, Bettman, & Johnson, 1993) and theorists in social cognition and persuasion (e.g., Chaiken, Liberman, & Eagly, 1989; Petty & Cacioppo, 1986), recognize that the type of process that operates and the information that is utilized in judgment and choice are contingent on a variety of contextual variables. Thus, Fazio's (1990) MODE Model postulates that the appraisal process is influenced by the motivation and opportunity to process the available information, as well as the availability of an overall attitude. The important role of motivation and opportunity in the evaluation of choice alternatives was investigated by Sanbonmatsu and Fazio (1990), who provided experimental participants with information about the attributes of two department stores: Browns and Smiths. Although Smiths had an inferior camera department, overall it was described more favorably than Browns. Consequently, participants formed more favorable global attitudes toward Smiths than Browns. After participants read about and formed global evaluations of the stores, they were given the task of deciding which store they would shop at to buy a camera under conditions of high or low fear of invalidity (Kruglanski & Freund, 1983) and high or low time pressure. A choice of Smiths reflected a reliance on global attitudes to make the decision because, again, it was described far more favorably than Browns. A choice of Browns, in contrast, reflected the usage of specific attribute knowledge because that store had the superior camera department. In this study and a follow-up, the researchers demonstrated that when participants were both motivated and had ample time to make a good decision, they were more likely to engage in the effortful processing of retrieving their attribute knowledge and choose Browns. However, when they had limited time or lacked the opportunity to make a good choice, participants were more likely to rely on their global attitudes and select Smiths. Thus, when the motivation or opportunity to make a good decision is limited, preexisting global attitudes toward the choice options are used to make a decision. However, when both motivation and opportunity are high, a more effortful, feature-based rule may be used to assess a target. Similarly, when an overall attitude does not exist in memory, an analysis of the individual features or outcomes is necessary to evaluate the alternatives (Sanbonmatsu, Kardes, & Gibson, 1991).

Attitudes and the Weighting of Information. Attitudes serve as the primary basis for the valuation of options. For example, attitudes guide evaluations of the potential costs and benefits associated with a new job or an alternative brand of TV. Interestingly, the perceived probabilities or weights of outcomes are frequently accounted for as well by the attitudes held toward different options or routines. That is, the overall attitude toward an alternative is often based on considerations of probability or weight. For example, many persons have a negative attitude toward playing the lottery. Obviously, this attitude is not based on an unfavorable evaluation of the multimillion dollar prize associated with winning, but rather is derived from a dim view of the chances of winning. The negative overall attitude reflects the low probability of winning entailed by the lottery.

Attitudes Guide the Processing of Information. Attitudes further influence assessments by guiding the gathering, interpretation, assimilation, and recall of information about choice options and other attitude objects (for reviews, see Eagly & Chaiken, 1993; Fazio, 1990; Kunda, 1990; Pratkanis & Greenwald, 1989). Information that is dissonant with attitudes is sometimes avoided unless it can be readily refuted (Frey, 1986). In addition, evidence that is inconsistent with attitudes is often discounted or rejected (e.g., Houston & Fazio, 1989; Lord, Ross, & Lepper, 1979). In the absence of information, assumptions are often made that are consistent with preexisting attitudes (e.g., Hatfield & Sprecher, 1986; Sanbonmatsu, Kardes, & Sansone, 1991). Moreover, information and events are often construed in a manner that is consistent with a perceiver's initial attitudes (e.g., Cooper & Jahoda, 1947; Fazio & Williams, 1986; Hastorf & Cantril, 1954). Thus, attitudes guide the processing of information, which in turn influences featured-based assessments of choice options, the situation, and other attitude objects.

ATTITUDES GUIDE THE APPRAISAL OF SITUATIONS, GOALS, ROUTINES, AND OTHER DECISION-RELEVANT CONSTRUCTS

As suggested earlier, one of the central roles of attitudes in decision making is to guide the evaluation of choice options. Attitudes are used in the comparison of different choice options and in the decision to implement a particular response. If only a singular option is considered (Sanbonmatsu, Posavac, Kardes, & Mantel, 1998), a negative attitude toward it may lead to the search for alternative courses of action.

Attitudes guide the evaluation of additional constructs that determine choice. In particular, appraisals of the situation or decision task may be guided by attitudes. A given situation, of course, may be interpreted and appraised in different ways. For example, a faculty member's criticism of a graduate student's work may be construed positively as "helpful feedback" or, negatively, as "high-handed bullying." The evaluation that is formed, of course, will influence the sorts of choice responses that are considered. If the comments are appraised to be constructive, the student might consider different ways to utilize the feedback. In contrast, if the comments are construed as "baseless criticism," the student might instead consider different methods of payback. Naturally, the student's attitudes toward the faculty member and feelings about his or her own research are all likely to play a role in how the comments are construed and, thus, the sorts of choice options that are considered.

Attitudes may also influence decisions by helping to determine the goals that operate in a given context, as well as the effort that is directed toward achieving those goals. For example, a student can approach a meeting with a faculty member with the explicit goals of behaving professionally and learning. Strong and positive attitudes toward these goals will tend to ensure a constructive response toward the comments of the faculty member even if he or she is perceived to be somewhat out of line.

Finally, attitudes affect a variety of meta-assessments that influence choice. In the course of making a judgment or decision, people often assess the adequacy of their information, the appropriateness of their judgmental standards, and the quality of their thinking. Attitudes are necessary to appraise these important facets of judgment and decision making. In some instances, a negative appraisal of one's thought processes may lead to rethinking or the gathering of additional information, thus altering the manner in which the decision is made.

ATTITUDES GUIDE DECISIONS IN CONJUNCTION WITH OTHER CONSTRUCTS

Again attitudes are the stored evaluations or feelings associated with an object. Once activated, these evaluations or feelings serve as an impetus to action that moves individuals to approach opportunities and avoid threats. Attitudes, however, do not do this alone; they guide behavior and decisions in concert with other constructs. Attitudes are always toward some object— that is, they are always associated with a representation of some choice option, person, event, issue, procedure, behavior, goal, norm, rule, or target in memory. For an attitude to guide evaluation, the representation of the attitude object must be activated, which in turn may activate the attitude (see Lord & Lepper, 1999). Basically, then, the attitude object must be recognized, identified, or cognized at some processing level for an attitude to play a role in choice (although not necessarily a conscious level; see Smith, Fazio, & Cejka, 1996; Zajonc, 1980). Thus, for a positive attitude toward a goal to influence decision making, the goal must be activated and, in turn, activate the attitude.

Constructs such as norms, goals, routines, and the self are often conceived as competitors with attitudes, the presumption being that behavior
is influenced by either attitudes *or* these alternative constructs, with one
precluding the operation of the other. For example, in many predictive
models of the attitude-behavior relation (e.g., Ajzen & Fishbein, 1980; Bentler & Speckart, 1979), social norms and attitudes are conceptualized as alternative determinants of choice. However, in our view, constructs such as
norms, goals, routines, and scripts do not belong in the same theoretical
category as attitudes. Rather, these are representations of the attitude objects with which attitudes are associated. Attitudes are better conceived as
the evaluations or feelings that guide appraisals of goals, routines, norms,
behaviors, and other attitude objects—that is, as a distinct class of determinants that work jointly with object and response constructs to influence behavior. To use an automotive analogy, we would suggest that attitudes and
constructs such as goals and routines are not both types of engines or both
types of fuel. Rather, we might characterize attitudes as the fuel and routines as the engine; both are distinct components that together make an automobile go (although unlike fuel, attitudes are not always necessary to
make a person go). When attitudes are conceptualized as the feelings and
evaluations that guide appraisals, rather than as an alternative to goals or
scripts, their relevance to models of motivation and decision making becomes more apparent.

ATTITUDES GUIDE DECISIONS IN CONJUNCTION
WITH CHOICE OPTION REPRESENTATIONS

As indicated previously, one of the central roles of attitudes in decision
making is to guide the assessment of decision alternatives. For an attitude
to guide such appraisals and influence choice, however, the representation
of the choice option must be activated or generated. Basically, a person
must think of the option if the attitude toward the option is to influence the
decision that is made.

Hence, the attitude or attitudes toward a response option play a role in
choice primarily when the option is activated or considered. Under what conditions is a choice option likely to be considered in a decision task? Research
by Posavac, Sanbonmatsu, and Fazio (1997) indicated that two critical determinants are the salience of the choice alternative in the decision context and
the accessibility of the choice alternative in memory. The ease with which a
representation of a option may be retrieved or activated from memory, of
course, varies considerably. When the association between an alternative
and the choice task or choice category is strong, the alternative is more
likely to be activated and selected. This was demonstrated by Posavac et al.

(1997), who asked experimental participants to select charities for a donation. The researchers observed that the more accessible the representation of a charitable organization was for a participant, the more likely the charity was selected as the donation recipient. It was found, however, that the importance of the accessibility of choice options is moderated by the salience of the choice options. Frequently choice alternatives are specified or present in the decision context. For example, restaurant menus list and describe different food items, whereas in supermarkets different brands are present on the shelves. Posavac et al. (1997) observed that when a list of different charitable organizations was presented, the accessibility of representations of the charities in memory was far less predictive of participants' donations. Their pattern of findings indicates that a choice option is especially likely to be considered if it is specified or present in the decision context. However, if a choice option is not highly salient, the accessibility of the representation of the choice option from memory plays an important role in determining whether it is considered and chosen.

The attitudes toward a response option, then, are especially likely to be activated and to influence choice when the response option is salient in the choice context or is highly accessible from memory. This was confirmed by Posavac et al. (1997), who found that participants were more likely to choose their favorite charities for a donation if those options were salient in the choice context or when the options were accessible in memory. When the alternative charities were not salient or readily accessible from memory, participants were less likely to make choices that were consistent with their attitudes—that is, they were less likely to choose the charities that they actually preferred the most.

ATTITUDES AND ROUTINES

Thus far we have used the terms *choice options* and *routines* somewhat interchangeably. Routines, however, are a particular class of choice options that are well learned, familiar, and accessible. We suggest that in natural settings the routinization of an option and the qualities of attitudes toward the option tend to go hand in hand. Individuals are particularly likely to have well-developed, favorable, and accessible global attitudes toward options that are routine. Thus, routines tend to be chosen in a decision task not only because they are especially likely to be considered, but also because attitudes toward them tend to be favorable and accessible.

The literature on conditioning (e.g., Greenspoon, 1955; Skinner, 1938) and automaticity (e.g., Shiffrin & Schneider; 1977; Smith, Branscombe, & Bormann, 1988) suggests that choice options will develop this profile if they are frequently and consistently selected with a positive outcome. For example, a consumer who consistently and frequently purchases Sony products that perform well is likely to develop highly positive attitudes toward Sony as well as a highly accessible representation of the Sony brand. The impact of this sort of reward schedule was investigated by Betsch, Haberstroh, Glockner, Haar, and Fiedler (2001), who manipulated the frequency with which a routine needed to be selected to achieve task goals. The researchers demonstrated that when a routine was strengthened through frequent selection in a choice task, it was more likely to be chosen later in a new but similar decision environment. We suggest that this sort of schedule or procedure can be seen as a basic conditioning paradigm that serves to strengthen the favorableness of attitudes toward the routine and that strengthens the association between the routine and the decision category or task.

Obviously, not all options that first come to mind are those that are highly favored. In some instances, an option may be readily accessible from memory because it was recently considered or observed in a previous setting. Moreover, often the routines that most readily come to mind are those that people are trying to inhibit or suppress. For example, the first thing a recovering alcoholic may consider under pressure is drinking, even though his or her feelings about alcohol may have become largely negative.

THE FUNCTIONAL UTILITY OF STRONG ATTITUDES AND ROUTINES

The development of global attitudes and the acquisition of strong routines facilitate choice in a number of important ways. It diminishes the need to search for options and integrate information about their merits, and thus increases both the speed and ease with which options can be generated and evaluated. Moreover, it often contributes to better decisions particularly when the time or motivation to deliberate is limited. In contrast, when a choice option is relatively novel, individuals are less likely to have a well-developed global attitude toward it. As a consequence, the evaluation of nonroutine options generally requires a time-consuming and laborious assessment of the attributes and consequences.

The drawback of strong routines and global attitudes, of course, is that environmental changes may occur that diminish their utility. If individuals are unaware of the changes, they may persist with a strong routine even when better alternatives are available. This was nicely demonstrated by Betsch, Haberstroh, and colleagues (2001), who observed that participants who had acquired strong routines in one decision environment persisted in choosing the routine in a subsequently encountered similar decision environment, even though the routine had been rendered obsolete.

ATTITUDES DO NOT PLAY A ROLE
IN ALL DECISIONS AND BEHAVIOR

Evaluation is not always the primary determinant of the selection of a choice option or routine. Increasingly research indicates that there are multiple bases for a decision (for a review, see Betsch, Haberstroh, & Hohle, 2002). For example, decisions may be guided by the familiarity of choice options (Gigerenzer et al., 1999) or the extent to which response options are perceived to be consistent with learned rules or procedures (e.g., Betsch, Haberstroh, & Hohle, 2002; Klein, 1999; Ross, Lussier, & Klein, chap. 18, this volume). Moreover, many decisions are not prompted by an affective or evaluative appraisal of the situation. Thus, attitudes do not always influence choice; they play a central role in decisions that involve evaluative processes.

More generally, attitudes do not directly influence most behavior. Most instances of behavior are not consciously chosen. Rather most are molecular actions that are part of biologically prewired or learned sequences that are elicited by the preceding acts and the current stimulus situation. Often consistently and frequently performed action patterns become learned to the point that they are elicited automatically by situational, proprioceptive, and behavioral cues without intervening appraisal processes. Thus, most behavior is habitual or reflexive (e.g., Bentler & Speckart, 1979; Ouellette & Wood, 1998; Triandis, 1980; Verplanken, Aarts, van Knippenberg, & van Knippenberg, 1994; Verplanken, Myrbakk, & Rudi, chap. 13, this volume) and occurs without an explicit consideration or evaluation of alternatives. Consequently, some categories of behavior are better predicted by past behavior or habit, opportunities, resources, skills, and abilities than by attitudes (for reviews, see Eagly & Chaiken, 1993; Liska, 1984).

Nevertheless, attitudes frequently play a role in the appraisals of situations that trigger a learned response or in the appraisal of molar courses of action or routines that involve sequences of automatic subscripts or subroutines. That is, it is the attitudes toward a general routine that may motivate or prompt a person to engage in an automatic sequence of behaviors. Thus, although attitudes may not have a proximal role in the elicitation of the specific molecular acts in a sequence or routine, it may be a distal determinant. Furthermore, as Abelson (1982) suggested, scripts often have choice points in which attitudes guide decisions. That is, attitude-guided decision making is often embedded in habits and scripts. For example, in a restaurant script, patrons sit down at a table, receive a menu, and then choose among menu items using their attitudes. Thus, attitudes operate together with routines and habits in different ways to influence action.

Some researchers suggest that the influence of attitudes is limited to behavior that is motivated, deliberated on, and voluntary. Thus, structural models of the attitude-behavior relation, such as the theory of reasoned action, are presented as theories of volitional behavior. However, these conceptualizations assign a role to attitudes that is much too narrow. Many nonvolitional acts are prompted by particular goals, the appraisals of which are often determined by attitudes. Moreover, the situational appraisals that lead to specific automatic response patterns may be similarly attitude guided. Thus, even in the elicitation of nonvolitional behavior, attitudes often play an important role by guiding the appraisal of situations and goals.

THE RELEVANCE OF THE ATTITUDES LITERATURE TO UNDERSTANDING CHOICE

The present chapter attempted to integrate research on attitudes with basic decision theory. We reviewed some of the important work on attitudinal processing and suggested that attitudes guide the evaluations or appraisals that determine choice. We noted that attitudes do not do this alone; the influence of attitudes is dependent on the activation of the associated attitude object. Thus, for the attitudes toward a choice option to guide choice, the choice option must be generated or identified. Consequently, routines that are accessible in memory or salient in the decision context, and that have strong and positive attitudes associated with them, are particularly likely to be chosen in a decision task. Finally, we noted that attitudes are best conceptualized as constructs that work together with goals, routines, and norms to determine choice rather than as an alternative or competing factor.

Some researchers may think that framing decision making in terms of attitudinal processes is unnecessary and that the relevance of the attitudes literature is limited. However, the linkage is valuable in that it connects decision theory with a wealth of research on basic evaluative processes. Specifically, the attitudes literature affords considerable insight into how the affect and evaluations associated with choice options and other representations are acquired, stored, and accessed, and how affective and evaluative predispositions can be effectively measured and changed. More directly, the research lends tremendous understanding to the processes through which appraisals and evaluations form and the moderating personality and contextual variables. Finally, research was reviewed that directly examined the relation between attitudes and choice that is relevant to decision theorists.

ACKNOWLEDGMENT

This article was supported by a National Institute of Mental Health grant (61364) to the first author.

REFERENCES

Abelson, R. P. (1982). Three modes of attitude-behavior consistency. In M. P. Zanna, E. T. Higgins, & C. P. Herman (Eds.), *Consistency in social behavior: The Ontario Symposium* (Vol. 2, pp. 131–146). Hillsdale, NJ: Lawrence Erlbaum Associates.

Ajzen, I., & Fishbein, M. (1980). *Understanding attitudes and predicting social behavior.* Englewood Cliffs, NJ: Prentice-Hall.

Anderson, N. H. (1974). Cognitive algebra. In L. Berkowitz (Ed.), *Advances in experimental social psychology* (pp. 1–101). New York: Academic Press.

Bargh, J. A., Chaiken, S., Govender, R., & Pratto, F. (1992). The generality of the automatic attitude activation effect. *Journal of Personality and Social Psychology, 62,* 893–912.

Bentler, P. M., & Speckart, G. (1979). Models of attitude-behavior relations. *Psychological Review, 86,* 452–464.

Betsch, T., Haberstroh, S., Glockner, A., Haar, T., & Fiedler, K. (2001). The effects of routine strength on adaptation and information search in recurrent decision making. *Organizational Behavior and Human Decision Processes, 84,* 23–53.

Betsch, T., Haberstroh, S., & Hohle, C. (2002). The effects of routine strength on adaptation and information search in recurrent decision making. *Theory and Psychology, 12,* 453–488.

Betsch, T., Plessner, H., Schwieren, C., & Gütig, R. (2001). I like it but I don't know why: A value-account approach to implicit attitude formation. *Personality and Social Psychology Bulletin, 27,* 242–253.

Cacioppo, J. T., Gardner, W. L., & Berntson, G. G. (1997). Beyond bipolar conceptualizations and measures: The case of attitudes and evaluative space. *Personality and Social Psychology Review, 1,* 3–25.

Cacioppo, J. T., & Tassinary, L. G. (1989). The concept of attitudes: A psychophysiological analysis. In H. Wagner & A. Manstead (Eds.), *Handbook of social psychophysiology* (pp. 309–346). New York: Wiley.

Chaiken, S., & Baldwin, M. W. (1981). Affective-cognitive consistency and the effect of salient behavioral information on the self-perception of attitudes. *Journal of Personality and Social Psychology, 41,* 1–12.

Chaiken, S., Liberman, A., & Eagly, A. H. (1989). Heuristic and systematic processing within and beyond the persuasion context. In J. S. Uleman & J. A. Bargh (Eds.), *Unintended thought* (pp. 212–252). New York: Guilford.

Cooper, E., & Jahoda, M. (1947). The evasion of propaganda: How prejudiced people respond to anti-prejudice propaganda. *Journal of Psychology, 23,* 15–25.

Eagly, A. H. (1992). Uneven progress: Social psychology and the study of attitudes. *Journal of Personality and Social Psychology, 63,* 693–710.

Eagly, A. H., & Chaiken, S. (1993). *The psychology of attitudes.* Fort Worth, TX: Harcourt Brace Jovanovich.

Einhorn, H. J., & Hogarth, R. M. (1981). Behavioral decision theory: Processes of judgment and choice. *Annual Review of Psychology, 32,* 53–88.

Fazio, R. H. (1990). Multiple processes by which attitudes guide behavior: The MODE model as an integrative framework. In M. P. Zanna (Ed.), *Advances in experimental social psychology* (pp. 75–109). San Diego, CA: Academic Press.

Fazio, R. H., Sanbonmatsu, D. M., Powell, M., & Kardes, F. R. (1986). On the automatic activation of attitudes. *Journal of Personality and Social Psychology, 50,* 229–238.

Fazio, R. H., & Williams, C. J. (1986). Attitude accessibility as a mediator of the attitude-perception and attitude-behavior relations: An investigation of the 1984 presidential election. *Journal of Personality and Social Psychology, 51,* 505–514.

Fishbein, M. (1963). An investigation of the relationships between beliefs about an object and the attitude toward that object. *Human Relations, 16,* 233–240.

Fishburn, P. C. (1974). Lexicographic orders, utilities and decision rules: A survey. *Management Science, 20,* 1442–1471.

Fiske, S. T., & Pavelchak, M. A. (1986). Category based versus piecemeal-based affective responses: Developments in schema triggered affect. In R. M. Sorrentino & E. T. Higgins (Eds.), *Handbook of motivation and cognition: Foundations of social behavior* (pp. 167–203). New York: Guilford.

Frey, D. (1986). Recent research on selective exposure to information. In L. Berkowitz (Ed.), *Advances in experimental social psychology* (Vol. 19, pp. 41–80). San Diego, CA: Academic Press.

Gigerenzer, G., Todd, P. M., & the ABC Research Group. (1999). *Simple heuristics that make us smart.* Oxford: Oxford University Press.

Greenspoon, J. (1955). The reinforcing effect of two spoken sounds on the frequency of two responses. *American Journal of Psychology, 68,* 409–416.

Greenwald, A. G., & Banaji, M. R. (1995). Implicit social cognition: Attitudes, self-esteem, and stereotypes. *Psychological Review, 102,* 4–27.

Hastorf, A. H., & Cantril, H. (1954). They saw a game; A case study. *Journal of Abnormal and Social Psychology, 49,* 129–134.

Hatfield, E., & Sprecher, S. (1986). Measuring passionate love in intimate relationships. *Journal of Adolescence, 9,* 383–410.

Houston, D. A., & Fazio, R. H. (1989). Biased processing as a function of attitude accessibility: Making objective judgments subjectively. *Social Cognition, 7,* 51–66.

Kahneman, D., & Miller, D. T. (1986). Norm theory: Comparing reality to its alternatives. *Psychological Review, 93,* 136–153.

Kahneman, D., & Tversky, A. (1979). Prospect theory: An analysis of decision under risk. *Econometrica, 47,* 263–291.

Katz, D. (1960). The functional approach to the study of attitudes. *Public Opinion Quarterly, 24,* 163–204.

Klein, G. (1999). *Sources of power: How people make decisions.* Cambridge, MA: MIT Press.

Kruglanski, A. W. (2001). That Avision thing@: The state of theory in social and personality psychology at the edge of the new millennium. *Journal of Personality and Social Psychology, 80,* 871–875.

Kruglanski, A. W., & Freund, T. (1983). The freezing and unfreezing of lay-inferences: Effects on impressional primacy, ethnic stereotyping, and numerical anchoring. *Journal of Experimental Social Psychology, 19,* 448–468.

Kunda, Z. (1990). The case for motivated reasoning. *Psychological Bulletin, 108,* 480–498.

Lazarus, R. S. (1966). *Psychological stress and the coping process.* New York: McGraw-Hill.

Liska, A. E. (1984). A critical examination of the causal structure of the Fishbein/Ajzen attitude-behavior model. *Social Psychology Quarterly, 47,* 61–74.

Lord, C. G., & Lepper, M. R. (1999). Attitude representation theory. In M. P. Zanna (Ed.), *Advances in experimental social psychology* (Vol. 31, pp. 265–343). San Diego, CA: Academic Press.

Lord, C. G., Ross, L., & Lepper, M. R. (1979). Biased assimilation and attitude polarization: The effects of prior theories on subsequently considered evidence. *Journal of Personality and Social Psychology, 37,* 2098–2109.

Lynch, J. G., Marmorstein, H., & Weigold, M. F. (1988). Choices from sets including remembered attributes and prior overall evaluations. *Journal of Consumer Research, 15,* 169–184.

McGuire, W. J. (1985). Attitudes and attitude change. In G. Lindzey & E. Aronson (Eds.), *Handbook of social psychology* (3rd ed., Vol. 2, pp. 233–346). New York: Random House.

Oskamp, S. (1977). *Attitudes and opinions.* Englewood Cliffs, NJ: Prentice-Hall.

Ouellette, J. A., & Wood, W. (1998). Habit and intention in everyday life: The multiple processes by which past behavior predicts future behavior. *Psychological Bulletin, 124,* 54–74.

Payne, J. W. (1976). Task complexity and contingent processing in decision making: An information search and protocol analysis. *Organizational Behavior and Human Decision Processes, 16,* 366–387.

Payne, J. W., Bettman, J. R., & Johnson, E. J. (1993). *The adaptive decision maker.* New York: Cambridge University Press.

Petty, R. E., & Cacioppo, J. T. (1981). *Attitudes and persuasion: Classic and contemporary approaches.* Dubuque, IA: William C. Brown.

Petty, R. E., & Cacioppo, J. T. (1986). The elaboration likelihood model of persuasion. In L. Berkowitz (Ed.), *Advances in experimental social psychology* (Vol. 19, pp. 123–205). San Diego, CA: Academic Press.

Posavac, S. S., Sanbonmatsu, D. M., & Fazio, R. H. (1997). Considering the best choice: Effects of the salience and accessibility of alternatives on attitude-decision consistency. *Journal of Personality and Social Psychology, 72,* 253–261.

Pratkanis, A. R., & Greenwald, A. G. (1989). A sociocognitive model of attitude structure and function. *Advances in Experimental Social Psychology, 22,* 245–285.

Russo, J. E., & Dosher, B. A. (1983). Strategies for multiattribute binary choice. *Journal of Experiment Psychology: Learning, Memory, and Cognition, 9,* 676–696.

Sanbonmatsu, D. M., & Fazio, R. H. (1990). The role of attitudes in memory-based decision making. *Journal of Personality and Social Psychology, 59,* 614–622.

Sanbonmatsu, D. M., Kardes, F. R., & Gibson, B. D. (1991). The role of attribute knowledge and overall evaluations in comparative judgment. *Organizational Behavior and Human Decision Processes, 48,* 131–146.

Sanbonmatsu, D. M., Kardes, F. R., & Sansone, C. (1991). Remembering less and inferring more: The effects of the timing of judgment on inferences about unknown attributes. *Journal of Personality and Social Psychology, 61,* 546–554.

Sanbonmatsu, D. M., Posavac, S. S., Kardes, F. R., & Mantel, S. (1998). Selective hypothesis testing. *Psychonomic Bulletin and Review, 5,* 197–220.

Savage, L. J. (1954). *The foundations of statistics.* New York: Wiley.

Shavitt, S. (1990). The role of attitude objects in attitude functions. *Journal of Experimental Social Psychology, 26,* 124–148.

Shiffrin, R. M., & Schneider, W. (1977). Controlled and automatic human information processing: II. Perceptual learning, automatic attending, and general theory. *Psychology Review, 84,* 127–190.

Skinner, B. F. (1938). *The behavior of organisms: An experimental analysis.* New York: Appleton-Century-Crofts.

Slovic, P., Lichtenstein, S., & Fischhoff, B. (1985). Decision making. In R. C. Atkinson, R. J. Hernstein, G. D. Lindsey, & R. D. Luce (Eds.), *Handbook of experimental psychology* (Vol. 2, pp. 673–738). New York: Wiley.

Smith, E. R., Branscombe, N. R., & Bormann, C. (1988). Generality of the effects of practice on social judgment tasks. *Journal of Personality and Social Psychology, 54,* 385–395.

Smith, E. R., Fazio, R. H., & Cejka, M. A. (1996). Accessible attitudes influence categorization of multiply categorizable objects. *Journal of Personality and Social Psychology, 71,* 888–898.

Tesser, A. (1978). Self-generated attitude change. In L. Berkowitz (Ed.), *Advances in experimental social psychology* (Vol. 11, pp. 289–338). San Diego, CA: Academic Press.

Thompson, M. M., Zanna, M. P., & Griffin, D. W. (1995). Let's not be indifferent about (attitudinal) ambivalence. In R. E. Petty & J. A. Krosnick (Eds.), *Attitudinal strength: Antecedents and consequences* (pp. 361–386). Hillsdale, NJ: Lawrence Erlbaum Associates.

Triandis, H. C. (1980). Values, attitudes, and interpersonal behavior. In H. E. Howe, Jr., & M. M. Page (Eds.), *Nebraska Symposium on Motivation* (Vol. 27, pp. 195–259). Lincoln: University of Nebraska Press.

Tversky, A. (1972). Elimination by aspects: A theory of choice. *Psychological Review, 79,* 281–299.

Tversky, A., Sattath, S., & Slovic, P. (1988). Contingent weighting in judgment and choice. *Psychological Review, 95,* 371–384.

Verplanken, B., Aarts, H., van Knippenberg, A., & van Knippenberg, C. (1994). Attitude vs general habit: Antecedents of travel mode choice. *Journal of Applied Social Psychology, 24,* 285–300.

Von Neumann, J., & Morgenstern, O. (1947). *Theory of games and economic behavior.* Princeton, NJ: Princeton University Press.

Wilson, T. D., Dunn, D. S., Kraft, D., & Lisle, D. J. (1989). Introspection, attitude change, and attitude-behavior consistency: The disruptive effects of explaining why we feel the way we do. In L. Berkowitz (Ed.), *Advances in experimental social psychology* (Vol. 22, pp. 287–338). San Diego, CA: Academic Press.

Wilson, T. D., Lindsey, S., & Schooler, T. Y. (2000). A model of dual attitudes. *Psychological Review, 107,* 101–126.

Wood, W. (1982). Retrieval of attitude relevant information from memory: Effects on susceptibility to persuasion and on intrinsic motivation. *Journal of Personality and Social Psychology, 42,* 798–810.

Zajonc, R. B. (1980). Feeling and thinking: Preferences need no inferences. *American Psychologist, 35,* 151–175.

Zanna, M. P., & Rempel, J. K. (1988). Attitudes: A new look at an old concept. In D. Bar Tal & A. W. Kruglanski (Eds.), *The social psychology of knowledge* (pp. 315–334). Cambridge, England: Cambridge University Press.

II

THE ROUTINES OF DECISION MAKING: BASIC RESEARCH

7

Development of Experience-Based Judgment and Decision Making: The Role of Outcome Feedback

Nigel Harvey
University College London

Ilan Fischer
Ben Gurion University of the Negev

Experience often allows us to improve our ability to reach our goals in judgment and decision-making tasks. This experience may be direct: We gain it as we tackle tasks on repeated occasions. Alternatively, it may be indirect: We gain it as we observe others repeatedly attempting the tasks. Of course experience with the task is not the only way that decision making can be improved. We can blindly take the advice of or be guided by someone more experienced in the task or we can let them educate us about how the system underlying the task works and then use inferential techniques to determine the best way to proceed.

Research has shown that decision-making tasks are differentially susceptible to experience-based learning. In what follows, we provide a brief review of the evidence for this. First, however, it is useful to make a distinction between experience that includes feedback and experience that does not. It is in the former case, when feedback is present, that significant improvements are likely to occur. In the latter case, when people perform the task repeatedly without finding out anything about the results of their efforts, improvements are usually negligible.

Improvements produced by feedback depend on the *type* of feedback that is provided. Outcome feedback merely informs performers of what happened. Simple performance feedback gives them details about the quality of each judgment or decision. Cognitive feedback provides them with more highly processed information. For example, it could provide them with a summary of various aspects of their performance over a large number of attempts at the task. We are primarily concerned with the effects of outcome feedback.

We discuss the role of experience in five types of judgment and decision-making tasks: multiple-cue probability learning, advice-taking, confidence judgment, probability estimation, and dynamic decision making. We have selected these tasks for two reasons. First, examining them demonstrates that it is not possible to make broad generalizations about the effects of outcome feedback that hold across a range of judgment and decision-making tasks. Second, by analyzing and comparing effects of different types of experience in different tasks, it is possible to formulate a tentative model to explain how experience has the effects that it does.

MULTIPLE-CUE PROBABILITY LEARNING

Multiple-cue probability learning (MCPL) tasks have been intensively studied over the last 40 years (Cooksey, 1996; Hammond, 1996; Slovic & Lichtenstein, 1971). Typically, people are required to estimate or predict a criterion variable given a number of cue variables. For example, they may make judgments about people's annual salaries on the basis of information about these people's age, their weight, and the distance they live from the center of town. The investigator can use regression analyses to estimate both the external (environmental) relation between criterion values and the cues and the internal (cognitive) relation between judged values and the cues. By comparing regression weights in the two analyses and extracting various correlations from the data (e.g., between judged and criterion values), it is possible to measure how well people can perform the task.

Undoubtedly, one of the most startling findings to emerge from this body of work has been that experience with outcome feedback improves performance on MCPL tasks only when there are no more than two or three cues related to the criterion and when this relation is a linear one. Even then the learning process "is slow and requires outcomes ... over a long period of time (trials ranging into the hundreds)" (Hammond & Boyle, 1971, p. 106). As a result, "there is no alternative to a long series of trials, if the learner is limited to outcomes as feedback" (Hammond, 1971, p. 904). When there are more than two or three cues or when cues are related to the criterion in a nonlinear fashion, presence of outcome feedback does not produce learning (Todd & Hammond, 1965) and, indeed, may even impede it (Hammond, Summers, & Deane, 1973).

Outcome feedback is highly effective in producing learning in motor skills (e.g., Schmidt, 1975), which, according to some authorities (e.g., Welford, 1968), are not intrinsically different from cognitive skills. Why then does outcome feedback fail to produce learning in MCPL tasks, in which good performance would certainly count as a cognitive skill? Two answers to this question have been proposed.

Brehmer (1980) argued that people do not have the cognitive mechanisms that efficient performance of probabilistic task requires. They form deterministic hypotheses. When these hypotheses fail, they "tend to assume that there is no rule at all, rather than to seriously consider that the rule may be probabilistic in character ... people simply do not have the cognitive schemata needed for efficient performance in probabilistic tasks" (Brehmer, 1980, pp. 231–233). Thus, for Brehmer, the problem is a general one. People cannot learn to perform *any* reasonably complex probabilistic inference tasks. The difficulty they experience is revealed by, but not restricted to, MCPL tasks.

For Todd and Hammond (1965), the problem is more task-specific. In MCPL tasks, outcome feedback does not provide people with the information they need to improve their performance. In particular, it does not allow them to determine in a straightforward way which cues they are weighting too heavily and to which they are giving insufficient weight. For example, suppose they judge Mr Smith's salary to be $80,000, but outcome feedback informs them that it is actually $110,000. This information does not allow them to ascertain, for example, whether their judgment relied too much or too little on his weight or too much or too little on the distance he lives from the center of town. In other words, it gives them no direct information about how they should change their judgment policy in the future to ensure that their performance at the task improves.

These two conflicting hypotheses peacefully coexisted for almost 20 years. Rather than determining which was true, researchers became interested in how to improve performance in MCPL tasks, whichever was true. They found that providing people with task information was effective in this respect (Doherty & Balzer, 1988; Balzer, Doherty, & O'Connor, 1989). Task information tells people how the cues are related to the criterion (and to each other) in the external environment. It gives them guidance about how to relate their judgments to the cues to ensure that those judgments produce the closest possible match to the criterion. As Björkman (1972) pointed out, task information should not be regarded as feedback. It does not produce experience-based learning; it produces improvements in performance via a feedforward or guidance process. (For example, it could benefit someone's first attempt at an MCPL task.) It is misleading to treat it as a type of cognitive feedback.

Returning to the two alternative accounts for the failure of outcome feedback to produce performance improvements in all but the simplest MCPL task, we can still ask whether Brehmer (1980) was correct to claim that this problem extends to all probabilistic tasks or whether Todd and Hammond

(1965) were right to formulate a more task-specific account of it. To answer this question, we must turn to recent work on advice taking.

ADVICE TAKING

One can take advice about which course of action to adopt or about the numerical value of some variable (e.g., a sales forecast). Here we deal with the latter type of advice taking. It has been studied systematically using a task that is similar to the one typically employed in the MCPL paradigm. The cues comprise pieces of advice from a number of different sources about the value of some criterion variable. Advice from some sources is better than that from others. Judges use the advice to make their own estimate for the value of the criterion variable. Outcome feedback can then be provided to inform them of its true value.

The advice-taking and MCPL paradigms differ in one crucial respect. In the former case, the cues, criterion, judgment, and outcome feedback all refer to the same variable (e.g., sales volume); in the latter case, the cues (e.g., age, weight, distance of residence from the center of town) refer to variables that are different from the variable specified by the criterion, judgments, and outcome feedback (e.g., annual salary). In the advice-taking task, outcome feedback informs judges about not only the error in their own judgment, but also the error in each piece of advice. As a result, it provides them directly with information about how much they should rely on each cue. Thus, Todd and Hammond's (1965) argument about why outcome feedback is of little benefit in MCPL tasks does not hold for advice-taking tasks. They would expect outcome feedback to improve people's use of advice. Of course advice-taking and MCPL tasks are both probabilistic. Consequently, Brehmer (1980) would predict outcome feedback to be just as ineffective in advice taking as it has been found to be in MCPL tasks.

Fischer and Harvey (1999) examined learning in an advice-taking task. People had to forecast product sales on the basis of advice about those sales received from four different sources (marketing manager, product manager, etc.). Without outcome feedback, there was no learning; judges' forecasts were consistently worse than those obtained by simply averaging the four pieces of advice. With outcome feedback, learning was rapid. Within 10 trials, judges' forecasts were as good as those obtained by taking the simple average of the four pieces of advice. Thus, the results favored Todd and Hammond's (1965) hypothesis for the ineffectiveness of outcome feedback in MCPL tasks over that of Brehmer (1980). Whether outcome feedback benefits performance in probabilistic tasks depends on the detailed structure of the task.

Although Fischer and Harvey (1999) found that learning was rapid when outcome feedback was provided, it soon reached an asymptote. Even after

80 trials, people's forecasts were still no better that those obtained by taking the simple average of the advice. Why was this? Because of the probabilistic nature of the task, the difference between the outcome feedback and the advice from a particular source on a single trial provided only an approximate estimate of the long-run error to be expected from that source. To get a better estimate, the difference between the feedback and advice would have had to have been averaged over trials. Doing this for all four sources to determine the judgment weight to assign to each source must have imposed unrealistic cognitive demands on the judges. Fischer and Harvey (1999) obtained some support for this interpretation by running another experiment. Judges were provided with decision support, which informed them of the mean error made by each adviser from the start of the experiment. Under these conditions, they were able to produce forecasts that outperformed those obtained by taking the simple average of the four pieces of advice on each trial.

A stronger test between the Todd and Hammond (1965) and Brehmer (1980) hypotheses was reported by Harries and Harvey (2000). In their experiment, the same underlying formal system of equations relating four cue variables to a criterion variable was framed as an advice-taking task for one group of people and an MCPL task for another group. For both groups, the aim was to predict sales of a consumer product. For the advice-taking group, these judgments were made on the basis of advisory forecasts received from four different sources varying in forecasting ability. For the MCPL group, they were made on the basis of four different pieces of information (number of sales outlets, competitors' promotional spending, etc.) that varied in predictive validity. As expected, learning was much faster in the advice-taking group. Even at the end of the experiment, forecasting performance was poorer in the MCPL group. In other words, there was a clear difference between the two groups that was not predicted by Brehmer's (1980) hypothesis, but that was consistent with Todd and Hammond's (1965) arguments.

Harries and Harvey's (2000) experiment also produced an unexpected finding. Error on the first trial of the experiment was much less in the advice-taking task than in the MCPL task. Clearly, this could not have arisen from differential ease of use of outcome feedback because, at that stage of the experiment, no such feedback had been received. Instead it must have occurred because the expectations about the task that people generated after reading the experimental instructions were more useful in the advice-taking task. The description of the task that those instructions provided allowed them to use the extralaboratory experience they had gained prior to the start of the experiment to put greater constraints on their responses than the description of the task for the MCPL condition did. More specifically, people in the advice-taking task tend to assume that the best estimate of the true value lies within the range of advice. In fact without any evidence favoring one adviser over another, they tend to take the median estimate and, given the way advice tends to be distributed in the environment, this is a reasonable strategy (Harries, Yaniv, & Harvey, in press; Yaniv, 1997). In the MCPL task, in contrast, criterion values are not constrained in the same way: There is no reason for them to be more likely to be within the range of cue values than outside that range.

This work suggests that we need to take account of experience outside the laboratory prior to an experiment as well as experience inside the laboratory during that experiment when modeling the cognitive processes underlying performance of laboratory-based tasks. Some of the work discussed in the next section serves to reinforce this conclusion.

CONFIDENCE JUDGMENT

People can judge the likelihood that something is true or will happen in various ways. They can express their confidence in it by giving a confidence rating, they can estimate the number of times out of a total number of possible times it will or did occur, or they can assess its probability of occurrence. Here we focus on the effects of experience on confidence judgments. In the next section, we deal with probability estimation.

Confidence judgments are used primarily to express the likelihood that an action or a decision will be effective. Research on confidence in the effectiveness of actions has been reviewed by Harvey (1994) and Bjork (1999). It is clear from this body of work that people do not have the sort of privileged access to their own cognitive processes that would allow them to directly assess the strength of the memory traces on which their skill depends (Koriat, 1995). One possibility is that they use heuristics to determine how likely their actions are to be effective. For example, experience at the task is likely to improve performance, and so confidence in the effectiveness of actions should be higher after greater experience at the task. Also experience at a task is likely to be more beneficial if it includes outcome feedback that informs the performer of how effective their actions are.

Of course experience and feedback do not always serve to improve performance. However, people do not appear to recognize the situations in which they are likely to fail. In these situations, they still apply their heuristics. As a result, their confidence judgments are biased in ways that are diagnostic of the heuristics they use. Consider, for example, an experiment reported by Harvey, Garwood, and Palencia (1987). People were given one of two types of training to improve their ability to sing a musical interval. Some people practiced singing the interval: They could hear the results of their own attempts and so received some feedback about their effectiveness. Other people merely listened to an expert singer produce the interval. After their training session, both groups were tested: On each of 24 trials, they attempted to sing the interval; after each attempt, they rated their confidence that they had succeeded. Two findings are of interest here. First, people's performance at the task did not improve over the 24 test trials, but their confidence in the effectiveness of their performance increased. Clearly they expected their experience with feedback during the test session to benefit their performance. Second, there was no difference between the two groups' performance during the test session, but those who had merely listened to someone else singing during training were less confident throughout the test session than those who had been singing during training. Thus, people expect active practice with feedback to be more effective than passive practice without it.

Other experiments have also shown that confidence in performance increases with practice even when there is no change in the quality of performance (e.g., Adams & Goetz, 1973; Marteau, Johnston, Wynne, & Evans, 1989; Marteau, Wynne, Kaye, & Evans, 1990). Following Sterman (1994), we could say that people have an internal mental model of their task. This model can be used to generate expectations about how different variables (e.g., experience, outcome feedback) affect performance. Those expectations then influence confidence in performance.

This "mental model" approach to explaining biases in confidence judgments is rather more flexible than the account in terms of heuristics. Although the mental model of the task generates expectations about performance, and can therefore be seen as providing guidance about how to make judgments about performance, we must also assume that the model is a product of experience with the task (or with a set of closely related tasks). With greater experience, the model should reflect the task more accurately, produce better expectations about performance, and, hence, offer better guidance for judgments about performance. Experience and feedback can produce better feedforward influences on judgment.

The research on confidence judgments reviewed earlier reveals biases that suggest that extralaboratory experience with tasks similar to the experimental one has feedforward effects: It generates expectations about the effects of experience with the experimental task. However, this research provides no evidence that these biases decrease with experience at the experimental task. In other words, experience within the laboratory has not been shown to modify the initial expectations that people have about the effects of that experience. There are various ways in which to interpret this. Perhaps insufficient experience was provided to allow modification of the mental models of the tasks. Alternatively, the structural complexity of the tasks may have made it difficult or impossible for people to use outcome feedback to refine their mental models of them (cf. Paich & Sterman, 1993).

Finally, it is possible that expectations were not generated by potentially modifiable mental models that provide cognitive representations of the task in the manner that Sterman (1994) suggested. Instead they may have been produced by simple and relatively inflexible heuristics of the sort proposed by Harvey (1994) and Bjork (1999).

We know that confidence judgments are biased because differences and changes in them do not match differences or changes in performance. However, these judgments do not allow us to determine whether people are overconfident or underconfident in their performance in an absolute sense. As a result, we cannot say whether the increases in confidence in the absence of increases in performance that were observed in the studies cited before made confidence judgments better (because people were initially underconfident) or worse (because people were overconfident from the start). To decide this, we have to be able to compare likelihood judgments to an objective scale that measures performance quality. Likelihood judgments that are made by estimating probability allow us to do this.

PROBABILITY ESTIMATION

There is an extensive literature on how well people can estimate the probability of a statement being correct or an action being effective. Recent reviews of it include those by McClelland and Bolger (1994) and Harvey (1997). Here we focus on the effects that experience with and without outcome feedback has on the quality of this type of judgment.

Paese and Sniezek (1991) asked people to estimate the probability that a measure of baseball pitchers' performance would fall within an interval they had specified. No feedback was given. Accuracy did not increase with experience of the task, but confidence did. Overall, people were overconfident at the task. Hence, it is not unreasonable to conclude that experience increased overconfidence (viz. made judgments worse) rather than decreased underconfidence (viz. made judgments better). Paese and Sniezek (1991) suggested that confidence increased because "the belief that one has had a lot of practice on a judgment task should serve as evidence that judgments are likely to be accurate" (p. 102). In other words, people were using a heuristic of the type discussed in the previous section. Problems arose because the heuristic was inappropriate, but participants did not realize that it was. Therefore, Paese and Sniezek (1991) suggested that "an interesting question for future research concerns whether provision of feedback after each judgment trial would reduce or eliminate the increase in confidence due to practice" (p. 125).

If outcome feedback is effective in reducing bias in probability estimates, experts who have been exposed to such feedback over a long period should make accurate judgments. Studies of weather forecasters (Murphy & Winkler, 1977), horseracing aficionados (Hoerl & Fallin, 1974; Johnson & Bruce, 2001), and financial analysts (Whitecotton, 1996) show that they often do. However, some studies have shown probability estimation to be poor in experienced judges (Christensen-Szalanski & Busheyhead, 1981; Tomassini, Solomon, Romney, & Krogstad, 1982), and others have shown it to be poorer than estimates made by relatively inexperienced people (Yates, McDaniel, & Brown, 1991). Furthermore, in those studies that have shown beneficial effects of experience, it is not possible to attribute those effects to outcome feedback per se. This is because experts are likely to have also received more guidance and cognitive feedback than those people with whom they are compared.

Experimental studies have also produced mixed results. Outcome feedback has been found to reduce underconfidence biases in some cases (Petrusic & Baranski, 1997; Subbotin, 1996), but not others (Björkman, Juslin, & Winman, 1993; Keren, 1988; Winman & Juslin, 1993). It has also been found to reduce overconfidence in some studies (Winman & Juslin, 1993; Zakay, 1992, computerized experiment), to have had no effect on the bias in others (Baranski & Petrusic, 1994; Keren, 1988; Subbotin, 1996; Zakay, 1992, paper-and-pencil experiment), and occasionally even to increase it (Petrusic & Baranski, 1997).

Harvey and Fischer (2004) argued that the conflicts in these results may have arisen because all studies in the literature suffer from methodological problems. These problems include failure to incorporate a no-feedback control condition, examination of the mean difference between feedback and no-feedback groups without analysis of how this difference changes over the session, failure to ensure that improvements in calibration are not caused fortuitously by changes in performance rather than by changes in probability estimation, and failure to exclude the possibility that such improvements are driven by expected rather than actual effects of feedback.

In an attempt to resolve the issue of feedback effectiveness, Harvey and Fischer (2004) carried out a study that did not suffer from these problems. People had to assess the probability that a decision they made would be effective. On each trial, they saw a satellite move some way across their computer screen. At this point, they selected one of a number of guns to intercept it and then estimated the probability that interception would occur. In feedback conditions, they then saw the satellite continue on its way either to be intercepted or not intercepted by a missile shot from the gun they had selected. In no-feedback conditions, they did not see this. There was both a hard version of the task (selection from 30 guns) and an easy one (selection from 10 guns).

Overconfidence appeared only on the first block of trials: Although interception rate was slightly below 50%, mean judged probability of interception was above that value. In the hard task condition, interception rate rose slowly to about 80% over the eight trial blocks; in the easy task condition, it rose more rapidly to above that figure. In both cases, outcome feedback was highly effective. Overconfidence disappeared by the second block. From then on, increases in interception rate from block to block were closely tracked by changes in mean estimated probability of interception. Without feedback, this tracking did not occur; mean estimated probability of interception remained fairly constant around its initial value of 60%. However, interception rate showed a slight but significant improvement. As a result, mean overconfidence decreased significantly over blocks—even in the absence of feedback. Additional analyses showed that Yates' (1982) slope index increased over blocks only when outcome feedback was provided: This implies that the effects of feedback were corrective rather than expectation-driven.

This study appears to provide the first good evidence that outcome feedback provides an effective means to correct probability judgments. The primary task (gun selection) could be characterized as a cognitive skill. Whether our findings generalize to situations in which the primary task is in other domains (e.g., knowledge, perception, motor skill) remains an open question.

DYNAMIC DECISION MAKING

In dynamic decision-making tasks, the choice made from a set of options at one point in time determines the options that will be available to the decision maker at a later point in time (e.g., Haberstroh, Betsch, Glöckner, Haar, & Stiller, chap. 12, this volume; Shanteau, Friel, Thomas, & Raacke, chap. 14, this volume). The most thoroughly studied tasks of this type are those in which the output of some system must be brought into and maintained within a target range by altering the settings of one or more control parameters. These tasks are variously known as judgmental control or complex problem-solving tasks. Reviews of studies that have examined how well people perform them can be found in Frensch and Funke (1995) and Kerstholt (1996).

People can learn to control simple dynamic systems. For example, Dienes and Fahey (1995) studied people's performance on Berry and Broadbent's (1984) sugar production task. Participants were told to imagine that they were in charge of a factory that produces sugar. Their goal was to achieve and maintain an output of 9,000 tons by changing the size of the workforce. Initially sugar output was 6,000 tons, and there were 600 workers. On each trial, people entered a number between 1 and 12 to indicate how many hundred workers they wished to use on that occasion. They then received outcome feedback that specified how much sugar was produced by these workers. Participants were not informed explicitly that this output was determined by the equation $S_t = 2W - S_{t-1} + N$, where S_t was the sugar output in thousands on the trial in question, S_{t-1} was the sugar output in thousands on the previous trial, W was the number of workers in hundreds that the participant specified, and N was a random noise term that was -1, 0, and $+1$ with equal frequency. In the first block of 40 trials, mean number of trials on which production was no more than 1,000 off target was 7.9. In the second block of 40 trials, the corresponding figure was significantly higher at 15.3 trials. In other words, learning occurred.

When systems are more complex, similar levels of experience with feedback fail to produce improvements in performance. For example, Broadbent, Fitzgerald, and Broadbent (1986, Exp. 2) studied people's ability to control a system involving 22 interrelated equations. The system was initiated away from its stable position so that the change in output with successive iterations depended both on the system's own movement toward its stable point and on the participant's manipulation of the input variables. The authors compared the proximity of an output variable to its target on each of 20 iterations of the system when participants had control with its proximity to the target on those iterations when the system was moving autonomously. On fewer than half of the 20 iterations, it was better when people had control. Thus, there was no evidence that people learned to control this system. Many similar results are reviewed in Frensch and Funke (1995).

It is reasonable to argue that people would need much more experience to show evidence of learning to control more complex systems. Given the difficulty of the task, we could also argue that providing them with incentives would facilitate the learning process. However, experiments by Sterman and his colleagues (e.g., Diehl & Sterman, 1995; Kampmann & Sterman, 1998; Paich & Sterman, 1993) have shown that, even with incentives and after a great deal of experience, people fail to learn to control highly complex systems. For example, Paich and Sterman (1993) asked people to make pricing and capacity decisions for a product in a simulated market. After 50 years of simulated experience with outcome feedback, people still failed to show any improvement in their performance in the dynamically complex conditions of the task.

What accounts for this failure to learn? First, it is difficult to interpret outcome feedback (cf. Hogarth, chap. 4, this volume; Kardes, Muthukrishnan, & Pashkevich, chap. 8, this volume). This may be because it is delayed or patterned over time. By way of analogy, consider a spring balance with a small weight on it. The task is to lengthen the spring by a specified amount by adding to the weight. If the correct weight is added, there will be some transient bounce causing the spring to be too long and too short by successively smaller amounts before it reaches the target length. In systems control tasks, such transient behavior can extend over a number of iterations of the system and mislead judges about whether they have made the correct decision. For example, they may initially incorrectly think that they have changed the control parameter too much because the transient response has caused the output to overshoot the target. As a result, they partially reverse their decision on the next iteration. After decay of the transient response of the system, this would lead to undershooting the target. However, the judge has no chance to realize this because the new control decision produces another misleading transient response, and so on.

Complexity of a system can be regarded as a function of the number of variables, parameters, and equations that are needed to define it. We have suggested that more complex systems are more difficult to control. As with MCPL tasks, people find it more difficult to reach some criterion level of performance when they have to keep track of more information. However, our discussion of the misperception of feedback suggests that, for a system of given complexity (in the earlier sense), control is more difficult when the behavior of the system is more complex. As May (1976) pointed out, there are some simple systems comprising just a single equation, a single parameter, and a single variable that can produce complex behavior. These are nonlinear systems. Again extrapolating from what we know about performance in MCPL tasks, we should not be surprised to find that controlling them is difficult to learn.

One such simple system is the noisy logistic map, defined by the equation $S_t = WS_{t-1}(1 - S_{t-1}) + N$. As with Berry and Broadbent's (1984) task, S is the variable to be controlled, W is a parameter under control of the judge, and N is a random noise term. However, the behavior of this system is more complex. When W is greater than 1.0, but less than or equal to 3.0, S, which always lies between 0.0 and 1.0, has a single asymptotically stable value that increases with W. For W above 3.0, but less than or equal to 3.4, the system asymptotes to a stable state in which S alternates between a relatively high value and a relatively low one. The mean distance between these two values increases with W. For W above 3.4, but less than or equal to 3.57, the system produces unpredictable chaotic behavior.

Harvey (1990) studied people's ability to control this system. People were told to imagine they were psychiatrists giving drug treatments to patients with affective disorders. System output was multiplied by 50 and represented patients' mood score. A score of 29 to 31 was defined as normal. Patients who were initially depressed (mood score below 29) required antidepressants to render them normal. As higher dosages increased W by a greater amount, patients who were more depressed required more antidepressant. Other patients were either manic (mood consistently above 31) or manic-depressive. Manic-depressive patients' moods either alternated above and below the normal range (corresponding to W between 3.0 and

3.4) or were unpredictable (corresponding to W between 3.4 and 3.57). Both manic and manic-depressives needed to be treated with lithium (which reduced W). As higher doses of lithium reduced W by a greater amount, unpredictable manic-depressives needed more of the drug than alternating manic-depressives, and alternating manic-depressives required more of it than manics.

People were able to learn to treat depressives and manics fairly quickly. This was presumably because the difference between the patient's "natural" mood and the target mood was related to the required drug dosage in an almost linear manner. Some learning also occurred for the alternating manic-depressives, but it was much slower. This was presumably because the cue needed to guide treatment was less easy to appreciate: The required drug dosage was related to the size of the difference between successive moods. Finally, no learning was evident for the unpredictable manic-depressives. This was presumably because the output sequence provided no cue to guide treatment. These results suggest that, in addition to problems in interpreting feedback, there is a second factor that makes it difficult for people to improve their performance in judgmental control tasks: the availability and usability of information relevant to the required decision.

These two factors do not exhaust those that determine the difficulty of learning system control. However, they do emphasize the problems of generalizing about the effects of experience and feedback not just across tasks, but also across variants of a given task.

As a final anecdotal aside, we should mention that, although experience with feedback failed to improve people's ability to bring the chaotic behavior of the unpredictable manic-depressives under control in Harvey's (1990) experiment, that behavior could be controlled by the experimenter who wrote the program for the computer-controlled task. It was simply necessary to give a large dose of lithium to bring the behavior out of the chaotic region and then use information in the output to fine tune the treatment. It appears that this strategy can be inferred via relevant education (viz. reading books), but not via pure experience with the task. (It may be that a period of free exploration of the system [viz. just changing the control parameter and observing the effects of this without the requirement to achieve a particular target] would have much the same effect.)

SUMMARY

Work on the role of feedback in the five different types of judgment and decision-making tasks discussed here has not been brought together before. By dealing with it all in a single review, we hoped to identify the distinct contributions made by research in each area, as well as to glean additional insight by comparing findings across areas. Here we first summarize some of the broad conclusions produced by this exercise. Then we bring them together into a tentative, but reasonably coherent, model designed to explain how the interplay between feedback and expectations (feedforward) governs the level of performance as experience accumulates in any type of judgment and decision-making task.

First, whether outcome feedback produces learning depends on how easily it can be interpreted in a manner that gives judges information about how their performance can be improved. We have seen that they find it easier to interpret in advice taking than in MCPL tasks and in simple dynamic decision-making tasks than in complex ones.

Second, comparison of performance in MCPL and advice-taking tasks on the first trial of an experiment (Harries & Harvey, 2000) indicates that people use instructions and information they are given to formulate expectations that constrain their judgments. These expectations must derive from extralaboratory experience at real-life tasks (for naive participants, at least). Research on confidence judgments and probability estimation throws further light on expectation formation. Increases in confidence in the absence of increases in performance can be interpreted in terms of the failure of heuristics that are generally useful because they do not normally fail. Failure to make use of feedback in relatively complex dynamic decision-making tasks can also be interpreted in this way: Because feedback in most judgments and decision-making tasks is immediate, people wrongly expect it to arrive immediately in complex, dynamic decision-making tasks.

Viewing overconfidence in probability estimation tasks as arising from inappropriate use of a heuristic implies that the bias is quite robust. This is because heuristics are generally viewed as rather inflexible means of making judgments. Although people's selection of a heuristic from the set of those possible to use for the task may depend on the relative importance of accuracy and speed (Payne, Bettman, & Johnson, 1993), the selected heuristic is generally regarded as immutable. Therefore, it is important to determine whether outcome feedback can reduce overconfidence.

Our review of work dealing with this question revealed a plethora of conflicting findings. We suggested that methodological problems that plague studies in this area were responsible for these conflicts. By recognizing these problems and then removing them, Harvey and Fischer (2004) obtained clear evidence that outcome feedback can eliminate overconfidence. This result can be interpreted as evidence that feedback merely counteracts the effects of the expectations produced by heuristics. However, certain features of the results, together with Sterman's (1994) work on dynamic decision making, imply that the expectations are modified. Feedback does not just inform people how to modify their previous response to improve their performance on the next occasion; it also, over the longer term, gives them information that allows them to build a mental model of their task that, as it becomes more sophisticated, can be used to produce increasingly accurate expectations.

Thus, for Sterman (1994), outcome feedback is involved in two nested, closed loops of information processing. Consider the faster inner loop first. People use stimulus information to make a judgment or decision. This has an effect on the external environment that is returned as outcome feedback. This feedback enables people to improve their judgment or decision. In its turn, this improved judgment or decision has another effect on the environment that is again returned as outcome feedback, and so on. Now consider the slower outer loop. As before, judgments or decisions have their effects on the environment that are returned as outcome feedback. However, in this case, it does not have a direct effect on the next decision. Instead, in conjunction with instructions and other information that the person has received about the task, it is used to develop and refine a mental model of the task. This, in turn, allows the judges to produce expectations about the quality of their judgments or the effects of their decisions. These expectations then influence the judgments or decisions that are made.

The mental model integrates feedback received on many different occasions, and the results of this integration are used to produce expectations. The outer loop operates relatively slowly, and therefore the mental model must be retained in long-term memory. In contrast, the inner loop acts to modify the previous judgment or decision made in circumstances similar to the present ones. It operates relatively quickly and is more likely to make use of working memory to retain information about the judgments or decisions that will be modified. (One could also argue that the inner loop is more likely to depend on implicit processing and the outer loop is more likely to involve explicit processing.)

Sterman's two-loop model means that the direct effects of feedback and the effects of expectations produced by the mental model must combine in some way to influence the judgments or decisions that people make. (In this respect, it is analogous to Pew's [1974] two-loop model of visuomotor tracking that also involves integration of feedback and feedforward effects on behavior.) Of course when no feedback is provided, performance must be driven solely by the mental model in an open-loop fashion. The mental model may also facilitate interpretation of feedback in complex dynamic tasks—or, if it is inappropriate, impair that interpretation.

Sterman's (1994) two-loop model leaves certain questions unanswered. We have argued that performance on the first trial of judgment or decision-making task must depend on top–down feedforward processes alone. These initial expectations are more useful in some tasks (advice taking) than others (MCPL). These initial expectations cannot be derived from feedback obtained within the experiment. Where do they come from? Our suggestion is that information and instructions provided by the experimenter enable participants to categorize the task in some way. This, in turn, allows them to search a long-term store of mental models of tasks until they find one appropriate to the task at hand. This is retrieved and used to develop initial expectations of the first trial. Later feedback can be used either to refine it or, if the mismatch between expectations and performance is too great, reject it. If it is rejected, the search of the long-term store of mental models must be repeated. In processing terms, this adds a third loop to Sterman's (1994) two-loop model.

This elaboration of Sterman's (1994) model can be applied to all the tasks we have discussed. Figure 7.1 depicts a version of it developed to account for judgments of the probability that performance in a skilled task will be successful (Harvey & Fischer, 2004). The three-loop model has two interesting implications. First, people retain mental models of previous tasks that they have performed both inside and outside the laboratory and apply them to new tasks that they are given. This notion appears consistent with the role that many ecological psychologists give to extralaboratory information (e.g., Gigerenzer & Todd, 1999; Oaksford & Chater, 2001). Second, people categorize the tasks they perform in some way. Possible typologies for judgment and decision-making tasks have been the subject of recent debate (Funke, 1995; Hammond, 2000; Harvey, 2001).

The basic model we have described implies that mental models are acquired only via direct experience with the task. However, there is no reason that they should not be derived from other sources, such as observation of someone else performing the task or via an educational process. Indeed we suggested at the end of the last section that adequate mental models for certain complex, dynamic decision-making tasks cannot be acquired via ex-

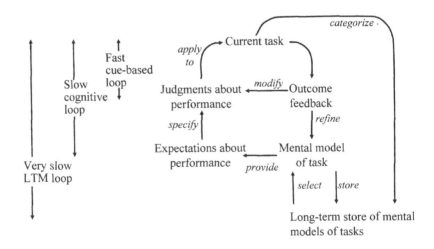

FIG. 7.1. Three-loop model to account for changes in people's estimates of the probability of success in a skilled task.

perience alone, but require educational input. Experience-based learning is often effective, but it is not the only way to improve judgments and decisions.

REFERENCES

Adams, J. A., & Goetz, E. T. (1973). Feedback and practice as variables in error detection and correction. *Journal of Motor Behavior, 5*, 217–224.

Balzer, W. K., Doherty, M. E., & O'Connor, R. O., Jr. (1989). Effects of cognitive feedback on performance. *Psychological Bulletin, 106*, 410–433.

Baranski, J. V., & Petrusic, W. M. (1994). The calibration and resolution of confidence in perceptual judgments. *Perception and Psychophysics, 55*, 412–428.

Berry, D. C., & Broadbent, D. E. (1984). On the relationship between task performance and associated verbalisable knowledge. *Quarterly Journal of Experimental Psychology, 36*, 209–231.

Bjork, R. A. (1999). Assessing our own competence: Heuristics and illusions. In D. Gopher & A. Koriat (Eds.), *Attention and Performance XVII Cognitive regulation of performance: Interaction of theory and application* (pp. 435–459). Cambridge, MA: MIT Press.

Björkman, J. (1972). Feedforward and feedback as determiners of knowledge and policy: Notes on a neglected issue. *Scandinavian Journal of Psychology, 13*, 152–158.

Björkman, M., Juslin, P., & Winman, P. (1993). Realism of confidence in sensory discrimination: The underconfidence phenomenon. *Perception and Psychophysics, 54*, 75–81.

Brehmer, B. (1980). In one word: Not from experience. *Acta Psychologica, 45*, 223–241.

Broadbent, D. E., Fitzgerald, P., & Broadbent, M. H. P. (1986). Implicit and explicit knowledge in the control of complex systems. *British Journal of Psychology, 77*, 33–50.

Christensen-Szalanski, J. J., & Busheyhead, J. B. (1981). Physicians' use of probabilistic inference in a real clinical setting. *Journal of Experimental Psychology: Human Perception and Performance, 7*, 928–935.

Cooksey, R. W. (1996). *Judgment analysis: Theory, methods, and applications*. San Diego: Academic Press.

Diehl, E., & Sterman, J. D. (1995). Effects of feedback on complexity of dynamic decision making. *Organizational Behavior and Human Decision Processes, 62*, 198–215.

Dienes, Z., & Fahey, R. (1995). Role of specific instances in controlling a dynamic system. *Journal of Experimental Psychology: Learning, Memory and Cognition, 21*, 848–862.

Doherty, M. E., & Balzer, W. K. (1988). Cognitive feedback. In B. Brehmer & C. R. B. Joyce (Eds.), *Human judgment: The SJT view* (pp. 163–197). Amsterdam: North Holland, Elsevier.

Fischer, I., & Harvey, N. (1999). Combining forecasts: What information do judges need to outperform the simple average? *International Journal of Forecasting, 15*, 227–246.

Frensch, P. S., & Funke, J. (Eds.). (1995). *Complex problem solving. The European perspective*. Hillsdale, NJ: Lawrence Erlbaum Associates.

Funke, J. (1995). Experimental research on complex problem solving. In P. A. Frensch & J. Funke (Eds.), *Complex problem solving: The European perspective* (pp. 243–268). Hillsdale, NJ: Lawrence Erlbaum Associates.

Gigerenzer, G., & Todd, P. M. (1999). Fast and frugal heuristics: The adaptive toolbox. In G. Gigerenzer, P. M. Todd, & the ABC Research Group (Eds.), *Simple heuristics that make us smart* (pp. 3–34). Oxford: Oxford University Press.

Hammond, K. R. (1971). Computer graphics as an aid to learning. *Science, 172*, 903–908.

Hammond, K. R. (1996). *Human judgment and social policy: Irreducible uncertainty, inevitable error, unavailable injustice*. Oxford: Oxford University Press.

Hammond, K. R. (2000). *Judgments under stress*. Oxford: Oxford University Press.

Hammond, K. R., & Boyle, P. J. R. (1971). Quasi-rationality, quarrels and new conceptions of feedback. *Bulletin of the British Psychological Society, 24,* 103–113.

Hammond, K. R., Summers, D. A., & Deane, D. H. (1973). Negative effects of outcome-feedback in multiple-cue probability learning. *Organizational Behavior and Human Performance, 9,* 30–34.

Harries, C., & Harvey, N. (2000). Taking advice, using information and knowing what you are doing. *Acta Psychologica, 104,* 399–416.

Harries, C., Yaniv, I., & Harvey, N. (in press). Combining advice: The weight of a dissenting opinion in the consensus. *Journal of Behavioral Decision Making.*

Harvey, N. (1990). Judgemental control of the behaviour of a dynamical system. In K. J. Gilhooly, M. T. G. Keane, R. H. Logie, & G. Erdos (Eds.), *Lines of thinking: Reflections on the psychology of thought* (Vol. 1, pp. 337–352). Chichester: Wiley.

Harvey, N. (1994). Relations between confidence and skilled performance. In G. Wright & P. Ayton (Eds.), *Subjective probability* (pp. 321–352). New York: Wiley.

Harvey, N. (1997). Confidence in judgment. *Trends in Cognitive Science, 1,* 78–82.

Harvey, N. (2001). Studying judgment: General issues. *Thinking and Reasoning, 7,* 103–118.

Harvey, N., & Fischer, I. (2004). *Metacognitive adjustment: Subjective tracking of changes in skilled performance.* Manuscript in preparation.

Harvey, N., Garwood, J., & Palencia, M. (1987). Vocal matching of pitch intervals: Learning and transfer effects. *Psychology of Music, 15,* 90–106.

Hoerl, A. E., & Fallin, H. K. (1974). Reliability of subjective evaluations in a high incentive situation. *Journal of the Royal Statistical Society, 137,* 227–230.

Johnson, J. E. V., & Bruce, A. C. (2001). Calibration of subjective probability judgments in a naturalistic setting. *Organizational Behavior and Human Decision Processes, 85,* 265–290.

Kampmann, C., & Sterman, J. D. (1998). *Feedback complexity, bounded rationality, and market dynamics.* Working paper, System Dynamics Group, Sloane School of Management, MIT, Cambridge, MA.

Keren, G. (1988). On the ability of monitoring non-veridical perceptions and knowledge: Some calibration studies. *Acta Psychologica, 67,* 95–119.

Kerstholt, J. H. (1996). *Dynamic decision making.* Wageningen: Ponsen & Looijen bv.

Koriat, A. (1995). Dissociating knowing and the feeling of knowing: Further evidence for the accessibility model. *Journal of Experimental Psychology: General, 124,* 311–333.

Marteau, T. M., Johnston, M., Wynne, G., & Evans, T. R. (1989). Cognitive factors in the explanation of the mismatch between confidence and competence in performing basic life support. *Psychology and Health, 3,* 172–182.

Marteau, T. M., Wynne, G., Kaye, W., & Evans, T. R. (1990). Resuscitation: Experience without feedback increases confidence but not skill. *British Medical Journal, 300,* 849–850.

May, R. M. (1976). Simple mathematical models with very complicated dynamics. *Nature, 261,* 459–467.

McClelland, A. G. R., & Bolger, F. (1994). The calibration of subjective probabilities: Theories and models 1980–94. In G. Wright & P. Ayton (Eds.), *Subjective probability* (pp. 453–482). New York: Wiley.

Murphy, A. H., & Winkler, R. L. (1977). Can weather forecasters formulate reliable probability forecasts of precipitation and temperature? *National Weather Digest, 2,* 2–9.

Oaksford, M., & Chater, N. (2001). The probabilistic approach to human reasoning. *Trends in Cognitive Sciences, 5,* 349–357.

Paese, P. W., & Sniezek, J. A. (1991). Influences on the appropriateness of confidence in judgement: Practice, effort, information, and decision-making. *Organizational Behavior and Human Decision Processes, 48,* 100–130.

Paich, M., & Sterman, J. D. (1993). Boom, bust, and failures to learn in experimental markets. *Management Science, 39,* 1439–1458.

Payne, J. W., Bettman, J. R., & Johnson, E. J. (1993). *The adaptive decision maker.* Cambridge: Cambridge University Press.

Petrusic, W. M., & Baranski, J. V. (1997). Context, feedback and the calibration and resolution of confidence in perceptual judgments. *American Journal of Psychology, 110*, 543–572.

Pew, R. W. (1974). Human perceptual-motor performance. In B. H. Kantowitz (Ed.), *Human information processing* (pp. 1–39). Hillsdale, NJ: Lawrence Erlbaum Associates.

Schmidt, R. A. (1975). A schema theory of discrete motor skill learning. *Psychological Review, 82*, 225–260.

Slovic, P., & Lichtenstein, S. (1971). Comparison of Bayesian and regression approaches to the study of information processing in judgment. *Organizational Behavior and Human Performance, 6*, 649–744.

Sterman, J. (1994). Learning in and about complex systems. *System Dynamics Review, 16*, 291–330.

Subbotin, V. (1996). Outcome feedback effects on under- and overconfident judgments (General Knowledge Tasks). *Organizational Behavior and Human Decision Processes, 66*, 268–276.

Todd, F. J., & Hammond, K. R. (1965). Differential feedback in two multiple-cue probability learning tasks. *Behavioral Science, 10*, 429–435.

Tomassini, L. A., Solomon, I., Romney, M. B., & Krogstad, J. L. (1982). Calibration of auditors' probabilistic judgments: Some empirical evidence. *Organizational Behavior and Human Performance, 30*, 391–406.

Welford, A. T. (1968). *Fundamentals of skill.* London: Methuen.

Whitecotton, S. M. (1996). The effects of experience and decision on the slope, scatter and bias of earning forecasts. *Organizational Behavior and Human Processes, 66*, 111–121.

Winman, A., & Juslin, P. (1993). Calibration of sensory and cognitive judgments: Two different accounts. *Scandinavian Journal of Psychology, 34*, 135–148.

Yaniv, I. (1997). Weighting and trimming: Heuristics for aggregating judgments under uncertainty. *Organizational Behavior and Human Decision Processes, 69*, 237–244.

Yates, J. F. (1982). External correspondence: Decompositions of the mean probability score. *Organizational Behavior and Human Decision Processes, 30*, 132–156.

Yates, J. F., McDaniel, L. S., & Brown, E. S. (1991). Probabilistic forecasts of stock prices and earnings: The hazards of nascent expertise. *Organizational Behavior and Human Decision Processes, 49*, 60–79.

Zakay, D. (1992). The influence of computerized feedback on overconfidence in knowledge. *Behavior and Information Technology, 11*, 329–333.

8

On the Conditions Under Which Experience and Motivation Accentuate Bias in Intuitive Judgment

Frank R. Kardes
University of Cincinnati

A. V. Muthukrishnan
Hong Kong University of Science and Technology

Vladimir Pashkevich
University of Cincinnati

Commonsense suggests that judgmental bias should decrease as experience or motivation increases. As experience increases, the amount of relevant semantic, episodic, and procedural knowledge that is stored in memory increases, and this knowledge should help decision makers use externally provided information about the various decision options more intelligently. As motivation increases, decision makers should be more likely to search for and use a relatively large amount of judgment-relevant information and less likely to rely on simple heuristic cues as a basis for judgment. Contrary to these commonsensical notions, we review empirical evidence indicating that, under some conditions, experience and motivation can accentuate some forms of judgmental bias. We also draw parallels on the roles of experience and motivation in judgment and decision making.

One of the earliest theoretical frameworks to challenge the commonsense position was Arkes' (1991) debiasing theory. This framework suggests that different types of judgmental biases require different types of debiasing procedures, and it is important to match the appropriate procedure with the appropriate bias. Arkes argued that most judgmental biases belong to one of three possible categories: (a) strategy-based biases, or biases resulting from an overreliance on simple heuristic cues (such as the prediction heuristics investigated by Tversky & Kahneman, 1974, and the choice heuristics examined by Payne, Bettman, & Johnson, 1993); (b) association-based errors, or unwanted side effects of an associative memory system (e.g., priming effects, explanation/imagination effects, salience effects, vividness effects, pseudodiagnostic hypothesis testing); and (c) psychophysically based biases (e.g., framing effects, assimilation and contrast effects involving comparison to a standard).

According to Arkes (1991), increasing motivation or incentives for accuracy encourages decision makers to rely less heavily on simplifying heuristic cues in favor of more thorough and systematic information processing. However, increasing motivation or incentives for accuracy should have no effect on memory-based or psychophysically based biases. Considering alternatives (Hirt, Kardes, & Markman, 2004; Hirt & Markman, 1995) reduces memory-based biases by encouraging decision makers to focus on multiple hypotheses rather than on a single focal hypothesis (Sanbonmatsu, Posavac, Kardes, & Mantel, 1998). Psychophysically based biases are reduced by encouraging decision makers to adopt a different reference point from the status quo or to adopt multiple reference points. Debiasing procedures that are effective for one type of bias are hypothesized to be ineffective for the other types.

However, empirical evidence for Arkes' (1991) debiasing theory is mixed (e.g., motivation increases the use of some heuristics and decreases some memory-based biases; Lerner & Tetlock, 1999). Moreover, Arkes' framework is mute with respect to the role of experience in debiasing judgment. We suggest that experience can either help or hurt decision making depending on the nature of the experience (see also Hogarth, chap. 4, this volume). Unambiguous experience is informative because it is not open to multiple interpretations, and it enables people to differentiate among competing alternatives (Harvey & Fischer, chap. 7, this volume; Sedlmeier, chap. 5, this volume). By contrast, ambiguous experience is uninformative about the relative standing of the various choice options in terms of specific key benefits or overall quality (Ha & Hoch, 1989; Hoch & Ha, 1986). Interestingly, people rarely distinguish between unambiguous and ambiguous experience. Consequently, people frequently assume that they learn much from experience even when experience is ambiguous and uninformative (Muthukrishnan, 1995; Muthukrishnan & Kardes, 2001).

EFFECTS OF EXPERIENCE ON JUDGMENT AND CHOICE

Ellsberg (1961) defined *ambiguity* as a "... quality depending on the amount, type, and reliability and unanimity of information" (p. 657). Further, he identified *objectively* ambiguous contexts as those in which "... available information is scanty or obviously unreliable or highly conflicting; or where expressed expectations of different individuals differ widely" (pp. 660–661). This broad definition is consistent with more recent conceptualizations that describe ambiguity as caused by missing information that is relevant and that could be known (e.g., Camerer & Weber, 1992; Frisch & Baron, 1988; Heath & Tversky, 1991). We adopt this conceptualization and operationalize ambiguity in terms of the amount and type of information available in the decision context, which determines the ease with which brands can be compared.

In some choices, brand comparisons can easily reveal an option that is superior to all others. We consider such choices as those characterized by little ambiguity. When choice sets are characterized by high ambiguity, even side-by-side comparisons may not reveal which option is superior. Ambiguity of this nature is widely prevalent in the marketplace. Often consumers may come across choice sets in which each brand may have advantages in terms of some attributes but disadvantages in terms of others (Ha & Hoch, 1989). Although the brands in the choice set are described in terms of the same attributes, the attribute values differ and, across the brands, attributes are negatively correlated. Therefore, choices may involve making trade-offs on key attribute dimensions, and this increases uncertainty (Shafir, Simonson, & Tversky, 1993; Tversky & Shafir, 1992).

Consumers may also encounter choice sets in which each option contains a unique set of key attributes, but all the options emphasize the same benefits. In these cases again, side-by-side comparisons of brands will not yield a clearly superior option because of consumer uncertainty regarding the efficacy of these different attributes in rendering certain benefits. In addition, in several instances, consumers may have information about only a few brands available at the time of a choice, and they may have to retrieve information from memory about the other brands that may be in their consideration set. Such choices are termed *mixed* choices (Alba, Hutchinson, & Lynch, 1991). In such choices, consumers may not always have perfect memory for information about a previously encountered brand. Imperfect memory can hinder brand comparison on an attribute-by-attribute basis and this increases ambiguity.

Muthukrishnan (1995)

How does experience influence preference for a previously chosen (incumbent) brand when the product experience and decision context are ambiguous? Muthukrishnan (1995) reasoned that the beliefs formed during extensive experience with a brand are qualitatively different from the information available at the point of purchase for a competitor brand.

Therefore, the preference for a previously chosen and experienced brand persists in a subsequent choice occasion even when there is an objectively superior competitor brand available. Overconfidence about the superiority of the chosen brand is the primary mechanism by which experience causes persistent preference for the previously chosen incumbent brand. In choices in which both the product and decision context are ambiguous, experience can strengthen beliefs to the point of overconfidence. In such instances, experience may inhibit rather than facilitate learning (Alba & Hutchinson, 1987; Einhorn & Hogarth, 1978, 1981). In the Einhorn and Hogarth (1978) model, confidence is an increasing monotonic function of feedback (Harvey & Fischer, chap. 7, this volume; Hogarth, chap. 4, this volume). Assuming that the positive qualities of a brand are greater than its negative qualities (which is likely in most marketplace choices), confidence increases with additional trials of the same brand even when these additional trials are uninformative. With extensive experience, consumers feel overconfident about the superiority of the previously chosen brand and exhibit persistent preference for this brand even when there is a competitor brand that is objectively superior to the incumbent brand.

Subjects first read a story that provided information about the key natural ingredients contained in skin lotions and the benefits derived from these attributes. Subjects were then shown a brand-by-attribute matrix that described four fictitious brands in terms of several attributes. One of these alternatives was superior to all other brands in the choice set. Hence, it was expected that every subject would choose this brand. The experience and belief crystallization manipulations were then administered in some experiments. Subjects in the Limited Experience condition were asked to try the chosen brand once, whereas those in the Extensive Experience condition were asked to try the chosen brand six times. Next, the belief crystallization manipulation was administered. Because this manipulation also could enhance subjects' overconfidence about the superiority of the incumbent brand by making its benefits very salient, we expected the effect of belief crystallization to be the same as extensive experience. Subjects in the High Belief Crystallization condition rated their beliefs about the benefits of the chosen brand (after either one trial or six trials) on an eight-item scale. Each item pertained to a separate benefit (e.g., promotes healthy skin texture, restores lost moisture, etc.). Subjects in the Low Belief Crystallization condition were assigned an unrelated task.

Next, we asked subjects to return after 2 days to complete the experiment. On returning, subjects were asked to assume that they were going on a shopping trip to buy lotions. This time they happened to visit another store that did not stock the original set of brands. Instead they came across two new brands, of which one was superior to the other brand as well as the previously chosen incumbent in terms of the attribute values. At this critical choice, subjects chose either the incumbent brand or the better of the two new brands.

The objective of Experiment 1 was to investigate the effects of extensive experience or belief crystallization on preference for an incumbent over a superior new brand when the context in the subsequent choice does not facilitate attribute-by-attribute comparisons. Therefore, when subjects chose between the incumbent and the new brand on Day 2, they did not have the attribute information about the incumbent available in front of them. It was hoped that this constraint for memory heightened ambiguity in the decision context. It was expected that except when experience and crystallization of beliefs were both at a low level, subjects should persist with their status quo choice. The results support this prediction. Whereas the proportion of those who chose the incumbent brand was only 14% in the Limited Experience-Low Belief Crystallization condition, it was significantly above 50% in the other three conditions. In addition, subjects exhibited lower confidence in the superiority of the (objectively inferior) incumbent in the former condition than in the other three conditions. Thus, the results of this experiment suggest that even uninformative additional experience with a chosen brand can cause overconfidence in its superiority and thereby cause persistent preference for the incumbent brand. However, as the results of Experiment 2 reveal, this advantage for the incumbent brand obtains only when the decision context is highly ambiguous. When there was opportunity to compare the incumbent brand and the new superior brand on attribute-by-attribute basis, a majority of subjects chose the new brand despite having extensive experience with the incumbent.

In Experiment 3, ambiguity in the choice context was manipulated by making subjects choose from a choice set in which the two competing brands possessed different, nonoverlapping sets of attributes. Note that even if information about the competing brands is available readily, contexts of this nature also do not offer an opportunity to compare brands on attribute-by-attribute basis especially for those consumers who are not experts in the product category. For example, how does one compare a brand that contains aloe vera, cocoa butter, and apricot extracts as key ingredients with another that contains vitamin E, jojoba extracts, and papaya extracts? In such choice contexts also, extensive experience with a chosen brand caused persistent preference for that brand.

Debiasing Unwarranted Brand Loyalty

In Experiment 4, the relative attractiveness of the incumbent brand in the initial choice set was varied. In one condition, in terms of the attribute values, the incumbent was portrayed to be the best brand available. In the other condition, the incumbent was portrayed as the second best with another superior brand available. However, just before subjects made a choice, they were told that this superior brand is not available in the market anymore and the subjects needed to choose among the other three brands. It was predicted that, in the latter condition, a majority of subjects would switch over to the new, superior challenge brand in the subsequent choice even though they had extensive experience with the incumbent. Our results indeed support this prediction (64% in the former condition and only 21.5% in the latter condition exhibited status quo bias).

In Experiment 5, we offered subjects an opportunity to try the new, superior brand before the critical choice on Day 2. This manipulation significantly mitigated the status quo preference for the incumbent brand. The five experiments together offer support to our proposition when the product category and decision context are both ambiguous, extensive experience with a brand causes overconfidence in the superiority of this brand even when there is an objectively superior competitor and thus causes persistent preference for the incumbent.

Muthukrishnan and Kardes (2001)

In a follow-up study, we investigated the conditions under which and the process that underlies the persistent preference for attributes (rather than brands). First, subjects chose a brand based on a target set of attributes. Next, the amount of experience with this brand was manipulated. After a delay, subjects were told that the original brands were unavailable, and subjects were asked to choose between two new brands: one containing the target attributes and the other containing a different set that was at least as relevant and efficient as the target set. A choice of the brand that contains the target set by itself may not constitute persistent preference for these attributes because it may reflect mere inertia (Jeuland, 1979). However, if the consumer considers the target attributes to be superior even in the face of additional information that suggests that the two sets render certain benefits with equal efficacy, there is evidence for choice based on premature cognitive commitment. Thus, Muthukrishnan and Kardes (2001) considered two components of preference persistence—the tendency to persist with the focal attributes in subsequent choices and the tendency to associate certain key benefits of the product primarily with the target attribute(s) even under neutral evidence.

The critical element in their theoretical framework is the interaction between the initial choice context and additional experience with the chosen brand. When the initial choice is made in an unambiguous context, consumers can readily form a theory that links the positive outcome with the salient attributes of the brand even with a single trial of the brand. For example, in a choice context in which one brand is better than all other brands in terms of the aloe vera contents, consumers can readily associate any positive outcome of experience with this attribute of aloe vera. Additional trials strengthen this theory. Psychological research offers a robust finding that consumers often misinterpret neutral information as supporting a previously held hypothesis (confirmation bias; see Fischhoff & Beyth-Marom, 1983; Haberstroh et al., chap. 12, this volume; Klayman & Ha, 1987; Sanbonmatsu et al., 1998). Thus, the additional trials, which offer no information beyond that offered by the initial trial, are considered as evidence that supports the theory of an association between a positive outcome and the salient attributes. With additional trials, the perception of having accumulated substantial evidence in support of the hypothesis also increases. Such confirmatory processing of information results in causality overestimation (Sanbonmatsu, Akimoto, & Biggs, 1993).

Behavioral decision theory research has also identified another bias in hypothesis testing—the pseudodiagnosticity effect (Beyth-Marom & Fischhoff, 1983; Fischhoff & Beyth-Marom, 1983). This effect occurs when people assess the extent to which the available evidence supports the focal hypothesis, but neglect the extent to which the available evidence supports alternative hypotheses (Doherty et al., 1979; Fischhoff & Beyth-Marom, 1983; Haberstroh et al., chap. 12, this volume; Sanbonmatsu et al., 1998). Due to this tendency as well as the propensity to make inductive inferences (Klar, 1990), after uninformative additional experience, consumers whose initial preferences were certain may associate the positive benefits of the brand predominantly to the focal set of attributes. For example, after using a lotion with aloe vera as the key ingredient, people may infer that the extra moisture in their skin is due to aloe vera without testing whether other ingredients can also create the same degree of moisture. In subsequent decisions, people often actively search for information that bears on the validity of the focal theory and neglect information that bears on the validity of alternative theories (Mynatt, Doherty, & Dragan, 1993; Sanbonmatsu et al., 1998). Therefore, preference for the focal attribute(s) persists through subsequent choices even when the brand that originally offered the focal attributes is no longer available.

However, in the initial choice, contexts that induce a high degree of ambiguity create preference uncertainty both before and immediately after choice. This initial uncertainty lingers on and prevents consumers from acquiring extreme confidence in their preferences even after extensive experience. Further, the relatively greater deliberation that occurs in high-ambiguity choice contexts reinforces prior learning that two different sets of attributes render the same benefits with equal efficacy. Thus, these contexts preclude a focal theory or hypothesis that links the positive outcome with any target set of attributes. Because there is no focal hypothesis to begin with, even with additional experience consumers do not consider the positive outcomes of the brand to be unique; if they do consider them unique, they cannot associate the outcome with any specific attributes. When the choice context causes high uncertainty in terms of preference, consumers tend to defer choice or seek additional information (Bettman, Johnson, Luce, & Payne, 1993; Dhar, 1997; Tversky & Shafir, 1992). Because of consumers' need for additional learning, in subsequent decisions consumers tend to choose information in an appropriate manner so as to test the relative efficacy of the attributes. Thus, the tendencies to resolve uncertainty and seek additional, diagnostic information weaken persistent preference for the attributes of a previously chosen brand.

The first three experiments employed a 2 (Ambiguity in the Initial Choice Context) X 2 (Experience) between-subjects factorial design using different manipulations of ambiguity across experiments. The levels of experience were manipulated as six additional trials after an initial trial before choice (Extensive Experience) or no additional trial after the initial trial (Limited Experience). Subjects were asked to read a story that provided information about the key ingredients of the products. This story familiarized subjects with the importance of the key attributes of natural lotions and the benefits derived from these attributes. Subjects were then shown a brand-by-attribute matrix that described four brands in terms of seven attributes. Subjects were asked to inspect the information carefully and then make a choice.

Next, the ambiguity of the choice context was manipulated. In the Low Ambiguity context, all four brands were described in terms of the same attributes. Except on a minor attribute (lemon grass), the focal brand possessed better values than the other brands in the choice set. Within this condition, one half of subjects had vitamin E, jojoba extracts, and papaya extracts (Set A) as the key attributes, and the other half saw aloe vera, cocoa butter, and apricot extracts (Set B) as the key attributes. The brands did not vary in terms of three other attributes.

In the High Ambiguity condition, the four brands were classified into two subcategories. Although four attributes were common to the two subcategories, three key attributes did not overlap across the two subcategories (one subcategory contained the Set A attributes of vitamin E, jojoba extracts, and papaya extracts; the second subcategory contained the Set B attributes of aloe vera, cocoa butter, and apricot extracts). Except on a minor attribute of lemon grass, the brands did not vary in terms of the values of the nonunique attributes. Thus, in the Low Ambiguity condition, there was only one brand superior to others; in the High Ambiguity condition, there were two brands that could be potentially considered equally attractive.

Subjects in the Extensive Experience condition were asked to try the brand they liked six more times. The cover story given to those in the Extensive Experience condition was that previous research had shown that people can evaluate lotions more accurately after a series of trials. Subjects in the

Limited Experience condition were not given any additional trial. A pretest revealed the uninformative nature of extensive experience. Subjects in all conditions were asked to return after 2 days to complete the experiment.

On returning, subjects were given the critical choice task. They were asked to assume that once again they needed to buy lotions. This time they happened to visit another store that did not stock the original set of brands. Instead they encountered two new brands for which descriptions were provided in a matrix. One of the two brands was described in terms of Set A attributes, and the other was described in terms of Set B attributes. Thus, for those in the Low Ambiguity condition, depending on the attribute set they received on Day 1, Set A or Set B served as the focal attributes, and the other served as the competitor. For those in the High Ambiguity condition, attributes of the brand they had chosen served as the focal attributes, and the other set of attributes served as the competitor. Before making the critical choice, subjects were asked to try the "two" brands of lotion. The same lotion was presented in two different containers with their real names concealed. Subjects were asked to either choose one of the two brands or express indifference between the two.

After the choice task, subjects once again experienced the "two" brands after a 30-minute delay during which time tasks not relevant to this chapter were administered. Subjects were asked to rate the superiority of one set of attributes over the other based on their most recent experience (of the two identical brands with different attribute descriptions). Subjects responded to three 9-point scales that measured the superiority (in terms of rendering certain benefits) of the three, nonoverlapping attributes that described the brands in Set A vis-à-vis those contained in Set B. The purpose of this task was to test the extent to which neutral, irrelevant information in the form of experiencing the two identical "brands" was overweighed in different experimental conditions.

Following another 30-minute delay after the superiority rating task, subjects were told that they would choose a brand of lotion once again, but were asked to acquire additional information before making another choice. Subjects then received a set of six envelopes that contained information on six attributes that did not overlap across Sets A and B on Day 1. The envelopes were sealed, but on the outside of each envelope the attribute label as well as an alphabetical label appeared. Subjects were told that each envelope contained additional information on the respective attribute. Further, they were instructed that because of cost constraints they could buy no more than two envelopes. Subjects were asked to indicate the two envelopes they wanted to buy by writing the alphabetical labels on a separate choice record.

The key dependent variable was the proportion of subjects that chose the brand that contained the focal attributes at Time 2. As expected, a greater proportion of subjects persisted with the focal attributes under low ambiguity in the initial choice combined with extensive, but uninformative experience than in any of the other three conditions. Subjects' perceptions of the superiority of the focal attributes followed the same pattern as their choices.

In addition, in the selection of additional information, subjects in the Low Ambiguity-Extensive Experience condition exhibited pseudodiagnosticity. Diagnostic hypothesis testing involves selecting a pair of attributes that lead to the same benefit, one of which is the focal attribute and the other the competitor. However, pseudodiagnostic (selective) information selection would involve asking for information for two attributes (that lead to two different benefits) of the brand chosen earlier. Additional analyses revealed that the choice of the focal attributes by the subjects in the Low Ambiguity-Extensive Experience condition was mediated by their tendency to be pseudodiagnostic in information selection. In Experiment 1B, we found that the judged relevance of the focal attributes increased because of extensive experience combined with low ambiguity in the initial choice context. This judgment in turn led to persistent preference for the focal attributes.

In consumer decisions, it is common that the competing brands contain both advantages and disadvantages. For example, in a choice set, Brand A may contain more of Attribute 1 and less of Attribute 2, and Brand B may contain more of Attribute 2 and less of Attribute 1. Ambiguity occurs when a consumer considers these two attributes as equally relevant for the decision. In Experiment 1C, high ambiguity was manipulated via such choice sets. The results of this experiment paralleled those of Experiments 1A and 1B.

Thus, in these three experiments, we examined how ambiguity interacts with product experience and influences persistent preference for the focal attributes in subsequent choices. We also examined the effects of these factors on the tendency to consider a set of focal attributes to be superior to a set of equally efficient competing attributes after having "neutral" experience (trying the same lotion under different descriptions). When the initial choice set induces greater ambiguity, and thereby greater preference uncertainty, there is a lesser likelihood of developing persistent preferences even after extensive experience. However, when there is little ambiguity in the initial choice, even uninformative additional experience creates persistent preferences for the focal attributes. We found that the tendency to confirm one's prior theory is the process that leads to persistent preference for the focal attributes.

Experiment 2 examined preference persistence for a seemingly irrelevant attribute. This experiment also used an additional manipulation that determined whether the attribute–brand outcome association was strong or weak, which in turn determined the degree of preference persistence.

When an irrelevant attribute was salient in the initial choice context, extensive experience with a brand caused consumers to judge the focal attributes to be the causes of the benefits they derived from the product use.

Debiasing Unwarranted Attribute Loyalty

Providing information about a superior but unavailable comparison brand decreases attribute loyalty by increasing uncertainty about initial preferences. A superior comparison referent causes the consumer to infer that the option he or she chose does not reflect his or her true preference. With additional experience, this belief may be held with a greater certainty, and thus the belief may acquire sufficient strength to induce the consumer to switch from the focal attributes in a subsequent choice. Thus, extensive experience may lead to lesser preference persistence for the focal attributes.

Comparative deliberation also decreases attribute loyalty. When ambiguity in the initial choice context was low, experience caused persistent preferences for the target set of attributes because it increased pseudodiagnostic hypothesis testing. This process suggests that attribute preference persistence should decrease when consumers are provided an opportunity to deliberate on an alternative set of attributes.

Although attribute preference persistence was consistently greater in the Low Ambiguity-High Experience condition than in the remaining three conditions, significantly more than 50% of subjects in the latter three conditions switched to the new set of attributes. We predicted that the choice pattern in these conditions would be 50% preferring the focal attributes and the other 50% preferring the competing set of attributes. One explanation for the significantly greater preference for the competing set of attributes may be that when the evidence supporting one conclusion is weak, people jump to the opposite conclusion (e.g., if Set A is not the best, Set B may be the best; McKenzie et al., 2002; Sanbonmatsu et al., 1998). Another possibility is variety seeking. In this instance, prior learning does not count. Instead people just want to try the new attributes without making any conclusions about their superiority vis-à-vis the focal attributes. In our ongoing research, we intend to tease apart the two explanations.

EFFECTS OF MOTIVATION ON JUDGMENT AND CHOICE

Just as it is the case that experience can help or hurt intuitive judgment, so too it is the case that motivation can help or hurt intuitive judgment. Unambiguous experience provides relevant information that can improve judgment accuracy. Ambiguous experience provides irrelevant information that people often misinterpret as relevant. Simply put, people believe that they learn a lot from experience even when experience is actually irrelevant. Similarly, the motivation to process information thoroughly and systematically can improve judgment accuracy when a relatively large amount of relevant information is available. However, when a relatively large amount of irrelevant information is available, motivation can lead people to over-interpret and overuse information that they would be better off not having.

Mantel and Kardes (1999) investigated the effects on preference judgment of two different motivational variables—need for cognition and involvement. *Need for cognition* is an individual difference variable that pertains to the degree to which people enjoy performing effortful cognitive activities (Cacioppo, Petty, Feinstein, & Jarvis, 1996). As need for cognition increases, people prefer to allocate more effort to judgment tasks. This preference generalizes to all cognitive tasks regardless of the importance or consequentiality of the task. By contrast, *involvement* is a situational variable manipulated by varying the personal importance or consequentiality of the task (Petty & Cacioppo, 1986; Petty, Cacioppo, & Schumann, 1983). Involvement increases as the personal importance or consequentiality of the task increases, and as involvement increases the amount of cognitive effort allocated to the task increases.

Prior research has shown that these two variables have conceptually similar effects in stimulus-based judgment tasks: As need for cognition or involvement increases, the likelihood of effortful systematic information processing increases and the likelihood of low-effort heuristic processing decreases (Cacioppo et al., 1996). However, Mantel and Kardes (1999) hypothesized that need for cognition and involvement would have diverging effects in memory-based judgment tasks. Specifically, it was predicted that need for cognition would enhance memory performance (Cacioppo et al., 1996), and therefore encourage attribute-based processing even when people would be better off not engaging in attribute-based processing. In contrast, involvement was predicted to increase systematic processing regardless of whether people focused on specific attributes or global attitudes.

When people focus on specific attributes and perform an attribute-by-attribute comparison of two objects that are described sequentially, the attributes of the object described last (vs. first) draw more attention and are weighed more heavily in judgment (Tversky, 1977). This occurs because comparison cannot begin until information about the object described last is encountered and because this information is more accessible from memory due to recent activation. Consequently, the unique features of the object described last are overweighed and the unique features of the other object are underweighed in comparative judgment. Mantel and Kardes (1999) found that this direction-of-comparison effect was more pronounced when the need for cognition was high (vs. low), and this effect was reduced when involvement was high (vs. low). Although prior research has shown that many different types of judgment biases decrease as need for cognition increases (Cacioppo et al., 1996), Mantel and Kardes (1999) demonstrated that the direction-of-comparison effect increases as need for cognition increases. Moreover, this effect was mediated by selective recall for the unique features of the brand described last, consistent with the implications of selective hypothesis-testing theory (Sanbonmatsu et al., 1998).

Accountability

The expectation that one will be asked to explain or justify one's judgments and decisions to others is another important motivational variable (Lerner & Tetlock, 1999). Like the need for cognition and involvement, accountability often increases the amount of effort that is allocated to a judgment task. However, unlike the need for cognition and involvement, accountability raises self-presentational concerns that have a powerful influence on the manner in which information is processed. When a person is concerned about pleasing others—such as a boss, peer, or spouse—the person often makes judgments and decisions that are consistent with the perspectives of others, provided that these perspectives are known in advance. Conversely, when the perspectives of others are unknown, accountability increases preemptive self-criticism or the tendency to think in more self-critical, flexible, and creative ways. Rather than adopting a single perspective, multiple perspectives are considered because this increases the likelihood of making a decision that can be justified to many different constituencies regardless of their personal perspectives, preferences, and backgrounds.

Consistent with the commonsense position that any motivational variable that increases the amount of effort allocated to a judgment task should reduce judgmental bias, accountability has been shown to reduce a large number of judgmental biases, including heuristic processing, schema-based processing, the fundamental attribution error, inconsistent cue utilization, order effects, anchoring effects, priming effects, mood effects, overconfidence, the conjunction fallacy, and groupthink (Lerner & Tetlock, 1999). However, in stark contrast to the commonsense position, accountability has been shown to increase some judgmental biases, including the status quo effect (Tetlock & Boettger, 1994), the dilution effect (Tetlock & Boettger, 1989), the attraction effect (Simonson, 1989), and the compromise effect (Simonson, 1989).

TOWARD A GENERAL THEORY OF DEBIASING

Why do experience and motivation reduce some types of judgmental biases but increase others? Arkes (1991) suggested that heuristic-based errors, memory-based errors, and psychophysically based errors require debiasing techniques unique to each of these three categories. Gilbert, Pelham, and Krull (1988) suggested that some types of biases occur because people process information too little (underprocessing), and other types occur because people process information too much (overprocessing). Motivation helps when underprocessing is likely, but hurts when overprocessing is likely. Similarly, Peracchio and Meyers-Levy (1997) suggested that judgment is most accurate when the amount of cognitive resources available for information processing matches the amount needed to perform a judgment task. This perspective suggests that motivation and task difficulty should produce interactive effects on judgment. A different type of interaction is implied by drive theory (Hull, 1943; Pelham & Neter, 1995). According to drive theory, high levels of motivation increase the likelihood that a dominant, well-learned behavior will be performed. Consequently, motivation should help when a judgment task is easy, but hurt when a judgment task is difficult. Finally, Lerner and Tetlock (1999) rejected broad theories of the effects of motivation on judgment and suggested that each judgment bias is influenced by a unique set of mediating and moderating variables, and consequently each judgment bias should be investigated singularly.

Considering Alternatives

We suggest a compromise between the focus on broad categories versus singular biases. More than three categories of biases are needed to capture the richness of the judgment literature. Although many biases are mediated by unique sets of processes, some commonalities and regularities are observed across biases. The distinctions among heuristic-based, memory-based, and psychophysically based biases are undoubtedly important, but additional distinctions should be considered as well. For example, some types of biases involve a focus on a single hypothesis (selective hypothesis testing), and the best way to reduce these biases is to encourage people to consider multiple alternative hypotheses (Sanbonmatsu et al., 1998). Encouraging people to consider multiple hypotheses improves many different types of judgments that are mediated by selective hypothesis testing, including hindsight bias (Sanna, Schwarz, & Stocker, 2002), overconfidence (Hoch, 1985; Koriat et al., 1980), the perseverance effect (Lord et al., 1984), the explanation effect (Hirt et al., 2004; Hirt & Markman, 1995; Koehler, 1991), functional fixedness (Galinsky & Moskowitz, 2000), confirmation bias (Galinsky & Moskowitz, 2000), omission neglect (Sanbonmatsu, Kardes, Houghton, Ho, & Posavac, 2003), and pseudodiagnostic attribute preference persistence (Muthukrishnan & Kardes, 2001).

Processing Fluency

Although considering multiple hypotheses is often useful, it is important to recognize that considering alternatives can backfire as a debiasing technique when the process of retrieving or generating alternatives is experienced as difficult (Hirt et al., 2004; Sanna et al., 2002). Ease of retrieval/generation is used as a heuristic cue for inferring whether a relatively large or small number of alternative hypotheses is possible. Retrieving/generating few alternatives is typically experienced as easy, and this implies that many alternative hypotheses exist. Ironically, retrieving/generating many alternatives is typically experienced as difficult, and this implies that few alternative hypotheses are plausible even though many alternatives were actually retrieved or generated. Ease of retrieval/generation is less likely to be used as a heuristic cue when involvement is high (Schwarz, 1998) or when the need for cognitive closure (the preference to reach a judgment or conclusion quickly; Kruglanski & Webster, 1996) is low (Hirt et al., 2004). Processing fluency is also discounted when prior knowledge is low because retrieval/generation is always experienced as difficult when one is unknowledgeable about a particular topic (Schwarz, 1998).

Considering Criteria

Another debiasing technique that merits further investigation is considering the criteria that should be used ideally as bases for judgment prior to considering the available evidence. Criteria should be considered early in the judgment process due to possible interference effects: The criteria implied by the information that happens to be available in a given context may interfere with the ability to retrieve or generate other criteria. Predecisional criteria consideration has been shown to reduce attribute preference persistence (Muthukrishnan & Kardes, 2001) and omission neglect (insensitivity to missing relevant information; Sanbonmatsu et al., 2003). This technique appears to be effective primarily for constructed judgments (Bettman et al., 1998) because online judgment construction involves allowing the available evidence to determine the criteria that are used as bases for judgment rather than vice versa. Judgment construction is particularly problematic when important information is missing or when the available evidence varies dramatically across contexts. In addition to reducing pseudodiagnostic information processing and omission neglect, predecisional criteria consideration may reduce the magnitude of preference reversals induced via direction-of-comparison (Kardes & Sanbonmatsu, 1993; Mantel & Kardes, 1999) framing (Kahneman & Tversky, 1979), compatibility (Shafir, 1995; Tversky, Sattah, & Slovic, 1988), evaluability (Hsee, Loewenstein,

Blount, & Bazerman, 1999), and analyzing reasons (Wilson & Schooler, 1991) manipulations.

The available research evidence suggests that no single debiasing technique is a panacea for the wide range of judgmental biases discovered by decision researchers. Instead it is important to match specific techniques to undo the specific problematic processes underlying the various classes of biases. Experience and motivation can either increase or decrease judgmental bias depending on the nature of the information used as a basis for judgment and the manner in which this information is used. Relevant experience helps, but irrelevant experience hurts because people assume that they learn a lot from experience even when experience is uninformative. Motivation helps when underprocessing or minimal information processing is likely, but motivation hurts when overprocessing or overinterpretation of the available evidence is likely. A clearer understanding of the processes that mediate heuristic thinking, attention and memory-based biases, psychophysically based biases, selective hypothesis testing, and judgment construction will have important implications for developing more effective debiasing techniques.

REFERENCES

Alba, J. W., Hutchinson, J. W., & Lynch, J. G. (1991). Memory and decision making. In T. S. Robertson & H. H. Kassarjian (Eds.), *Handbook of consumer behavior* (pp. 1–49). Englewood Cliffs, NJ: Prentice-Hall.

Arkes, H. R. (1991). Costs and benefits of judgment errors: Implications for debiasing. *Psychological Bulletin, 110,* 486–498.

Bettman, J. R., Johnson, E., Luce, M. F., & Payne, J. W. (1993). Correlation, conflict, and choice. *Journal of Experimental Psychology: Learning, Memory, and Cognition, 19,* 931–951.

Bettman, J. R., Luce, M. F., & Payne, J. W. (1998). Constructive consumer choice processes. *Journal of Consumer Research, 25,* 187–217.

Beyth-Marom, R., & Fischhoff, B. (1983). Diagnosticity and pseudodiagnosticity. *Journal of Personality and Social Psychology, 45,* 1185–1195.

Cacioppo, J. T., Petty, R. E., Feinstein, J. A., & Jarvis, W. B. G. (1996). Dispositional differences in cognitive motivation: The life and times of individuals varying in need for cognition. *Psychological Bulletin, 119,* 197–253.

Camerer, C., & Weber, M. (1992). Recent developments in modeling preferences: Uncertainty and ambiguity. *Journal of Risk and Uncertainty, 5,* 325–370.

Dhar, R. (1997). Consumer preference for a no-choice option. *Journal of Consumer Research, 24,* 215–231.

Doherty, M. E., Mynatt, C., Tweney, R., & Schiavo, M. (1979). Pseudodiagnosticity. *Acta Psychologica, 43,* 11–21.

Einhorn, H. J., & Hogarth, R. M. (1978). Confidence in judgment: Persistence of the illusion of validity. *Psychological Review, 85,* 395–416.

Einhorn, H. J., & Hogarth, R. M. (1981). Behavioral decision theory: Processes of judgment and choice. *Annual Review of Psychology, 32,* 53–88.

Ellsberg, D. (1961). Risk, ambiguity and Savage axioms. *Quarterly Journal of Economics, 75,* 643–669.

Fischhoff, B., & Beyth-Marom, R. (1983). Hypothesis evaluation from a Bayesian perspective. *Psychological Review, 90,* 239–260.

Frisch, D., & Baron, J. (1988). Ambiguity and rationality. *Journal of Behavioral Decision Making, 1,* 149–157.

Galinsky, A. D., & Moskowitz, G. B. (2000). Counterfactuals as behavioral primes: Priming the simulation heuristic and consideration of alternatives. *Journal of Experimental Social Psychology, 36,* 384–409.

Gilbert, D. T., Pelham, B. W., & Krull, D. S. (1988). On cognitive busyness: When person perceivers meet person receivers. *Journal of Personality and Social Psychology, 57,* 733–740.

Ha, Y. W., & Hoch, S. J. (1989). Ambiguity, processing strategy, and advertising-evidence interactions. *Journal of Consumer Research, 16,* 354–360.

Heath, C., & Tversky, A. (1991). Preference and belief: Ambiguity and competence in choice under uncertainty. *Journal of Risk and Uncertainty, 4,* 5–28.

Hirt, E. R., Kardes, F. R., & Markman, K. D. (2004). Activating a mental simulation mind-set through generation of alternatives: Implications for debiasing in related and unrelated domains. *Journal of Experimental Social Psychology, 40,* 374–383.

Hirt, E. R., & Markman, K. D. (1995). Multiple explanation: A consider-an-alternative strategy for debiasing judgments. *Journal of Personality and Social Psychology, 69,* 1069–1086.

Hoch, S. J. (1985). Counterfactual reasoning and accuracy in predicting personal events. *Journal of Experimental Psychology: Learning, Memory, and Cognition, 11,* 719–731.

Hoch, S. J., & Ha, Y. W. (1986). Consumer learning: Advertising and ambiguity of product experience. *Journal of Consumer Research, 13,* 221–233.

Hsee, C. K., Loewenstein, G. F., Blount, S., & Bazerman, M. H. (1999). Preference reversals between joint and separate evaluations of options: A review and theoretical analysis. *Psychological Bulletin, 125,* 576–590.

Hull, C. L. (1943). *Principles of behavior.* New York: Appleton-Century-Croft.

Jeuland, A. (1979). Brand choice inertia as one aspect of the notion of brand loyalty. *Management Science, 25,* 671–682.

Kahneman, D., & Tversky, A. (1979). Prospect theory: An analysis of decision under risk. *Econometrica, 47,* 263–291.

Klar, Y. (1990). Linking structures and sensitivity to judgment-relevant information in statistical and logical reasoning tasks. *Journal of Personality and Social Psychology, 59,* 841–858.

Klayman, J., & Ha, Y.-W. (1987). Confirmation, disconfirmation, and information in hypothesis testing. *Psychological Review, 94,* 211–228.

Koehler, D. J. (1991). Explanation, imagination, and confidence in judgment. *Psychological Bulletin, 110,* 499–519.

Koriat, A., Lichtenstein, S., & Fischhoff, B. (1980). Reasons for confidence. *Journal of Experimental Psychology: Human Learning and Memory, 6,* 107–118.

Kruglanski, A. W., & Webster, D. M. (1996). Motivated closing of the mind: "Seizing" and "freezing." *Psychological Review, 103,* 263–283.

Lerner, J. S., & Tetlock, P. E. (1999). Accounting for the effects of accountability. *Psychological Bulletin, 125,* 255–275.

Lord, C. G., Ross, L., & Lepper, M. R. (1984). Considering the opposite: A corrective strategy for social judgment. *Journal of Personality and Social Psychology, 47,* 1231–1243.

Mantel, S. P., & Kardes, F. R. (1999). The role of direction of comparison, attribute-based processing, and attitude-based processing in consumer preference. *Journal of Consumer Research, 25,* 335–352.

McKenzie, C. R. M., Lee, S. M., & Chen, K. K. (2002). When negative evidence increases confidence: Change in belief after hearing two sides of a dispute. *Journal of Behavioral Decision Making, 15,* 1–18.

Muthukrishnan, A. V. (1995). Decision ambiguity and incumbent brand advantage. *Journal of Consumer Research, 22*, 98–109.

Muthukrishnan, A. V., & Kardes, F. R. (2001). Persistent preferences for product attributes: The effects of the initial choice context and uninformative experience. *Journal of Consumer Research, 28*, 89–104.

Mynatt, C. R., Doherty, M., & Dragan, W. (1993). Information relevance, working memory, and the consideration of alternatives. *Quarterly Journal of Experimental Psychology, 46A*, 759–778.

Payne, J. W., Bettman, J. R., & Johnson, E. J. (1993). *The adaptive decision maker.* Cambridge, England: Cambridge University Press.

Pelham, B. W., & Neter, E. (1995). The effects of motivation on judgment depends on the difficulty of the judgment. *Journal of Personality and Social Psychology, 68*, 581–594.

Peracchio, L. A., & Meyers-Levy, J. (1997). Evaluating persuasion-enhancing techniques from a resource-matching perspective. *Journal of Consumer Research, 24*, 178–191.

Petty, R. E., & Cacioppo, J. T. (1986). The elaboration likelihood model of persuasion. In L. Berkowitz (Ed.), *Advances in experimental social psychology* (Vol. 19, pp. 123–205). San Diego, CA: Academic Press.

Petty, R. E., Cacioppo, J. T., & Schumann, D. W. (1983). Central and peripheral routes to advertising effectiveness: The moderating role of involvement. *Journal of Consumer Research, 10*, 135–146.

Sanbonmatsu, D. M., Akimoto, S. A., & Biggs, E. (1993). Overestimating causality: Attributional effects of confirmatory processing. *Journal of Personality and Social Psychology, 65*, 892–903.

Sanbonmatsu, D. M., Kardes, F. R., Houghton, D. C., Ho, E. A., & Posavac, S. S. (2003). Overestimating the importance of the given information in multiattribute consumer judgment. *Journal of Consumer Psychology, 13*, 289–300.

Sanbonmatsu, D. M., Posavac, S. S., Kardes, F. R., & Mantel, S. P. (1998). Selective hypothesis testing. *Psychonomic Bulletin & Review, 5*, 197–229.

Sanna, L. J., Schwarz, N., & Stocker, S. L. (2002). When debiasing backfires: Accessible content and accessibility experiences in debiasing hindsight. *Journal of Experimental Psychology: Learning, Memory, and Cognition, 28*, 497–502.

Schwarz, N. (1998). Accessible content and accessibility experiences: The interplay of declarative and experiential information in judgment. *Personality and Social Psychology Review, 2*, 87–99.

Shafir, E. (1995). Compatibility in cognition and decision. In J. R. Busemeyer, R. Hastie, & D. L. Medin (Eds.), *Decision making from the perspective of cognitive psychology: The psychology of learning and motivation* (Vol. 32, pp. 247–274). New York: Academic Press.

Shafir, E., Simonson, I., & Tversky, A. (1993). Reason-based choice. *Cognition, 49*, 11–36.

Simonson, I. (1989). Choice based on reasons: The case of attraction and compromise effects. *Journal of Consumer Research, 16*, 158–174.

Tetlock, P. E., & Boettger, R. (1989). Accountability: A social magnifier of the dilution effect. *Journal of Personality and Social Psychology, 57*, 388–398.

Tetlock, P. E., & Boettger, R. (1994). Accountability amplifies the status quo effect when change creates victims. *Journal of Behavioral Decision Making, 7*, 1–23.

Tversky, A. (1977). Features of similarity. *Psychological Review, 84*, 327–352.

Tversky, A., & Kahneman, D. (1974). Judgment under uncertainty: Heuristics and biases. *Science, 185*, 1124–1131.

Tversky, A., Sattath, S., & Slovic, P. (1988). Contingent weighting in judgment and choice. *Psychological Review, 95*, 371–384.

Tversky, A., & Shafir, E. (1992). Choice under conflict. *Psychological Science, 6*, 358–361.

Wilson, T. D., & Schooler, J. W. (1991). Thinking too much: Introspection can reduce the quality of preferences and decisions. *Journal of Personality and Social Psychology, 60*, 181–192.

CHAPTER

9

Using Expertise and Experience for Giving and Taking Advice

Helmut Jungermann
Katrin Fischer
Technical University of Berlin

There are situations when a person interacts with another person to arrive at a decision. For instance, a private investor meets in a bank with a financial advisor because he or she wants to invest money. Or a patient in a hospital has to choose whether to undergo surgery or chemical therapy, or do nothing, and discusses the situation with a doctor. We call these situations *dyadic decision situations*. We focus on situations where there is some legal responsibility and a special relation between the client, who formally has to make and sign the decision, and the advisor, who is to help the client make a decision by making a recommendation on which option to choose.[1]

From the traditional decision-theoretic perspective, the situation looks simple enough: There is a decision maker, the client, who asks for and gets information about the options, explores and evaluates the options, and then chooses one of them. There is an advisor, an expert, who provides substantial information about facts and judgments regarding components of the problem, who may elicit clients' preferences, and who finally provides an integrative evaluation of the options. The client can then make a deliberate and informed choice.

However, this perspective does not capture important components of the situations described earlier (i.e., the interaction between investor and

---

[1]We use the term *advisor* equivalently to the terms *advice-giver*, *consultant*, and *agent*, and the term *client* equivalently to the terms *advice-seeker*, *judge*, and *principal*. These terms are used for the same roles in dyadic decisions on other theoretical conceptions and research communities.

advisor or between patient and doctor). These situations share a feature that actually provides the rationale for the relation between advisor and client: *Expertise and experience are asymmetrically distributed.* This is also one of the features that distinguishes these situations from the advice-giving-and-taking situations that have been examined recently, for instance, by Harvey and Fischer (1997; chap. 7, this volume), Harvey, Harries, and Fischer (2000), Jonas and Frey (2003), Kray (2000), Sniezek (1999), Sniezek and Buckley (1995), Sniezek and van Swol (2001), and Yaniv and Kleinberger (2000). This asymmetry constitutes the situation: Person A, lacking expertise in a certain domain (e.g., an ill person), asks Person B (e.g., a doctor) because of his or her expertise, and Person B gives Person A a piece of advice because of this expertise. It is irrelevant whether the asymmetry actually exists or is only assumed by one or both persons involved in the situation (e.g., a private investor may be taken in by a false investment advisor, or a doctor may be deluded by a doctor as a patient).

We argue that this asymmetry in expertise, which we call *informational asymmetry*, favors that advisors and clients use different decision-making strategies and neither strategy is the "classical" optimizing strategy of exploring and evaluating the set of options. In particular, we suggest that clients often focus on the advisor rather than on the options, and we present some empirical evidence for the influence of the advisor. Finally, we propose a general model of the factors determining a client's decision based on our theoretical assumptions and recent empirical research.

DIFFERENCES IN KNOWLEDGE BETWEEN ADVISOR AND CLIENT

We are not aware of empirical research on quantitative and qualitative differences in knowledge between advisors and clients in the kind of situations we are addressing. Although it would be interesting to study such differences in detail, in particular the beliefs of advisors and clients with respect to each other's knowledge, major characteristics of the informational asymmetry can be reasonably assumed without specific empirical evidence due to the structure of situation and task (see Table 9.1).

Advisors are, by definition, experts in dyadic decisions. They have developed their expertise by professional training as well as from practical experience. What kind of expertise do they have? Most important, if advisors are really experienced, they have seen many clients with different problems, ideas, knowledge, goals, and so on. In statistical terms, they perceive an individual client as one single "point" of a broad distribution of clients. They have generalized knowledge. Compared with their clients, they have extensive knowledge regarding the relevant (e.g., medical, financial) facts. They

TABLE 9.1
Differences in Knowledge Between Advisor and Client

Advisor	Client
1. Generalized knowledge about client's problems	1. Individual knowledge about personal problem
2. Extensive knowledge about relevant facts	2. Little knowledge about relevant facts
3. Statistical knowledge (possibly technical database) about client's goals and values	3. Limited awareness (no database) about personal goals and values
4. Professional experience with decision outcomes, coping behaviors, and client's biases	4. Little if any experience with problem-related decision consequences, coping possibilities, and judgment demands
5. Explicit knowledge of decision strategies, implicit decision competence, and routines	5. No explicit procedural expertise, implicit (unrelated) competence
6. Professional expertise with client's decision-making behavior	6. Little if any experience with advisor's decision strategies

know the set of options, their clients' features, and the success that the choice of options has had for clients with particular features in the past. For instance, a surgeon knows at least his personal statistics of success and failure; often he knows the general statistics as well. Yet advisors have more expertise: They have explicit or implicit statistical knowledge about their clients' goals and values based on their training or a technical database. For instance, married middle-age teachers with two children look primarily for a safe investment, whereas single professors are more interested in risky investment with a high potential. Advisors have seen many clients and know the outcomes of many decisions, they know how clients experience and cope with consequences (e.g., regret), how their preferences have changed, and how biased their judgments often are (e.g., wishful thinking) due to greed or fear. Sometimes advisors have explicit knowledge of how to arrive at a decision, but more often their procedural knowledge is implicit. They have developed routines of decision making, may be originating from professional training but primarily determined by long experience. They know that they have and use these routines even if they may be unable to verbalize them precisely. Finally, advisors know something about their clients' decision-making process. They know at least that their clients do not use a decision analytic strategy or else clients would have confronted the advisor more often with their procedure and its result.

Clients are usually laypersons with respect to the problem. They seek advice from professional advisors because they do not have their knowledge and competence. Yet what knowledge do they have and what knowledge do they not have? Clients have knowledge about their own personal problems, of course, such as their financial situation or their disease, and they sometimes have second-hand knowledge about similar problems through relatives, friends, or the media. However, they do not have systematic and generalized knowledge about the problem, and therefore they do not have the "glasses" to understand their problem appropriately. Compared to advisors, clients have little and rather selective knowledge about the relevant facts. For instance, a private investor does not know all investment alternatives, their history and prospects, their interaction with his or her age, marital status, income, assets, and so on. Clients have some limited awareness of their goals and values, although often ill defined and structured, and they have some selective knowledge about other people's preferences, such as their friends' or the general public's. For instance, patients may know whether or how they want to live, which pain they will be able to tolerate in the short and long run, or which restrictions they are willing to accept. But they only have access primarily to their personal feelings and preferences. Because the situation is often new and unfamiliar to clients, they have no personal knowledge regarding the real consequences that choices might have for them, how they might be able to cope with unfavorable outcomes, with regret or ambiguity, how their preferences might change over time, and how their judgments may be biased. Some clients may realize, however, that the advisor has seen many clients and knows of things they do not and cannot know. All clients have made decisions in their lives, but they have little if any explicit knowledge about decision procedures. They have no technical competence how to identify, modify, or evaluate options systematically. Finally, clients know little about advisors' decision making. The advisors' procedure for generalizing a piece of advice remains mostly obscure. Because of their lack of expertise, clients will often be unable to understand how a recommendation was generated, what the rationale for a recommendation is, or which alternatives there might have been but were discarded.

DIFFERENCES IN STRATEGY
BETWEEN ADVISOR AND CLIENT

The informational asymmetry has consequences for the strategy of both advisors and clients (see Table 9.2). There is indirect evidence for advisors' behavior from research on experts' decision processes (see e.g., Lipshitz, Klein, Orasanu, & Salas, 2001; Shanteau, Friel, Thomas, & Raacke, chap. 14, this volume), and there is direct evidence for clients' behavior from recent empirical studies (see e.g., Harvey et al., 2000).

Advisors do not have to search and evaluate the complete set of options to identify the best option (i.e., they do not apply an optimizing strategy even if they are able to). They are experts; because of their expertise, they rely on their professional experience and routines. They provide informa-

TABLE 9.2
Differences in Strategy Between Advisor and Client

Advisor	Client
1. Is aware of client's (in)competence, relies on experience and routines	1. Cannot and does not want to explore all options, asks for advice
2. Knows that a recommendation is expected, is prepared to explain and justify	2. Expects a recommendation and is willing to pay for it
3. Applies a pattern-matching strategy	3. Directs attention to recommended option, searches and stores information selectively
4. Focuses on clients and their features, categorizes clients	4. Focuses on advisors and their features, evaluate their credibility
5. Decision: recommendation of the matching option(s)	5. Decision: acceptance or rejection of the advice

tion about the options, but they also know that the client lacks the competence to really understand and integrate the information. Advisors know that clients expect a recommendation, possibly accompanied by a justification. Therefore, they have to be prepared to explain the reasons why and how they arrived at their advice. Advisors do not explore the options from scratch when meeting a client, be it a patient or an investor. Experts can work efficiently and successfully with a pattern-making strategy, as demonstrated by Klein and others (e.g., Klein, 1989; Ross, Lussier, & Klein, chap. 18, this volume). In the situations we are dealing with, expert advisors can rely on mentally or technically prestored knowledge about options, patterns of client features, and established degrees of matching. For *experienced* consultants, it might take no time at all to find the right option; for *less experienced* consultants, the strategy might require a longer search process. To identify the right option, advisors must focus on the clients and their features. They must use their knowledge about the domain, their experience, and mostly some forms to elicit relevant and specific information from their clients, and they must then categorize the individual client. In a bank, for instance, clients are often categorized according to their age, profession, income, marital status, number of children, risk attitude, and other criteria. This strategy implies that advisors can and tend to generate, communicate, and recommend one or only a few options. The advisor's decision is simply to *recommend the matching option(s) or not to recommend an option* (if no justifiable match could be identified). We found evidence for this advice strategy in a study with students who met with financial advisors in banks presumably to discuss an investment of DM 70.000. Our "student mystery shoppers" had been trained before the meeting: They all told the advisor the same story, asked a number of specific questions, and made some statements intended to elicit particular comments and suggestions by the advisor (e.g., regarding the risks of shares). The finding of interest in this context was that advisors generally offered an investment recommendation very early in the meeting, not at the end of the meeting based on an extensive discussion.

Clients also do not apply an optimizing strategy. Because they do not have the experience and routines, they cannot generate and explore the set of possible options and search the best one. That is why they ask for professional advice. Clients do not want to spend the time and effort that an optimizing strategy demands. They expect a recommendation, and they are willing to pay for it. They assume that the recommendation is the result of a thorough analysis of their situation and problem, but they do not want to understand in detail the process that led to a recommendation. Therefore, clients tend to direct their attention primarily to the recommended option. Nonrecommended options represent counterfactual alternatives that are dim, less vivid, and less available than the recommended option (Kahneman & Miller, 1986). The attention focus can have a number of effects on how people search and encode information about the options, as has been shown, for instance, by Legrenzi, Girotto, and Johnson-Laird (1993) and Cherubini, Mazzocco, and Rumiati (2003). In an experimental study by Fischer (2002), participants had to choose between four multiattribute options. Before making their choice, they could demand information about the options using an information display board. Before the beginning of the information search, one group received a recommendation of an option; another group did not receive a recommendation. The data show that the first group asked for more information between attributes and less information within attributes than the second group. That is, the first group focused on searching information to confirm or disconfirm the advice, whereas the second group searched information in a balanced way. Furthermore, the first group asked for less information than the second group. The first group also recalled relatively more information about the recommended option than about the nonrecommended options, indicating that the advice induced selective information encoding in favor of the recommended option. Because the situation is unfamiliar and the domain complex, clients focus on the advisor and his or her advice. They form an impression of the advisor's personality and credibility. Under the condition of informational asymmetry, clients will not apply a belief adjustment strategy. Such a strategy has been suggested and empirically demonstrated for situations when advisors and clients are operating on the same informational level (e.g., when friends or students in experimental settings adjust their prior beliefs depending on the advice and the weight they give this advice; Hogarth & Einhorn, 1992). Yet patients or private investors often do not have specific prior beliefs to adjust, but only rather vague assumptions. Therefore, we suspect that clients often largely rely on their trust in the advisor and that their decision is not between options, but whether to accept or reject the advice.

THE SUBTLE INFLUENCE OF ADVICE

The foregoing analytic distinctions and theoretical assumptions can serve as a starting point for many empirical studies. A key question concerns the ways in which advice can influence a client's evaluation of the given options. Let us assume that the options in a given situation have a number of features (i.e., they are multidimensional). This assumption is valid for medical treatment options as well as financial investment options. In a multi-attribute utility framework (e.g., Keeney & Raiffa, 1976), multidimensional options can be described as sets of values on relevant attributes, and the attributes have weights depending on the decision maker's goals. According to the additive model, the overall evaluation of an option is the sum of its utilities of the attribute values, each weighted by the weight of the respective attribute. In this framework, two individuals may evaluate options differently because either their utility functions or their weights differ.

Experts and nonexperts are known to differ often in the importance they assign to features of the given options because experts have broad knowledge about clients' goals and values, whereas clients have only limited awareness about their personal goals and values (see Table 9.1). One way in which the recommendation by an expert can influence the decision-making process of a client may be the shifting of the client's a priori weights toward the weights implied by the recommendation. In two experiments, we examined whether and how the influence of advice may be reflected in a change of participants' importance judgments.

Experiment I

The participants in this experiment, all women, had to choose between two prenatal diagnostic screening methods for trisomy 21: amniocentesis and chorionic villi sampling (CVS). They received a booklet containing medical information about the methods; they were asked to read the booklet and use it in the course of their decision-making process. The methods were described on five attributes: physical risks to the fetus, physical risks to the mother, waiting period until the test result is known, test reliability, and costs of the test. After reading the material, participants were asked to assign their personal weights to the five attributes by distributing 100 points among the attributes. They were then informed about the weights that another person—an advisor—had provided. For Group A ($N = 27$), this was a genetic counselor; for Group B ($N = 29$), this was their best friend. In a pretest, participants rated the genetic counselor as significantly more competent and credible in the given situation than a best friend.

The weights of the advisor (counselor/friend) were the same in both groups. They were constructed so that they differed in a specific way from the weights that another group of participants had provided in a pretest: On average these participants had rated the first and second attributes as equally important (about 30 points). The weights of the advisor were set as 25 points for the first and 35 points for the second attribute, indicating that the advisor judged the second attribute (risks to the mother) clearly as more important than the first attribute (risks to the fetus). The weights provided by the participants to the first two attributes were not equal, but the first attribute was assigned a higher weight (38,89 by Group A, 41,31 by Group B) than the second attribute (34,63 by Group A, 31,21 by Group B).

After being informed about the weights of the counselor (Group A) or friend (Group B), participants were asked to reconsider their first importance ratings. They had the option of changing their ratings, but were not required to do so. Two questions arose: First, would participants change their weights due to the proposed weights? If so, would they change the weights for all attributes? Second, is the occurrence of changes dependent on the source of the advice? Would participants be more influenced by a counselor or a best friend?

Table 9.3 shows the results. The importance ratings of the two groups before the presentation of the advisor's weights do not differ significantly (i.e., both groups assign about the same weights to the five attributes). In Group B, the analysis of the changes between the first and second ratings shows that no significant changes occurred for any of the five attributes (paired samples t tests). In Group A, however, significant changes occurred for the first attribute (risks to the fetus; $t = 6,15$, $p < .05$) and second attribute (risks to the mother; $t = -2,71$, $p < .05$), whereas no changes occurred for the other three attributes. The data and analyses provide answers to the questions posed earlier. First, changes of the weights did occur as a re-

TABLE 9.3
Mean Attribute Weights Before and After Presentation of Advisor's Weights

Variable	Group A		Group B		Advisor's Weights
	First Weight	Second Weight	First Weight	Second Weight	
Risks to the fetus	38,89	32,96	41,31	39,41	25
Risks to the mother	34,63	38,89	32,21	33,41	35
Waiting period	10,74	11,30	8,97	10,00	15
Test reliability	14,44	13,15	15,79	16,31	15
Costs of the test	2,96	3,70	1,72	2,07	15

sult of advice. Second, weights were changed only for the two most important attributes and not for the less important attributes. Third, changes occurred only when the advice came from a competent and credible source (the genetic counselor).

Finally, a look at the data in Table 9.3 shows that when changes did occur, the weights shifted strongly toward the weights of the advisor. In fact the expert's advice reversed the importance that participants assigned to the first two attributes. Before the advice was given, Group A considered the first attribute as more important than the second attribute (38,89 vs. 34,63), but after the advice they considered the second attribute as more important than the first attribute (38,89 vs. 32,96).

Experiment 2

In the first study, the weights of the advisor were explicitly stated. This is in a way equivalent to a situation where an advisor presents and explains his or her arguments with respect to the given options. Yet could a piece of advice also influence participants' weights in a more subtle way—for instance if the advisor only recommends an option without making explicit the underlying importance judgments?

As in Experiment 1, participants had to choose between amniocentesis and CVS. Here both methods were described only in terms of the three attributes risks to the fetus, risks to the pregnant mother, and costs of the test. The previously mentioned pretest with other participants showed that the first and second attributes were rated as equally important, whereas the third attribute was rated as less important. Participants first had to read a booklet with the information about the methods. In this booklet, the option amniocentesis had a better value in terms of the first attribute (risks to the fetus) and the option CVS had a better value in terms of the second attribute (risks to the mother). Both options did not differ in terms of the third attribute (costs). After reading the information, participants had to assign weights to the three attributes and make a choice between the two diagnostic methods.

After reading the booklet, but before weighting and choosing, Group A was given a recommendation in favor of amniocentesis by a genetic counselor, whereas CVS was endorsed to Group B. Group C did not get any advice. We assume that if an expert recommends amniocentesis, a person can and will infer that this expert assigns greater weight to the first attribute than to the second attribute because amniocentesis had a better value for the first attribute. In contrast, if an expert recommends CVS, this recommendation suggests that the advisor considers the second attribute to be more important because CVS had a better value for this attribute. We expected that participants would adjust their attribute weights for the first and second attributes depending on the recommendation they were given. Group A should weight the first attribute as more important, Group B should judge the second attribute as more important, and in Group C the weights for the first and second attributes should not differ.

Table 9.4 shows the data. After being recommended amniocentesis (Group A), participants' weights of the first attribute were significantly higher than their weights of the second attribute (53,80 vs. 42,80; paired samples t test: $t = 3,15$, $p < .05$). After being recommended CVS (Group B), the weights of the second attribute were significantly higher than those of the first attribute (39,65 vs. 58,26; paired samples t test: $t = -4,13$, $p < .05$). Without advice, participants rated the first and second attributes as equally important. Participants seem to have inferred experts' weights of the attributes and adjusted their own weights to those of the expert.

The subtle influence of advice observed in this experiment can be expected to occur especially when the recommendation is not accompanied by an explicit discussion or explanation of the importance judgments underlying the advice. However, this is not a rare occurrence when medical or financial advice is given.

Should advisors and/or clients be worried about the kind of influence a recommendation demonstrated in these studies? Not necessarily because clients often want clear and unambiguous advice (i.e., the recommendation of what to do). They expect to change their minds as a result of the information provided by the advisor, whether it be explicitly or implicitly communicated. They should be worried only if they cannot trust the advisors to do their best in finding the best option for their client. Jonas and Frey (2003) showed that students in the role of advisors (e.g., travel agents), when they gave a recommendation, presented information about the given options rather selectively—namely, selecting information that supported the recommended option. However, before giving the recommendation, they searched the relevant information in a balanced way—more balanced and

TABLE 9.4
Mean Attribute Weights Inferred From Expert's Advice

Variable	Attribute 1: Risks to the Fetus	Attribute 2: Risks to the Mother	Attribute 3: Costs
Group A Recommendation: Amniocentesis	53,80	42,80	3,40
Group B Recommendation: Chorionic villi sampling	39,65	58,26	2,09
Group C No recommendation	47,00	49,57	3,43

comprehensively than students in the role of clients. In a business or medical context, motives for making a recommendation may not always be purely altruistic, but financial advisors as well as medical doctors can generally be assumed to at least give priority to the satisfaction of their clients because that strategy pays off better in the long run.

A GENERAL MODEL OF CLIENTS' DECISIONS ABOUT ADVICE

In the previous sections, we argued that clients often rely on their trust in the advisor, and that their decision is then whether to accept or reject the advice, rather than identify and choose the best option. We have presented some empirical evidence for the influence of an expert's advice. In this section, we present a general descriptive model of the factors determining a client's decision (see also Jungermann, 1999). We propose that the decision to accept or reject the advice has four determinants: the judgment of the advisor regarding the recommended option, the judgment of the client regarding the recommended option, the advisor's credibility, and the client's confidence. The first two factors are related to the recommended option: the quality of the option as judged by the advisor, usually based on pro and con arguments, and the quality of the option as judged by the client him or herself, based on plausibility, soundness, and assumed risks and benefits. The other two factors are related to the client's evaluation of the judgments: the perceived quality of the advisor's judgment, based on his or her credibility, and the perceived quality of the client's own judgment, based on his or her personal competence and confidence.

If this model is correct, clients' behavior can no longer be explained by their evaluations of the options alone (as advisors and clients believe or pretend to believe). Rather, acceptance as well as rejection of a recommended option can result from different evaluations. We illustrate the argument with four prototypical cases. (a) A client *accepts* the recommended option when the evaluations of both advisor and client are positive, the client considers the advisor trustworthy, and has confidence in his or her own judgment. (b) Clients *reject* the advice when they neither think that the option is good nor trust the advisor. These two cases are trivial. More interesting are the next two cases. (c) A client might *accept* the option recommended by the advisor although he or she personally evaluates the option negatively, but the advisor is perceived as trustworthy, and thus the client follows the advice. This pattern might be typical for situations when patients have to decide about a medical treatment: They think the recommended option is terrible, but they trust their doctor. (d) Clients might *reject* an option recommended by an advisor although they think it is a good one, but they do not trust the advisor. This pattern might be frequent in situations of financial investment, when the client can find no fault in the recommended fund, but has the feeling that the advisor's priority is selling this fund and not the satisfaction of the client. In these two cases, the client is in conflict between his or her own assessment of the quality of an option and the recommendation by an expert. We assume that a client generally follows a recommendation in situations like the ones discussed here simply because it is difficult for a client, due to the lack of expertise, to hold against an advisor's arguments in favor of the recommended option. Clients reject advice only if they have good reasons for distrust or if they have high confidence in their personal different opinion.

The influence of an expert's recommendation was demonstrated impressively in a recent study by Gurmankin, Baron, Hershey, and Ubel (2002) with 102 participants. The authors presented (on the World Wide Web) hypothetical treatment scenarios in which the treatment choice that maximized health was obvious. They varied physicians' recommendations across the scenarios in three ways: (a) physicians' recommendations supporting what maximized health, (b) physicians' recommendations that went against what maximized health, and (c) no physicians' recommendations. The data show that a significant number of participants' decisions were strongly influenced by experts' advice. Physicians' recommendations against the treatment that maximized health pulled subjects away from the treatment decision they made when no recommendation was given. This is the third case discussed in the previous paragraph: An expert's advice can lead people to make decisions that go against what is best and against what they would prefer without the advice. The authors also asked participants to provide reasons for their decisions from a list of eight alternatives developed from pilot studies. Of particular interest were their explanations when they followed the physicians' recommendation, whether the physician advised the best option or advised against it: "I believe the physician had important additional information that should influence my decision" (41%), "The physician had information about my risk that went beyond the data given in the question" (17%), "Physicians know best" (13%), "I don't like having the responsibility of making my own medical decision" (9%), "I don't trust myself to make the right decision" (6%). Clearly the participants in this study focused on the expert's advice and not on the options.

Experimental studies have shown that all four factors affect how people make use of advice. Although the experiments were run in different settings (mostly informational symmetry) and with different tasks (mostly probabilistic estimates), the structure of the relation between advisor and client allows a generalization of the findings. Sniezek and Buckley (1995) confirmed that advisors' assessments of the quality of their own advice do influence how advice is used by judges (as clients are called in this research paradigm). Harvey et al. (2000) showed that judges' use of advice is influenced by their assessments of its quality. Harvey and Fischer (1997) demonstrated that judges do take into account both their own and their advisors' levels of experience in the domain when deciding how much use to make of advice.

The four-factor model resembles the dual-process theories popular in research on persuasion: Petty and Cacioppo's (1986) elaboration-likelihood model and Chaiken's (1980) heuristic-systematic model. In both models, individuals are assumed to process a message carefully if they are motivated and able to do so. They use the central route or a strategy of systematic processing. Whether persuasion occurs is primarily determined by the strength of the argument. If individuals are unable or unmotivated to process carefully, they use the peripheral route or a strategy of heuristic processing; in that case, cues, heuristics, and other factors besides the pure consideration of the argument determine whether persuasion occurs. One important factor with this type has been shown to be the credibility of the source. In terms of our own model, in situations of low informational asymmetry (i.e., when clients are highly competent and involved), they focus on the options at stake, and the advisor's arguments and explanations of the given recommendation primarily determine the client's decision. In situations of high informational asymmetry (i.e., when clients have little knowledge in the domain), they focus on the advisor, and it is his or her credibility that primarily determine the client's decision.

The model suggests a number of questions. In particular, how are these factors weighted? They may contribute in a compensatory manner to the decision about how to use advice. It has been argued by many, however, that trust and credibility are often more important to decision makers than accuracy (i.e., more important than a thorough analysis of the advised option), implying a noncompensatory mechanism (e.g., March, 1994). In dyadic decision situations with informational asymmetry, trust and credibility bridge the gap that exists between expert and laypeople with respect to the matter to be decided, and we may therefore assume that trust and credibility play a key role. There is a large body of research on the role of trust and credibility in social interaction, of course, but few studies have looked at their role in advisor–client interactions. In a large survey, Oehler (1995) found that the quality of advisors in a bank were rated as much more important by customers than the bank's conditions and offers. Trust depends on the experience of failures and successes in the past. Yaniv and Kleinberger (2000) observed that positive and negative reputational information gathered across a series of episodes had a differential impact on the resulting weighting policy. Advisors' reputations were rapidly formed and asymmetrically revised. A poor advisor was discounted more than a good advisor was credited in the process of weighting. However, clients often do not have experience of failures and successes (e.g., a patient confronting surgery, parents considering amniocentesis). Other factors then become important, such as how much confidence an advisor has in his or her judgment. Sniezek and Buckley (1995) found that in the case of a disagreement between two advisors, judges gave more weight to the opinion of the advisor who expressed his opinion with more confidence. Other factors are how good the advisor can explain the recommendation or how carefully the advisor tries to fine tune the recommendation to the individual needs and wants of the client. The general credibility of the institution can also become a significant factor.

SOME CONCLUSIONS AND SUGGESTIONS

In certain dyadic decision situations, we find informational asymmetry between the persons involved. This is the case when an expert is asked for advice by a decision maker who has no expertise in the domain where a decision must be made (e.g., when a doctor is asked by a patient or when an investment consultant is asked by a client). The advisor generally has more relevant knowledge than the client or else the client would not demand the consultant's advice.

Because of this informational asymmetry, consultants need not and clients cannot apply an optimizing decision strategy in the usual sense (i.e., explore the set of possible options, and identify and choose the best one). Advisors can use their expertise and experience to use a client-focused pattern-matching strategy that helps them categorize the client and find the matching option(s). Clients must base their decision more on trust in the advisors and their institutions than on analysis, and consequently they use an advisor-focused strategy that helps them decide whether to accept or reject the advice. These strategies represent generally efficient mental short cuts for both advisors and clients, saving them an unnecessary or impossible search for the best option. Both strategies can become dysfunctional of course: if advisors apply the pattern-matching strategy automatically, without considering the specific case, and if patients or investors blindly follow the advice they are given only because they trust the advisor.

An interesting question is what advisors think about their clients' strategy and what clients believe about their advisors' strategy. We assume that both advisors and clients have some insight into their own strategy: Advisors are aware that they often do not check all possible options, but treat their patient or client as "a case" (heart insufficiency, neurodermitis, etc.; married teacher with two kids) at least in the beginning. Clients look for and stay with the doctor they trust because she was the family doctor since childhood or because they have had good experiences with him for a long time. We assume further that both also have a pretty good idea of the other's strategy: Advisors know about the importance of trust and credibility as decisive factors for their clients' decisions, and they spend as much effort on building trust and credibility as on generating good advice. Clients are aware that they are primarily cases, and not individuals, for the advisor. However, neither advisors nor clients would probably agree with this description because they both would feel that this represents a suboptimal solution to the problem: The optimal solution is the search for the best of all options. This is the declared common goal of the interaction. Because this strategy is practically inefficient for the advisor and practically impossible for the client, they use a strategy that is nonoptimal from a strict decision-theoretic point of view. The discrepancy between the official strategy and actual strategies produces those strange dialogues between patients and doctors in a hospital or clients and investment advisors in a bank, in which both parties pretend to rationally discuss all relevant information and explore all options, but know quite well that the decision process runs differently.

We have said that advisors need not and that clients cannot use the rational optimizing strategy. Maybe they should apply a decision analytic approach. Probably not, according to Fischhoff (1985) and, in particular, Ubel and Loewenstein (1997), who analyzed precisely and convincingly the difficulties and weaknesses of the decision analytic approach for the interaction between doctor and patient if the patient's signature of his or her informed consent is required. Yet the analysis of the situation and the empirical data presented in this chapter do not offer a better recipe for prescription or optimization. How should advisors advise and how should clients decide if they want "to do their best"? It may generally be easier to develop criteria and tools for designing advice-giving-and-taking interaction for advisors than for clients. Advisors can be provided with sound knowledge through instruction or a technical database, and this knowledge could help them optimize a pattern-matching strategy as a first screening-strategy, which then may be followed by a more thorough analysis of the individual case. Such strategies have been proposed, for instance, by Beach (1990). Advisors can also be trained to communicate their strategy, explain their recommendation, and offer alternatives. Clients could be helped by explicitly distinguishing the relevant attributes of the available options and the weights one could give them. Also clients could be supported by documenting the decision process, and thus giving them a chance to discuss the situation with others. Furthermore, they should be encouraged to demand a second (expert's) opinion. Most important, we may need primarily "support systems that guide people to appropriate sources of advice" (Harvey et al., 2000, p. 271). The "appropriate sources" would be trustworthy agencies—institutions that do not pursue their own interests, but whose only goal is to provide information and give advice. Such institutions exist, for instance, in the health domain.

REFERENCES

Beach, L. R. (1990). *Image theory: Decision making in personal and organizational contexts.* Chichester, England: Wiley.

Chaiken, S. (1980). Heuristic versus systematic information processing and the use of source versus message cues in persuasion. *Journal of Personality and Social Psychology, 39,* 752–766.

Cherubini, P., Mazzocco, K., & Rumiati, R. (2003). Rethinking the focusing effect in decision-making. *Acta Psychologica, 113,* 67–81.

Fischer, K. (2002). *Wenn guter Rat teuer ist. Patienten-Entscheidungen im medizinischen Kontext* [When wisdom is precious: Patients' decisions in a medical context]. Paper presented at the 43 Kongress der Deutschen Gesellschaft für Psychologie, Berlin, Germany.

Fischhoff, B. (1985). Cognitive and institutional barriers to "informed consent." In M. Gibson (Ed.), *To breathe freely* (pp. 169–185). Totowa, NJ: Rowan & Allanheld.

Gurmankin, A., Baron, J., Hershey, J. C., & Ubel, P. A. (2002). The role of physicians' recommendations in medical treatment decisions. *Medical Decision Making, 22,* 262–271.

Harvey, N., & Fischer, I. (1997). Taking advice: Accepting help, improving judgment, and sharing responsibility. *Organizational Behavior and Human Decision Processes, 70,* 117–133.

Harvey, N., Harries, C., & Fischer, I. (2000). Using advice and assessing its quality. *Organizational Behavior and Human Decision Processes, 81,* 252–273.

Jonas, E., & Frey, D. (2003). Information search and presentation in advisor-client interactions. *Organizational Behavior and Human Decision Processes, 91,* 154–168.

Jungermann, H. (1999). *Advice giving and taking.* Proceedings of the 32nd Hawaii International Conference on System Science (HICSS-32), Institute of Electrical and Electronics Engineers, Inc. (IEEE), Maui, Hawaii.

Kahneman, D., & Miller, D. T. (1986). Norm theory: Comparing reality to its alternatives. *Psychological Review, 93,* 136–153.

Keeney, R. L., & Raiffa, H. (1976). *Decisions with multiple objectives: Preferences and value-tradeoffs.* New York: Wiley.

Klein, G. A. (1989). Recognition-primed decisions. In W. B. Rouse (Ed.), *Advances in man-machine system research* (Vol. 5, pp. 47–92). Greenwich, CT: JAI Press.

Kray, L. J. (2000). Contingent weighting in self-other decision making. *Organizational Behavior and Human Decision Processes, 83,* 82–106.

Legrenzi, P., Girotto, V., & Johnson-Laird, P. N. (1993). Focusing in reasoning and decision-making. *Cognition, 49,* 37–66.

Lipshitz, R., Klein, G., Orasanu, J., & Salas, E. (2001). Taking stock of Naturalistic Decision Making. *Journal of Behavioral Decision Making, 14,* 331–352.

March, J. G. (1994). *A primer on decision making.* New York: The Free Press.

Oehler, A. (1995). *Die Erklärung des Verhaltens privater Anleger* [The explanation of private investors' behavior]. Stuttgart: Schäffer-Poeschel Verlag.

Petty, R. E., & Cacioppo, J. T. (1986). The elaboration likelihood model of persuasion. In L. Berkowitz (Ed.), *Advances in experimental social psychology* (Vol. 19, pp. 123–205). Orlando: Academic Press.

Sniezek, J. A. (1999). *Judge advisor systems theory and research and applications to collaborative systems and technology.* Proceedings of the 32nd Hawaii International Conference on System

Science (HICSS-32), Institute of Electrical and Electronics Engineers, Inc. (IEEE), Maui, Hawaii.

Sniezek, J. A., & Buckley, T. (1995). Cueing and cognitive conflict in judge-advisor decision making. *Organizational Behavior and Human Decision Processes, 62*, 159–174.

Sniezek, J. A., & van Swol, L. M. (2001). Trust, confidence, and expertise in a judge-advisor system. *Organizational Behavior and Human Decision Processes, 84*, 288–307.

Ubel, P. A., & Loewenstein, G. (1997). The role of decision analysis in informed consent: Choosing between intuition and systematicity. *Social Science and Medicine, 44*, 647–656.

Yaniv, I., & Kleinberger, E. (2000). Advice taking in decision making: Egocentric discounting and reputation formation. *Organizational Behavior and Human Decision Processes, 83*, 260–281.

10

Positive and Negative Transfer Effects in Groups

Torsten Reimer
Anne-Louise Bornstein
Klaus Opwis
Department of Psychology, University of Basel

In the literature on group decision making and problem solving, it is often mentioned but rarely tested that groups may benefit from developing routines (Gersick & Hackman, 1990). In particular, routines may help groups effectively reduce coordination requirements when solving interdependent tasks. A group that has developed a routine for solving a problem does not have to negotiate about each new task and about which group member will carry out which single step of the task (Malone & Crowstone, 1994). However, as we know from the literature on learning transfer (VanLehn, 1996) and routine decision making (Betsch, Haberstroh, & Hoehle, 2002), acquiring a routine sometimes impairs rather than improves performance. Such a negative learning transfer is most likely if problem solvers are provided with a novel task that shares surface features with the learning task but requires a different problem solution (VanLehn, 1989). If the acquisition of a routine leads to improved group performance, crucial to continued improvement is whether groups are able to detect changes in the task environment and adequately respond to novel task demands. Are groups more likely than individuals to detect such changes and adapt their routine to novel tasks?

On the one hand, there are studies indicating that groups outperform individuals in error correction, which may help groups cope with a situation in which their routine must be performed out of order. For example, Michaelsen, Watson, and Black (1989) reported empirical evidence that groups outperformed their best group members in multiple-choice tests on various tasks. Stasson and Bradshaw (1995) confirmed these results in the domain of mathematical reasoning. In a similar vein, Hinsz (1990), who used a memory task, also found that groups were more effective in error checking than individuals. From this perspective, groups may be more likely to adapt their routine to a task that requires different problem-solving procedures. On the other hand, research on group decision making has also revealed that effects that occur in individuals are often enhanced if decisions are made by homogeneous groups in which group members share common strategies (Hinsz, Tindale, & Vollrath, 1997). In accordance with this general finding, our studies aimed at testing the claim that transfer effects are stronger in homogeneous groups than in individuals because of systematic differences in the way groups and individuals adapt their routine to novel tasks. The persistency hypothesis assumes that homogeneous groups, in which group members share a routine, are in general more likely to stick to their acquired routine than individuals. This assumption of systematic differences in inertia is based on studies demonstrating that groups tend to accentuate preferences or decisions that are held by a majority (Hinsz et al., 1997). However, if groups use strategies more reliably and consistently than individuals, transfer effects should also be enhanced in homogeneous groups, irrespective of whether this transfer is positive or negative.

TRANSFER EFFECTS IN INDIVIDUALS

In general, transfer effects are most likely to occur if problem solvers have routinized a problem-solving procedure that they can easily apply to a novel task. Typically, problem-solving procedures that are routinized have been applied repeatedly and do not need extensive consideration. Such routines are usually linked to a certain class of problems and come to mind as an option when the problem solver recognizes a particular decision problem (for an overview on various definitions, see Betsch et al., 2002; Betsch, Haberstroh, Glöckner, Haar, & Fiedler, 2001; for a distinction between routines and habits, also see Verplanken, Myrbakk, & Rudi, chap. 13, this volume; Sanbonmatsu, Prince, Vanous, & Posavac, chap. 6, this volume). Problem solvers who have access to a routine tend to transfer their routine to novel but similar tasks. In general, routines are likely to be transferred to novel tasks if the transfer and learning tasks are perceived as similar (Ross, 1989). However, whether using a routine is a good idea and whether the acquisition of a routine enhances or impairs performance depends on the structural similarity between the transfer and learning tasks.

Accordingly, in the literature on learning transfer (VanLehn, 1989), two forms of transfer are distinguished: A *positive transfer effect* arises if the acquisition of a routine enhances performance compared with a control condition. Positive transfer requires that a problem solver chooses an appropriate routine (schema selection), that this routine is properly adapted to the transfer task (instantiation), and that it is correctly executed (execution). Hence, positive transfer is most likely to occur if participants are presented with tasks that share surface features as well as problem spaces and problem solutions. Transfer tasks can then be solved by analogy, which usually does not require an exhaustive understanding of problems (Van-Lehn, 1996). Compared with problem solving by analogy, gaining positive transfer effects is more challenging when problem isomorphs are provided that consist of different stimuli (Kotovsky, Hayes, & Simon, 1985; Ross, 1989). In this situation, positive transfer may be facilitated by fostering self-explanations and self-monitoring (Chi, Bassok, Lewis, Reimann, & Glaser, 1989; Chi, de Leeuw, Chiu, & LaVancher, 1994), which enables problem solvers to develop more abstract schemata that are dissociated from the specific contents of the learning task.

However, in the literature on learning transfer, there is also evidence that acquiring a routine can impair performance by forming an *Einstellung* that narrows the search for alternative problem solutions (see VanLehn, 1989, 1996, for various examples). In analogy to the concept of positive transfer, negative transfer may be defined by a situation in which the knowledge of a routine results in a worse performance compared with a control condition. *Negative transfer effects* are most likely to occur when participants are presented with identical stimuli in the training and the testing phase but different responses are expected. In these situations, a problem solver may not notice a change in task demands and insist on an inappropriate routine. The classic experiments by Luchins (1942) on the water-jug problem provide a conclusive example for the existence of such a "familiarity effect" that may impair performance. In these experiments, problem solvers were given a series of problems that could be solved by the same sequence of operations. After a while, participants were given a novel task for which an alternative, simpler sequence of operations existed. However, many problem solvers still used their routine, which they had successfully applied before, without becoming aware of the change in task demands (see also Betsch et al., 2001; Haberstroh, Betsch, Gloeckner, Haar, & Stiller, chap. 12, this volume, for a further example of a negative transfer effect).

TRANSFER EFFECTS IN GROUPS

What do we expect if we apply this approach on positive and negative transfer effects to a group context? Can we make any predictions on whether such transfer effects are enhanced or diminished when a group is faced with a transfer task? The literature on group decision making suggests that there are systematic differences in how individuals and groups adapt a routine to novel tasks. More specifically, there is strong evidence that homogeneous groups tend to make more reliable and consistent decisions compared with individuals. As Hinsz et al. (1997) demonstrated in their review on information processing in groups, homogeneous groups often accentuate decisions made by the single group members. In general, if individuals process information in a specific (and even biased) way, homogeneous groups usually tend to show an even stronger bias. However, if a bias or tendency is unlikely to occur in individuals, it is even less likely that this effect will appear in groups. For example, Nagao, Tindale, Hinsz, and Davis (1985) studied group effects on the neglect of base rates when giving probability judgments. If a group consisted of individuals who tended to neglect base rates, this effect was facilitated by the group setting—that is, the groups neglected base rates to a greater extent than individuals. In a similar vein, Argote, Devadas, and Melone (1990) showed that groups tend to overuse representativeness information—an effect that was also common among their individuals.

The accentuation approach also provides a feasible framework from which to derive predictions on transfer effects in problem-solving groups. More specifically, the rationale of our empirical studies was based on the following consideration: If groups use strategies and heuristics more reliably and consistently than individuals, transfer effects should also be enhanced in groups, irrespective of whether this transfer is positive or negative. Thus, according to the persistency hypothesis, stronger transfer effects should occur in groups than in individuals.

What follows from this with regard to performance? According to the persistency hypothesis, group performance depends on whether a positive or negative transfer effect occurs in individuals: If a transferred routine is appropriate and if we therefore expect positive transfer in individuals, homogeneous groups should surpass the individuals. However, if an inappropriate routine is applied by individuals causing a negative transfer effect, the persistency hypothesis predicts worse performance in groups than in individuals. That is, in the case of positive transfer, bonus effects are expected in the group, and in the case of negative transfer, process losses should arise.

In what follows, we describe an empirical study that supports the persistency hypothesis in a problem-solving context. First, we introduce an experimental task that was developed to test these predictions on transfer effects in groups by asking participants to solve Tower of Hanoi problems either individually or in pairs (Reimer, 2001a, 2001b). Transfer effects were produced by first teaching individuals one of two different procedures for solving the Tower of Hanoi problem. Next, participants were asked to solve several transfer tasks either individually or in pairs. Whereas one of the two routines could be directly applied to the transfer tasks (positive transfer), the second routine led to a long detour (negative transfer).

THE EXPERIMENTAL TASK

The Tower of Hanoi problem consists of three pegs and a fixed number of disks of different sizes (Simon, 1975). The original task is to move all the disks from the left to the right peg under the following constraints (see Fig. 10.1): (a) Only one disk may be moved at a time, (b) only the disk that is on the top of the pyramid may be moved, and (c) a larger disk may never be placed on top of a smaller disk. A problem with n disks requires a minimum of $2^n - 1$ moves.

There are several procedures that guarantee an optimal solution of the Tower of Hanoi problem (Simon, 1975). To produce transfer effects, we first taught participants one of two procedures (described next): either the goal-recursion (R) or the move-pattern procedure (M). These procedures differ in two aspects that make them suitable for studying transfer effects within the Tower of Hanoi problem: (a) Only the R procedure and not the M procedure can be directly applied to a transfer task in which the start peg is the middle peg. Hence, for a person who acquired the R procedure, positive transfer should arise, whereas negative transfer should occur if somebody has learned the M procedure. (b) The two procedures lead to different pat-

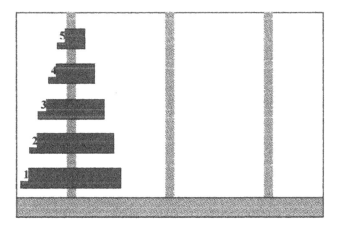

FIG. 10.1. The Tower of Hanoi problem, as presented on a computer screen for a problem with five disks. A disk could be moved by clicking on the disk first and then on the peg to which it should be moved. If a player tried to move a disk onto a smaller disk an error message appeared on the screen. All disks were numbered throughout to make it easier to apply the move-pattern procedure (see text for description).

terns of move latencies. Thus, differences in move latencies can be used as an indicator of which procedure was applied and to what extent problem solvers insisted on their routine.

The Goal-Recursion Procedure

The R procedure is based on a chunking strategy. Each problem with $n > 1$ disks can be decomposed into three subproblems (see Fig. 10.2): (a) a problem consisting of $n - 1$ disks, (b) a problem consisting of moving the largest disk from the start peg onto the goal peg, and (c) a second problem consisting of $n - 1$ disks.

For example, the five-disk problem in Fig. 10.1 can be decomposed into two four-disk problems and the move of a single disk: (a) First, the four-disk pyramid (consisting of disks 2–5) has to be moved from the start peg onto the middle peg; (b) in the next step, the largest disk (number 1) can be moved onto the goal peg; and (c) finally, the four-disk pyramid has to be moved again, this time from the middle peg onto the goal peg. Further, the four-disk problem can also be decomposed into two three-disk problems and the move of a single disk. Thus, the R procedure is based on a chunking strategy by dividing a problem into subproblems until only one disk remains.

The Move-Pattern Procedure

The M procedure is based on a stimulus-driven instead of a goal-driven strategy, without the formulation of any subgoals. According to this procedure, one has to pay attention to the *position* of a disk and to its *parity* (see

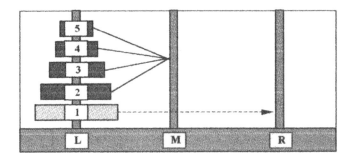

FIG. 10.2. The goal-recursion procedure (R). A five-disk problem can be simplified by decomposing the pyramid into two four-disk problems and one one-disk problem. In the first step, the marked four-disk pyramid, which is blocking the movement of the largest disk, should be moved onto the middle peg (first four-disk problem). In the second step, the largest disk (with the number 1) should be moved onto the goal peg (one-disk problem), and finally, the four-disk problem should be moved from the middle onto the right peg (second four-disk problem).

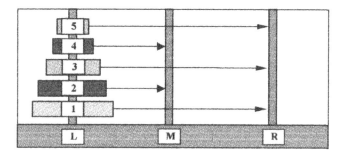

FIG. 10.3. The move-pattern procedure (M). The move-pattern procedure is based on the position and the parity of the disks. Odd-numbered disks are moved from the left to the right, from the middle to the left, and from the right to the middle. Even-numbered disks are moved the other way around, that is, from the left to the middle, from the middle to the right, and from the right to the left.

Fig. 10.3): Odd-numbered disks should always be moved from the left to the right, from the middle to the left, and from the right to the middle. Even-numbered disks are moved the other way around, from the left to the middle, from the middle to the right, and from the right to the left. Moreover, the same disk should never be moved twice in one row. This constraint guarantees that it is always clear which disk should be moved next.

According to the M procedure, the disk with the number 5 in Fig. 10.1 should be moved onto the right peg because it is an odd-numbered disk. Next, disk number 4 should be moved onto the middle peg because the same disk should never be moved twice in one row and because it is an even-numbered disk.

Original Versus Transfer Tasks

If all the rules are strictly adhered to, the two procedures lead to identical moves and to an optimal solution. This functional equivalence holds for any number of disks. However, this is only true as long as the start peg is the left peg. If the task is slightly modified by starting with the middle peg instead of the left peg, the R procedure still guarantees an optimal solution, whereas the M procedure results in a long detour. The M procedure can be applied to such a transfer task, but it requires twice as many moves as the goal-recursion procedure. To solve this new task with the M procedure, the entire tower must be moved first onto the left peg and then onto the right peg. To ensure this difference, we slightly changed the original move-pattern procedure, which is not restricted to a certain start or goal peg (Simon, 1975), by linking the move patterns to the left, middle, and right peg instead of the start and the goal peg.

How can this setting be used to produce positive and negative transfer effects? Because both procedures guarantee an optimal problem solution with original tasks, problem solvers who learn either the R or M procedure should gain from their knowledge and should solve the original tasks almost perfectly. However, expectations for transfer tasks differ with respect to the two procedures: The acquisition of the R procedure should foster positive transfer, whereas negative transfer should occur among problem solvers who have routinized the usage of the M procedure because, in the latter condition, problem solvers are provided with a similar set of stimuli for which the acquired routine is no longer appropriate.

Move Latencies as an Indicator of the Strategy Applied

Although the two procedures lead to identical moves with original tasks, they differ in the amount of planning required and therefore result in different patterns of move latencies (Reimer, 2001a). If the M procedure is applied, the cognitive effort is almost the same for all moves (even though the decision as to which disk should be moved next may vary among different game situations). Thus, a player who applies the M procedure moves disks relatively regularly. According to the R procedure, however, at the very beginning as well as in situations in which a new subtower has to be solved, extensive planning is required. These "first moves" should take a long time, whereas subsequent moves (i.e., all other moves) should be carried out quickly to execute the planned recursion smoothly without extensive interruptions. Hence, ideally, applying the R procedure results in high latencies for the first moves and short latencies for subsequent moves.

In general, the extent to which a player spends more time on first moves than on subsequent moves can be quantified by the following strategy index (S):

$$S = FM \: / \: SM,$$

where FM is the mean time for first moves and SM is the mean time for subsequent moves. Because the two procedures differ in the extent of chunking and planning, on average, participants who are taught the R procedure score higher on the strategy index than participants who are taught the M procedure ($S_R > S_M$). Thus, the strategy index may also be used as a measure of the extent to which participants in the M condition change their strategy to a chunking strategy when solving transfer tasks.

EMPIRICAL EVIDENCE FOR THE PERSISTENCY HYPOTHESIS

In what follows, we describe a study that was designed to (a) test for differences in performance between pairs and individuals and, in particular, to test whether bonus effects occur in the R condition and process losses in the M condition (*performance hypothesis*); (b) test the claim that pairs insist more strongly on their procedure than do individuals, which should result in a lower (higher) strategy index for the M pairs (R pairs) than the M individuals (R individuals) (*persistency hypothesis*); and (c) assess to what extent the potential differences in performance are mediated by the strategy index (*mediation hypothesis*). In this study (see Reimer, 2001a, for details), groups always consisted of group members who had been taught the same procedure (homogeneous groups). Group members moved in turns throughout and had no opportunity to communicate with each other. The issues of group composition and communication are addressed later.

Overview of the Study

The design consisted of three factors. First, participants were individually taught either the R or M procedure (factor procedure). Second, participants solved problems either individually (I) or in pairs (P) (factor group). Finally, type of task was varied as a within-subjects factor (original vs. transfer tasks). The 90 students who participated in the study were randomly distributed among experimental conditions (15 pairs in the conditions R–P and M–P and 15 individuals in the conditions R–I and M–I).

Each participant first was individually taught the R or M procedure and then completed a computerized training run on the respective procedure. In the testing phase, participants were asked to solve two original and two transfer tasks (one four- and one five-disk problem each) in as few moves as possible. The opportunity to correct or undo moves by moving a disk twice in a row was explicitly mentioned in the instructions. If a person tried to place a larger disk on top of a smaller one, an error message appeared on the screen.

Performance: Number of Moves

For the following analyses, measures were aggregated across the four- and five-disk problems throughout. Problems with four disks are solvable in 15 moves, and problems with five disks require 31 moves. Thus, the minimum number of moves is 23 irrespective of the task condition—that is, regardless of whether original or transfer tasks are solved.

TABLE 10.1
Means of the Number of Moves and of the Strategy Index
According to Procedure (Goal Recursion vs. Move Pattern),
Group (Individuals vs. Pairs), and Task (Original vs. Transfer Tasks)

| | Goal Recursion | | Move Pattern | |
Problem	Individuals	Pairs	Individuals	Pairs
	Number of Moves			
Original problem				
M	24.83	23.47	25.87	23.50
SD	3.79	0.72	4.53	0.60
Transfer problem				
M	25.20	23.57	39.97	46.77
SD	5.14	0.73	7.07	9.84
	Strategy Index			
Original problem				
M	1.16	1.08	1.04	1.02
SD	0.04	0.04	0.03	0.02
Transfer problem				
M	1.18	1.09	1.10	1.02
SD	0.04	0.03	0.09	0.04
N	15	15	15	15

Table 10.1 shows the mean number of moves that were required by the individuals and pairs. As expected, an analysis of variance (ANOVA) with the factors procedure (R vs. M), group (I vs. P), and task (original vs. transfer tasks) revealed an interaction of task × procedure [$F(1,56) = 115.51$; $p < .01$].

Whereas in the goal-recursion condition, the original tasks as well as the transfer tasks were solved very well (Moriginal = 24.15; Mtransfer = 24.38), in the move-pattern condition, many more moves were required for the transfer than for the original tasks (Moriginal = 24.68; Mtransfer = 43.37). This result indicates a positive transfer effect in the R condition and a negative transfer effect in the M condition.[1] The negative transfer effect also caused the two main effects of procedure and task (see Table 10.1): Overall, participants performed less well in the M condition than in the R condition, and the transfer tasks were solved less well than the original tasks. However, in

[1]In the Introduction, transfer effects were defined by differences in performance between a learning condition and a control condition. A follow-up study (Reimer, 2002), in which a control condition was included, confirmed that the number of moves that were required for solving the transfer tasks was higher (lower) in the M condition (R condition) than in the control condition, in which participants had not been taught any procedure.

accordance with the persistency hypothesis, there were also differences between the M pairs and M individuals. The M pairs had much more difficulty solving the transfer tasks than the M individuals. In the remaining three conditions, a ceiling effect occurred indicating that both procedures had been learned very well. However, the few errors that arose in these conditions can be attributed almost exclusively to the individuals. Thus, whenever the participants had access to an appropriate routine, the pairs tended to outperform the individuals. This pattern is also in accordance with the persistency hypothesis. Overall, the pairs required fewer moves than the individuals within the original tasks, and the R pairs also tended to outperform the R individuals within the transfer tasks.

Are the observed process losses in the M pairs really due to differences in persistency? This question was addressed by three measures: the strategy index, the number of moves that were in accordance with the M procedure (M moves), and the number of correcting moves (CMs). Because of the ceiling effect in the R condition, the following analyses on differences between pairs and individuals in persistency and on the mediation hypothesis were restricted to the M condition.

Move Latencies

Because the distribution of latencies was positively skewed, each latency per move was transformed first by taking the logarithm. As expected, participants in the R condition had much higher strategy indices than participants in the M condition throughout (see Table 10.1). This holds true for original tasks as well as for transfer tasks.

An ANOVA on the strategy index within the M condition revealed a main effect of group, indicating higher strategy indices for the individuals than for the pairs throughout. This main effect (which also occurred in the R condition; see Table 10.1) may be explained by the time required by the pairs when taking turns. Additionally, there was also a significant main effect of type of task. Overall, participants showed higher strategy indices when solving transfer tasks compared with original tasks. However, the two main effects were also qualified by a significant interaction [$F(1,28) = 5.16$; $p < .05$]. As can be seen in Table 10.1, the M individuals had a much higher strategy index in the transfer tasks than in the original tasks [$t(14) = 2.70$; $p < .05$], whereas the M pairs did not change the way in which they structured the problem-solving process [$t(14) = 0.44$; ns]. This result is in line with the persistency hypothesis: The M individuals tried to change to a chunking strategy, whereas the M pairs did not significantly change the way they structured the problem-solving process.

TABLE 10.2
Intercorrelations Between the Number of Moves (Criterion) and the
Predictors (Strategy Index, SI, Latencies for First Moves, FM, and Latencies
for Subsequent Moves, SM) and β Coefficients of a Stepwise Regression
Analysis Within the Move-Pattern Condition (Transfer Tasks)

Variable	Number of Moves	SI	FM	SM	β
Individuals					
Number of moves	—				
SI	−.73**	—			−.73**
FM	−.67**	.87**	—		−.15
SM	.23	−.41	.09	—	−.08
M	39.97	1.10	3.73	3.40	
SD	7.07	0.09	0.26	0.13	
Pairs					
Number of moves	—				
SI	−.66**	—			−.66**
FM	−.57*	.90**	—		.09
SM	.28	−.38	.08	—	.04
M	46.77	1.02	4.25	4.15	
SD	9.84	0.04	0.15	0.07	

Note. Only the strategy index (SI) entered the regression equation.
R^2 (individuals) = .53; R^2 (pairs) = .43.
*$p < .05$. **$p < .01$.

To show that the observed process losses in the M condition are due to these differences in persistency, an analysis of covariance (ANCOVA) on the number of moves was run using the strategy index as a covariate. This analysis revealed that the observed process losses disappear if differences in the strategy index are controlled. As we demonstrated earlier, the M pairs performed less well than the M individuals ($F = 4.72$; $p < .05$). The two conditions also differed in their strategy index ($F = 9.78$; $p < .01$). Additionally, the strategy index was related to performance ($F = 22.72$; $p < .01$; see Table 10.2). When the effect of the strategy index on the number of moves was statistically controlled, the differences in performance between the M pairs and M individuals vanished ($F = 0.89$; ns). Hence, the process losses in the M pairs were mediated by the strategy index.

Number of Move-Pattern Moves and of Correcting Moves

As a further measure of the extent of persistency, we additionally classified each single move as to whether it was in accordance with (move-pattern moves, MMs) or contradicted (no MMs) the move pattern described by the

TABLE 10.3
Mean Number of Move-Pattern Moves (MMs) and Correcting Moves (CMs)
in the Move-Pattern Condition (Transfer Tasks)

| | Individuals | | Pairs | | |
Variable	M	SD	M	SD	t
Number of moves	39.97	7.07	46.77	9.84	−2.17*
Number of MMs	29.37	13.29	41.87	16.05	−2.32*
Number of moves that are not MMs	10.60	6.90	4.90	7.59	2.15*
Number of CMs	1.43	1.07	3.07	2.20	−2.59*
Number of correct CMs	0.93	0.68	1.53	0.88	−2.10*
Number of wrong CMs	0.50	0.63	1.53	1.59	−2.35*

Note. *$p < .05$.

M procedure. As is shown in Table 10.3, which refers to the transfer tasks, overall, the M pairs carried out relatively more moves that were in accordance with the M procedure than did the M individuals [interaction of group (individuals vs. pairs) × move (MMs vs. no MMs): $F(1,28) = 5.34$; $p < .05$].

Research on group decision making has shown that the group context can enhance performance by facilitating effective error-checking strategies (e.g., Hinsz, 1990; Stasson & Bradshaw, 1995). To test for differences in the quantity and quality of mutual corrections, we separately analyzed the corrections of single moves (see Table 10.3). A move can be defined as a correcting move (CM) if a disk is moved twice in a row. Note that a correcting move may be either correct ("correct CM") or wrong ("wrong CM"). Such a classification is possible because the distance to the goal state can be computed for each single state of the game—that is, the minimum number of moves that are required to solve the problem. This distance was computed twice, once before and once after each CM. Then three situations can be distinguished: (a) The number of required moves is diminished by one step (correct CM); (b) this number does not change; or (c) after a CM one more move is required than before. All moves of Conditions (b) and (c) were classified as wrong CMs—that is, CMs that did not diminish the number of required moves.

As the single comparisons in Table 10.3 show, the M pairs corrected more moves overall and carried out more correct as well as wrong CMs. However, whereas the individuals had many more correct than wrong CMs, these two numbers did not differ in the pair condition. Thus, the relative frequency of correct CMs was much higher in the M individuals than in the M pairs, indicating that the pairs compensated less well for errors than did the individuals.

ARE THE PROCESS LOSSES DUE
TO PERSISTENCY OR DISTRACTION?

The study corroborates the claim that homogeneous groups differ from individuals in the way they react to changes in the environment by adapting a routine to novel tasks. First, as expected, the experimental paradigm instigated positive as well as negative transfer effects in individuals, thus providing a useful framework for testing the proposed hypotheses on transfer effects in groups. Whereas participants who had been taught the goal-recursion procedure did not have any serious problems solving the transfer tasks (positive transfer), within the move-pattern condition a negative transfer effect occurred. Second, in accordance with the expected differences in performance, the M pairs performed worse on the transfer tasks than did the M individuals, which supports the performance hypothesis.

Can the observed process losses also be explained by mutual distraction? A very powerful approach to explaining process losses in problem-solving groups rests on the simple assumption that group members distract each other when solving problems or making decisions. According to the distraction hypothesis, process losses often arise because paying attention to other group members may diminish cognitive capacity and cognitive effort that should be allocated to the task at hand to find a reasonable problem solution (Baron, 1986; Hinsz et al., 1997; Reimer, 2001a). Distraction effects are most likely if cognitive load is high because of task difficulty and coordination load. However, in the current setting, the observed process losses do not seem to be due to mere mutual distraction in the pairs. It cannot be ruled out that participants distracted each other when joining a dyad, but it is unlikely that such distraction was mainly responsible for the poor performance in the M pairs. If this were the case, similar process losses should have been observed in the other pair conditions, too. Rather, the results may be better explained by differences in persistency: Measures of the move latencies, the number of move-pattern moves, and the quality of corrections uniformly indicate that the M pairs needed many more moves to solve the transfer tasks because they insisted more strongly on using their routine than did the M individuals, who reacted much more flexibly and tried to adopt a chunking strategy. Moreover, the finding that the dyads performed better than the individuals when their acquired routine was appropriate also rules out that strong distractor effects appeared in the pairs throughout. However, it may be reasonable to assume that the M pairs insisted more strongly on their acquired routine because they expected severe mutual distraction if they tried to change and adapt their routine. From this study, it is not clear whether the dyads needed more time to become aware that their routine was no longer appropriate or whether they stuck to their routine to avoid coordination losses.

ARE THE PROCESS LOSSES DUE TO PERSISTENCY RESTRICTED TO HOMOGENEOUS GROUPS?

Interestingly, as another study revealed, participants who are taught the M procedure perform less well if they solve transfer tasks in uniform pairs (MM pairs) than in mixed pairs (MR pairs)—that is, when they join a participant who was taught the R procedure (see Reimer, Opwis, & Bornstein, 2002, for such a mixed-pair condition). However, despite these objective differences in performance, the M participants judged their performance to be much better when they solved problems in a uniform, MM, condition than in a mixed, MR, condition. Thus, it is reasonable to assume that it is the unanimity in particular that put the pairs at a disadvantage. According to this interpretation, persistency was fostered by the fact that both members had learned the same inappropriate procedure and that this unanimity diminished the likelihood that the M pairs would detect at an early stage of the problem-solving process that their routine was no longer appropriate.

In line with this reasoning, it should be stressed that the persistency hypothesis assumes that groups are homogeneous—that is, that a group comprises group members who share a common strategy. If groups are heterogeneous, the psychological processes may be totally different, in particular, if at least one group member knows the correct solution of a problem. In this case, performance more likely depends on whether this group member is able to demonstrate the correct solution (Laughlin & Ellis, 1986; for further evidence on the truth-wins principle, see Hinsz et al., 1997).

DOES THE PRINCIPLE OF INERTIA ALWAYS YIELD POOR GROUP DECISIONS?

Homogeneous groups often seem to behave like "ocean steamers," but this behavior may be adaptive and rational in the long run because groups often need much time and effort to work out an efficient problem-solving procedure. The most obvious advantage for a group in following the principle of inertia is in saving time and energy because routines need not be actively managed; subsequently, they reduce coordination requirements (Gersick & Hackman, 1990). In a situation in which changing a routine requires extensive coordination processes (high coordination load), it may be advisable to insist on a routine compared with a situation in which the adaptation of a routine is less resource consuming. In general, following the principle of inertia may be useful if the process losses due to persistency are less severe than the process losses due to coordination processes that are required by the adaptation of a routine. In line with this reasoning, it might be interesting to test whether groups consider those costs by testing whether coordination load moderates persistency in groups.

Moreover, in situations in which the ocean steamer is on the right course and a routine is appropriate, groups may be expected to surpass individuals by better compensating for individual errors and facilitating positive transfer (Hinsz et al., 1997). In the study presented earlier, the bonus effects were much weaker than the process losses due to a ceiling effect in the R condition. Thus, it would be worthwhile to further test the assumption that routine problem solving in groups may also enhance performance in situations in which group members have access to an appropriate routine. For example, studies on the simple heuristics approach (Gigerenzer & Goldstein, 1999; Gigerenzer, Todd, & the ABC Research Group, 1999) revealed that individuals often prefer to keep track of cues that were useful in prior decisions instead of exhaustively comparing all available information. The Take the Last (TTL) heuristic provides a powerful tool that yields robust and reasonable decisions in many choice tasks. With respect to this approach, it would be interesting to study whether groups use the TTL heuristic more reliably and consistently than individuals, which should help groups minimize coordination losses (for an application of other simple heuristics to the context of group decision making, see Reimer & Hoffrage, 2003; Reimer & Katsikopoulos, in press).

IS THE PRINCIPLE OF INERTIA RESTRICTED TO A SITUATION IN WHICH GROUP MEMBERS HAVE NO OPPORTUNITY TO COMMUNICATE WITH EACH OTHER?

Whether communication enhances or reduces the observed process losses may be another interesting issue for future research, likewise the question of whether the findings can be generalized to groups that consist of more than two members. In general, we can speculate that the larger the group, the stronger the transfer effects, assuming a group consists of homogeneous group members who share the same routine. Thus, there is no strong reason to assume that the observed persistency effects are restricted to dyads. This prediction rests on the finding in research on group decision making that the number of group members is correlated with the extent of accentuation (Hinsz et al., 1997). Accordingly, we can assume that the findings of this study should also generalize to larger homogeneous groups. As far as the communication issue is concerned, there is evidence that communication enhances performance in pairs who were not taught a routine, but who have to develop a common strategy for solving Tower of Hanoi problems (Reimer, Neuser, & Schmitt, 1997; Reimer, 2001a). In this study, the dyads had no opportunity to discuss or exchange their ideas. This may prevent groups from using effective error-checking methods and developing an appropriate procedure. Conversely, communication may also enhance the risk of mutual distraction, which can impair performance. Moreover, whether communication improves or impairs performance may depend on when a communication takes place. Whereas communication may be helpful in a situation in which a "first move" has to be set and in which planning is required (for empirical evidence, see Reimer, 2001a), it is possible that extensive communication in a phase of subsequent moves may impair performance by interrupting the problem-solving process. Because communication instigates meta-cognitive thinking (Brand, Reimer, & Opwis, 2003) and facilitates the development of abstract problem representations (Schwartz, 1995), it may also help groups to lower the risk of negative transfer. However, this does not necessarily mean that communication enhances individual performance on subsequent tasks (Laughlin & Sweeney, 1977) unless group members receive additional incentives for individual learning (see Slavin, 1995).

REFERENCES

Argote, L., Devadas, R., & Melone, N. (1990). The base-rate fallacy: Contrasting processes and outcomes of group and individual judgment. *Organizational Behavior and Human Decision Processes, 46*, 296–310.

Baron, R. S. (1986). Distraction–conflict theory: Progress and problems. *Advances in Experimental Social Psychology, 19*, 1–40.

Betsch, T., Haberstroh, S., Glöckner, A., Haar, T., & Fiedler, K. (2001). The effects of routine strength on adaptation and information search in recurrent decision making. *Organizational Behavior and Human Decision Making, 84*, 25–53.

Betsch, T., Haberstroh, S., & Hoehle, C. (2002). Explaining routinized decision making: A review of theories and models. *Theory & Psychology, 12*, 453–488.

Brand, S., Reimer, T., & Opwis, K. (2003). Effects of metacognitive thinking and knowledge acquisition in dyads on individual problem solving and transfer performance. *Swiss Journal of Psychology, 62*, 251–261.

Chi, M. T. H., Bassok, M., Lewis, M. W., Reimann, P., & Glaser, R. (1989). Self-explanations: How students study and use examples in learning to solve problems. *Cognitive Science, 13*, 145–182.

Chi, M. T. H., de Leeuw, N., Chiu, M. H., & LaVancher, C. (1994). Eliciting self-explanations improves understanding. *Cognitive Science, 18*, 439–477.

Gersick, C. J. G., & Hackman, J. R. (1990). Habitual routines in task-performing groups. *Organizational Behavior and Human Decision Processes, 47*, 65–97.

Gigerenzer, G., & Goldstein, D. G. (1999). Betting on one good reason: The take the best heuristic. In G. Gigerenzer, P. M. Todd, & the ABC Research Group (Eds.), *Simple heuristics that make us smart* (pp. 75–95). New York: Oxford University Press.

Gigerenzer, G., Todd, P. M., & the ABC Research Group. (1999). *Simple heuristics that make us smart*. New York: Oxford University Press.

Hinsz, V. B. (1990). Cognitive and consensus processes in group recognition memory performance. *Journal of Personality and Social Psychology, 59,* 705–718.

Hinsz, V. B., Tindale, R. S., & Vollrath, D. A. (1997). The emerging conceptualization of groups as information processors. *Psychological Bulletin, 121,* 43–64.

Kotovsky, K., Hayes, J. R., & Simon, H. A. (1985). Why are some problems hard? Evidence from Tower of Hanoi. *Cognitive Psychology, 17,* 248–294.

Laughlin, P. R., & Ellis, A. L. (1986). Demonstrability and social combination processes on mathematical intellective tasks. *Journal of Experimental Social Psychology, 22,* 177–189.

Laughlin, P. R., & Sweeney, J. D. (1977). Individual-to-group and group-to-individual transfer in problem solving. *Journal of Experimental Psychology: Human Learning and Memory, 3,* 246–254.

Luchins, A. S. (1942). Mechanization in problem solving—the effect of Einstellung. *Psychological Monographs, 54*(6), 95.

Malone, T. W., & Crowstone, K. (1994). The interdisciplinary study of coordination. *ACM Computing Surveys, 26*(1), 87–119.

Michaelsen, L. K., Watson, W. E., & Black, R. H. (1989). A realistic test of individual versus group consensus decision making. *Journal of Applied Psychology, 74,* 834–839.

Nagao, D. H., Tindale, R. S., Hinsz, V. B., & Davis, J. H. (1985). *Individual and group biases in information processing.* Paper presented at the 93rd annual convention of the American Psychological Association, Los Angeles, CA.

Reimer, T. (2001a). Kognitive Ansätze zur Vorhersage der Gruppenleistung: Distraktion, Kompensation und Akzentuierung. *Zeitschrift für Sozialpsychologie, 32*(2), 107–128.

Reimer, T. (2001b). Attributions for poor group performance as a predictor of perspective-taking and subsequent group achievement: A process model. *Group Processes and Intergroup Relations, 4,* 31–47.

Reimer, T. (2002). *Negativer Lerntransfer in Gruppen.* Paper presented at the 43rd meeting of the German Association of Psychology, Berlin.

Reimer, T., & Hoffrage, U. (2003). Information aggregation in groups: The approach of simple group heuristics (SIGH). In R. Alterman & D. Kirsch (Eds.), *Proceedings of the Twenty-Fifth Annual Conference of the Cognitive Science Society* (pp. 982–987). Boston: Cognitive Science Society.

Reimer, T., & Katsikopoulos, K. (in press). The use of recognition in group decision-making. *Cognitive Science.*

Reimer, T., Neuser, A., & Schmitt, C. (1997). Unter welchen Bedingungen erhöht die Kommunikation unter den Gruppenmitgliedern die Koordinationsleistung in einer Kleingruppe? *Zeitschrift für experimentelle Psychologie, 3,* 495–518.

Reimer, T., Opwis, K., & Bornstein, A.-L. (2002). Routine problem solving in groups. In W. Gray & C. Schunn (Eds.), *Proceedings of the Twenty-Fourth Annual Conference of the Cognitive Science Society* (pp. 780–785). Mahwah, NJ: Lawrence Erlbaum Associates.

Ross, B. (1989). Distinguishing types of superficial similarities: Different effects on the access and use of earlier problems. *Journal of Experimental Psychology: Learning, Memory, and Cognition, 13,* 629–639.

Schwartz, D. L. (1995). The emergence of abstract representation in dyad problem solving. *Journal of the Learning Sciences, 4,* 321–354.

Simon, H. A. (1975). The functional equivalence of problem solving skills. *Cognitive Psychology, 7,* 268–288.

Slavin, R. E. (1995). *Cooperative learning.* Boston: Allyn & Bacon.

Stasson, M. E., & Bradshaw, S. D. (1995). Explanations of individual–group performance differences. *Small Group Research, 26*(2), 296–308.

VanLehn, K. (1989). Problem solving and cognitive skill acquisition. In M. Posner (Ed.), *Foundations of cognitive science* (pp. 526–579). Cambridge, MA: MIT Press.

VanLehn, K. (1996). Cognitive skill acquisition. *Annual Review of Psychology, 47,* 513–539.

11

Mood and the Use of General Knowledge Structures in Judgment and Decision Making

Herbert Bless
Eric R. Igou
University of Mannheim, Germany

Perhaps with the exception of Mr. Spock from the USS Enterprise, presumably all of us have had the experience that our judgments and decisions are often influenced by our feelings. Not surprisingly, then, the notion that judgments and decisions are influenced by how we feel is not new at all. The scientific interest in this issue has manifested itself in a long tradition of philosophical speculation (e.g., Descartes, 1961/1649) and psychological thinking (e.g., Freud, 1940; James, 1890). Quite in line with Mr. Spock's view, most of these traditional positions hold that affect reduces individuals' ability to think rationally about the social world, and that affective states thus impair individuals' judgments and decisions (see Forgas, 2000). More recent research suggests, however, that affect is not necessarily creating irrationalities, but that affective states often provide a useful source for the regulation of cognitive processes. In the present chapter, we address this latter aspect by discussing how mood influences individuals' processing and decision-making strategies. Given the scope of the present chapter, we do not elaborate on other aspects on the interplay of affect and decision making (e.g., postdecisional affect, anticipated affect, or memories of past affects; for an overview, see Schwarz, 2000).

There is ample evidence that individuals' judgments and decisions reflect the valence of the affective state at the time of the judgment. For example, individuals in positive mood states seem to be more optimistic, overestimate the likelihood of positive events, and underestimate of the likelihood of negative events (e.g., Johnson & Tversky, 1983; Nygren, Isen, Tylor, & Dulin, 1996; see also Deldin & Levin, 1986). Such findings are complemented by vast evidence suggesting that evaluative judgments are congruent with individuals' affective state. On the one hand, it has been argued that mood-congruent judgments reflect the increased accessibility of mood-congruent information (Bower, 1981; Forgas, 1995). On the other hand, it has been suggested that individuals use their affective state as a source of information and rely on a "How do I feel about it?" heuristic (see Schwarz & Clore, 1988; Bless, 2001a, for a review of the two accounts). The general notion that individuals' affective states provide a basis for judgments and decisions is also captured by the "affect heuristic" (Slovic, Finucane, Peters, & MacGregor, 2002). The corresponding evidence suggests that the affect associated with a decision alternative may influence decisions, but also judgments of probabilities, risks, and benefits (see also Mellers, Schwartz, & Ritov, 1999).

Besides the notion that affect may serve as information that is either integrated with other information or even provides the only basis for judgments and decision, it is argued that affective states may influence how individuals form judgments and decisions. In this respect, much of the available evidence indicates that positive moods increase the reliance on heuristics, whereas moderately negative moods elicit more careful, step-by-step analyses (see Schwarz, 2000). For example, in the judgment and decision domain, results reported by Hertel and colleagues (Hertel, Neuhof, Theuer, & Kerr, 2000) suggest that positive affect increases the likelihood that individuals heuristically imitate the behavior of other players in a "chicken game," whereas negative affective states lead to more analytic reasoning on the moves and structure of the game. These results are consistent with the observation that negative mood states elicit more extensive processing and focusing on one attribute at a time (Luce, Bettman, & Payne, 1997). Moreover, investigating the impact of mood in a more applied domain of decision making, Elsbach and Barr (1999) reported that individuals in negative affective states more carefully executed the steps of a structured decision protocol. The general conclusion of more heuristic processing under positive moods and more analytic processing under negative moods is also in line with research by Isen and colleagues. This research, for example, demonstrated that happy participants showed faster and more efficient decision making (Isen & Means, 1983), reduced contentious strategies (Carnevale & Isen, 1986), and more creative solutions in problem solving (Isen, Daubman, & Nowicki, 1987; for overviews, see Isen, 1987, 1993).

Heuristics can be considered as general knowledge structures that are applied to specific situations. Such general knowledge structures may be related to different contents—for example, scripts (Abelson, 1981), stereotypes (Macrae & Bodenhausen, 2000), policies (Beach, 1990), habits (Verplanken et al., chap. 13, this volume), routines (Betsch, chap. 3, this volume,

Haberstroh et al., chap. 12, this volume), or content-free processing rules (see Fiske & Taylor, 1991). Independent of the various forms of general knowledge structures, it is suggested that these general knowledge structures may routinely be applied to specific situations, resulting in a "business as usual" procedure. As an alternative to such a processing strategy, individuals may rely less on their prior general knowledge, but attend more to the specifics of the situation at hand. In the present chapter, we propose that individuals' affective states influence the choice of these processing strategies. In general, individuals in happy moods are more likely to rely on general knowledge structures using a top–down strategy, whereas individuals in sad moods are more likely to rely on the specifics of the present situation using a bottom–up strategy. In the remainder of this chapter, we present evidence from various domains underlining this assumption. We first address general knowledge structures that comprise different contents (stereotypes, scripts, peripheral persuasive cues, prior judgments) and emphasize the relation between mood and content-free general knowledge in form of processing rules. We then address various theoretical accounts for the available evidence and discuss evidence that allows us to test competing predictions.

MOOD AND THE RELIANCE ON GENERAL KNOWLEDGE: A FIRST LOOK AT THE EMPIRICAL EVIDENCE

Mood and Stereotyping

When forming judgments about other persons, individuals may apply two different strategies (Fiske & Neuberg, 1990). On the one hand, judgments can be primarily based on the target person's category membership. In this case, judgments reflect the perceiver's general knowledge about the category to which the target is assigned (i.e., the implications of the stereotype). On the other hand, judgments may be primarily based on available individuating information about a specific target person. In this case, individuals cannot respond "as usual" (i.e., they cannot apply their general knowledge in form of stereotypes, but respond to the specifics of a given situation). In this case, the impact of category membership information is attenuated.

Distinguishing between category-based and individuating information-based judgments, a number of studies have investigated the relation between individuals' affective state and the impact of stereotypes on social judgments. For example, Bodenhausen, Kramer, and Süsser (1994) presented participants in different mood states with descriptions of an alleged student misconduct and asked participants to determine the target's guilt. Happy participants rated the offender as more guilty when he was identified as a member of a group stereotypically associated with the described offense than when this was not the case. This impact of the stereotype, however, was not observed for participants in a neutral mood. Similarly, Bodenhausen, Sheppard, and Kramer (1994) observed that sad participants were less affected by an applicable stereotype than neutral mood participants (for related evidence, see also Bless, Schwarz, & Wieland, 1996). Consistent with these findings, Forgas and Fiedler (1996) reported that happy individuals were more likely to rely on heuristic group category information in low-relevance intergroup situations. Thus, in summary, the available evidence suggests that stereotypes have more impact on individuals in a happy rather than a sad or neutral mood.

Mood and Brand Extensions

The conceptual logic of the stereotypes studies described earlier can be extended to other domains. For example, in the consumer domain, products can be evaluated on either specific attributes or implications of the brand image (Aaker & Keller, 1990) to which the product belongs. Investigating the impact of individuals' affective state, we provided happy, neutral, or sad mood participants with a detailed description of a newly launched car that was ostensibly either a very prestigious or a less prestigious brand (Bless, Igou, & Kuschmann, 2002). The obtained findings strongly support the conclusions from the mood and stereotyping research. As can be seen in Fig. 11.1, happy but not sad participants were strongly influenced by the varia-

FIG. 11.1. Evaluation of product line extension as a function of mood and fame of brand.

tion of the brand. Specifically, happy participants evaluated the new car more positively when it was launched by a prestigious rather than a less prestigious brand. This effect is equivalent to the increased impact of stereotypes under happy moods. In contrast, sad participants were unaffected by the brand manipulation because they were presumably elaborating on the specifics of the presented car.

Mood and Scripts

Similar conclusions about the relation between mood and general knowledge structures can be derived from research investigating the relation between affective states and the impact of scripts on information processing (Bless, Clore et al., 1996). In a series of studies, different mood states were induced before participants were provided with information about well-known activities (e.g., "going out for dinner"), for which they were likely to have a well-developed script (Graesser, Gordon, & Sawyer, 1979). Some of this information was script typical ("the hostess placed the menus on the table"), whereas other information was script atypical ("he put away his tennis racket"). After a short delay, participants received a surprise recognition test assessing their memory for the daily activities information presented to them. This recognition test comprised information that was script typical or script atypical; half of the information had actually been presented and the remaining half was new information. The obtained findings support the assumption that being in a happy mood fosters reliance on general knowledge structures.

Specifically, happy participants were more likely than sad participants to "recognize" statements that were typical for the script as having been presented, and this effect was independent of whether the statements were actually presented. Presumably, this reflects that reliance on a script allows individuals to infer script-typical behaviors, resulting in good recognition of typical behaviors that were actually presented as well as erroneous recognition of script typical behaviors that were not ("intrusion errors"). As expected, this influence was not obtained for atypical information, reflecting that this information could not be inferred from the script. Again these findings strongly suggest that happy moods increase the impact of general knowledge structures on individuals' information processing.

Mood and the Encoding of Persuasive Messages

The distinction between more routine-based processing strategies and strategies that address the specifics of a given situation can also be found in the persuasion domain. When forming an attitude judgment in response to a persuasive message, individuals may carefully consider the content of the message and pay close attention to the implications of the presented arguments. However, instead of engaging in a thorough consideration of message content, individuals may alternatively rely on general knowledge in the form of heuristic cues, such as the communicator's expertise or likability or the sheer length of a message (Chen & Chaiken, 1999; Petty & Cacioppo, 1986; for the relation between attitudes and decisions see Sanbonmatsu et al., chap. 6, this volume).

Researchers interested in the interplay of affect and cognition have investigated the impact of mood on these two alternative mechanisms. In this research, different affective states were induced, and participants were subsequently exposed to persuasive messages that included either strong or weak arguments. In general, participants in sad (or neutral) moods reported more favorable attitudes toward the advocated position when they were exposed to strong rather than weak arguments. In contrast, happy participants were less influenced by the message quality and were equally persuaded by strong and weak arguments. This general pattern has been replicated in a number of studies using a range of different mood inductions and persuasive messages about a variety of attitudinal issues (e.g., Bless, Bohner, Schwarz, & Strack, 1990; Bless, Mackie, & Schwarz, 1992; Mackie & Worth, 1989; Wegener & Petty, 1994; Worth & Mackie, 1987). These findings have been complemented by the observation that attitudes of recipients in positive but not neutral moods reflect the presence of heuristic cues (Mackie & Worth, 1989; Worth & Mackie, 1987).

Mood and Prior Judgments

Prior judgments about similar or related situations can be conceptualized as another form of general knowledge structure. If so, the evidence reported earlier suggests that individuals in happy moods should be more likely to rely on prior judgments than individuals in sad moods when required to form a new, but related judgment. Evidence from different domains supports this hypothesis. For example, in the domain of person perception, individuals in an elated mood have been found to be more likely to show halo effects than individuals in a depressed mood and to be less influenced by detailed person descriptions (see Sinclair & Mark, 1992, for a review). Similarly, Bless and Fiedler (1995) reported that specific judgments about a target person were more strongly influenced by preceding general trait judgments about the target when participants were in a happy rather than a neutral or sad mood. In the persuasion domain, we observed that when happy participants were asked to report an attitude judgment, they were more likely than sad individuals to rely on a prior formed global judgment of a persuasive message (Bless et al., 1992).

Mood and the Reliance on the Ease
of Retrieval Heuristic

Although in general the evidence for an increased reliance on heuristic processing seems quite compelling, a closer look reveals a rather surprising gap. In particular, there is surprisingly little evidence available on what is perhaps one of the most prominent heuristics—the ease of retrieval heuristic (Tversky & Kahneman, 1973). One might argue that the ease of retrieval heuristic is just another form of heuristic, another form of general knowledge. Note, however, that the heuristics discussed before provide content (e.g., a stereotype provides information about the traits and behaviors of a typical group member, a script about "going out for dinner" provides information about the typical sequence of events in a restaurant). In contrast, the ease of retrieval heuristic does not provide such content, but operates more like a processing rule (e.g., "If an exemplar of a category comes to mind easily—there must be many instances of it"; see Fiske & Taylor, 1991, for content-free schemas).

Evidence of the impact of mood on the reliance on the ease of retrieval heuristic is reported by Isen and colleagues (Isen, Means, Patrick, & Nowicki, 1982), who confronted participants with a similar scenario as in the original Tversky and Kahneman research. Participants were presented with a list of female and male names. In one condition, the male names were more famous; in another condition, the female names were more famous. Later participants were asked to estimate the number of male and female names on the list. Participants in a happy mood were more likely than participants in a neutral mood to overestimate the proportion of male to female names when the respective names were famous.

On first glance, the findings reported by Isen and colleagues (1982) suggest that happy individuals relied on the ease of retrieval heuristic. Famous names came to mind more easily, and by applying the ease of retrieval heuristic happy participants inferred a higher proportion of this category. However, these findings (just as the original Tversky and Kahneman studies) do not allow for a direct test of whether individuals relied on ease of retrieval or on the content that came to mind. On the one hand, participants may have overestimated the proportion of males (or female) names because the famous names came to mind more easily. On the other hand, instead of relying on the ease with which the information came to mind, happy participants may have simply based their judgment on the content—in this case, on the names that came to mind. For example, when more male than female names came to mind, participants may have concluded that the list comprised more male than female names. Note that this latter explanation does not require a subjective experience in the form of the experienced ease of retrieval (for a more extensive discussion of this issue, see Schwarz, Bless et al., 1991).

Addressing the ambiguity of the ease versus the content explanation, Schwarz et al. (1991) offered a paradigm that allows one to disentangle the two accounts. Participants were asked to recall either 6 or 12 examples of assertive behaviors, and they were subsequently asked to rate their assertiveness. Pretests had demonstrated that participants could retrieve 6 behaviors easily, whereas recalling 12 behaviors was accompanied with difficulty. Within this paradigm, the ease and content explanations allow for different predictions. If participants base their judgment on the content that comes to mind, they should rate themselves as more assertive the more information is recalled—that is, when 12 rather than 6 assertive behaviors were made more accessible. Conversely, if participants base their judgment on the ease with which the content comes to mind, they should rate themselves as more assertive when the relevant information comes to mind easily—that is, when they recalled 6 (easy) rather than 12 (difficult) assertive behaviors. The results of a series of studies support this latter explanation (for additional evidence and extensions, see Dijksterhuis, Macrae, & Haddock, 1999; Rothman & Schwarz, 1998; Wänke, Bless, & Biller, 1996; for an overview, see Schwarz, 1998).

Relying on this paradigm, Ruder and Bless (2003) investigated whether individuals' affective state influenced the reliance on the ease of retrieval heuristic. In these studies, participants in different affective states were asked to recall (generate) either few or many arguments in favor of a particular position (e.g., favoring a change in the educational system). Pretests had assured that generating few arguments was experienced as easy, whereas generating many arguments was manageable but experienced as difficult.

As can be seen in the upper part of Fig. 11.2, participants' attitudes toward a change in the educational system were a function of their affective state and the ease of retrieval reflected in a significant interaction. Specifically, happy participants reported more favorable attitudes when they had generated few rather than many arguments. In combination with prior results (Schwarz et al., 1991; Wänke et al., 1996), this finding suggests that happy individuals based their judgment on the ease with which the arguments came to mind. A reversed pattern was obtained for participants in a sad mood. Sad participants reported more favorable attitudes when they had generated many rather than few arguments. In combination with prior results, this later finding suggests that sad individuals relied on the content of the generated arguments and did not take into account the ease with which these arguments were generated.

Additional evidence supports the conclusion that happy individuals more strongly rely on the ease of retrieval heuristic than sad individuals. Specifically, further data rule out that (a) individuals' affective state influenced the experienced ease of retrieval (rather than the reliance on it; Experiment 1, 3, and 4), or (b) happy or sad participants generated arguments

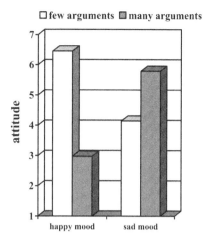

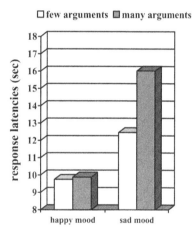

FIG. 11.2. Attitudes and response latencies as a function of mood and number of generated arguments (Ruder & Bless, 2003).

of different quality (Experiment 2). Further supporting evidence emerged from the analyses of individuals' response latencies (Experiment 4). It was hypothesized that if happy mood increases the reliance on the ease of retrieval heuristic, happy individuals should be faster at reporting a judgment than sad individuals, and that happy individuals' judgmental latencies should be rather independent of whether many or few arguments had been generated. As can be seen in the lower part of Fig. 11.2, the obtained findings support these hypotheses. Moreover, the results indicate that sad individuals (who are assumed to rely less on the experienced ease, but more on the content of the activated information) required more processing time the more arguments were generated—presumably because sad participants needed to evaluate and integrate the various arguments with respect to the various attitude questions, unlike happy participants who based their judgments on the experienced ease.

In summary, the reported evidence addressing the relation between individuals' affective state and the reliance on stereotypes, brand image, scripts, prior judgments, and the ease of retrieval heuristic provides a consistent pattern. Across the various domains, happy rather than sad individuals are more likely to rely on general knowledge structures. In the next section, we discuss (a) alternative explanations that may account for these findings, and (b) possibilities to empirically disentangle the various explanations.

THEORETICAL ACCOUNTS

The Mood and General Knowledge Structure Assumption

Various explanations have been offered to account for the finding that happy mood increases the reliance on stereotypes, scripts, heuristic cues, and so on. Our own approach builds on previous theorizing on the informative function on affective states (Schwarz, 1990; Schwarz & Bless, 1991), which holds that affective states inform the individual about the psychological nature of the current situation. In line with other theorizing (cf. Frijda, 1988), we assume that individuals usually feel good in situations that are characterized by positive outcomes and/or do not threaten their current goals. In contrast, individuals usually feel bad in situations that threaten their current goals either due to the presence of negative outcomes or the lack of positive outcomes. If different situations result in different affective states, individuals may consult their affect as a usually valid and quick indicator of the nature of the current psychological situation. If so, positive affective states may inform the individual that the current situation poses no problem, whereas negative affective states may signal that the current situation is problematic.

However, what follows from the signal that the current situation is problematic or benign? The present approach holds that it would be highly adaptive for individuals to differentially rely on their general knowledge structures—in the form of scripts, stereotypes, or other heuristics—depending on the nature of the current psychological situation (Bless, 2001b). If being in a positive mood informs us that the present situation poses no particular problem, this "business as usual" signal may increase the likelihood that we rely on general knowledge structures, which usually serve us well. In contrast, problematic situations are usually deviations from normal, routine situations. If so, individuals would be poorly advised to rely on the knowledge they usually apply. Instead successfully dealing with problematic situations requires one to focus on the specifics of the current situation. Thus, individuals' current affective state may influence the degree to which they rely on their general knowledge structures, mediated by the impact of affective states on the interpretation of the current situation. Specifically, individuals in positive affective states may feel more confident about relying on activated general knowledge structures that are potentially applicable to the situation. In contrast, individuals in negative affective states may feel less confident to rely on general knowledge structures and more likely to focus on the data at hand. This mood-dependent reliance on general knowledge structures versus the data at hand would direct individuals' attention toward the information that is presumably most useful in the current situation.

Alternative Accounts

Although the empirical evidence discussed earlier is in line with the proposed mood and general knowledge assumption (see also Fiedler, 1991, for a model implying similar predictions), other explanations may similarly account for the observed findings. Various approaches hold that happy mood reduces individuals' amount of processing, and their reliance on heuristics and other forms of general knowledge structure results from their reduced amount of processing. These accounts incorporate consistent evidence that general knowledge structures allow the individual to reduce the complexity of information processing at different stages, and they often promote a parsimonious and efficient processing (Fiske & Taylor, 1991).

First, it has been argued that being in a good mood limits processing capacity due to the activation of a large amount of interconnected positive material stored in memory (e.g., Mackie & Worth, 1989). Hence, individuals in a good mood may default to less taxing strategies and more strongly rely on general knowledge structures that allow a simplified processing. Second, accounts based on mood maintenance motivation (Isen, 1987; Wegener & Petty, 1994) argue that individuals in happy moods avoid investing cognitive effort in tasks unless doing so promises to maintain or enhance their positive mood. Hence, individuals in a good mood may rely on general knowledge structures to avoid more effortful cognitive processing. Third, based on the affect-as-information hypothesis, it has been argued that negative affective cues signal problematic and positive affect cues signal unproblematic situations. As a result, negative affective cues may motivate a systematic processing, whereas individuals in positive moods are not motivated to expend cognitive effort unless called for by other goals (see Schwarz, 1990).

Although these three approaches come from different starting points, they share the conclusion that increased reliance on general knowledge structures under happy moods results from happy moods decreasing the amount of information processing. For the present purpose, we do not further differentiate between these three accounts, but compare their common implications to the presented mood and general knowledge assumption.

Comparing the Different Theoretical Accounts

Obviously, all of the discussed assumptions imply that general knowledge structures are more influential under positive than under negative mood conditions. Hence, they cannot be distinguished by assessing the impact of general knowledge structures per se. Conceptually, the key issue is if mood affects processing motivation or capacity and these deficits, in turn, increase reliance on general knowledge structures (Alternative A), or, alternatively, if mood influences reliance on general knowledge structures in a way that is not mediated by deficits in processing motivation and/or capacity (Alternative B; Bless & Schwarz, 1999). In the former case (Alternative A), reliance on general knowledge structures is a consequence of reduced elaboration under happy moods: Given deficits in motivation or capacity, happy individuals are not able or willing to elaborate on the details and hence need to rely on general knowledge structures when making a judgment. In the latter case (Alternative B), reliance on general knowledge structures is an antecedent of reduced elaboration under happy moods: Given a "business-as-usual" signal, happy individuals rely on general knowledge structures and do not need to elaborate on the details (unless situational constraints elicit an elaboration of these details, as discussed next).

Although the various approaches all lead to the prediction that general knowledge structures are more influential under positive than under negative mood conditions, they do, however, lead to different additional predictions, which allow empirical testing. Two of these predictions pertain to the performance on a secondary task and the impact of information that is inconsistent with the implications of the general knowledge structure. We address these two aspects in turn.

Secondary Tasks. One way to test the competing accounts described earlier is to assess the cognitive effort individuals are willing or able to spend in a dual-task paradigm. In this paradigm, it is assumed that efficient processing of one task enables individuals to allocate more resources to the other task, resulting in improved performance on that task. In the studies on mood and scripts described previously (Bless, Clore et al., 1996), we applied this dual processing paradigm. Participants listened to a tape-recorded story comprising well-known activities and, as discussed before, the recognition data suggested that happy individuals are more likely to rely on general knowledge structures in form of scripts. While listening to the tape-recorded story, participants worked on a secondary task—namely, a concentration test that assessed how much effort participants were able and willing to allocate to it. The competing approaches have different implications with respect to performance on the secondary task: If happy moods reduce processing motivation or capacity, they should not only impair performance on the primary task, but also performance on a secondary task. In contrast, a different prediction results from the mood and general knowledge assumption. This account makes no assumption about mood-dependent differences in processing motivation or processing capacity. If happy moods elicit reliance on general knowledge structures pertaining to the primary task, the primary task should be less taxing (e.g., Macrae, Milne, & Bodenhausen, 1994). The obtained findings strongly support this latter account. While working simultaneously on a secondary task, happy participants showed better performance at that task than sad participants. The presumption is that by relying on a script, happy participants freed up resources that could be applied to the secondary task, which resulted in their improved performance. If happy participants' reliance on the script were due to reduced processing motivation or processing capacity, the respective deficit should also have impaired their secondary task performance, which was not the case.

The Impact of Stereotype-Inconsistent Information. It is well documented that dealing with stereotype-inconsistent information requires considerable cognitive resources (Stangor & Duan, 1991). If individuals are willing and able to allocate sufficient resources that are necessary for processing inconsistent information, inconsistent information should be particularly salient and should receive special weight in judgment formation. Note that such an increased impact of inconsistent information is more likely according to the mood and general knowledge assumption, rather than according to the assumption that happy moods reduce extensive processing. The latter assumption would predict that happy individuals may use the stereotype simply as a peripheral cue that simplifies their task, resulting in an attenuated impact of the inconsistent information. However, if happy moods increase the reliance on general knowledge structures, but do not elicit processing constraints, happy individuals should allocate additional resources to the inconsistent information, which should in turn render the inconsistent information more influential.

Support for this latter account can be found in different studies that have addressed the impact of inconsistent information under different mood conditions. Specifically, stereotype-inconsistent information has been found to be especially influential when individuals were in positive rather than negative affective states (Bless, Schwarz, & Wieland, 1996; see also Krauth-Gruber & Ric, 2000). Similarly, suggesting that happy individuals are particularly attending to inconsistent information, Dovidio, Gaertner, and Loux (2000) reported an increased recall of stereotype-inconsistent information under happy mood conditions.

CONCLUDING REMARKS

The present approach holds that happy and sad individuals differently rely on general knowledge structures. It is argued that the increased impact of general knowledge structures is presumably due to the signal function of affective states (Schwarz, 1990), and positive affective states may inform the individual that the current situation poses no problem, whereas negative affective states may signal that the current situation is problematic. If being in a positive mood informs us that the present situation poses no particular problem, this "business as usual" signal may increase the likelihood that we rely on general knowledge structures, which usually serve us well. In contrast, problematic situations are usually deviations from normal, routine situations. If so, individuals would be poorly advised to rely on the knowledge they usually apply. These considerations are strongly supported by the reported findings pertaining to a wide spectrum of general knowledge structures. Moreover, the obtained findings are in line with research more directly related to classic domains of decision making (e.g., Elsbach & Barr, 1999; Hertel et al., 2000; Isen, 1987; Luce et al., 1997, see also Schwarz, 2000). The reported findings also suggest that happy individuals' reliance on general knowledge structures is presumably not (or not necessarily) due to motivational or capacity deficits.

With respect to the impact of mood on processing style, it is important to note that the impact of mood on the use of activated general knowledge structures is only one aspect of the interplay of multifaceted influences. In addition, mood may also influence whether (a) a new knowledge structure is established (e.g., Bless, Hamilton, & Mackie, 1992), or (b) individuals are able to switch between knowledge structures. With respect to the latter, it has been suggested that the processing under happy moods is characterized by a higher flexibility than the processing under sad mood (e.g., Murray, Sujan, Hirt, & Sujan, 1990). Supporting the notion of a higher flexibility under happy moods, Haberstroh and colleagues (chap. 12, this volume) found that happy participants were more likely to abandon an inadequate routine and create new hypotheses (and new routines) than sad participants.

In closing, we briefly address why the mood-dependent reliance on general knowledge structures might be a highly adaptive mechanism. Most important, the two different processing perspectives (focus on general knowledge vs. focus on the specifics of the situation) direct individuals' attention toward the information that is presumably most useful in a given situation. Problematic situations are usually deviations from normal, routine situations. If so, individuals would be poorly advised to rely on the knowledge they usually apply. Instead successfully dealing with problematic situations requires that the individual focus on the specifics of the given situation. In contrast, unproblematic situations require less attention to the specifics of the situation. In this case, it would be highly adaptive to save processing resources allocated to the specifics of the situation and direct these resources toward other tasks (Bless, Clore et al., 1996). Such a mechanism would be particularly beneficial if it allowed the redirecting of processing attention when certain aspects of the situation require additional attention (e.g., as in the case of inconsistent information; Bless, Schwarz, & Wieland, 1996). Finally, individuals would be well advised to generate and test new, creative inferences beyond the information given in safe, rather than problematic, situations (Isen, 1987). Presumably, individuals' affective states serve as a quick and usually valid indicator for the nature of the situation (Schwarz, 1990), and this information in turn influences individuals' reliance on general knowledge structures versus the specifics of the situation. If so, individuals' affective states provide a useful source for the regulation of cognitive processes and the interpretation of the social situation. Thus, affective states elicit judgments and decision-making strategies that most often match the requirements of the situation. Looking at affective states from such a perspective, we would not be well advised if we tried—just like Mr. Spock from our introduction example—to exclude the impact of our feelings on our decision making.

ACKNOWLEDGMENT

The reported research was supported by the Sonderforschungsbereich 504 "Rationalitätskonzepte, Entscheidungsverhalten und ökonomische Modellierung" at the University of Mannheim, Germany.

REFERENCES

Aaker, D., & Keller, K. (1990). Consumer evaluations of brand extensions. *Journal of Marketing, 54*, 27–41.

Abelson, R. P. (1981). The psychological status of the script concept. *American Psychologist, 36*, 715–729.

Beach, L. R. (1990). *Image theory: Decision making in personal and organizational contexts.* New York: Wiley.

Bless, H. (2001a). The consequences of mood on the processing of social information. In A. Tesser & N. Schwarz (Eds.), *Blackwell handbook in social psychology* (pp. 391–412). Oxford, England: Blackwell.

Bless, H. (2001b). The relation between mood and the use of general knowledge structures. In L. L. Martin & G. L. Clore (Eds.), *Mood and social cognition: Contrasting theories* (pp. 9–29). Mahwah, NJ: Lawrence Erlbaum Associates.

Bless, H., Bohner, G., Schwarz, N., & Strack, F. (1990). Mood and persuasion: A cognitive response analysis. *Personality and Social Psychology Bulletin, 16*, 331–345.

Bless, H., Clore, G., Schwarz, N., Golisano, V., Rabe, C., & Wölk, M. (1996). Mood and the use of scripts: Does happy mood make people really mindless? *Journal of Personality and Social Psychology, 71*, 665–679.

Bless, H., & Fiedler, K. (1995). Affective states and the influence of activated general knowledge. *Personality and Social Psychology Bulletin, 21*, 766–778.

Bless, H., Hamilton, D. L., & Mackie, D. M. (1992). Mood effects on the organization of person information. *European Journal of Social Psychology, 22*, 497–509.

Bless, H., Igou, E. R., & Kuschmann, T. (2002). *The impact of mood on brand extensions*. Unpublished manuscript, Universität Mannheim.

Bless, H., Mackie, D. M., & Schwarz, N. (1992). Mood effects on encoding and judgmental processes in persuasion. *Journal of Personality and Social Psychology, 63*, 585–595.

Bless, H., & Schwarz, N. (1999). Sufficient and necessary conditions in dual process models: The case of mood and information processing. In S. Chaiken & Y. Trope (Eds.), *Dual process theories in social psychology* (pp. 423–440). New York: Guilford.

Bless, H., Schwarz, N., & Wieland, R. (1996). Mood and the impact of category membership and individuating information. *European Journal of Social Psychology, 26*, 935–959.

Bodenhausen, G. V., Kramer, G. P., & Süsser, K. (1994). Happiness and stereotypic thinking in social judgment. *Journal of Personality and Social Psychology, 66*, 621–632.

Bodenhausen, G. V., Sheppard, L. A., & Kramer, G. P. (1994). Negative affect and social judgment: The differential impact of anger and sadness. *European Journal of Social Psychology, 24*, 45–62.

Bower, G. H. (1981). Mood and memory. *American Psychologist, 36*, 129–148.

Carnevale, P. J., & Isen, A. M. (1986). The influence of positive affect and visual access on the discovery of integrative solutions in bilateral negotiation. *Organizational Behavior and Human Decision Processes, 37*, 1–13.

Chen, F., & Chaiken, S. (1999). Heuristic and systematic information processing. In S. Chaiken & Y. Trope (Eds.), *Dual process theories in social psychology* (pp. 73–96). New York: Guilford.

Deldin, P. J., & Levin, I. P. (1986). The effect of mood induction in a risky decision-making task. *Bulletin of the Psychonomic Society, 24*, 4–6.

Descartes, R. (1961). *Passions of the soul: Essential works of Descartes* (L. Blair, Trans.). New York: Bantam Books. (Original publication 1649)

Djiksterhuis, A., Macrae, N. C., & Haddock, G. (1999). When recollective experiences matter: Subjective ease of retrieval and stereotyping. *Personality and Social Psychology Bulletin, 25*, 760–768.

Dovidio, J. F., Gaertner, S. L., & Loux, S. (2000). Subjective experiences and intergroup relations: The role of positive affect. In H. Bless & J. P. Forgas (Eds.), *The message within: The role of subjective experience in social cognition and behavior* (pp. 340–371). Philadelphia, PA: Psychology Press.

Elsbach, K. D., & Barr, P. S. (1999). The effects of mood on individuals' use of structured decision protocols. *Organization Science, 10*, 181–198.

Fiedler, K. (1991). On the task, the measures and the mood in research on affect and cognition. In J. Forgas (Ed.), *Emotion and social judgments* (pp. 83–104). Oxford: Pergamon.

Fiske, S. T., & Neuberg, S. L. (1990). A continuum of impression formation from category-based to individuating processing: Influences of information and motivation on attention and interpretation. In M. P. Zanna (Ed.), *Advances in experimental social psychology* (Vol. 23, pp. 1–74). Orlando, FL: Academic Press.

Fiske, S. T., & Taylor, S. E. (1991). *Social cognition.* New York: McGraw-Hill.

Forgas, J. P. (1995). Mood and judgment: The affect infusion model (AIM). *Psychological Bulletin, 117,* 39–66.

Forgas, J. P. (Ed.). (2000). *Feeling and thinking: The role of affect in social cognition. Studies in emotion and social interaction, second series* (pp. 253–280). New York: Cambridge University Press.

Forgas, J. P., & Fiedler, K. (1996). Us and them: Mood effects on intergroup discrimination. *Journal of Personality and Social Psychology, 70,* 28–40.

Freud, S. (1940). *Gesammelte Werke.* Frankfurt: Fischer.

Frijda, N. H. (1988). The laws of emotion. *American Psychologist, 43,* 349–358.

Graesser, A. C., Gordon, S. E., & Sawyer, J. D. (1979). Memory for typical and atypical actions in scripted activities: Test of a script pointer + tag hypothesis. *Journal of Verbal Learning and Behavior, 18,* 319–332.

Hertel, G., Neuhof, J., Theuer, T., & Kerr, N. L. (2000). Mood effects on cooperation in small groups: Does positive mood simply lead to more cooperation? *Cognition and Emotion, 14,* 441–472.

Isen, A. M. (1987). Positive affect, cognitive processes, and social behavior. In L. Berkowitz (Ed.), *Advances in experimental social psychology* (Vol. 20, pp. 203–253). San Diego: Academic Press.

Isen, A. M. (1993). Positive affect and decision making. In M. Lewis & J. M. Haviland (Eds.), *Handbook of emotions* (pp. 261–277). New York: Guilford.

Isen, A. M., Daubman, K. A., & Nowicki, G. P. (1987). Positive affect facilitates creative problem solving. *Journal of Personality and Social Psychology, 52,* 1122–1131.

Isen, A. M., & Means, B. (1983). The influence of positive affect on decision making strategy. *Social Cognition, 2,* 18–31.

Isen, A. M., Means, B., Patrick, R., & Nowicki, G. (1982). Some factors influencing decision-making strategy and risk-taking. In M. S. Clark & S. T. Fiske (Eds.), *Affect and cognition: The 17th annual Carnegie Symposium on Cognition* (pp. 243–261). Hillsdale, NJ: Lawrence Erlbaum Associates.

James, W. (1890). The principles of psychology. In R. M. Hutchins (Ed.), *The great book of the Western world* (p. 348). Chicago: Encyclopaedia Brittanica, LIII.

Johnson, E., & Tversky, A. (1983). Affect, generalization, and the perception of risk. *Journal of Personality and Social Psychology, 45,* 20–31.

Krauth-Gruber, S., & Ric, F. (2000). Affect and stereotypic thinking: A test of the mood-and-general-knowledge-model. *Personality and Social Psychology Bulletin, 26,* 1587–1597.

Luce, M., Bettman, J., & Payne, J. W. (1997). Choice processing in emotionally difficult decisions. *Journal of Experimental Psychology: Learning, Memory, and Cognition, 23,* 384–405.

Mackie, D. M., & Worth, L. T. (1989). Cognitive deficits and the mediation of positive affect in persuasion. *Journal of Personality and Social Psychology, 57,* 27–40.

Macrae, C. N., & Bodenhausen, G. V. (2000). Social cognition: Thinking categorically about others. *Annual Review of Psychology, 51,* 93–120.

Macrae, C. N., Milne, A. B., & Bodenhausen, G. V. (1994). Stereotypes as energy-saving devices: A peek inside the toolbox. *Journal of Personality and Social Psychology, 66,* 37–47.

Mellers, B., Schwartz, A., & Ritov, I. (1999). Emotion-based choice. *Journal of Experimental Psychology: General, 128,* 332–345.

Murray, N., Sujan, H., Hirt, E. R., & Sujan, M. (1990). The influence of mood on categorization. A cognitive flexibility interpretation. *Journal of Personality and Social Psychology, 59,* 411–425.

Nygren, T. E., Isen, A. M., Tyler, P. J., & Dulin, J. (1996). The influence of positive affect on the decision rules in risk situations: Focus on outcome (and especially avoidance of loss) rather than probability. *Organizational Behavior and Human Decision Processes, 66,* 59–72.

Petty, R. E., & Cacioppo, J. T. (1986). The elaboration likelihood model of persuasion. In L. Berkowitz (Ed.), *Advances in experimental social psychology* (Vol. 19, pp. 124–203). New York: Academic Press.

Rothman, A. J., & Schwarz, N. (1998). Constructing perceptions of vulnerability: Personal relevance and the use of experiential information in health judgments. *Personality and Social Psychology Bulletin, 24,* 1053–1064.

Ruder, M., & Bless, H. (2003). Mood and the reliance on the ease of retrieval heuristic. *Journal of Personality and Social Psychology, 85,* 20–32.

Schwarz, N. (1990). Feelings as information: Informational and motivational functions of affective states. In R. M. Sorrentino & E. T. Higgins (Eds.), *Handbook of motivation and cognition: Foundations of social behavior* (Vol. 2, pp. 527–561). New York: Guilford.

Schwarz, N. (1998). Accessible content and accessibility experiences: The interplay of declarative and experiential information in judgment. *Personality and Social Psychology Review, 2,* 87–99.

Schwarz, N. (2000). Emotion, cognition, and decision making. *Cognition and Emotion, 14,* 433–440.

Schwarz, N., & Bless, H. (1991). Happy and mindless, but sad and smart? The impact of affective states on analytic reasoning. In J. P. Forgas (Ed.), *Emotion and social judgments* (pp. 55–71). Oxford: Pergamon.

Schwarz, N., Bless, H., Strack, F., Klumpp, G., Rittenauer-Schatka, H., & Simons, A. (1991). Ease of retrieval as information: Another look at the availability heuristic. *Journal of Personality and Social Psychology, 61,* 195–202.

Schwarz, N., & Clore, G. L. (1988). How do I feel about it? Informative functions of affective states. In K. Fiedler & J. P. Forgas (Eds.), *Affect, cognition, and social behavior* (pp. 44–62). Toronto: Hogrefe International.

Sinclair, R. C., & Mark, M. M. (1992). The influence of mood state on judgment and action: Effects on persuasion, categorization, social justice, person perception, and judgmental accuracy. In L. L. Martin & A. Tesser (Eds.), *The construction of social judgment* (pp. 165–193). Hillsdale, NJ: Lawrence Erlbaum Associates.

Slovic, P., Finucane, M., Peters, E., & MacGregor, D. G. (2002). The affect heuristic. In T. Gilovich, D. Griffin, & D. Kahneman (Eds.), *Heuristics and biases. The psychology of intuitive judgment* (pp. 397–420). Cambridge: Cambridge University Press.

Stangor, C., & Duan, C. (1991). Effects of multiple task demands upon memory for information about social groups. *Journal of Experimental Social Psychology, 27,* 357–378.

Tversky, A., & Kahneman, D. (1973). Availability: A heuristic for judging frequency and probability. *Cognitive Psychology, 5,* 207–232.

Wänke, M., Bless, H., & Biller, B. (1996). Subjective experience versus content of information in the construction of attitude judgments. *Personality and Social Psychology Bulletin, 22,* 1105–1113.

Wegener, D. T., & Petty, R. E. (1994). Mood management across affective states: The hedonic contingency hypothesis. *Journal of Personality and Social Psychology, 66,* 1034–1048.

Worth, L. T., & Mackie, D. M. (1987). Cognitive mediation of positive affect in persuasion. *Social Cognition, 5,* 76–94.

12

The Impact of Routines on Deliberate Decisions: The Microworld-Simulation COMMERCE

Susanne Haberstroh
Tilmann Betsch
University of Erfurt

Andreas Glöckner
Deutsche Lufthansa AG

Thomas Haar
Anja Stiller
University of Heidelberg

Research on habitual or routinized decision making has been conducted, for the most part, using two different approaches. First, in laboratory experiments, habit or routine strength is usually measured in a controlled laboratory setting. Researchers employing this approach are interested in the impact of the strength of routine or habit on various facets of current decisions. These include the attitude–behavior relation (e.g., Verplanken, Aarts, van Knippenberg, & Moonen, 1998) or the elaborateness of information search (e.g., Aarts, Verplanken, & van Knippenberg, 1997; Verplanken, Aarts, & van Knippenberg, 1997; for an overview of routine effects, see Betsch, Haberstroh, & Höhle, 2002). Second, in applied research on recurrent decision making, researchers study decisions with a view to the realistic consequences in a natural environment, such as the decisions of fire fighters or sports referees (Omodei, McLennan, & Wearing, chap. 15, this volume; Plessner, chap. 17, this volume). Novices are compared to experts who have developed their expertise over a long period of time (see e.g., Shanteau, Friel, Thomas, & Raacke, chap. 14, this volume; Omodei et al., chap. 15, this volume). Employing this approach, exact experimental control often has to be traded against the more realistic setting and the more generality of the results (for an overview see e.g., Salas & Klein, 2001).

In recent years, however, decision researchers have adopted a third method, which was previously used in the field of problem solving (e.g., Dörner, Kreuzig, Reither, & Stäudel, 1983): the use of microworld-simulations (e.g., Betsch, Brinkmann, Fiedler, & Breining, 1999; Betsch, Fiedler, & Brinkmann, 1998; Omodei & Wearing, 1995; Shanteau et al., chap. 14, this volume). In this type of study, participants are confronted with a computer-based decision scenario, in which they have to solve novel decision tasks. To mirror the complexity of real-world decisions, these decision tasks are embedded in a rather complex environment. However, in contrast to naturalistic decision tasks, all parameters are under experimental control.

The advantages of microworld-simulations, compared with other research methods, are threefold. First, by using microworld-simulations, the researcher does not have to rely on the measurement of routines that participants bring into the laboratory. Rather, routines can be induced in the course of the experiment, and thus can be controlled more exactly. Second, microworld-simulations include several decision trials, in comparison with most experimental decision tasks, which often involve one-shot decisions (Goldstein & Hogarth, 1997). Participants can experience the consequences of their decisions directly, learn from these consequences, and change their behavior contingent on situational requirements. Thus, the decisions are more realistic in terms of consequences, which participants experience directly than in most experiments, but in this case there is no loss of the advantages of experimental control. Third, prior knowledge is under experimental control. In our microworld-simulation, we excluded the influence of prior knowledge on current decisions by locating the microworld in a fictitious environment. This enabled us to induce routines without having to take into account participants' existing experience in the given domain.

The literature on problem solving contains numerous examples of microworld-simulations (e.g., "LOHAUSEN"; Dörner et al., 1983). For our purposes, however, the microworld had to fulfill two conditions that were not met by existing tools. It was not only desirable to induce routines in our participants; we also wanted to experimentally manipulate routine strength and investigate its effect on recurrent decisions. In addition, because we were interested in deliberate decisions in which no constraints were imposed on the decision makers, we wanted our participants to completely understand the underlying payoff structure for their decisions. Other microworld-simulations have a complex structure, in which all parameters influence each other and in which the decision maker's actions can change the environment. This structure makes it difficult, if not impossible, for participants to understand the underlying payoff structure of the simulation. In our microworld-simulation, participants have to adapt to a given environment, in which all consequences are predetermined and cannot be changed by the decision maker. Thus, in contrast to other tools, this specific microworld-simulation is characterized by bounded complexity. In fact, the underlying structure of our microworld-simulation resembles the gambling paradigm, which is the basis for most decision research (Goldstein & Hogarth, 1997). In this paradigm, participants have to choose between several options, each of which is characterized by the outcomes and their probabilities. Outcomes and probabilities are usually numerically stated and cannot be changed by actions of the decision maker. In our microworld-simulation, the same structure is employed (i.e., the options differ with respect to their outcomes and the probabilities of these outcomes, which are kept constant during trials). In contrast to the gambling paradigm, these outcomes and probabilities are not stated, but have to be learned and inferred from recurrent decision trials. Moreover, the microworld-simulation differs from the gambling paradigm in that it offers a richer environment, in which information about the options can be looked up and in which a larger number of decisions has to be made.

Based on these considerations, we developed a microworld-simulation called COMMERCE[1] (Betsch, Haberstroh, & Glöckner, 2000). This microworld allows the investigation of the impact of routines on deliberate decisions. It is important to emphasize in advance what is meant by the term *routine*. We define a routine as a behavioral option that comes to mind as a solution when the decision maker is confronted with a certain decision-making situation involving particular goals and context conditions (Betsch, Haberstroh, Glöckner, Haar, & Fiedler, 2001; Betsch, Haberstroh, & Höhle, 2002). In contrast to the definition of *habit* (see e.g., Verplanken, Myrbakk, & Rudi, chap. 13, this volume), this definition does not contain the automatic instantiation of a behavior in a given situation. We developed COMMERCE to study routinized decisions that are not automatized. In this chapter, we give an overview of COMMERCE and describe the decision scenario as well as one typical trial. We then outline some studies in which it has been applied.

THE MICROWORLD-SIMULATION COMMERCE

Overview

COMMERCE simulates a fictitious decision scenario, in which industrial goods (robots) are traded (for an overview, see Fig. 12.1). Participants assume the role of a stockpile manager of a large firm that rents out robots of

---

[1]A demo version of COMMERCE can be downloaded at http://www.mpr-online.de (Vol. 5, No. 2, 2000).

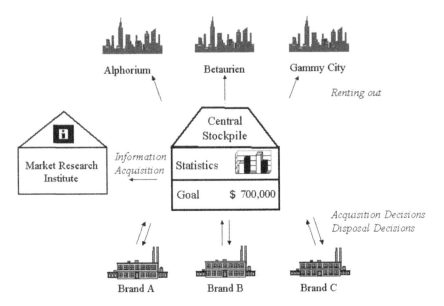

FIG. 12.1. Overview of COMMERCE.

three brands to three markets. The goal is to maximize profit in one given market (primary market). To achieve this goal, participants have to manage the stockpile according to the market's demands. They can acquire new robots (i.e., ordering new robots into the stockpile so they can be rented out to the three markets) or dispose of robots (i.e., sending back robots that are not rented out). Participants have to observe the market to adapt to it. Robots that are rented out in the primary market have to be accumulated in the stockpile by acquiring them repeatedly. Robots that are not rented out have to be disposed of to minimize stockpiling costs. Participants have two sources of information for their acquisition and disposal decisions: They can contact a market research institute, which provides them with forecast information about the three markets in the current trial. Furthermore, in each trial, they get complete feedback about the consequences of their decisions in the previous trial. Achieving the goal requires participants to repeatedly acquire the brands of robots that are rented out and to dispose of those robots not rented out in the primary market. Both behaviors have to be performed repeatedly because the number of robots that can be traded in one trial is limited. By repeatedly favoring one brand of robots, participants learn a routine (i.e., they learn a preference for a certain brand given the primary market). Routine strength can be manipulated by altering the frequency of acquisition choices needed to achieve the goal. Routine effects can be assessed in subsequent games, in which the environment changes, so that the previously established routine becomes inadequate as a solution to the new game. In this new game, it is possible to observe how long participants keep to the routine option, although they get negative feedback for choosing it. To rule out influences of other sorts of prior knowledge on participants' behavior, the scenario is situated in an unknown location. Specifically, participants are told that in the distant future people have colonized the moon. Participants play the role of a stockpile manager for a large firm, which rents out robots to emerging cities on the moon, in which residential facilities are to be built.

One Trial in COMMERCE

To illustrate how our requirements to manipulate routines and bounded complexity were met, we now describe one trial in COMMERCE as it appeared to our participants.

One trial represents 1 month in the microworld-simulation. Within each trial, participants can inspect stockpile and financial statistics, consult the market research institute, search for feedback regarding the consequences of the previous trial, and alter the stockpile by acquiring or disposing of robots. They can perform as many actions as they wish in a free order. After each trial, the payoffs in the markets are calculated by the program. If the goal (i.e., a certain profit in the primary market) is achieved, the game is terminated. If this is not the case, another trial begins. At the beginning of each trial, the participant is presented with a start window containing the most important statistics and an action menu.

Figure 12.2 shows the start window of COMMERCE. The start window contains all the important information (trial counter, stockpile statistics, financial statistics) and action buttons for all possible actions.[2] The stockpile statistics (upper left part of the screen) show three colored bars labeled with the names of the brands. The columns represent the current absolute number of robots of each brand in the stockpile. Below the stockpile statistics, financial statistics are presented. This figure shows the current profit made in the three markets (Alphorium, Betaurien, and Gammy City) in chart format. The bar of one market is red (light grey in Fig. 12.2), indicating that this is the primary market in which profits have to be maximized to a given amount. Furthermore, this table contains the momentary change in profit in a gain–loss row. In each trial, participants can perform each of the six actions represented by the action buttons. It is up to the participant to choose the number and order of actions within each trial. Usually partici-

---

[2]The "exit" button is only included in the demo version and was not visible to the participants in our experiments.

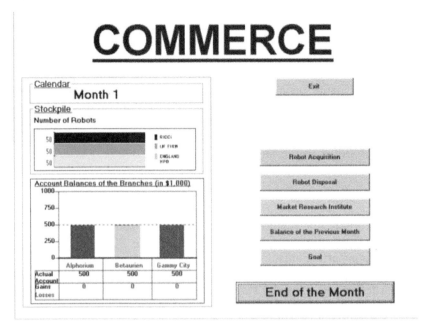

FIG. 12.2. Start window of COMMERCE.

pants first inspect the goal setting. The goal includes the announcement of the primary market (e.g., Betaurien), in which profits have to be maximized to a given amount (e.g., $700,000). The other two markets, Alphorium and Gammy City, are not to fall below a certain threshold (e.g., $100,000). The goal is kept constant during a game and has to be reached as quickly as possible (i.e., in a minimum of trials). To find out which robots are rented out in the primary market, participants have two sources of information. Their first option is to contact the Market Research Institute. Participants are told that the Market Research Institute provides dichotomous information about the development of the three brands in the three markets in the current trial (e.g., "Ricci will/will not be rented out in Betaurien"). In the instruction, participants are told that the Market Research Institute "is not always right." In fact it has a hit rate of 80%. When participants consult the Market Research Institute, they can retrieve the forecast information in a 3 (brand) × 3 (market) matrix, resembling the "Mouse lab" developed by Johnson and colleagues (Johnson, Payne, Schkade, & Bettman, 1986). The second source for the participants is the inspection of the "Balance of the previous month." This information also contains a 3 (brand) × 3 (market) matrix, in which the actual losses and gains obtained in the previous month are shown. By inspecting these pieces of information, participants are completely informed about the success of their actions in the previous trials. To achieve the goal, participants have to change the stockpile according to the market's demand. Those robots that are rented out produce gains, whereas robots that are not rented out produce losses due to stockpiling costs. Therefore, participants have to accumulate those robots that are successful in the stockpile and dispose of those robots that are not successful. To do so, they can order those robots that they assume to be successful from the earth into the stockpile ("Robot Acquisition"). Likewise, they can send robots that are not successful back to earth ("Robot Disposal"). In each trial, the number of robots that can be acquired or disposed of is limited. When participants have performed all the actions they chose, they can end the month/trial. The program now updates payoff and profit statistics. A feedback page pops up, indicating whether the goal has been achieved. If it has been achieved, the program self-terminates. If it has not been achieved, participants have to continue with a new trial.

Manipulating Routine Strength

In COMMERCE, a routine is the option (brand) that has turned out to be most beneficial for the goal to maximize profit in a certain market and that has been repeatedly acquired over trials. By means of choice repetition, participants are assumed to establish an association between the goal (= achieve profit in a certain market) and the routine (= choose Brand A when you order robots). Routine strength is operationalized by the frequency with which the routine option has been chosen during the learning game. The rationale behind this is that choice repetition has been proposed to be a powerful mean to strengthen situation–behavior associations in an organism (e.g., Hull, 1943; Ronis, Yates, & Kirscht, 1988; see also Verplanken et al., chap. 13, this volume). Consequently, to induce a strong routine, choice frequency for the routine option has to be higher than to induce a weak routine. Therefore, the game has to be more difficult to be solved for a strong routine. A more difficult game means that participants need more trials to solve the game and, therefore, the routine option is preferred more frequently. COMMERCE offers several ways to manipulate the difficulty of the game. In the studies we report in this chapter, the difficulty of the game was manipulated by the rent prices. The rent prices refer to the gain a robot achieves when it is rented out. Everything else being equal, there is an inverse relationship between rent prices and the number of choice repetitions needed to win the game. The smaller the rent prices, the more often the best performing option has to be acquired to achieve a stockpile capacity that yields the required amount of profit.

EXPERIMENTING WITH COMMERCE

We have employed COMMERCE in several studies. These studies aimed at answering various questions with regard to recurrent decision making. First, we wanted to show routine maintenance effects in deliberate decision making in unconstrained situations as well as how routine strength moderates this effect. Second, we investigated effects of participants' mood on recurrent decisions and the subjective interpretation of the decision situation. Third, COMMERCE was extended by an information search tool, which allowed us to study the effects of behavioral routines on information search patterns. Because all studies had the same structure, we first describe how routines were induced and how routine maintenance was assessed in all our studies.

Assessing Routine Maintenance and Deviation

We developed COMMERCE to study the effects of prior behavioral knowledge and new evidence on decisions in a controlled environment. Routine maintenance and deviation were measured using the following methods. In a learning game, participants learned a routine (i.e., they learned to prefer a brand) and were given the goal to maximize profit in a certain market. The routine option had a rent-out probability of 80%. The other two options had rent-out probabilities of 50% and 20%, respectively. During the course of the learning game, participants learned which robot is best at being rented out. It took participants on average 32 trials in the strong routine condition and 16 trials in the weak routine condition to complete the learning phase. After a time lapse, participants played a new game in COMMERCE: the test game. In this game, we observed participants' behavior in a situation in which the routine became obsolete. For this purpose, we changed the pay-off structure in the test game. The goal setting was the same, but the three options differed from the learning game. In the experimental group, the option set again contained the routine option plus two new options, which were unfamiliar to the participants. However, the routine option no longer promoted the goal (maximize profit in market X). Due to a gain probability of 40%, participants had to dispose of this option instead of acquiring it. The other two options were new and had gain probabilities of 70% and 10%. We compared this experimental condition to a control condition, in which all three options were unfamiliar. As a main dependent variable, we assessed the acquisition and disposal decisions regarding the "target option," which was the former routine option in the experimental condition or a new option in the control condition. More frequent acquisition of this option in the experimental than in the control condition indicated a routine maintenance effect. Second, patterns of information search could be analyzed because all movements in the information matrix were recorded. Finally, in the last study, we describe an additional tool that was developed to study the information search process more closely.

Do Routines Affect Deliberate Decisions?

In our first study (Betsch et al., 2001, Study 1), the primary aim was to investigate how routinized decision makers adapt to situations in which their routines no longer serve their goals. We focused on unconstrained situations, leaving participants ample time to inspect all relevant information. We assumed that routine strength influences the willingness of the participants to deviate from their inadequate routines.

The procedure in the experiment follows the prior description. In a learning game, a routine was induced and its strength was manipulated. In the test game, we compared an experimental group (for which the option set contained the former routine, which now only had a gain probability of 40% and two new options) and a control group, for which all three options were unfamiliar. As a dependent variable, we compared the difference of acquisition and disposal decisions regarding the target option, which was either the former routine option (in the experimental group) or a new option (in the control group). A positive difference indicates that the routine was maintained in the test game. A negative difference indicates an adaptation to the new situation because the target option is disposed of.

We analyzed the first half and the second half of test trials separately (Fig. 12.3 shows the means). The results for the strong routine condition show that, in the first half of the trials, participants in the experimental group (black columns) maintained their routine (i.e., they acquired the target option more than they disposed of it). In contrast to that, participants in the control condition (light columns), for which the target option carried a new label, acquired less of the target option. However, in the second half of trials, this pattern is significantly reversed. Now all participants have realized that this option produces more losses than gains and, consequently, dispose of this option. Because participants in the experimental group have acquired more of the target option in the first half of the game, they now dispose of this option more than participants in the control group. This cross-over pattern does not show for weak routine participants. In fact, there are no significant differences between the experimental and control groups for weak routine participants.

Taken together, this first study shows that even in unconstrained situations, in which participants could look up all relevant information and in which no time pressure was employed, participants maintain their behavioral routine. This effect only occurred if the routine was strong. Weak routines did not significantly influence the behavior 1 week after the learning

Strong routine

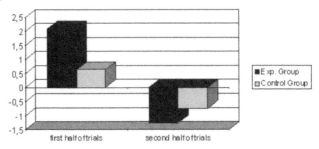

Weak routine

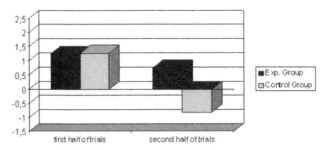

FIG. 12.3. Difference of acquisition and disposal of target option depending on routine strength and trials in Study 1.

game. This study also provided evidence for the suitability of COMMERCE to study recurrent decision making in an unconstrained environment.

The Malleability of Routine Effects

In the first experiment, we showed that routines can influence unconstrained, deliberate decisions. In the next step, we were interested in the malleability of these influences. Do interpersonal differences have an impact on these routine effects?

From social cognition research, we know that positive and negative moods can have tremendous influence on all kinds of cognitive processes. For example, positive mood enhances memory for positive information, whereas negative information can be recalled more easily in negative mood (Bower, 1981). Mood also influences the information-processing style: Positive mood leads to more creativity and flexibility in problem solving or decision making (e.g., Forgas & Fiedler, 1996; Isen, Daubman, & Nowicki, 1987), whereas negative mood promotes a more systematic processing of information (for an overview, see Clore, Schwarz, & Conway, 1994; see also Bless &

Igou, chap. 11, this volume). Fiedler (1990, 1991) argued that information processing is guided by two forces—passive conservation of information and active transformation of information. Passive conservation means a stimulus-driven maintenance of the input, whereas active transformation describes a theory-driven drawing of inferences on the basis of the stimulus input. All information processing is assumed to include both cognitive tasks—conservation and transformation—to different degrees. Fiedler argued that positive mood promotes information transformation, whereas negative mood promotes the passive conservation of the information given (for a similar model, see Bless, 2001; Bless & Igou, chap. 11, this volume).

Applying this reasoning to routinized decision making, we hypothesized that positive mood should lead to a longer routine maintenance than negative mood. A behavioral routine can be understood as a stored knowledge structure. If people in a good mood process incoming information on the basis of these established theories about the world, they should rely more on the routine than people in a bad mood. Bad mood leads to stimulus-driven information processing. If people in a bad mood adhere strictly to the information presented in the test phase, they should realize more easily that the routine is no longer successful, and that instead another option should be acquired to reach the goal. Therefore, bad mood should lead to a faster deviation from the routine.

However, the overt decision behavior is a rather strict measure for the subtle mood influences, so that we employed an additional, more sensitive measure for mood influences. Mood should influence overt decision behavior by changing the interpretation of the decision situation. Therefore, we measured these interpretations more directly by the use of think-aloud protocols. In the last couple of years, many researchers have shown that the think-aloud procedure is an appropriate tool to study cognitive processes in decision making (e.g., Adelman, Gualtieri, & Stanford, 1995; Barber & Roehling, 1993). In our study, we expected that participants in a good mood refer to their prior knowledge regarding the options more often, whereas participants in a bad mood try to conserve the current information with which they are provided. This procedure should allow us to measure mood influences on a more fine-graded level than the overt behavior we observe.

In this study (Stiller, 2001), basically the same design was employed as in the first study. However, only the strong routine condition was employed, and the test game was conducted after a short distraction task in the same session. Again participants first played the learning game. Afterward, they were instructed to the think-aloud procedure. We asked participants to voice every thought that came to their mind without explaining or editing what they say. Participants then practiced this procedure with an unrelated decision task. Mood was manipulated by using 5-minute film clips, which—according to pretests—led to a good or bad mood. After watching the films, participants played the test game. They were instructed to think aloud during playing the first 10 trials of the game. As dependent variables, we compared (a) the decision behavior between good and bad mood participants and between experimental and control group, and (b) the think-aloud protocols between the good and bad mood participants.

Regarding the decision behavior, the results of Study 1 could be replicated. Again participants in the experimental condition maintained their routine (i.e., they falsely acquired more of the target option in the first half of trials than participants in the control condition). However, the results did not reveal any differences regarding the routine choices between good and bad mood participants. Participants in a good mood did not maintain the routine longer than participants in a bad mood.

To analyze the verbal data, we used a category system, which we arrived at by considering the theoretical assumptions by Fiedler (1990, 1991). Here we report the data of the two most important combined categories (altogether the category system comprised seven categories): (a) conservation of the stimulus input/inspection of information: This category comprised all utterances in which the presented information were repeated and edited to completely represent the stimulus data (e.g., in the Market Research Institute, "Oh, I see, this time only the third robot will rent out"); and (b) active transformation and interpretation of information: This category comprised all utterances in which the stimulus material was interpreted on the basis of prior knowledge and subjective theories (e.g., "Robot A will not rent out—I don't believe this information—Robot A is a good one").

Thus, the first category included stimulus-driven, bottom–up processes. This category comprised processes aimed at understanding and consolidating the current stimulus data without going beyond the information given in the situation. Based on Fiedler's (1990, 1991) theoretical assumptions, these processes should have been promoted by negative mood. The second category included theory-driven processes. These processes incorporated knowledge acquired outside the current decision situation. The stimulus data were actively interpreted on the basis of such knowledge or subjective theories. This category therefore comprised all references to the contents of the learning game. These processes should have been promoted by positive mood.

Analyzing the verbal protocols, we found the expected differences regarding the first category. Participants in a bad mood indeed more often tried to comprehend the information to fully represent the decision situation than participants in a good mood. They also more often repeated pieces of information, which were presented in the game. However, the hypotheses regarding theory-driven processes in the second category could not be confirmed. Good mood and bad mood participants did not differ in referring to the learning game or in the degree they actively interpreted the given information.

Taken together, this study first shows that the results of the prior study could be replicated: Participants maintained their routine despite negative evidence. Second, in contrast to our hypotheses, this effect was not influenced by the mood manipulation we employed. Participants in a good mood did not differ from participants in a bad mood regarding the overt decision behavior. Third, on the more sensitive measure, think-aloud protocols, mood effects were partly found in the expected direction. Participants in a bad mood engaged more in information repetition and comprehension. No differences were found for theory-driven processes like information interpretation.

The nonexpected results regarding overt decisions could be due to the fact that the think-aloud procedure influenced the decision behavior (van Someren, Barnard, & Sandberg, 1994). The influence of this additional task that participants had to perform sufficed to rule out the rather subtle mood influences we expected on overt behavior. Therefore, in a third study, we replicated the second one without the think-aloud procedure (Haar, 2001). The dependent variables were the acquisition and disposal decisions in the test phase. We expected negative mood participants to be more successful in finishing the game than positive mood participants because they were thought to rely less on their prior knowledge, which was now inadequate. The better performance should have manifested itself in two manners: (a) Participants in a bad mood should have made more profit in the primary market at the end of the game because they should have closely followed the advice given by the Market Research Institute. Therefore, they should have realized faster which option was successful in the test game. (b) For the same reason, participants in a bad mood should have acquired a lower number of robots of the target option and more robots of the now best performing brand than participants in a good mood.

Surprisingly, the results show the opposite pattern. At the end of the game, participants in a good mood made more profit in the primary market than participants in a bad mood (i.e., they were more successful). This result indicates that good mood participants adapted faster to the new environment. In fact the stockpile statistics showed that, at the end of the game, participants in a good mood had less robots of the target option (the now inadequate former routine) in their stockpile than participants in a bad mood. Additionally, they had more of the now best performing option in their stockpile. Both findings indicate that good mood participants adapted better to the new situation than participants in a bad mood.

It was argued earlier that bad mood participants should be more successful because they pay more attention to the information given in the new environment. This should have enabled them to quickly find out which option performs best in this new situation. Good mood participants, in contrast, should have been influenced by their prior knowledge and should, consequently, have maintained their routine longer.

However, sticking too strictly to the advice provided by the Market Research Institute also might have hindered bad mood participants from solving the game. Because the Market Research Institute only gave correct advice in 80% of the cases, following this advice closely should sometimes have led to inadequate choices. Consequently, this strategy might not have been as successful as we initially expected. In fact this is what an additional analysis showed. Figure 12.4 shows to what extent participants followed the advice given by the Market Research Institute regarding the target option. The bold line depicts the behavior of a fictitious person who always followed the advice provided by the Market Research Institute (option will rent out vs. will not rent out) and who always acquired or disposed of the maximum number of robots (10 in this game). The dotted line shows the behavior of good mood participants; the solid line shows the behavior of participants in a bad mood. The three lines basically have a similar trend indicating that participants in both groups considered the information of the Market Research Institute in their decisions. However, participants in a bad mood did so in a much stricter way. The bold and solid lines are almost identical throughout the whole game. Of course relying on this strategy will successfully finish the game. However, because the Market Research Institute only has a hit rate of 80%, this strategy is not the optimal solution to the game.

Participants in a good mood behaved differently. In the beginning of the game (i.e., for approximately 10 to 12 trials), they also closely followed the advice. They then seem to have developed a new hypothesis about the structure of the game (e.g., "Robot A does not seem to be the most promising option in this game. I have to clear the stockpile of this option"). In the remaining trials, they relied stronger on this new hypothesis than on the information provided by the Market Research Institute. Consequently, they kept on disposing of this option, although sometimes the Market Research

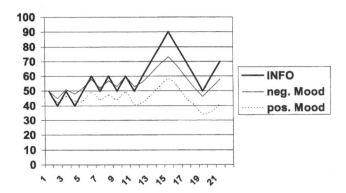

FIG. 12.4. Acquisition and disposal behavior of the target option compared with the Market Research Institute in Study 3.

Institute advised them not to do so. In fact this strategy is more successful in finishing the game than strictly going with the information given.

The two studies combined show that recurrent decision making can be influenced by the mood of the participants. Good mood does not necessarily lead to prolonged routine maintenance, as we expected. However, participants in a good mood interpreted the new information in a more active way, which is in line with the models proposed by Fiedler (1990, 1991) or Bless (2001; see also Bless & Igou, chap. 11, this volume). In contrast, participants in a bad mood were data driven and prone to follow the given information in a more rigid way. Consequently, they were less successful in adapting to new situations. These differences are also evident on examination of the think-aloud protocols, which we employed to depict the underlying processes of decision making. Bad mood participants more often repeated and conserved the information given in the new situation than good mood participants. This measure is in line with their overt behavior in the third study.

Behavioral Routines and Information Search

Up to this point, we have not reported any data regarding information search. In all of the experiments discussed so far, we neither obtained differences in information search between participants with a strong or a weak routine nor between participants in a good or bad mood. All participants looked up the relevant pieces of information. In the next study, we focus on the influence of routine strength on information search. The pattern we obtained so far shows that strong and weak routine participants in fact looked up information revealing the inadequacy of the routine in the new environment to the same degree. Therefore, it seems that strong and weak routine participants decided differently based on the same pieces of information. Weak routine participants deviated from the routine, whereas participants with a strong routine kept on acquiring this option. A strong routine seems to have led participants to neglect counterevidence, which might promote routine maintenance in subsequent choices. However, if strong routine participants tend to neglect counterevidence, why does this tendency not show up in the search pattern? Based on this observation, we should expect a confirmatory search pattern for strong routine participants. In accordance, new information that favors the routine option should more likely be considered than information that disfavors the routine. In COMMERCE, the information search is limited. The Market Research Institute only provides dichotomous information ("Brand A will rent out/will not rent out in Betaurien"). It might be the case that effects of routine strength on information search can only evolve if the information is richer and not as easily assessed.

The pattern of information search should also be influenced by other factors. From previous research, we know that the emergence of confirmatory information search is also moderated by context factors (Frey, 1981). For instance, changes in the environment that make the situation appear novel can lower confirmatory tendencies or even cause such tendencies to occur in the opposite direction. This means that confirmatory tendencies should only occur if the formerly acquired knowledge about the options is applicable to the new situation. If the new situation is perceived as novel, the acquisition of new information should not be biased by prior knowledge because it is not applicable to this new situation.

These hypotheses were tested in another study. We expected a pronounced difference regarding the information search pattern depending on the framing of the new situation. If the new situation is framed as familiar, a confirmatory search should be observed. If the new situation is framed as unfamiliar, participants might even prefer disconfirming evidence. This effect should only occur for strong routine participants. Weak routine participants should be less confident in the hypothesis that the routine is a good choice and should show fewer biases in information search. Therefore, for them no difference regarding framing of the situation was expected.

Based on these considerations, we developed an extended version of COMMERCE, which allowed studying information search behavior more precisely (Betsch et al., 2001, Exp. 2). After learning a routine, participants had to make a final decision, which was said to be of extraordinary importance. To make this decision, participants were given the opportunity to search for information in an extended version of the Market Research Institute. In contrast to the former version, which provided three dichotomous pieces of information for each brand (e.g., "Ricci will be rented out/will not be rented out in Betaurien"), the new matrix contained eight headings of reports for each brand. The headings consisted of one statement, which summarized a longer report that participants could order to help them make their decision. The headings always implied whether the information was favoring (e.g., "RICCI improves manufacturing standards") or disfavoring (e.g., "Low scores for RICCI in an expert rating") the option. Thus, it was obvious whether the report would support the respective option.

Participants first had to make a tentative decision for one option and then they had to choose which report they wanted to read before making a final decision. We analyzed whether participants chose confirming or disconfirming evidence with respect to their tentative decision. Additionally, in this new decision, we varied the frame of the situation. The new situation was described as either similar to the learning game ("Your task is now the same as before, although now an administration complex will be built instead of residential facilities") or as an unfamiliar situation ("Your task is not the same as before because now an administration complex will be built instead of residential facilities").

The results regarding the tentative decision show that in both routine strength conditions most participants chose the routine option. The information search data show that, as expected, strong routine participants showed a pronounced preference for confirming evidence if the new situation was described as familiar (confirming evidence pro routine and contra the other two options). If the task has been described as being novel, strong routine participants did not show any confirming tendencies, but even revealed a slight tendency toward disconfirmation (disconfirming evidence contra routine and pro the other two options). Weak routine participants showed a moderate tendency for confirmatory search without being affected by the task framing.

The results of this study support the notion that routines can impact information acquisition in deliberate, unconstrained situations. Strong routine participants showed the most pronounced tendency for confirmatory search if the task is framed as being similar to the learning game. In contrast, strong routine participants also discarded confirming tendencies if the task were described as novel. Weak routine participants were not affected by the manipulation of task novelty. This study shows that, in addition to studying the impact of routine strength on decision behavior and the interpretation of the decision task, COMMERCE also allows studying information search behavior and the impact of routine strength on confirmatory search tendencies.

CONCLUSIONS

This chapter aimed to demonstrate how recurrent decision making can be studied using the microworld-simulation COMMERCE. This microworld differs from previous tools (e.g., Shanteau et al., chap. 14, this volume) mainly by its reduced complexity. In COMMERCE, the environment is not altered by the decision of the actor. The payoff structure is fixed (i.e., forecast information and outcome are prescheduled). Consequently, after a few trials, the decision maker is able to fully understand the underlying structure of the microworld and can make informed decisions. The decision maker has to adapt to the given environment, but cannot change it. This structure, which is easy to understand, should make it even harder to observe routine effects at all.

In four studies, we demonstrated that COMMERCE is in fact an appropriate tool to study recurrent decision making and identify genuine routine effects. COMMERCE allows the researcher to induce routines and vary routine strength under highly controlled laboratory conditions. We could show that strong routines (repetition frequency about 30 times) lead participants to maintain their routine in a new environment, in which the routine no longer promotes the goals of the decision maker. The overt behavior and subjective perception and interpretation of this new environment are influenced by the participants' mood. Participants in a bad mood stick closer to information than participants in a good mood. COMMERCE was also successfully applied to studying information search behavior. Participants with a strong routine showed pronounced confirmatory tendencies in their information search. However, this effect did not occur if the new situation was framed as unfamiliar. In this case, participants with a strong routine even showed disconfirmatory information search. In addition to these applications, COMMERCE offers the possibility to study a multitude of questions in the domain of recurrent decision making.

REFERENCES

Aarts, H., Verplanken, B., & van Knippenberg, A. (1997). Habit and information use in travel mode choices. *Acta Psychologica, 96,* 1–14.

Adelman, L., Gualtieri, J., & Stanford, S. (1995). Examining the effect of causal focus on the option generation process: An experiment using protocol analysis. *Organizational Behavior and Human Decision Processes, 61,* 54–66.

Barber, A. E., & Roehling, W. V. (1993). Job postings and the decision to interview: A verbal protocol analysis. *Journal of Applied Psychology, 78,* 845–856.

Betsch, T., Brinkmann, J., Fiedler, K., & Breining, K. (1999). When prior knowledge overrules new evidence: Adaptive use of decision strategies and the role of behavioral routines. *Swiss Journal of Psychology, 58,* 151–160.

Betsch, T., Fiedler, K., & Brinkmann, J. (1998). Behavioral routines in decision making: The effects of novelty in task presentation and time pressure on routine maintenance and deviation. *European Journal of Social Psychology, 28,* 861–878.

Betsch, T., Haberstroh, S., & Glöckner, A. (2000). COMMERCE: A microworld–simulation to study routine maintenance and deviation in repeated decision making. *Methods of Psychological Research, 5.* (online)

Betsch, T., Haberstroh, S., Glöckner, A., Haar, T., & Fiedler, K. (2001). The effects of routine strength on adaptation and information search in recurrent decision making. *Organizational Behavior and Human Decision Processes, 84,* 23–52.

Betsch, T., Haberstroh, S., & Höhle, C. (2002). Explaining routinized decision making—a review of theories and models. *Theory and Psychology, 12,* 453–488.

Bless, H. (2001). The consequences of mood on the processing of social information. In A. Tesser & N. Schwarz (Eds.), *Blackwell handbook in social psychology* (pp. 391–412). Oxford, England: Blackwell.

Bower, G. H. (1981). Mood and memory. *American Psychologist, 36,* 129–148.

Clore, G. L., Schwarz, N., & Conway, M. (1994). Affective causes and consequences of social information processing. In R. S. Wyer & T. K. Srull (Eds.), *Handbook of social cognition* (2nd ed., pp. 323–341). Hillsdale, NJ: Lawrence Erlbaum Associates.

Dörner, D., Kreuzig, H. W., Reither, F., & Stäudel, T. (1983). *Lohhausen. Vom Umgang mit Unbestimmtheit und Komplexität* (Lohhausen. Problem solving in uncertain and complex problems). Bern: Huber.

Fiedler, K. (1990). Mood-dependent selectivity in social cognition. In W. Stroebe & M. Hewstone (Eds.), *European review of social psychology* (pp. 1–32). New York: Wiley.

Fiedler, K. (1991). On the task, the measure, and the mood in research on affect and social cognition. In J. P. Forgas (Ed.), *Emotion and social judgment* (pp. 83–104). Oxford: Pergamon.

Forgas, J. P., & Fiedler, K. (1996). Us and them: Mood effects on inter-group discrimination. *Journal of Personality and Social Psychology, 70,* 28–40.

Frey, D. (1981). *Informationssuche und Informationsbewertung bei Entscheidungen* (Information seeking and information evaluation in decision making). Bern: Huber.

Goldstein, W. M., & Hogarth, R. M. (1997). Judgment and decision research: Some historical context. In W. M. Goldstein (Ed.), *Research on judgment and decision-making: Currents, connections and controversies* (pp. 3–65). Cambridge: Cambridge University Press.

Haar, T. (2001). *When you can't see the forest for the trees: Mood effects on cognitive style and performance in recurrent decision making.* Unpublished diploma thesis, University of Heidelberg.

Hull, C. L. (1943). *Principles of behavior.* New York: Appleton-Century-Crofts.

Isen, A. M., Daubman, K. A., & Nowicki, G. P. (1987). Positive affect facilitates creative problem solving. *Journal of Personality and Social Psychology, 52,* 1122–1131.

Johnson, E. J., Payne, J. W., Schkade, D. A., & Bettman, J. R. (1986). *Monitoring information processing and decisions: The mouse lab system.* Unpublished manuscript, Center for Decision Studies, Fuqua School of Business, Duke University.

Omodei, M. M., & Wearing, A. J. (1995). The Fire Chief microworld generating program: An illustration of computer-simulated microworlds an experimental paradigm for studying complex decision-making behavior. *Behavior Research Methods, Instruments & Computers, 27,* 303–316.

Ronis, D. L., Yates, J. F., & Kirscht, J. P. (1988). Attitudes, decisions and habits as determinants of repeated behavior. In A. R. Pratkanis, S. J. Breckler, & A. G. Greenwald (Eds.), *Attitude structure and function* (pp. 213–239). Hillsdale, NJ: Lawrence Erlbaum Associates.

Salas, E., & Klein, G. (Eds.). (2001). *Linking expertise and naturalistic decision making.* Mahwah, NJ: Lawrence Erlbaum Associates.

Stiller, A. (2001). *Affektive Einflüsse und die Relevanz von Handlungswissen bei Entscheidungen: Eine Auswertung von Protokollen des lauten Denkens* [The role of affective influences and behavioral knowledge in decisions: An analysis of think-aloud protocols]. Unpublished diploma thesis, University of Heidelberg.

van Someren, M. W., Barnard, Y. F., & Sandberg, J. A. C. (1994). *The think aloud method. A practical guide to modeling cognitive processes.* London: Academic Press.

Verplanken, B., Aarts, H., & van Knippenberg, A. (1997). Habit, information acquisition and the process of making travel mode choices. *European Journal of Social Psychology, 27,* 539–560.

Verplanken, B., Aarts, H., van Knippenberg, A., & Moonen, A. (1998). Habit versus planned behaviour: A field experiment. *British Journal of Social Psychology, 37,* 111–128.

13

The Measurement of Habit

Bas Verplanken
Vemund Myrbakk
Erik Rudi
University of Tromsø, Norway

We seldom do things for the first time. Most of our everyday behaviors are recurrences or variants of behaviors we have previously executed, most of which numerous times. The frequency of occurrence and the stability of behavior were central themes in the behaviorist tradition (e.g., Hull, 1943), and James (1890) already devoted an intriguing chapter about habit in his famous *The Principles of Psychology*. Although social psychologists never lost sight of the behavioral side of human functioning, the repetitive aspect of behavior has only received minimal attention in social psychology. In the decision-making area, it seems that repetition of choices has almost been neglected or has been studied in specific contexts such as decision making by experts (e.g., Shanteau, Friel, Thomas, & Raacke, chap. 14, this volume). However, given the prevalence of repeated over new behavior, there is good reason to pay more systematic attention to constructs like past behavior, repetitive choices, experience, routines, and habit. This chapter focuses on *habits* and addresses in particular the issue of the measurement of habit strength. We first discuss the habit construct in more detail and give a brief summary of some work that has been done on habits. We then review four instruments to measure habit strength. Finally, a study is presented in which these measures were used simultaneously.

THE CONSTRUCT

Verplanken and Aarts (1999) defined *habits* as ". . . learned sequences of acts that have become automatic responses to specific cues, and are functional in obtaining certain goals or end states" (p. 104). Some features in this definition should be highlighted. First, habits are learned, goal-directed acts. This refers to the fact that habits do not develop randomly, but are formed first and foremost because they serve us. Habits develop in a stable situation when a particular sequence of acts appears functional or efficient or gives us pleasure (cf. Bagozzi & Dholakia, chap. 2, this volume). This relates directly to the behaviorist approach: Stable behavior is established through a history of systematic repetition and reinforcement. Thus, the everyday early morning routines may include a range of habits, which make the transition from waking up to starting work at the office as convenient and efficient as possible. It is important to realize that this holds for any behavior that becomes habitual, including behaviors we may consider unhealthy, unadaptive, or pathologic (e.g., Verplanken & Faes, 1999). In each of these cases, habits may be analyzed in terms of their history of repetition and their functions.

Another important feature in the definition of habit is that habit is a form of automaticity, which is triggered by specific cues. This conceptualization thus suggests that habits are executed without much awareness or deliberation, which comes close to how the habit construct appears in everyday language (Bargh, 1994). Wood, Quinn, and Kashy (2002) nicely documented this aspect in a diary study. Using a signal-contingent diary procedure, they demonstrated that people are less likely to think about and have fewer emotions related to habitual than nonhabitual behaviors. In terms of social cognition models, habits may be considered as behavior that is guided by implicit structures like schemas or implicit attitudes, rather than by explicit evaluations of behavior or conscious decision making (cf. Sanbonmatsu, Prince, Vanous, & Posavac, chap. 6, this volume). These cognitive structures are activated by relevant cues, such as time cues (walk to the bus stop at 7.47 a.m.), location cues (stop for a coffee on my way to work), or internal stimuli (feeling hungry). Because habits are automatically triggered by cues, one may infer that control over behavior is primarily rooted in the environment, rather than in an individual's motives or conscious will. Aarts and Dijksterhuis (2000) demonstrated the notion of habits as goal-directed automatic behavior. Participants who had either strong or weak bike habits indicated whether various travel modes were realistic options for a number of travel destinations. Half of the participants were previously primed with travel goals that were related to bike use. It was found that participants with a strong bike habit responded more quickly when bike was combined with a travel destination. However, this speed advantage only occurred when participants were primed with a bike-related travel goal. These results not only suggest that habits are goal-directed cognitive structures, but also that goal activation is a necessary component for habit-related responses (cf. Aarts, Verplanken, & van Knippenberg, 1998; Bagozzi & Dholakia, chap. 2, this volume).

Habits can be distinguished from a number of other concepts that build on prior knowledge. For example, Abelson (1981) introduced the concept of a *script*. Scripts are sequences of acts that are executed automatically. However, scripts differ from habits in being rooted in culture and thus being shared by many individuals, such as the restaurant script (enter, give coat, be seated, study the menu, order, etc.). Some scripts have a normative flavor, such as the casual conversation before starting a formal meeting (Aarts & Dijksterhuis, 2003). Abelson also suggested the idea of a personal script, which comes close to our conception of habit. *Experts'* behavior usually also consists of a range of automatic acts. These behaviors may be prescribed or have been developed by experience so as to optimally serve the expert's work (e.g., Omodei, McLennan, & Wearing, chap. 15, this volume; Plessner, chap. 17, this volume; Ross, Lussier, & Klein, chap. 18, this volume; Shanteau et al., chap. 14, this volume). Although expert routines may certainly be highly automized, this needs not be the case, which distinguishes them from habits. Finally, habits may be distinguished from *routines* and *routinized decision making* (e.g., Betsch, Haberstroh, & Höhle, 2002; Betsch, Haberstroh, Glöckner, Haar, & Fiedler, 2001; Haberstroh et al., chap. 12, this volume). These authors defined routines as behavioral solutions to decision problems. As is the case with experts' behavior, routines may be automized, but need not be so. Furthermore, routines differ from habits in that a person does not necessarily need to have personal experience with the behavior, such as is the case when performing a task according to a manual. Therefore, unlike habits, routines do not always require a history of successful repetition.

CONSEQUENCES

What are the consequences of habit formation? First of all, habit formation implies the establishment of stable behavioral patterns. Indeed as demonstrated in numerous studies on attitude–behavior relations, measures of past behavior are reliable predictors of future behavior and may outperform established predictors of behavior like attitudes and intentions (Ouellette & Wood, 1998). Many of these behaviors are likely to have a habitual component. Although there is an ongoing debate as to how to interpret this general finding (e.g., Ajzen, 2002; Bagozzi & Dholakia, chap. 2, this volume), the strong behavior–behavior correlations can be interpreted as indications of stability. One question is whether the predictive value of past behavior is contingent on its frequency. Ouellette and Wood (1998) demonstrated in a meta-analysis of studies on intention–behavior relations that this is indeed the case. They found that for frequent behaviors past behavior was more predictive of future behavior ($r = 0.47$) than for infrequent behaviors (r = 0.25). The reverse was the case for the relationship between behavioral intentions, which can be considered as a representation of motivation and conscious will and future behavior. Infrequent behaviors were found more under the control of intentions (r = 0.64) than frequent behaviors (r = 0.12). These findings suggest that there may be two ways by which past experiences influence future behavior. One is through deliberate thinking and decision making, which occurs with infrequent behaviors. This route represents the process by which we may consider past experiences and incorporate these as input of a future decision. Models like the theory of planned behavior apply to this route (e.g., Ajzen, 1991, 2002). The second route may represent the result of a habit formation process. When behavior is repeated frequently, the effects of motivation and conscious may fade away, and control over behavior may be taken over by the automatic cue-response mechanism described earlier as the way a habit functions (Wood et al., 2002). Such a pattern was modeled earlier by Triandis (1980). He suggested that the probability of an act is predicted by a weighted function of habit and behavioral intention in such a way that the two weights are compensatory: A strong weight of the habitual component implies a weak influence of intention and vice versa (Verplanken & Aarts, 1999). Bagozzi and Dholakia (chap. 2, this volume) distinguished three roles of past behavior in goal setting and goal striving (i.e., past behavior as statistically controlling for unmeasured effects of other antecedents of behavior, past behavior as a direct predictor of goal-directed behavior, and past behavior as influencing the process of goal setting and goal striving). Our distinction between the habit and deliberate routes clearly fits Bagozzi and Dohlakia's second and third roles, respectively.

A study on travel mode choices illustrated this habit–intention balance (Verplanken, Aarts, van Knippenberg, & Moonen, 1998). Car owners kept a diary for 7 days, in which they registered where they went during these days and which mode of transportation they used for each trip. The proportion of trips made by car versus public transport was predicted by previously measured behavioral intentions to use the car and a measure of car use habit strength. It appeared that there was only a significant relation between intention and behavior when habit strength was weak. At moderate and high levels of habit strength, there was no significant relation between intention and behavior.

Habit formation may have other, perhaps more fundamental, effects. In a series of lab studies, it was demonstrated that habit attenuates the depth of processing during decision making. A strong habit in one particular travel mode (e.g., bike or car) appeared to be associated with using less information about available travel mode alternatives (Verplanken, Aarts, & van Knippenberg, 1997, Studies 1 and 2) and with using less information that described the nature of the choice situations (Aarts, Verplanken, & van Knippenberg, 1997; Verplanken et al., 1997, Study 3). In the latter study, the attention to information about travel situations was manipulated. It appeared that the relatively low level of information acquisition under strong habit conditions could be increased by having participants make their choices in a more deliberative fashion. However, this effect was only temporary; after half of the 27 trials, these participants returned to the low information acquisition level comparable with strong habit participants in the control group. This study suggested that even under ideal intervention conditions (e.g., motivated participants, no distraction), which can never be accomplished in real-life situations, it was difficult to have strong habit individuals pay more attention to new information. In general, the finding that strong habit individuals' behavior is not or only weakly related to attitudes and intentions, together with the apparently low interest for information, presents a grim picture for those who wish to influence habitual behavior through information campaigns and attitude change. If information is attended to and changes attitudes in the first place, the weak attitude–behavior link among strong habit individuals seriously limits the likelihood of success for such an approach.

MEASUREMENT

Eagly and Chaiken (1993) concluded in their book, *The Psychology of Attitudes*, that "... the role of habit *per se* remains indeterminate (...) because of the difficulty of designing adequate measures of habit" (p. 181). Indeed although research on habit in social psychology is scarce in the first place, the measurement issue has not been given much attention.

The first problem in the measurement of habit is that usually no distinction is made between past behavior and habit. Thus, indicators of behavioral frequency are mostly used as measures of habit. Although some of those indicators are smarter than others, such as indicators obtained by observation (e.g., Landis, Triandis, & Adamopoulos, 1978) or reports of ongoing experiences (Wood et al., 2002), most measures consist of some kind of self-report of past behavioral frequency. Because a history of repetition forms the basis of a habit, using past behavioral frequency as a measure of habit does not seem unreasonable. However, there are a number of problems with self-reported behavioral frequency as a measure of habit. The first is that, although habit implies repeated behavior, repeated behavior needs not necessarily involve habituation (Ajzen, 2002). A second problem is that we cannot be sure that there is a linear relation between behavioral frequency and habit. For instance, how many trials does it take to form a habit? Ronis, Yates, and Kirscht (1989) defined a *habit* as behavior that is repeated at least twice a month and has been performed at least 10 times. However, there is no empirical evidence to support such an absolute statement. When a habit has formed, does behavioral frequency keep on strengthening it? Behaviorist models of conditioning do not suggest such a relation. These models suggest that once a behavior has been established, repetition and reinforcement schedules are needed to sustain it, but *not* that repetition will infinitely strengthen a habit, which is basically what a measure of behavioral frequency suggests. Another problem with self-reported frequency measures is that such reports might be flawed. This holds in particular if a measure asks participants to recall instances of behavior. Such episodic memories are notoriously inaccurate, which can especially be expected when behavior is habitual. If there is a stable pattern of repeated behaviors (e.g., doing the weekly shopping), estimation strategies might yield relative accurate reports of behavioral frequency. However, this is not generally assumed to be the case (see Verplanken & Aarts, 1999, for more details of this argument). In addition, many factors may bias a self-reported behavioral frequency measure, such as recency and salience effects, which may influence the ease with which behavioral episodes can be retrieved from memory (e.g., Aarts & Dijksterhuis, 1999). In general, because retrieval of episodic memories of habitual behavior is difficult almost by definition, frequency estimates will be made by using a variety of different strategies and heuristics, which may all be vulnerable to biases and distortions (e.g., Betsch & Pohl, 2002; Haberstroh & Betsch, 2002; Schwarz & Wänke, 2002).

Some researchers used a variant of a self-reported frequency measure by asking how often a behavior was conducted in the past "without awareness" or "by force of habit" (e.g., Kahle & Beatty, 1987; Mittal, 1988; Towler & Shepherd, 1991; Wittenbraker, Gibbs, & Kahle, 1983). In addition to the potential problems of frequency estimates discussed earlier, these measures suffer from the problem that an item asks two questions at the same time (i.e., a frequency estimate and the question to what extent a behavior can be qualified as a habit). Also an attempt to measure a construct like habit with only one item is likely to result in an unreliable measure.

In all, although self-reported frequency of past behavior does not seem an unreasonable measure of habit strength at first sight, there are questions about the validity of these measures, and such reports may also be inaccurate and biased. In the following, we discuss two alternative measures of habit strength—the Response Frequency measure and the Self-Reported Habit Index.

The Response Frequency Measure

The Response Frequency (RF) measure was developed and used in a research program on traffic mode choices (e.g., Aarts, 1996; Aarts et al., 1997, 1998; Verplanken et al., 1997, 1998; Verplanken, Aarts, van Knippenberg, &

van Knippenberg, 1994). To measure travel mode choice habits, this measure presented participants with a number (e.g., 15) of travel destinations. For each destination, participants were requested to respond as quickly as possible to which transportation mode they would use. The idea behind the RF measure was that general habits (e.g., taking the car) are represented as behavioral schemas. When such a schema is activated, in this case by the travel destination vignettes (e.g., visiting a friend in town), it is supposed to elicit the dominant travel mode response of that schema—for instance, using the car. The measure has been validated in a number of studies and showed good psychometric properties (Aarts, 1996). The advantage of the RF measure is that it does not ask participants to make estimates or judgments about their own behavior or psychological processes. It is also a measure that was designed to be used in contexts where multiple behavioral choice options are available. The measure is also attractive for behaviors that are conducted in a variety of situations, such as travel mode or food choice. For these behaviors, the habit may consist of making a particular choice in different situations. For instance, the habitual car user may take the car for any trip—even to bring a letter to a nearby mailbox. The person who has a habit of taking fatty food may do so in a variety of food choice situations. In particular, the generality of such a habit may render it problematic and socially relevant (Dawes, 1998; Verplanken et al., 1994). The RF measure seems especially adequate in such contexts. However, the RF measure has its downsides as well. For instance, because participants are supposed to respond as quickly as possible, it is difficult to use in self-administered questionnaires. If participants are given the opportunity to think and deliberate, the measure may tap other constructs, such as attitudes or preferences, rather than habit. Another inconvenience is that a new version of an RF measure should be constructed for each particular context, which requires pilot work and pretesting of the vignettes.

The Self-Report Habit Index

Perhaps the most straightforward approach to the measurement of habit strength is to ask people directly to report on their habits. Of course, such an approach has a number of potential problems. In addition to problems that are inherent to all self-report instruments, such as their sensitivity to social desirability and consistency biases, the main problem might be that people usually have little access to psychological processes, which has been put forward in the seminal paper by Nisbett and Wilson (1977). To use self-reports of habit strength and to know which questions would measure it, we should first be sure that people agree on what habits are. However, there is no unequivocal lay conception of what a habit is. For instance, *habit* has a number of different connotations in addition to doing things often or regularly, such as the connotation of bad habits or addictive behavior (e.g., Sinclair, 1989). Therefore, measures that attempt to ask directly to report on habit, such as the self-reported habit frequency measure discussed earlier, may be low in validity.

Verplanken and Orbell (2003) took a different approach and constructed a 12-item self-report instrument to measure habit strength, which was named the Self-Report Habit Index (SRHI). The reasoning behind this measure was that whereas it might be difficult to report on habit strength as such, a more valid measure might ask to report on a number of qualities of habitual behavior that are easier to conceptualize. The habit concept was thus broken down into a number of components that characterize habits (i.e., a history of repetition, lack of awareness, lack of control, mental efficiency, and expressing self-identity). A history of repetition forms a core element of habits. Lack of control, lack of awareness, and mental efficiency represent three features of automaticity, which were put forward by Bargh (1994). Bargh distinguished a number of variants of automaticity according to whether one or more of four features (the fourth feature is lack of intention) are present. The three features included in the SRHI are typical for habitual behavior. Finally, the element of self-identity was included in the SRHI. This refers to the fact that habits may be considered as idiosyncratic behaviors, which may be part of a person's self-description. In some cases, a habit may even reflect attitudes or values that are central to the self-concept (cf. Verplanken & Holland, 2002). Whereas reporting on habit strength per se may be too difficult to provide a valid measure, reporting on these more specific aspects seems feasible if one is posed with the right questions.

The SRHI has been used in a number of studies measuring a variety of habits. As far as published studies to date are concerned, the SRHI has been used to measure habit strength of travel mode choices, eating candies, listening to music, watching a TV soap series, and chatting with colleagues (Verplanken, 2004; Verplanken & Orbell, 2003). In addition, the measure was used in a number of recent and as yet unpublished data sets measuring habits of buying on impulse, taking unhealthy snacks, fish consumption, fruit consumption, and thinking negatively about oneself. In all data sets collected so far, the internal reliability of the SRHI was excellent (coefficient alphas > 0.90). In addition, the index also showed a high test–retest reliability when administered 1 week later ($r = 0.91$; Verplanken & Orbell, 2003, Study 1). Verplanken and Orbell (2003) presented a number of studies that provided evidence for convergent validity of the measure. For instance, the SRHI correlated strongly with the RF measure and with measures of past behavioral frequency. The index also discriminated between behaviors that varied in frequency and between daily and weekly habits. The SRHI has been included as part of larger models. For instance, in a study on job satisfaction among nurses, Verplanken (2003) found that the habit of chatting with each other predicted nurses' attitude toward their ward, which in turn predicted job satisfaction.

Summary

To date, four measures of habit strength are available (i.e., self-reported frequency of past behavior, self-reported habit frequency, the response frequency [RF] measure, and the Self-Report Habit Index [SRHI]). The measures differ in a number of ways. In Table 13.1, five characteristics are summarized. The first characteristic refers to whether each measure requires participants to reflect on their own behavior. Bassili (1996) distinguished meta-judgmental measures (self-reflections) from operative measures (e.g., response latencies). Self-reported frequency of past behavior, self-reported habit frequency, and the SRHI can be qualified as meta-judgmental measures, whereas the RF measure is an operative measure. Meta-judgmental measures are easy to interpret, but are vulnerable to judgmental and motivational biases. Operative measures, such as the RF measure, avoid such biases, but their drawback is validity. The second characteristic concerns whether the measure is a single- or multiple-item instrument. Multiple-item instruments are more reliable than single-item instruments. The third characteristic is whether the measure asks participants to make behavioral frequency estimates, which is the case for self-reported frequency of past behavior and self-reported habit. Frequency estimates may be difficult to make and may be subject to biases especially when numeric estimates are involved. The fourth characteristic indicates whether the measure applies to decisions with multiple behavioral options. The RF measure was designed for such contexts. The other measures focus on one behavioral option. In this case, one behavioral option refers either to a yes-no de-

TABLE 13.1
Characteristics of the Four Habit Measures

	Habit Measure			
Characteristic	*SRF*	*SRHF*	*RF*	*SRHI*
Type of measure	Meta-judgmental	Meta-judgmental	Operational	Meta-judgmental
Single/multiple item	Single	Single	Multiple	Multiple
Frequency estimate	Yes	Yes	No	No
Focus on multiple options	No	No	Yes	No
Usable in self-administered questionnaires	Yes	Yes	Preferably not	Yes

Note. SRF = self-reported frequency; SRHF = self-reported habit frequency; RF = response frequency measure; SRHI = Self-Report Habit Index.

cision or a focus on one choice option, thereby ignoring alternative options. Finally, the measures are scored on whether they can easily be used in self-administered questionnaires. This is no problem for all measures except the RF measure, which requires a time pressure instruction. Although not impossible in self-administered questionnaires, the optimal fashion of administering the RF measure is by a research assistant in a controlled research environment.

A STUDY WITH FOUR MEASURES

To compare the four habit measures discussed earlier, a study was conducted that included the four measures simultaneously (i.e., self-reported frequency of past behavior, self-reported habit frequency, the RF measure, and the SRHI). The habit domain we chose was travel mode choices. The study was conducted among students at the University of Tromsø. The four measures were taken with respect to taking the bus and the car, which were the two most frequently used travel modes among this sample. The first aim was to inspect intercorrelations among the four measures within each travel mode alternative. The second aim was to inspect correlations between the two travel mode alternatives for each measurement method. It can be expected that habit strength of competing travel mode alternatives in a particular setting (in this case, going by bus or taking the car) are inversely related.

Method

A questionnaire was presented to 98 students at the University of Tromsø, Norway. There were 60 females and 38 males. Ages ranged from 19 to 43 years ($M = 24.5$ years). The questionnaire contained four measures of habit strength concerning traveling by bus and car, respectively. The four measures were self-reported frequency of past behavior, self-reported habit frequency, the RF measure, and the SRHI. Self-reported frequency of past behavior consisted of the question how many times the bus (car) was used during the past week. Self-reported habit frequency was asked by the question how many times the bus (car) was used during the past week by force of habit. An RF measure of habit was constructed in which 13 travel destinations were presented that could be reached by bus or car. Participants were asked to respond as quickly as possible for each destination by choosing among four alternatives (i.e., walk, bus, car, or taxi). Finally, the SRHI was presented for bus and car use, respectively A seven-point Likert scale format was used. Coefficient alphas were 0.93 and 0.96 for the bus and car SRHI, respectively. The measures were presented in a fixed order (i.e., the

SRHI for bus and car, the RF measure, self-reported frequency of past behavior for bus and car use, and self-reported habit frequency of bus and car use, respectively). All measures were coded such that high values indicate strong habits.

Results

Correlations Among the Habit Measures. Table 13.2 presents intercorrelations for the two sets of habit measures (i.e., self-reported frequency, self-reported habit frequency, the response frequency measure, and the Self-Report Habit Index), each set with respect to traveling by bus and traveling by car. Although there were some exceptions, the correlations among the four habit measures were relatively high *within* each travel mode alternative, thus demonstrating convergent validity. As for the correlations of particular measures *between* the two travel mode alternatives, a negative correlation between a particular measure of bus and car habit should be expected because bus and car were the most likely alternatives, which was exactly what was found. Note that in this case, the −0.90 correlation between the two RF measures is a methodological artifact because the RF measure asked participants to choose between travel mode choices, and was thus used to infer both a bus and a car habit in one measurement. It seems that the SRHI is better able to tap the expected inverse relationship between bus and car habits ($r = -0.59$), compared with the self-reported frequency of past behavior and self-reported habit measures ($r = -0.30$ and $r = -0.27$), respectively. The difference in correlations between the SRHI and the two other self-report measures are statistically significant ($z = 2.59$ and $z = 2.80$, $ps < .01$), respectively.

TABLE 13.2
Pearson Correlations, Means, and Standard Deviations of Four Measures
of Habit With Respect to Bus and Car Use, Respectively

Variable	1	2	3	4	5	6	7	8
1. SRF bus	—	0.74	0.50	0.59	−0.30	−0.38	−0.38	−0.39
2. SRHF bus		—	0.38	0.55	−0.21	−0.27	−0.28	−0.34
3. RF bus			—	0.73	−0.65	−0.58	−0.91	−0.71
4. SRHI bus				—	−0.48	−0.47	−0.64	−0.59
5. SRF car					—	0.90	0.73	0.69
6. SRHF car						—	0.68	0.69
7. RF car							—	0.76
8. SRHI car								—

Note. $p < .05$ for correlations larger then 0.20; $p < .01$ for correlations larger then 0.25; $p < .001$ for correlations larger then 0.33. SRF = self-reported frequency; SRHF = self-reported habit frequency; RF = response frequency measure; SRHI = Self-Report Habit Index.

Habit Qualities. Whereas the frequency and RF measures consist of one score indicating habit strength, the SRHI provides a profile of scores on the different facets of the index. In principle, this gives the possibility to distinguish among different variants of habits. Whereas most habits can be expected to be based on a history of repetition, some habits may be particularly characterized by mental efficiency, others by lack of control, lack of awareness, the self-identifying aspect, or some combination of these features. Although so far the SRHI has been shown to be fairly one dimensional, we explored this line of reasoning by subjecting the bus and car SRHIs to principle component analyses (PCA) and structural equation modeling (SEM). Both PCAs suggested a predominantly one-dimensional structure, although for the bus SRHI, two eigenvalues greater than one appeared. Yet inspection of a two-component solution yielded quite a similar structure for both travel modes. In this structure, one component was determined by the three frequency-related items (e.g., taking the bus is something I do frequently) and the other component by the three items indicating a lack of awareness (e.g., taking the bus is something I do without thinking). These two sets of items were subsequently averaged and subjected to a structural equation modeling analysis (AMOS 4). In the estimated model, the awareness and frequency components of each SRHI were tested as indicators of latent variables representing a bus and car habit, respectively. The two latent habit constructs were assumed to be (negatively) correlated because these were two alternative choice options. The model, although relatively simple, showed an excellent fit, *Chi-square*(1) = 1.24 (*p* = .27), *Goodness of Fit Index* = 0.99, *Adjusted Goodness of Fit Index* = 0.94, *Comparative Fit Index* = 0.99, *Root Mean Residuals* = 0.06, *Root Mean Square Error of Approximation* = 0.05. The model and estimates are presented in Fig. 13.1. The analysis thus portrays bus and car habits as alternative options (*r* = −0.70), which are predominantly characterized by frequency of occurrence and lack of awareness.

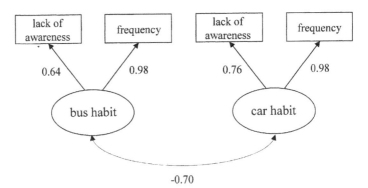

FIG. 13.1.   Latent variable model of bus and car habits as two alternative travel mode choices.

DISCUSSION AND CONCLUSIONS

Habit is an undervalued construct in social psychology. Whereas interest in other forms of schematic and automatic processes boomed during the last decade, research on habits remained scarce. We think undeservedly because a large portion of everyday behaviors might be characterized as habits. Undoubtedly, as expressed by the quote from Eagly and Chaiken (1993) earlier in this chapter, the problem of how to measure habit strength has been a major obstacle. Therefore, there is much to gain from investing in the development of reliable and valid habit measures, which seems most necessary in order to move habit research forward.

How should we evaluate the measures that were focused on in this chapter? Important criteria for such an evaluation are psychometric properties, conceptual clarity, external validity, vulnerability to biases, and practical aspects such as applicability and ease of using the measure. As for *psychometric properties*, internal reliability is not relevant for the two frequency measures, which consist of one item. It should be noted, however, that in general one-item measures suffer from being unreliable. The RF measure consists of multiple items (the vignettes). Because this measure consists of a count of the target behavior across the vignettes, a measure of internal reliability is not applicable. The SRHI is a multi-item instrument. It showed excellent internal reliability in the present study, as well as in the studies where it has been used so far. In the present study, the four measures showed good convergent validity, as was shown by the moderate to high intercorrelations for each travel mode alternative.

When it comes to *conceptual clarity*, the self-reported frequency measures are problematic. Although repetition of behavior is an important element of habit, not all repeated behavior are habits. Thus, a measure of past behavioral frequency is not necessarily a valid measure of habit (Ajzen, 2002). The self-reported habit frequency measure is difficult to interpret because of its confound of frequency and habit strength. The validity of the RF measure has been criticized for measuring intentions or preferences, rather than habit strength (Ajzen, 2002). This may particularly be the case when the measure is not properly administered (i.e., when respondents fill out the measure at their own pace instead of being under time pressure). The SRHI is an attempt to encompass the habit construct more fully by capturing the variety of aspects of the habit construct. Thus, this not only includes behavioral frequency, but also facets of automaticity (i.e., lack of awareness, lack of control, and mental efficiency). The present study also provided some evidence that demonstrates how the SRHI may be used to present habit profiles. That is, habits in different areas may have a different profile in terms of the facets of the SRHI. For instance, lack of control may be a particularly relevant feature of eating habits, whereas mental efficiency may be a salient aspect of driving a car. In the present study, the data suggest that in particular behavioral frequency and lack of awareness were the most salient qualities of travel mode choices. A similar approach was tentatively attempted on other data sets that included an SRHI. For instance, the most salient elements of habits to buy on impulse were frequency, self-identity, and the difficulty to control the behavior. The potential of the SRHI to distinguish among different habit qualities might be further investigated in future research. Clearly, whereas past behavioral frequency is undoubtedly an aspect of habit, the SRHI captures a much richer picture of what a particular habit might look like compared with other measures.

The external validity of the four measures is difficult to compare particularly because the measures have been applied in different contexts, and to date there are no systematic empirical comparisons of external validity. In our own research program on travel mode choices, both the self-reported frequency measure and the RF measure were found to predict information search behavior (Verplanken et al., 1997) as well as actual travel mode choices over a 7-day period (Verplanken et al., 1998). The SRHI was found to distinguish between daily and weekly executed behaviors (Verplanken & Orbell, 2003). As further evidence of external validity, the SRHI also performs well as part of larger models, such as in a study on chatting habits and job satisfaction (Verplanken, 2004), and in as yet unpublished studies on snacking habits, fish and meat consumption, fruit consumption, impulsive buying habits, and the dysfunctional habit of negative thinking, respectively.

The frequency measures might be most vulnerable to biases. Judgmental biases can particularly be expected when numerical frequencies are involved (e.g., biases due to recency or salience effects). The RF and particularly the SRHI seem less vulnerable to these problems. In the SRHI, the habit construct is broken down into elements that can well be reflected on, and there is no reason to suspect that biases may be problematic.

Finally, habit measures may be compared on practical aspects. Self-reported frequency of past behavior and the SRHI are convenient instruments. Both measures can be incorporated in self-administered questionnaires and do not require particular instructions. However, the RF requires pilot and pretest work for every new habit or habit context. In addition, it is preferably not used in self-administered questionnaires because it requires a time pressure instruction.

Is there a best habit measure? To answer this question, it should first be clear what the goal of the measurement is. A researcher may be interested in behavioral frequency and not necessarily in habituation. For instance, in the case of physical exercise, frequency may be more important information than habituation. In such cases, self-reported frequency of past behavior is the best measure. If the target behavior clearly involves making choices among multiple alternatives, the RF measure might be the right choice provided that the measure can be taken properly. The self-reported habit frequency measure should be disqualified because of its double-barreled and one-item nature, which comprises its validity and reliability. The SRHI is the better measure if one wishes to tap the degree to which a particular choice or behavior is habitual. This measure has multiple items, good psychometric properties, and is based on current notions of automaticity. In addition, it has a generic format and can easily be incorporated in questionnaires. A context to which the SRHI seems especially interesting to apply is to measure *change* in habit strength (i.e., habit formation or habit decay). In this context, behavioral frequency as a measure of habit may not work. Take, for example, medicine use. It can be assumed that a person who is put on long-term medication begins by taking medicine in a deliberative and thoughtful fashion. In due time, however, this may turn into a habit. A measure of behavioral frequency would be useless in this case because it can be assumed that the person immediately establishes a prescribed fixed schedule. The habituation in this case concerns medicine intake to become an automatic act, *not* a more frequent act. The SRHI might be a measure that taps this type of habituation, such as changes in the amount of thinking and the need to remind oneself of taking the medicine. In general, frequency measures cannot provide information about other features of habit such as the degree and quality of automaticity, which makes the SRHI a new and challenging instrument.

To date most researchers equate past behavioral frequency with habit, and thus use measures of past behavioral frequency as indicators of habit strength. However, this approach first ignores the fact that repeated behavior is not necessarily habitual behavior, and, second, that the habit construct is richer and more interesting than the mere repetition of behavior. A habit can be considered as a psychological construct and should be measured accordingly. Whereas in some contexts behavioral frequency gives important information, the SRHI does measure habit as a psychological construct. The SRHI gives researchers the opportunity to represent different qualities of habits and monitor changes in habit strength and habit qualities over time or as a result of interventions. This measure may thus contribute to the further development of future habit research.

REFERENCES

Aarts, H. (1996). *Habit and decision-making: The case of travel mode choice.* Unpublished dissertation, University of Nijmegen.

Aarts, H., & Dijksterhuis, A. (1999). How often did I do it? Experienced ease of retrieval and frequency estimates of past behavior. *Acta Psychologica, 103,* 77–89.

Aarts, H., & Dijksterhuis, A. (2000). Habits as knowledge structures: Automaticity in goal-directed behavior. *Journal of Personality and Social Psychology, 78,* 53–63.

Aarts, H., & Dijksterhuis, A. (2003). The silence of the library: Environment, situational norm, and social behavior. *Journal of Personality and Social Psychology, 84,* 18–28.

Aarts, H., Verplanken, B., & van Knippenberg, A. (1997). Habit and information use in travel mode choices. *Acta Psychologica, 96,* 1–14.

Aarts, H., Verplanken, B., & van Knippenberg, A. (1998). Predicting behavior from the past: Repeated decision-making or a matter of habit? *Journal of Applied Social Psychology, 28,* 1355–1374.

Abelson, R. P. (1981). Psychological status of the script concept. *American Psychologist, 36,* 715–729.

Ajzen, I. (1991). The theory of planned behavior. *Organizational Behavior and Human Decision Processes, 50,* 179–211.

Ajzen, I. (2002). Residual effects of past on later behavior: Habituation and reasoned action perspectives. *Personality and Social Psychology Review, 6,* 107–122.

Bargh, J. A. (1994). The four horsemen of automaticity: Awareness, intention, efficiency, and control in social cognition. In R. S. Wyer & T. K. Srull (Eds.), *Handbook of social cognition* (Vol. 1, pp. 1–40). Hillsdale, NJ: Lawrence Erlbaum Associates.

Bassili, J. N. (1996). Meta-judgmental versus operative indexes of psychological attributes: The case of measures of attitude strength. *Journal of Personality and Social Psychology, 71,* 637–653.

Betsch, T., Haberstroh, S., Glöckner, A., Haar, T., & Fiedler, K. (2001). The effects of routine strength on adaptation and information search in recurrent decision making. *Organizational Behavior and Human Decision Processes, 84,* 23–53.

Betsch, T., Haberstroh, S., & Höhle, C. (2002). Explaining routinized decision making: A review of theories and models. *Theory and Psychology, 12,* 453–488.

Betsch, T., & Pohl, D. (2002). Tversky and Kahneman's availability approach to frequency judgement: A critical analysis. In P. Sedlmeier & T. Betsch (Eds.), *Etc.: Frequency processing and cognition* (pp. 109–120). Oxford: Oxford University Press.

Dawes, R. M. (1998). Behavioral decision making and judgment. In D. T. Gilbert, S. T. Fiske, & G. Lindzey (Eds.), *The handbook of social psychology* (Vol. 1, pp. 497–548). New York: McGraw-Hill.

Eagly, A. H., & Chaiken, S. (1993). *The psychology of attitudes.* Fort Worth, TX: Harcourt Brace Jovanovich.

Haberstroh, S., & Betsch, T. (2002). Online strategies versus memory-based strategies in frequency estimation. In P. Sedlmeier & T. Betsch (Eds.), *Etc.: Frequency processing and cognition* (pp. 205–220). Oxford: Oxford University Press.

Hull, C. L. (1943). *Principles of behavior: An introduction to behavior theory.* New York: Appleton-Century-Crofts.

James, W. (1890). *The principles of psychology (Vol. 1).* London: Macmillan.

Kahle, L., & Beatty, S. E. (1987). The task situation and habit in the attitude-behavior relationship: A social adaptation view. *Journal of Social Behavior and Personality, 2,* 219–232.

Landis, D., Triandis, H. C., & Adamopoulos, J. (1978). Habit and behavioral intentions as predictors of social behavior. *Journal of Social Psychology, 106,* 227–237.

Mittal, B. (1988). Achieving higher seat belt usage: The role of habit in bridging the attitude-behavior gap. *Journal of Applied Social Psychology, 18,* 993–1016.

Nisbett, R. E., & Wilson, T. (1977). Telling more than we can know: Verbal reports on mental processes. *Psychological Review, 84,* 231–259.

Ouellette, J. A., & Wood, W. (1998). Habit and intention in everyday life: The multiple processes by which past behavior predicts future behavior. *Psychological Bulletin, 124,* 54–74.

Ronis, D. L., Yates, J. F., & Kirscht, J. P. (1989). Attitudes, decisions, and habits as determinants of repeated behavior. In A. R. Pratkanis, S. J. Breckler, & A. G. Greenwald (Eds.), *Attitude structure and function* (pp. 213–239). Hillsdale, NJ: Lawrence Erlbaum Associates.

Schwarz, N., & Wänke, M. (2002). Experiential and contextual heuristics in frequency judgement: Ease of recall and response scales. In P. Sedlmeier & T. Betsch (Eds.), *Etc.: Frequency processing and cognition* (pp. 89–108). Oxford: Oxford University Press.

Sinclair, J. (Ed.). (1989). *Collins cobuild English language dictionary.* London: Collins.

Towler, G., & Shepherd, R. (1991). Modification of Fishbein and Ajzen's theory of reasoned action to predict chip consumption. *Food Quality and Preference, 3,* 37–45.

Triandis, H. C. (1980). Values, attitudes, and interpersonal behavior. In H. E. Howe, Jr., & M. M. Page (Eds.), *Nebraska symposium on motivation, 1979* (pp. 195–259). Lincoln, NE: University of Nebraska Press.

Verplanken, B. (2004). Value congruence and job satisfaction among nurses: A human relations perspective. *International Journal of Nursing Studies.*

Verplanken, B., & Aarts, H. (1999). Habit, attitude, and planned behaviour: Is habit an empty construct or an interesting case of goal-directed automaticity? *European Review of Social Psychology, 10,* 101–134.

Verplanken, B., Aarts, H., & van Knippenberg, A. (1997). Habit, information acquisition, and the process of making travel mode choices. *European Journal of Social Psychology, 27,* 539–560.

Verplanken, B., Aarts, H., van Knippenberg, A., & Moonen, A. (1998). Habit, information acquisition, and the process of making travel mode choices. *British Journal of Social Psychology, 37,* 111–128.

Verplanken, B., Aarts, H., van Knippenberg, A., & van Knippenberg, C. (1994). Attitude versus general habit. *Journal of Applied Social Psychology, 24,* 285–300.

Verplanken, B., & Faes, S. (1999). Good intentions, bad habits, and effects of forming implementation intentions on healthy eating. *European Journal of Social Psychology, 29,* 591–604.

Verplanken, B., & Holland, R. W. (2002). Motivated decision making: Effects of activation and self-centrality of values on choices and behavior. *Journal of Personality and Social Psychology, 82,* 434–447.

Verplanken, B., & Orbell, S. (2003). Reflections on past behavior: A self-report index of habit strength. *Journal of Applied Social Psychology, 33,* 1313–1330.

Wittenbraker, J., Gibbs, B. L., & Kahle, L. R. (1983). Seat belt attitudes, habits, and behaviors: An adaptive amendment to the Fishbein model. *Journal of Applied Social Psychology, 13,* 406–421.

Wood, W., Quinn, J. M., & Kashy, D. A. (2002). Habits in everyday life: Thought, emotion, and action. *Journal of Personality and Social Psychology, 83,* 1281–1297.

THE ROUTINES
OF DECISION MAKING:
APPLIED RESEARCH

14

Development of Expertise in a Dynamic Decision-Making Environment

James Shanteau
Brian M. Friel
Rickey P. Thomas
John Raacke
Kansas State University

The decision maker must continually adjust to consequences, and in doing so, deviate from the clear course of laid out in advance.

—A. Toffler (1991)

For over a half century, decision-making research has focused on static choice and judgment. That is, time is "frozen" at the point of decision making. Probably the best-known example is the choice-between-bets task (Edwards, 1954). This is commonly called the *gambling paradigm* (Goldstein & Hogarth, 1997). Other examples include heuristics-and-biases word problems (Tversky & Kahneman, 1974) and fast-and-frugal heuristic tasks (Gigerenzer & Goldstein, 1996). In these studies, decision makers are shown a problem that is fixed at a point in time.

It has been clear to many investigators, however, that a dynamic focus is needed in decision research (e.g., see Anderson, 1971; Brehmer, 1995; Connolly, 1988; Hogarth, 1987; von Winterfeldt & Edwards, 1986). Most decision-making environments evolve over time, so that there is a past, present, and future to choice and judgment; past decisions impact present situations and present decisions impact future situations (see also work on routinized decision making by Betsch, Fiedler, & Brinkmann, 1998; Betsch, Glöckner, & Haberstroh, 2000; Betsch, Haberstroh, Glöckner, Haar, & Fiedler, 2001).

Despite these self-evident observations, little has changed in decision research over the years (Goldstein & Hogarth, 1997). Most research tasks remain static, with a preponderance of fixed-in-time decision problems. There are at least three reasons that might explain why dynamic decision making has received little attention.

First, there are few theories or models of dynamic decision making. Normative theories derived from either economics or statistics generally lack a temporal component; the Bayesian model of probability revision is a notable exception. Similarly, most descriptive models lack a temporal element, although some models have been proposed to account for belief updating and attitude revision (e.g., Anderson, 1971; Einhorn & Hogarth, 1986; Pitz, Downing, & Reinhold, 1967). Thus, it is difficult to conduct research on dynamic decisions when theories and models are lacking.

Second, there are relatively few decision tasks that include a temporal element. Interestingly, some of the earliest paradigms in decision research did contain a dynamic component—for example, the bookbags-and-poker chips task (Phillips & Edwards, 1966) and the multiple-cue-probability-learning (MCPL) task (Hammond, Summers, & Deane, 1973). At the time, both paradigms generated a great deal of research. However, they have been used less in recent years and have yet to be replaced by other dynamic tasks.

Third, there are a lack of tools and methods for evaluating behavior in dynamic tasks. Although it is relatively straightforward to assess choices and preferences in static environments, it is less obvious how to evaluate behavior in changing environments. This is particularly problematic in settings where past behavior influences present decision options. Describing interactions between past and present (or present and future) behavior has proved elusive.

Even standard dynamic variables, such as learning and fatigue, have received little attention in decision research. Indeed most researchers either ignore or attempt to eliminate such changes in participants' decisions. Yet it seems dubious to assume that behavior remains fixed over time in an experiment (e.g., Hogarth, chap. 4, this volume). Even fairly straightforward decision tasks can lead to surprisingly large changes within an experimental session (see Shanteau & Linin, 1990).

In the present study, each of these issues was addressed in the research design. Specifically, decisions are studied for a dynamic air traffic control environment using a novel approach to assessing skilled performance that may lead a new model of dynamic decision making.

DYNAMIC ELEMENTS IN DECISION MAKING

There are three ways that dynamic elements may impact judgment and decision making. The first is that stimulus environments change over time (i.e., many tasks have an inherently temporal component). In air traffic control, for instance, aircraft are constantly changing position regardless of whether the controller makes a decision. Other examples include fire fighting and power plan operations. In each case, it makes little sense to "stop time" to study a judgment or decision.

The second dynamic element is that the participants change over time. For instance, the strategies used and/or the values underlying decision making evolve from learning, adaptation, or prior experience. Conversely, the participant's performance may decline due to fatigue, boredom, or exhaustion. Thus, even if it is possible to stop time for the stimuli, temporal shifts often occur within the participant.

The final element involves the role of feedback within a scenario. Many tasks involve not just a single decision, but a series of ongoing decisions each based, in part, on outcomes from prior decisions (see Harvey & Fischer, chap. 7, this volume). For instance, driving a car or flying an aircraft involves a series of decisions with a built-in feedback loop. This illustrates what Connolly (1988) called "hedge clipping"—a series of interrelated decisions each tied to those that came before.

The present research incorporates each of these dynamic elements. Specifically, changing participant behavior (due to learning) is studied within an inherently dynamic environment (ongoing air traffic control) with a built-in feedback loop (involving hedge clipping).

MICROWORLDS

As defined by Rigas, Carling, and Brehmer (2002), "microworlds are computer simulations of certain reality aspects and are characterized by various degrees of complexity, dynamics, polytely, and intransparency" (p. 465). *Complexity* arises from multiple variables related through uncertain causal connections. *Polytely* refers to multiple, often contradictory, goals that require trade-offs. *Dynamics* within a microworld reflect automatic changes taking place over time. *Intransparency* means that not everything in the system is apparent and certain aspects must therefore be inferred. Thus, "in experiments with microworlds, the goals are ill-defined, only part of the needed information is available from the beginning, the decisions are dependent on time, there are several possible solutions, and there is more than one correct solution method" (Rigas et al., 2002, p. 465).

In the present research, a microworld simulation of air traffic control (ATC) is used. The microworld CTEAM (Controller Teamwork Evaluation and Assessment Methodology) was originally developed by the American Federal Aviation Administration (FAA; Bailey, Broach, Thompson, & Enos, 1999). Each operator learns to direct a series of aircraft within an air sector from takeoff to an ultimate destination. The aircraft are constantly moving, so that if the operator does nothing, the planes will continue on their present course. There are multiple possible solutions, each of which can get the aircraft to their intended destination. At the same time, it is essential to maintain appropriate separation between adjacent aircraft. In all, CTEAM meets the microworld specifications identified by Rigas et al. (2002): dynamics, complexity, polytely, and intransparency.

COCHRAN–WEISS–SHANTEAU (CWS) INDEX OF PERFORMANCE

As reviewed by Shanteau, Weiss, Thomas, and Pounds (2003), a variety of indexes and measures have been proposed to identify skilled or expert behavior. Some of these are direct, but unverifiable (i.e., formal certification or job titles). Thus, accredited subject matter experts (SMEs) are often used by researchers to provide a standard of comparison. Other approaches are verifiable, but difficult to apply in many domains (i.e., externally validated correct answers). Unfortunately, experts are frequently needed in precisely those domains where verifiable "gold standard" answers are unavailable. Some approaches, although compelling, are circular (e.g., using the consensus of already defined experts to establish criterion answers). In effect, this uses one group of experts to define the standards used to evaluate another group of experts. For a discussion of other approaches to expertise, see Omodei, McLennan, and Wearing (chap. 15, this volume).

There are, however, two necessary, but not sufficient, conditions that are both verifiable and noncircular, and do not require externally defined correct answers. The first condition, initially proposed by Einhorn (1974), is within-expert reliability or consistency. To be skilled, an expert should be able to repeat his or her judgment under similar circumstances. Unreliable judgments are a counterindication of skill or expertise. The second condition, defined by Hammond (1996), is the ability to differentiate or make discriminations. Experts should be able to discriminate stimulus cases using often subtle cues to which nonexperts may be insensitive.

To use CWS, an expert's responses are analyzed to generate measures of discrimination and inconsistency. Typically, variances are used to estimate discrimination and consistency. Examining variation in the candidate's responses to different stimuli gauges discrimination. Inconsistency is assessed by variation in the candidate's responses to the same stimuli.

CWS combines these two necessary conditions by forming a ratio of discrimination to inconsistency so that higher scores indicate more skilled performance. Thus, experts should be consistent in making fine discriminations. The use of a ratio is consistent with the formulation proposed by Cochran (1943) for assessing the quality of response instruments.

CWS has been successfully applied to several prior studies of expert judgment (see Shanteau, Weiss, Thomas, & Pounds, 2002). In a reanalysis of Ettenson (1984), for instance, CWS distinguished between expert and nonexpert auditors based on their assessments of a set of financial cases. In a reanalysis of a study of livestock judges by Phelps (1977), CWS separated specialists in swine judging from specialists in cattle judging. When applied to a study of personnel selection by Nagy (1981), CWS revealed that use of irrelevant information was more diagnostic than use of relevant information in differentiating experts from nonexperts.

In each of these applications, CWS was able to separate higher skilled performance from lesser skilled performance. Moreover, CWS did this without relying on an externally validated correct answer. Instead CWS made use of properties of the behavioral responses. For more information on the theory behind CWS, see Weiss and Shanteau (2003).

One limitation in previous applications of CWS, however, is that the decisions were made in response to static or fixed stimuli. In each case, participants viewed printed summaries of cases. Thus, CWS has yet to be applied to the more realistic situation of dynamic decision making. Therefore, one purpose of this research is to demonstrate the applicability of CWS in a dynamic task.

RESEARCH PREDICTIONS

For our study, we made five predictions. First, we expect that CWS will provide a useful tool for analyzing performance in a complex, constantly changing environment such as CTEAM. Thus, we believe the success that CWS had in assessing expertise in static, fixed environments will extend to dynamic, moving environments.

Second, we expect that CWS scores will increase with experience. If the old adage "practice makes perfect" is true, then the longer an operator practices with CTEAM, the better performance should be (as shown by higher CWS scores).

Third, we predict that CWS scores would vary as a function of task complexity. In this study, complexity was manipulated by adding more aircraft to the scenario (i.e., higher density). The more planes there are to handle, the more difficult the task—hence, lower CWS scores are anticipated.

Fourth, if higher CWS scores reflect better CTEAM performance, then the scores should be negatively correlated with ATC errors. That is, errors are counterindicative of expert performance—the greater the number of errors, the lower the CWS score should be. (Note that professional air traffic controllers rarely make errors. Hence, number of errors provides an insensitive measure of relative performance.)

Finally, CWS scores are expected to be lower in scenarios with restricted flight zones (i.e., areas where aircraft cannot fly). If a thunderstorm reduces the airspace available, then operators have less area to move aircraft through. Thus, when a restriction is present, operators should have a more difficult time routing aircraft to their destinations—hence, lower CWS scores are predicted.

METHOD

Project Overview

A 12-week longitudinal study involving naive participants was conducted, with three 2-hour sessions each week. The initial 4 weeks were devoted to instruction and familiarization; the final 8 weeks were used for data collection. The study had two manipulations of scenario difficulty. The first involved variations of aircraft density; the second involved the presence or absence of restricted airspace due to a thunderstorm. Three dependent measures were collected: (a) number of separation errors (aircraft within five scale miles of a sector boundary or another aircraft at the same altitude), (b) number of collisions, and (c) time through sector (the amount of time from an aircraft's first appearance on the screen until it reaches destination = TTS). We focused on TTS because it is the primary variable used by the FAA to evaluate ATC performance (Bailey et al., 1999).

Participants

Twelve Kansas State University undergraduates were paid $12 per 2-hour session. Two participants dropped out of the study—one after 13 sessions, the other after 23 sessions. Because their departure had nothing to do with performance, their data were included where appropriate. However, the same pattern of results was obtained when their data were excluded from the analyses.

Apparatus, Design, and Procedure

Participants were given the task of operating a single-sector version of CTEAM (see Fig. 14.1). CTEAM was presented on 17-inch monitors. The operator's task was to direct aircraft from starting points to exit gates (places at which the planes can leave a sector) or to destination airports. Control actions were made using *Kensington Expert Mouse* trackballs, similar to those used in real ATC.

Each aircraft and its associated information are represented by data blocks. A data block includes (a) aircraft call sign (designated by a number

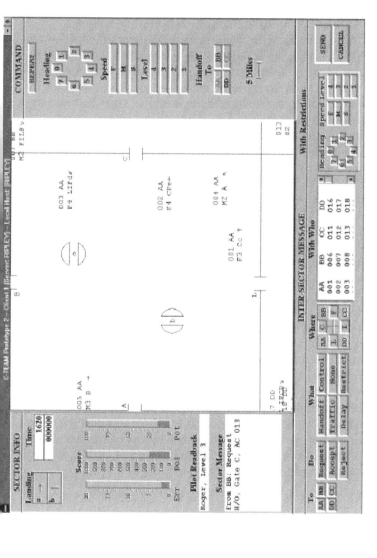

FIG. 14.1. Screen shot of single sector version of CTEAM. The central (white) area shows the sector to be controlled, with aircraft identified by datablocks (containing identifiers, route and destination, speed, heading, and elevation). To the right is the "command panel," where operators control the aircraft. To the left is the "feedback panel," containing updated scores on errors, delay times, and percent of aircraft reaching destination. At the bottom is the "communication panel," with message send-and-receive feedback. For more detailed information on CTEAM, see Bailey et al. (1999).

257

reflecting its order of appearance in the airspace; e.g., 016, and two letters corresponding to its sector of origin; e.g., AA), (b) speed (S = slow, M = medium, F = fast), (c) altitude (1–4, with higher numbers representing higher altitudes), and (d) destination (lowercase letters representing airports and uppercase letters representing the exit gates). The physical location of an aircraft is represented by an arrow that also indicates its heading.

Participants were instructed to avoid separation errors (i.e., when aircraft come within 5 miles of one another at the same altitude or the sector boundary). In the event of a separation error, the data blocks for the involved aircraft light up in red to warn the controller to issue commands for evasive maneuvers. Collisions are depicted by red plus signs and result in the aircraft disappearing from the screen. Airports are represented by the circles intersected by an open bar, which symbolize the runway direction.

Participants controlled speed, altitude, and heading by first selecting the aircraft using the trackball and then selecting the appropriate command on the "Command" panel. The aircraft data block changes from green to yellow to indicate that a command has been issued.

One advantage of CTEAM is that it allows experimenters to manipulate scenario characteristics. For example, aircraft density can be varied by specifying the number and timing of aircraft appearing in a scenario. Experimenters can also add a restricted airspace (RA) into the scenario, through which aircraft are not allowed to fly. Failure to avoid RA results in a collision error.

In the present study, participants were presented with six scenarios created by crossing three levels of Aircraft Density (Low = 12, Medium = 24, High = 36 aircraft) with two levels of RA (Present or Absent). To compare CWS scores across different densities, a common set of 12 aircraft from the Low scenario were embedded in the Medium and High scenarios.

In the 8 weeks of the study, participants completed three repetitions (hereafter called *replicates*) of the same scenario to estimate the Consistency component of CWS. Participants completed three sessions per week, yielding 24 sessions per participant. Two 2-week blocks of scenarios were created, each presented twice (see the design in Table 14.1). The order of scenario presentation was the same for all participants.

Analyses

CWS scores were calculated using the time between the aircraft's first appearance in the sector to the time it reached its destination (= TTS) as the dependent variable. For each participant in every session, Discrimination was calculated from the variance of TTS scores between different aircraft (i.e., the variance between TTS scores for aircraft taking different routes). Inconsistency was assessed from the variance of TTS scores for the same

TABLE 14.1
Order of Scenario Presentation Across Weeks

Block	Week	Day 1	Day 2	Day 3
1	1	Low	Med	Low/RA
	2	Med/RA	Low	Med
1	3	Low	Med	Low/RA
	4	Med/RA	Low	Med
2	5	Med	High	Med/RA
	6	High/RA	Med	High
2	7	Med	High	Med/RA
	8	High/RA	Med	High

aircraft across the three replicates (i.e., the variance within TTS scores for the same aircraft across replications). Discrimination was divided by Inconsistency to form the CWS ratio. Only those 12 aircraft common to all three aircraft densities were included in the CWS calculations.

Because ratio scores typically result in positive correlations between means and variances (in the present study, there was a positive correlation of $r = +.84$ between means and variances), CWS scores were transformed so they no longer violated the homoscedasticity assumption. The square root of each CWS score was used for analytic purposes. For presentation, the root mean squared (the average square root of the CWS scores squared) was used as a summary statistic (Weiss & Edwards, under review). "Objective" measures of performance (i.e., Collision Errors and Separation Errors) were also analyzed for comparison to CWS scores.

RESULTS

Scenario Complexity Manipulations

Root mean squares of CWS scores for each scenario condition are presented in Fig. 14.2. As shown by the solid bar to the far right, the High Density/no RA (no restricted airspace) condition produced a root mean square CWS value of 77.28; the Low/no RA and Medium/no RA density conditions produced root mean square CWS values of 152.53 and 172.33, respectively. A similar pattern was observed for the RA conditions (gray bars).

As anticipated, CWS scores declined for the higher density scenarios. Unexpectedly, the CWS results for the RA conditions were greater at each density level. Overall, the best performance was in the Low/RA condition; the worst performance was in the High/no RA condition.

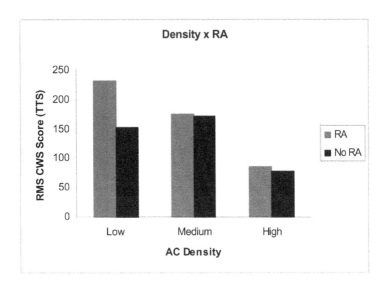

FIG. 14.2.   Root mean square CWS scores as a function of Aircraft (AC) Density and Restricted Airspace (RA).

To verify these findings, the data were analyzed by a 3 (Aircraft Density) × 2 (RA) repeated measures ANOVA. The main effects of Aircraft Density [$F(2, 20) = 14.71, p < .05, \eta^2 = .42$] and RA [$F(1, 10) = 5.17, p < .05, \eta^2 = .02$] were both statistically significant. The interaction was not significant [$F(2, 20) = 2.12, p > .05, \eta^2 = .04$]. These results confirm the graphical results in Fig. 14.2.

Initially, it had been predicted that scenarios with a restricted airspace would lead to lower CWS scores because there is less free space to use for the aircraft. However, both graphical and statistical analyses confirm that restrictions in the airspace actually improved performance. Possible reasons for this finding are considered in the Discussion.

Performance Improvements Over Time

Figure 14.3 shows CWS scores across sessions for the three density conditions. CWS scores can be seen to increase across the four sessions for the Low/no RA scenario (left panel). Similarly, the scores increased overall, except the last session for the Medium/RA scenario (bottom panel). For comparison, the scores for Medium/no RA scenario show a more modest increase (right panel). (Due to space limitations, only three graphs are shown here. However, similar results were obtained for the other conditions.)

Within each level of Aircraft Density, CWS scores were analyzed statistically over sessions. Linear trend analyses revealed significant increases for Low/no RA [$F(1, 10) = 5.99, p < .05$] and Medium/RA [$F(1, 9) = 7.44, p < .05$].

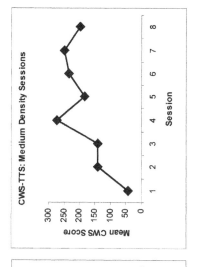

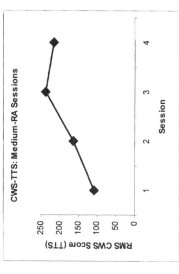

FIG. 14.3. Root mean square CWS scores for Low Aircraft Density/No Restricted Airspace (RA) as a function of sessions, Medium Aircraft Density/No RA, and Medium Aircraft Density/RA. Note: There are four sessions for some scenarios and eight sessions for others.

The apparent improvement for the Medium/no RA scenarios was marginally significant [$F(1, 10) = 4.35, p = .06$]. The linear trends were not significant for Low/RA [$F(1, 11) < 1$], High/no RA [$F(1, 8) = 2.03, p > .10$], and High/RA scenarios [$F(1, 9) < 1$].

Comparison to Objective Measures

To determine how well CWS did in capturing performance, the scores were compared to the "objective measures" of the number of collision errors, separation errors, and total errors (= collision errors + separation errors). The results in Table 14.2 give correlation values between CWS and these other measures. The center column shows the correlations for CWS scores (computed with the aircraft involved in collisions omitted). This analysis reveals moderately negative correlations with each of the three objective measures of errors. With the data for all aircraft included (even those involved in collisions), results in the right column show larger negative correlations with CWS. In all, these results reveal that CWS scores share some, but not all, of the variance with objective error data.

Comparison to Other Measures

Given that CWS scores are moderately correlated with the objective measures, the question remains: Does CWS add anything new? Why use CWS if objective error data are available? One answer can be seen in Fig. 14.4, which shows CWS scores for the Low/no RA sessions in which no errors were made. As can be seen, CWS scores increased across the sessions, although no errors were made. That is, CWS changes over sessions in which there is no change in the objective error data. Thus, CWS appears to provide a more sensitive measure of performance.

Another objective measure is raw TTS. As shown in Fig. 14.5, times for the Low/no RA condition did decline from the first to second sessions. However, times reached asymptote, whereas the CWS scores for the same conditions in Fig. 14.5 continued to show improvement. Also, as seen in Table 14.3, CWS scores were more strongly correlated with errors than are TTS

TABLE 14.2
Spearman Rank-Order Correlations Between CWS
and Objective Measures of Performance

Error	$CWS_{Without\ Collisions}$	$CWS_{With\ Collisions}$
Collision errors	−.24	−.52
Separation errors	−.34	−.36
Total errors	−.35	−.49

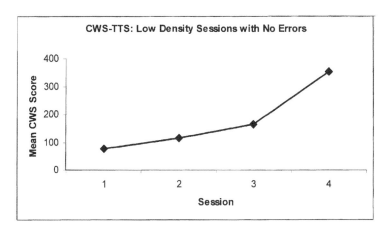

FIG. 14.4. Root mean square CWS scores in Low Aircraft Density/No Restricted Airspace as a function of sessions in which no errors were made.

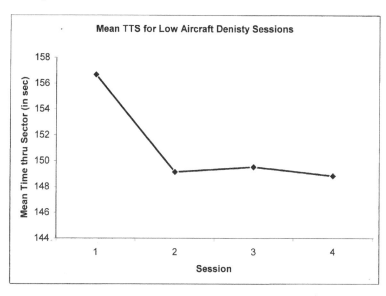

FIG. 14.5. Mean time through sector in Low Aircraft Density/No Restricted Airspace as a function of sessions.

TABLE 14.3
Spearman Rank-Order Correlations Between CWS (With and Without Crashes), Raw Time Through Sector, and Different Types of Errors

Error	$CWS_{Without\ Collisions}$	$CWS_{With\ Collisions}$	Time Though Sector
Collision errors	−.24	−.52	+.21
Separation errors	−.34	−.36	+.15
Total errors	−.35	−.49	+.19

values. This means CWS is more sensitive to improvements in performance than is a measure of time.

DISCUSSION

These results are relevant to the five predictions made initially. First, CWS provided a useful tool to study complex, dynamic behavior in a computer microworld such as CTEAM. Second, CWS scores generally increased with practice, suggesting that the index provides a useful measure of performance improvement. Third, CWS scores were sensitive to changes in task complexity due to changes in aircraft density. Fourth, CWS values were moderately negatively correlated with objective measures (i.e., collision and separation errors). Finally, CWS scores were unexpectedly higher in scenarios contained in restricted airspace. Each of these findings is discussed next.

Evaluation of Skills in Dynamic Environments

As shown here, CWS makes it possible to analyze decision performance in a complex, dynamic environment. Despite the complexity of the ATC task, the CWS approach provided insights into the behavior of operators in an ever-changing microworld. Many of the results were expected, but still confirmed by CWS (e.g., the decline in performance as airspace density increased).

It is worth commenting on the use of a technologically sophisticated microworld-simulation in this research. Unlike some microworld programs, CTEAM is more than an elaborate computer game. It was initially developed for internal purposes by the FAA and later made available to researchers (see Bailey et al., 1999). It joins a small group of other microworld-simulations of air traffic control (Ackerman & Cianciolo, 2002) and adds to the options available for investigating dynamic decision making (see also Omodei, McLennan, & Wearing, chap. 15, this volume; Omodei & Wearing, 1995). Beyond the analysis of individual expertise, CWS can also be used to study development of group or team decision making (Kameda, Tindale, & Davis, 2003).

Longitudinal Skill Development

As predicted, CWS scores reflected performance improvements for three of the scenarios. Figure 14.3, for instance, reveals a clear upward trend in performance. However, three other scenarios did not yield significant increases in CWS scores. One possible reason is that there were only two sessions of the Low/RA and High/RA scenarios (see the design in Table 14.1). This may not have allowed enough practice for participants to show performance improvements in these scenarios. In particular, given the relative difficulty of the High/RA scenario (participants averaged 4.10 errors per session), it is plausible that two sessions were insufficient to allow for skill development. There is obviously a need for further research on this issue.

Nonetheless, the finding that CWS scores were sensitive to performance improvements means the index could be used to assess skill development in trainees. For instance, the present results suggest that CWS could be used to compare different methods of training (or different durations of training). Also trainees' CWS score improvements might be used to determine whether all-or-none sink-or-swim training is preferable to gradual step-by-step instruction.

CWS might be used to evaluate other training issues, such as the role of outcome feedback in development of experienced-based decision making (see Harvey & Fischer, chap. 7, this volume). CWS could also be applied to evaluate different modes of thinking during training (see Hogarth, chap. 4, this volume).

Sensitivity of CWS to Task Complexity

In this study, task complexity was manipulated by varying the density of aircraft in the airspace. This reflects the strategy adopted by FAA researchers in previous applications of CTEAM (Bailey et al., 1999). Although there are likely to be other variables that impact complexity (such as the spacing of aircraft), variation of aircraft density is clearly a variable linked to task complexity.

It is notable that CWS scores were uniformly higher for more dense environments. As can be seen in Figs. 14.2 and 14.3, CWS scores varied as a function of the number of aircraft in the airspace. This finding held across other analyses not reported here for lack of space. Thus, CWS is sensitive to the density manipulation.

One implication of this finding is that CWS may provide a useful proxy measure of task complexity. Measuring or even defining complexity has been a vexing problem in previous research (e.g., Rigas et al., 2002). Although CWS was not intended as a means to define complexity, it may offer a novel approach to the problem of measuring complexity. Of course this will have to be verified in future research.

Comparison of CWS to Objective Measures

Because CWS is a novel approach to assessing performance in skilled tasks, it is worthwhile to compare it to other more traditional (i.e., objective) approaches. In the present study, there were several external indexes reported by CTEAM: Number of Collisions, Number of Separation Errors, and Times Through Sector. Although each of these external measures did show trends in the expected direction, CWS did a better job of capturing several aspects of performance. For instance, CWS scores were superior to error measurements in cases where few errors are made (see Fig. 14.4).

Two additional points are worth noting. First, professional air traffic controllers rarely make errors. Thus, the use of error measures for assessing performance has limited value (because of insensitivity) when dealing with professionals. Second, CWS analyses of TTS latencies proved to be more sensitive than assessment of raw TTS latencies (see Fig. 14.5). Given that the same data entries were used for each analysis, this shows that CWS is able to extract information that might otherwise be missed in an objective analysis of skilled performance.

It is not our purpose to suggest that objective measures never be used. Obviously, when external criteria are available, they should play an essential part in analyzing skilled behavior. As demonstrated here, however, CWS provides a useful tool that may supplement external measures, especially when those measures reach asymptote. Thus, CWS can be used to complement error measures by providing information that the objective measures do not.

We are now exploring an extension of CWS that allows a more fine-grained analysis of ongoing performance in continuous, dynamic settings. By continually updating CWS scores during a scenario, it should be possible to assess moment-by-moment changes in performance. This may help identify, for example, the sources of performance enhancers and performance detractors.

Do Restrictions Hurt?

We originally hypothesized that adding restrictions to the airspace ("no-fly" areas) would impede performance. Our logic was based on the belief that reducing options would inhibit the operators' decision-making flexibility. Unexpectedly, we found the opposite—CWS scores were higher when RA was introduced into the scenarios.

There are two possible explanations for this unexpected result. The first is that RA scenarios were always presented several days after corresponding scenarios with no RA (see Table 14.1). Experience with a particular level of aircraft density may account for the higher CWS scores in the RA conditions. This is consistent with the improvements shown by participants with practice.

The second explanation focuses on the Inconsistency component of CWS. The presence of RA leaves participants with fewer response options of where to direct aircraft. Thus, Inconsistency scores may have been lower because aircraft are less free to vary, leading to increased CWS scores. In fact scenarios with RA did yield lower values of Inconsistency than scenarios with no RA (Low/RA Inconsistency = 27.95, Low/no RA = 70.75; Medium/RA = 50.03, Medium/no RA = 187.85; High/RA = 238.31, High/no RA = 260.44). Thus, Inconsistency scores were lower when restrictions were imposed.

It would be interesting to examine the role of restrictions on decision performance in other dynamic microworld environments (e.g., fire fighting or power plant operations). Is it the case that a restriction of choice options always improves performance in other domains? Also are there some types of restrictions that improve performance while other types of restrictions impede performance?

Other Applications of CWS

It is relevant to speculate on other applications of CWS. For instance, Haberstroh, Betsch, Glöckner, Haar, and Stiller (chap. 12, this volume) looked at routinized decision making in a microworld-simulation (COMMERCE). When changes in the microworld rendered the routine choice obsolete, it took participants a considerable amount of time to adapt to the new situation. The stronger the routine, the harder it is for participants to quit their strategy, although the evidence clearly speaks against maintaining routine choices (see also Betsch, Haberstroh, Glöckner, Haar, & Fiedler, 2001; Betsch, Haberstroh, & Höhle, 2002). It might be interesting to apply CWS to examine changes in such routinized decision environments.

Similarly, CWS might be used as an index to evaluate factors that lead to deficits in performance, such as time pressure or environmental stress (e.g., Svenson & Maule, 1993). Alternatively, CWS could be used to evaluate efforts to teach improved decision-making skills (e.g., Baron & Brown, 1991). Finally, CWS might be valuable for examining variables that facilitate decision performance, such as positive affect (Isen & Labroo, 2003).

Finally, it may be worth using CWS in other areas of research outside the usual judgment and decision-making framework. For example, CWS could be extended to evaluate behavior in problem-solving contexts (e.g., see Brehmer, Dörner, and others).

Caveats

There are three caveats to the use of CWS that deserve mention. It is important to note, however, that other measures of skilled performance (e.g., correlations with objective criteria) share these restrictions.

First, CWS provides a relative, not an absolute, measure of performance. It is possible to determine, using CWS, which of two conditions or which of two operators produces better performance (an ordinal statement). However, it is not possible to say that performance in one condition is twice as good as another (a ratio statement).

Second, CWS is task and domain specific. The present results apply only to the specific scenarios used within the CTEAM microworld-simulation. There is no way to generalize performance from one task (e.g., air sector management) to another task (e.g., weather forecasting) in air traffic control. Further, we cannot make any predictions about performance in one domain (e.g., fire fighting) simulation based on performance in another domain (e.g., air traffic control).

Finally, the CWS components of Discrimination and Inconsistency were computed using variances in this study. In general, we feel that variances are often the most efficient (and most convenient) method for estimating CWS values, but it deserves mention that there are other estimation procedures. In Weiss and Shanteau (2003), an example calculation is presented for CWS analysis of categorical data using nominal counts. Thus, the CWS method is more flexible than was demonstrated here.

ACKNOWLEDGMENTS

This research was supported, in part, by the Federal Aviation Administration, Department of Transportation (Grant No. 90-G-026) and, in part, by the Office of Naval Research (Grant Award No. N00014-01-10917). We wish to acknowledge the helpful contributions of Clive Fullagar, Shawn Farris, and David Egleston in the planning and interpretation of this research. We are especially grateful to Natalie Nygaard and Christina Hrenchir for their assistance in gathering and analyzing the data. Finally, this research would not have been possible without advice and feedback from Ward Edwards and Julia Pounds at every stage.

REFERENCES

Ackerman, P. L., & Cianciolo, A. T. (2002). Ability and task constraint determinants of complex task performance. *Journal of Experimental Psychology: Applied, 8*, 194–208.

Anderson, N. H. (1971). Integration theory and attitude change. *Psychological Review, 78*, 171–206.

Bailey, L. L., Broach, D. M., Thompson, R. C., & Enos, R. J. (1999). *Controller teamwork evaluation and assessment methodology (CTEAM): A scenario calibration study* (DOT/FAA/AAM-99/24). Washington, DC: Federal Aviation Administration Office of Aviation Medicine. Available from: National Technical Information Service, Springfield, VA 22161.

Baron, J., & Brown, R. (Eds.). (1991). *Teaching decision-making to adolescents.* Hillsdale, NJ: Lawrence Erlbaum Associates.

Betsch, T., Fiedler, K., & Brinkmann, B. J. (1998). Behavioral routines in decision making: The effects of novelty in task presentation and time pressure on routine maintenance and deviation. *European Journal of Social Psychology, 28*, 861–878.

Betsch, T., Glöckner, A., & Haberstroh, S. (2000). COMMERCE—A micro-world simulation to study routine maintenance and deviation in repeated decision making. *Methods of Psychological Research, 5*(2). (online)

Betsch, T., Haberstroh, S., Glöckner, A., Haar, T., & Fiedler, K. (2001). The effects of routine strength on adaptation and information search in recurrent decision making. *Organizational Behavior and Human Decision Processes, 84*, 23–52.

Betsch, T., Haberstroh, S., & Höhle, C. (2002). Explaining routinized decision making—a review of theories and models. *Theory and Psychology, 12*, 453–488.

Brehmer, B. (1995). Feedback delays in complex dynamic decision tasks. In P. A. Frensch & J. Funke (Eds.), *Complex problem solving: The European perspective* (pp. 103–130). Hillsdale, NJ: Lawrence Erlbaum Associates.

Cochran, W. G. (1943). The comparison of different scales of measurement for experimental results. *Annals of Mathematical Statistics, 14*, 205–216.

Connolly, T. (1988). Hedge-clipping, tree-felling, and the management of ambiguity. In M. B. McCaskey, L. R. Pondy, & H. Thomas (Eds.), *Managing the challenge of ambiguity and change* (pp. 37–49). New York: Wiley.

Edwards, W. (1954). The theory of decision making. *Psychological Bulletin, 51*, 380–417.

Einhorn, H. J. (1974). Expert judgment: Some necessary conditions and an example. *Journal of Applied Psychology, 59*, 562–571.

Einhorn, H. J., & Hogarth, R. M. (1986). Judging probable cause. *Psychological Bulletin, 99*, 3–19.

Ettenson, R. (1984). *A schematic approach to the examination of the search for and use of information in expert decision making.* Unpublished doctoral dissertation, Kansas State University.

Gigerenzer, G., & Goldstein, D. G. (1996). Reasoning the fast and frugal way: Models of bounded rationality. *Psychological Review, 103*, 650–669.

Goldstein, W. M., & Hogarth, R. M. (1997). Judgment and decision making: Some historical context. In W. M. Goldstein & R. M. Hogarth (Eds.), *Research on judgment and decision making: Currents, connections, and controversies* (pp. 3–65). Cambridge, England: Cambridge University Press.

Hammond, K. R. (1996). *Human judgment and social policy.* New York: Oxford University Press.

Hammond, K. R., Summers, D. A., & Deane, D. H. (1973). Negative effects of outcome feedback in multiple-cue probability learning. *Organizational Behavior and Human Performance, 9*, 30–34.

Hogarth, R. M. (1987). *Judgement and choice* (2nd ed.). Chichester: Wiley.

Isen, A. M., & Labroo, A. A. (2003). Some ways in which positive affect facilitates decision making and judgment. In S. L. Schneider & J. Shanteau (Eds.), *Emerging perspectives on judgment and decision research* (pp. 365–393). Cambridge, England: Cambridge University Press.

Kameda, T., Tindale, R. S., & Davis, J. H. (2003). Cognitions, preferences, and social sharedness: Past, present, and future directions in group decision making. In S. L. Schneider & J. Shanteau (Eds.), *Emerging perspectives on judgment and decision research* (pp. 458–485). Cambridge, England: Cambridge University Press.

Nagy, R. H. (1981). *How are personnel selection decisions made? An analysis of decision strategies in a simulated personnel selection task.* Unpublished doctoral dissertation, Kansas State University.

Omodei, M. M., & Wearing, A. J. (1995). The Fire Chief microworld generating program: An illustration of computer-simulated microworlds as an experimental paradigm for studying complex decision-making behavior. *Behavior Research Methods, Instruments, & Computers, 27*, 303–316.

Phelps, R. H. (1977). *Expert livestock judgment: A descriptive analysis of the development of expertise.* Unpublished doctoral dissertation, Kansas State University.

Phillips, L., & Edwards, W. (1966). Conservatism in a simple probability inference task. *Journal of Experimental Psychology, 72*, 346–354.

Pitz, G. F., Downing, L., & Reinhold, H. (1967). Sequential effects in the revision of subjective probabilities. *Canadian Journal of Psychology, 21*, 381–393.

Rigas, G., Carling, E., & Brehmer, B. (2002). Reliability and validity of performance measures in microworlds. *Intelligence, 30,* 463–480.

Shanteau, J., & Linin, K. A. (1990). Subjective meaning of terms used in organ donation: Analysis of word associations. In J. Shanteau & R. J. Harris (Eds.), *Organ donation and transplantation: Psychological and behavioral factors* (pp. 37–49). Washington, DC: American Psychological Association.

Shanteau, J., Weiss, D. J., Thomas, R. P., & Pounds, J. C. (2002). Performance-based assessment of expertise: How can you tell if someone is an expert? *European Journal of Operations Research, 136,* 253–263.

Shanteau, J., Weiss, D. J., Thomas, R. P., & Pounds, J. C. (2003). How can you tell if someone is an expert? Empirical assessment of expertise. In S. L. Schneider & J. Shanteau (Eds.), *Emerging perspectives on judgment and decision research* (pp. 620–639). New York: Cambridge University Press.

Svenson, O., & Maule, J. (Eds.). (1993). *Time pressure and human judgement and decision making.* New York: Plenum.

Toffler, A. (1991). *Future shock.* New York: Bantam Books.

Tversky, A., & Kahneman, D. (1974). Judgment under uncertainty: Heuristics and biases. *Science, 185,* 1124–1131.

von Winterfeldt, D., & Edwards, W. (1986). *Decision analysis and behavioral research.* Cambridge, England: Cambridge University Press.

Weiss, D. J., & Edwards, W. (manuscript under review). *The mean for all seasons.*

Weiss, D. J., & Shanteau, J. (2003, Spring). Empirical assessment of expertise. *Human Factors, 45,* 104–114.

15

How Expertise Is Applied in Real-World Dynamic Environments: Head-Mounted Video and Cued Recall as a Methodology for Studying Routines of Decision Making

Mary M. Omodei
Jim McLennan
School of Psychological Science, La Trobe University, Australia

Alexander J. Wearing
Department of Psychology, University of Melbourne, Australia

In this chapter, we describe a methodology that permits detailed study of a decision maker's experiences in time-pressured, high-stakes, complex, dynamic, multiperson task environments. The methodology is minimally reactive and generates rich data in the form of verbal protocols allowing cognitive process tracing. In summary, the methodology involves a decision maker wearing a lightweight head-mounted video camera while engaged in a decision task. Subsequently, the decision maker views his or her own-point-of-view video footage with associated audio; this cues detailed recollections of the psychological processes (affects and cognitions) that generated intentions and actions.

We first describe the methodology and then report the findings from a research project in which we used the methodology to study decision-making processes of experienced fire officers in charge of managing emergency incidents (Incident Commanders).

HEAD-MOUNTED VIDEO AND CUED RECALL
AS A METHODOLOGY FOR STUDYING
DECISION MAKING IN COMPLEX, DYNAMIC
TASK ENVIRONMENTS

Methodological Challenges to Studying
Real-World Decision Processes

The rigorous study of real-world decision making poses serious methodological challenges. Current methodologies for obtaining data on decision-
making processes in complex, naturally occurring settings comprise either
(a) concurrent reporting procedures (on-task commentaries), or (b) retrospective interview procedures (posttask reviews).

One major challenge concerns possible "reactivity" of concurrent reporting methods. For example, there is good evidence that traditional think-
aloud techniques of the kind recommended by Ericsson and Simon (1993)
may distort the actual decision phenomena under investigation, as well as
posing a safety hazard in real-life task environments by distracting the decision maker from core attentional tasks (Bartl & Doerner, 1998; Dickson,
McLennan, & Omodei, 2000).

A second major challenge concerns the adequacy of standard retrospective reporting methods for obtaining comprehensive and accurate data on
psychological processes underlying observable decision actions. This challenge is not a trivial issue. Indeed Woods and Cook (1999) went so far as to
argue that the operation of hindsight bias (knowledge of outcome biases
our judgments about the processes that generated the outcome) renders
useless most current applications of postincident accident reporting as a
means to understand and prevent errors. Although such a radical rejection
of postincident reporting as a data-gathering methodology may be extreme,
there are grounds for calling into question the comprehensiveness and accuracy of data generated by conventional interview or questionnaire methods of eliciting postincident retrospections. We suggest that typical strategies for obtaining retrospective self-reports causes some psychological
processes to be much more likely to be recalled than others, leading to a
distorted understanding of the decision-making process in general, particularly when there is the possibility of decision maker error. What is less
likely to be recalled are those perceptual, affective, and motivational states
that are essentially preverbal or at least not verbalized during the flow of
the decision incident in question. There is abundant evidence, both anecdotal and experimental, of a pervasive human tendency when providing
self-reports to present an image of the self that is both self-enhancing and
self-consistent via processes of distortion and censoring (e.g., Swann, Griffin, Predmore, & Gaines, 1987). Thus, experiences least likely to be recalled

are those associated with actual or potential errors because such experiences constitute a negative self-assessment and, as such, are subject to self-enhancement/protection processes, including repression (Omodei, Wearing, & McLennan, 2002).

Clearly what is needed to study the application of expertise in naturalistic complex decision task environments are methodologies that are both minimally reactive and capable of generating comprehensive verbal protocols that are as free as possible from serious self-referent distortion. In the present volume, Plessner (sports referees, chap. 17) describes research examining how experts make decisions in real-world settings other than fire and related emergency incident management. The accounts given in this chapter can be contrasted fruitfully with the methodology we describe here.

The head-mounted video cued-recall interview procedure was developed specifically for use in the field. There are, of course, other strategies for studying decision making in complex task environments more amenable to rigorous control. One such strategy is the use of computer-generated complex decision scenarios. We have used the Networked Fire Chief micro-world-simulation to carry out controlled laboratory experiments (Omodei, Wearing, McLennan, Elliott, & Clancy, in press). In this volume, Haberstroh, Betsch, Glöckner, Haar, and Stiller (chap. 12) describe the use of the COM-MERCE microworld-simulation as a research tool.

Overview of the Head-Mounted Video Cued-Recall Procedure

What follows is a summary description; a more detailed account and discussion of the methodology can be found in Omodei, Wearing, and McLennan (1998). The essence of the methodology is to capture from the head of the participant a record of the central portion of his or her visual field during a decision episode. This recording, with accompanying audio, is then replayed to the subject as soon as is practical after the decision episode. During this replay, a free-recall procedure is adopted, in which the subject is encouraged to become psychologically re-immersed in the original incident and verbalize all recollections they might have, uncensored for relevance or appropriateness. Such recollections can include any perceptual, affective, or cognitive experiences that occurred at the time of the recorded episode. The tape is paused as needed to allow the subject sufficient time to articulate their spontaneous recollections, including recollections of any preverbal or otherwise fleeting experiences.

This uncensored recall procedure involves essentially an insider account of decision making, in which all evaluation and postincident analysis is suspended: The goal is not to probe beyond the initial experience, but to simply help the subject reexperience exactly what went on psychologically during the course of the incident. Evaluative and analytical judgments by either subject or interviewer are put on hold at least until after the full incident has been replayed. To get additional global information most specifically related to decision-making adequacy, two of our most useful probes used after the video replay cued procedure is finished are: (a) "If you could magically go back in time and do the whole thing again, what, if anything, would you do differently, and why?"; and (b) "Suppose it had not been you in charge but someone else rather less experienced, what is the most likely way he/she might have mis-handled the incident so it went badly wrong?" Both of these provide the participant with an opportunity to identify the most likely errors that could have been made. These two probes typically result in generating a large amount of relevant and sometimes unexpected information over and above that cued by the replay.

The Own-Point-of-View Perspective

The key element of both the capture of the head-mounted video footage and the subsequent free-recall debriefing procedure is the own-point-of-view perspective. This combination of an own-point-of-view video image with an own-point-of-view (insider) recall perspective is a particularly powerful method for stimulating the recall of the maximum amount of relatively uncontaminated information. The own-point-of-view perspective provides as close a match as is possible between the initial experience and the replayed image. This close correspondence is a powerful cue to the concurrent recall of other images and experiences not directly represented in the image captured by the relatively narrow camera angle. For example, while watching their replay, subjects often appear unable to distinguish that which is visible onscreen (captured by the relatively narrow camera angle) from that which was off to one side—it is as if they really do "see" this "missing" information onscreen.

The own-point-of-view perspective takes on an added dimension when one considers the effect of head movement on the image. Theoretical accounts of the link between motion and perception suggest that the experience of watching a video image taken from one's own head as one moves through an environment is fundamentally different—not only from that of watching a video taken of oneself, but also from watching a video taken from someone else's head. We suggest that head-mounted video images evoke the same psychological reactions that underlie the immersive experience of three-dimensional virtual reality (VR) simulations—when a person moves his or her head, the image displayed in the VR goggles changes accordingly. For example, the possibly quite jerky movement in the image resulting from one's head movement becomes an advantage as one watches one's own replay. While increasing psychological immersion is achieved by such image movement, the actual movement is quickly adapted to and becomes unnoticed (the same perceptual stabilization processes appear to occur during image watching as occur in naturally occurring movement).

The impact of the own-point-of-view perspective is further enhanced by the recording of concurrent audio information. In addition to the recorded verbal interactions, other sounds—ranging from one's footfall and breathing to external sounds of doors closing, alarms sounding, and radio traffic—augment the impact of the video images.

Advantages of the Own-Point-of-View Perspective

Video recording from an external perspective is often impossible or impractical (e.g., attempting to follow a fireground commander into a burning or collapsed building). Even when such an external video recording is possible, the own-point-of-view perspective provided by a head-mounted camera is by far the superior option for stimulating the recall of psychologically relevant data.

There are three advantages of the own-point-of-view perspective with respect to the video recording. First, as indicated earlier (and the main reason for its use), this perspective is the most accurate representation of the perceptual field that is possible to achieve. Consequently, it is a maximally powerful stimulus to the spontaneous recollection of those mental events that occurred while the recording was being made. The greater psychological immersion in the replayed incident generates a more representative and comprehensive set of recollections with less self-defensive justification. This psychological immersion allows for the recollection not only of specific cognitions, but also of perceptual, affective, and motivational states that were essentially preverbal or at least not verbalized during the original decision episode.

Second, it overcomes several of the observed disadvantages of an external video perspective with the subject in the field of view. Most notably, the increase in self-awareness (self-consciousness) induced by images of oneself in action has been shown to lead to self-protective attributions and selective reporting of those experiences participants feel is appropriate or expected by the enquirer (cf. Duval & Wicklund, 1972).

Third, the actual wearing of a head-mounted camera does not appear to generate the same level of self-consciousness as having an external video camera focused on oneself. Because it is out of sight, it is out of mind. We have been quite surprised at the extent to which wearing even a bulky head harness is forgotten by subjects who are involved in a current incident or activity.

A related concern was the extent to which the behavior of others in the subject's environment would be altered by his or her awareness of the camera on the subject's head. This would be particularly problematic should it result in changes in the way such persons interact with or respond to the subject. We have also been quite surprised at the rapidity with which others habituate to and thus become unaware of the camera. We suggest that because the subject wearing the camera acts "naturally," his or her interactions with others do not evoke self-consciousness in these others.

The two studies described next involved fire fighting and related emergencies. The two studies involved large-scale simulation exercises. Use of the methodology in operational settings is described in McLennan, Omodei, and Wearing (2001). The methodology has been used to study decision making in other contexts, including competitive sport (Omodei, McLennan, & Whitford, 1998) and sport umpiring (McLennan & Omodei, 1996).

Study I: Decision Making at Simulated Emergency Incidents: Introduction, Goal, and Method

This study involved Melbourne Metropolitan Fire Brigade Station Officers who were participating in a training course to prepare them for competitive promotion to the rank of Senior Station Officer. At the time we carried out the research, the only published empirical study of decision making by fire officers was that of Klein, Calderwood, and Clinton-Sirocco (1986). Klein et al. interviewed 26 fire officers, asking them to describe the decision processes involved at a fire or similar emergency that they had attended sometime during the preceding 2 years. Klein et al. concluded that emergency management decision making rarely involved weighing up alternatives and selecting the optimum course of action (as proposed by classical decision theory), but rather involved recognitional decision processes: A situation was recognized as an exemplar of a class of familiar incident types and one course of action was selected as being appropriate for the particular situation. Klein's Recognition Primed Decision (RPD) model of real-world decision making proposes that an experienced decision maker first engages in situation assessment and recognizes a situation as an exemplar of a class of situations associated with rules for dealing with them. The decision maker then mentally simulates the application of the rules to this particular instance to confirm their applicability. If confirmed, the rules are implemented. If not confirmed, the situation is reassessed and the cycle is repeated. According to the RPD model, what experienced decision makers do *not* do is select an optimal course of action from an array of alternatives. Our goal was to see whether data generated by our head-mounted video cued-recall technique was consistent with Klein's RPD model of time-pressured, high-stakes decision making by experienced fire officers (note that Ross, Lussier, & Klein, chap. 18, this volume, describe the RPD model and its application to training in more detail).

Participants were nine male officers with between 3 and 12 years experience at Station Officer rank ($M = 7.4$ years). Their promotion assessment was to be conducted by an examining panel that would evaluate their performance while in command of four fire-fighting vehicles and crews at a simulated emergency incident. In preparation for the examination, the nine officers took part in an intense program of role playing emergency incident simulation exercises and received critical feedback from a panel of observers.

Each officer wore the head-mounted camera while in command during such a role-played simulation exercise. The simulated emergencies were varied, including a toxic chemical spill at a factory, a fire in a building under construction, an entrapment in a tunnel, and a fire in a timber yard. Immediately after his exercise, each officer viewed a replay of his own-point-of-view video footage and verbalized his recalled experiences. These recollections were recorded on a VHS copy of the original 8mm video footage, including all the original communications and commands. All the material was then transcribed to generate a verbal protocol for subsequent analysis. To assist in analyses, a Cognitive Process Tracing Categorization Scheme (CPTCS) was developed to code recalled mental events. An annotated extract follows to show the nature of the protocols.

(The simulated emergency involved a fire in an office building under construction that threatened to spread to an adjoining shop and residence. Some construction workers were not accounted for. The officer had four appliance crews to call on. These would arrive at irregular intervals. The extract begins as the officer arrives and takes charge):

[radio transmission—instructions] Officer in charge of Teleboom (—an appliance with a hydraulic ladder—) 59, please acknowledge. I want you to get your men in B(reathing) A(pparatus). I want you to enter the building and perform a rescue. We have two people on the fourth floor.

[verbal instruction] Dave, I want you to get two 65s (—large fire hoses—) into the (—roof sprinkler system—) boosters, OK? I want you to boost it.

[cued recall] **Well, I thought I'll boost the hydrant system within the building. I am thinking ahead of the next appliance coming on-scene. I've given a task to the other appliance, I've told the crew to search the building. I thought 'I'll boost the building hydrant system and with the next crew to arrive I'll establish firefighting lines'. [Coded as Intention Formation and Action Generation: Evaluating Demands/Resources Balance; and Planning]**

[verbal request for information from bystander] How many people living there?

[verbal response] Four, I think.

[radio transmission—instructions] Incident Commander to Teleboom 59, would you split your crew up, please. I want two to do the rescue in the building and two to enter the shop. It is not known if there are residents still in there. I want them evacuated.

[cued recall] The initial crew I got to do the rescue in the building. There could be residents in the shop, but it was only an exposure. So I split the crew up: two to search the building, two to look after the shop exposure. [Coded as (i) Situation Assessment: Recognition, and (ii) Intention Formation and Action Generation: Prioritizing]

[radio transmission—report] VKN8 (—call sign of the central dispatch center—), Pumper 59 (—appliance number—), Victoria Street Control, wordback. Structure fire, respond Third Alarm. Fire involves a nine-story concrete building under construction. Two people to be rescued from the building. Rescue in progress. BA Stage 1 in operation.

[cued recall] I'm thinking I've got a crew rolling up here and I've got to allocate their tasks. [Coded as Intention Formation and Action Generation: Evaluating Demands/Resources Balance]

Table 15.1 consists of an extract from a protocol illustrating the cognitive process tracing analysis procedure.

Findings and Discussion

In relation to the goal of the study, several of the Klein et al. (1986) proposals were supported, notably the relatively large amount of cognitive activity devoted to situation assessment and lack of cognitive activity associated with selecting an optimal choice from among decision alternatives. The nine officers recalled 184 coded mental events: 45% related to Situation Assessment, 37% related to Intention Formation and Action Generation, and 18% related to Self-Monitoring and Self-Regulation. The most frequently recalled event category was Evaluating Demands/Resources Balance (13%), followed by Identify a Need for Specific Information (12%). There were no recalled instances of officers selecting a course of action from an array of alternatives. However, eight of the nine officers recalled pre-action simulations of possible scenario features or developments and possible alternative options. This finding of the importance of Pre-Priming processes as potential determinants of subsequent Situation Assessment and Intention Formation processes confirmed earlier findings by McLennan and Omodei (1996) in their studies involving interviews with fire officers and head-mounted video cued recalls by football umpires. All the officers reported experiences involving Self-Monitoring and Regulation, mostly noting the degree to which they were experiencing a sense of mastery and control. The

TABLE 15.1
Illustrative Cognitive Process Tracing Protocol Analysis

Transcript	Cues	Actions	Cognitions	Process
VI: Any hazards in there?		Seeks information		Risk assessment
R: There's a gas cylinder just inside the corner.	Information on threat			
VI: All right, there's two people missing. You stay with me.		Orders continued presence		Resource conservation
VI: (shouts to two crew entering building) Gas cylinder on ground floor!		Warns of danger		Risk reduction
Recall: I am just trying to ensure that the two crew know that there's a gas cylinder which is an extra hazard to look out for. Taking into account the size of the fire, I took that ground floor fire to be a small fire and what I hoped to do with these crew, after they extinguish the fire is to give them a rescue operation.			**Recognize threat (SAU4)** **Planning action (IN4)**	

Note. The incident involved a role-playing simulation of a fire in a building under construction. Cognitions were coded using the Cognitive Process Tracing Categorization Scheme (CPTCS) summarized in Table 15.2.

finding that almost one fifth of the total amount of cognitive activity involved self-monitoring and self-regulation of arousal level, emotions, and self-talk was unanticipated. The role of such processes has not been emphasized in most theoretical models of decision processes.

All the officers quickly formed a general strategy for managing the incident and rapidly committed their crews to this management strategy. In forming their strategy, officers drew on procedural knowledge about fire (and chemical) behavior, equipment capability, safety considerations, and standard operating procedures. Subsequent tactical decisions as the incident developed were driven by an officer's perceptions of an actual or potential change in the balance of the demands (risks, threats) of a situation and the resources available, either current or anticipated. Loss of resources—through either equipment failure such as a burst hose or non-arrival of anticipated resources—was disruptive of decision-making processes. Contrary to a key aspect of the Klein et al. (1986) proposed RPD model, we found no instances of officers mentally rehearsing the likely effectiveness of an action prior to implementation.

Although there was heavy reliance, overall, on recognitional decision processes as proposed by the Klein et al. (1986) RPD model, six officers recalled using complex analytical problem-solving processes. These occurred when any of the following circumstances arose: (a) the situation was opaque, (b) the officer had no previous experience with an emergency of this kind, or (c) task demands greatly exceeded available resources. Two types of complex analytical strategies were identified following Newell and Simon (1972): means–ends analysis and minimaxing:

> *Means–ends analysis: "Even though there are people unaccounted for, I won't start a search yet. There are 140 rooms (in the motel). I'll put the crew to containing the fire in the kitchen and when the next two appliances come on-scene I'll start those crews on search."*

> *Minimaxing: "Anyone in the warehouse was probably dead by now. I'll start two men in BA organizing the evacuation (–from an adjoining child care center–), I don't want a kindergarten of dead kids."*

We concluded that the type of decision process likely to be employed by an incident commander at an emergency depends on the nature of the task environment. If it is transparent and familiar, and adequate resources are available, then rapid, simple, recognitional decision processes are employed. If any of these characteristics is lacking, then slower, more complex, analytical problem-solving processes are likely to be employed.

The observing panel members judged three officers as highly skilled and three as relatively less skilled. The recall transcriptions from the two groups were examined. Compared with the less skilled officers, the highly skilled officers recalled: (a) fewer mental events associated with Situation Assessment, (b) more mental events associated with Intention Formation and Action Generation, and (c) fewer events associated with Self-Monitoring and Regulation. These findings suggest that more highly skilled emergency Incident Commanders are able to draw on appropriate task-related procedural knowledge more effectively.

Finally, returning to the original goal of investigating support for the Klein et al. (1986) RPD model provided by our head-mounted video cued-recall methodology, we concluded that the findings were mixed. We found that indeed the basis of time-pressured, emergency management decision making involves mostly recognitional processes derived from past experience, which generate a single-action sequence, not selection of an optimal choice of action from among an array of alternatives. However, we failed to find evidence of mental simulation of the likely effectiveness of an action prior to implementation. Instead we found evidence of a more dynamic process in which an action is implemented rapidly and modified as necessitated by feedback on the effectiveness of the actions implemented as events unfold. (The effectiveness of taking quick action in high-uncertainty, dynamic task environments and using feedback to guide subsequent corrective actions was noted previously by Kleinmuntz & Thomas, 1987.) The principal driver of such modifications was perceived changes in the demands (i.e., risks or threats)/resources balance (Fig. 15.1). We also found that, although simple recognitional processes predominate, in complex sit-

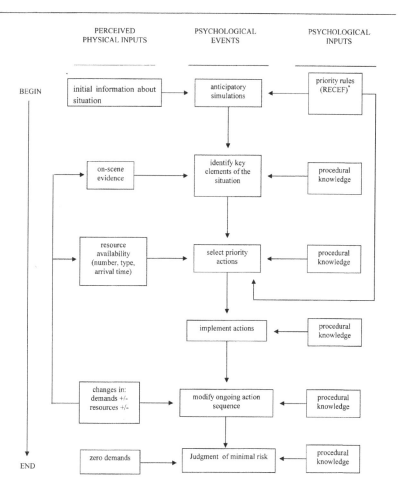

(*RECEF = Melbourne Fire Brigade priority rules: Rescue civilians, Exposures to be protected, Contain the fire, Extinguish the fire, Fire duties as needed)

FIG. 15.1. Fire-fighting decision sequence illustrating the dynamic nature of the process: the role of changes in the demands/resources balance and the importance of feedback from the task environment following implementation of actions.

uations characterized by lack of information, lack of prior experience, or where demands greatly exceed available resources, more complex, analytical problem-solving strategies are likely to be employed. These findings appear to have come about as a result of our use of the head-mounted video cued-recall methodology. Other methodologies seem to be less sensitive to the processes we identified.

Study 2: Good Versus Poor Decision Making Under Standardized Simulation Conditions: Introduction, Goal, and Method

Naturalistic Decision Making (NDM) accounts have been criticized as being descriptive and lacking in the ability to identify features of more versus less effective decision processes independent of observed decision outcome (e.g., Yates, 1998). Study 2 used standardized role-playing emergency incident simulations to investigate cognitive processes associated with relatively better versus poorer decision performance. Our goal was to identify decision processes associated with more versus less effective decision making by incident commanders in charge at simulated emergency incidents. In particular, we sought to test two hypotheses generated by our field research (McLennan, Omodei, & Wearing, 2001) that more effective decision making was likely to be associated with (a) more effective self-monitoring and emotional self-regulation, and (b) more rapid situation assessment. What follows is a summary; a more detailed account of the study, in the context of comparing NDM accounts of effective decision making with those of classical decision models, is in McLennan, Pavlou, and Omodei (in press).

Participants were 12 male candidates for promotion from Station Officer to Senior Station Officer. They had between 10 and 20 years experience in fire fighting and between 4 and 12 years experience as a Station Officer. The procedure resembled that of Study 1. However, all the different role-playing emergency incident simulations were constructed in such a manner to be of approximately equal difficulty. Also each officer's performance was assessed by a panel of two experienced senior fire officers on 10-point rating scales. The two sets of ratings correlated strongly ($r = .81$, $p < .01$), indicating adequate reliability of the performance ratings.

After assuming the role of Incident Commander (IC) wearing a head-mounted video camera in his simulation exercise, each officer undertook a cued-recall interview. The recall session was taped and transcribed as in the previous study. The transcripts were coded by two independent raters using the CPTCS (Table 15.2). Interrater agreement was high (Cohen's κ = .94).

TABLE 15.2

Percentage Frequencies of Use of Cognitive Activity Categories
Recalled by the Six More Skillful Incident Commanders Compared
With Those of the Six Less Skillful Incident Commanders

Cognitive Activity Category		IC Performance	
		Less Skill	More Skill
Situation Assessment/Understanding			
SAU1	identify relevant cues/features	5	1
SAU2	identify need for specific information	19	25
SAU3	attend to specific information	10	7
SAU4	recognize demand/threat/need	21	17
SAU5	anticipate a demand/threat/need	9	16
SAU6	inventory available resources	6	6
SAU7	anticipate future resources	6	7
SAU8	evaluate effects of an action	2	2
SAU9	evaluate conformity of an action to SOPs	5	0
SAU10	anticipate a situation development	0	0
SAU11	formulate/revise a situation conceptualization	17	18
	[*n* =	**81(32%)**	**87(38%)**]
Intention Formation/Action Generation			
IN1	remembering fact/rule/procedure	19	4
IN2	prioritizing actions	18	11
IN3	evaluating demands/resources balance	4	6
IN4	planning actions	17	17
IN5	generating a specific action	16	20
IN6	presimulating a possible scenario	0	0
IN7	simulating a possible development	1	0
IN8	evaluating and choosing among alternative actions	1	3
IN9	analyzing and problem solving	23	30
IN10	distributing/delegating decision making	2	9
IN11	nonproductive cognitions: wishing, wondering	0	0
	[*n* =	**96(37%)**	**116(51%)**]
Self-Monitoring and Regulation			
SM1	maintaining self-view consistency	3	0
SM2	noting negative affect	8	15
SM3	noting positive affect	6	8
SM4	noting level of control/mastery versus overload	29	31
SR1	control attentional focus	27	14
SR2	engage in self-talk	8	0
SR3	restrict information inflow	20	31
SR4	engage in physical activity	0	0
	[*n* =	**79(31%)**	**26(11%)**]
All cognitive activities	*N* =	**256**	**229**

Note. Percentages were calculated *within each* of the three major classes of cognitive activity categories.

Findings and Discussion

In summary, relatively poor IC performance seemed to be related to one of two decision themes: First, being overwhelmed by the demands of the unfolding emergency, being unable to form a plan, and struggling to manage the cognitive workload of the incoming information; and second, focusing on only one salient feature of the situation and failing to take into account emerging threats that rapidly nullified any original plan. By way of contrast, the more skillful ICs generally felt in control and behaved like the leaders they were supposed to be. They kept track of events, often making notes. They anticipated likely developments rather than merely reacting to events. They accepted the need to revise plans, and they reacted to new threats without undue concern or irritation.

Table 15.2 compares the pattern of cognitive activities recalled by the six relatively more skillful ICs with those of the six relatively less skillful ICs. Overall, the six more skillful ICs reported a significantly different pattern of cognitive activities for the three major categories of cognitive process [Situational Assessment and Understanding; Intention Formation and Action Generation; Self-Monitoring and Self-Regulation: χ^2 (5; $n = 485$) = 27.4, $p <$ .001]. The significant difference was accounted for by the less skillful ICs' relatively more frequent reporting of Self-Monitoring and Regulating cognitive activities. When Self-Monitoring and Regulating cognitive activities were excluded for the six more skillful ICs, their relative proportions of Situation Assessment and Understanding to Intention Formation and Action generation was 0.43 to 0.57. For the less skillful ICs, the proportions were 0.46 to 0.54, suggesting that the six less skillful ICs engaged in slightly more Situation Assessment and Understanding activities. However, the difference was not statistically significant.

Inspection of the content of the cued-recall verbalization protocols shed more light on the role of Self-Monitoring and Regulation cognitive activity in differentiating between the two groups. The content of such recollections by the less skillful ICs was uniformly negative:

> . . . I haven't taken in what the other officer has actually told me. He's told me we have a large fire on the container ship. Now the Captain walks in and I tell him that it appears we've got a fire. So I can see that things are being told to me and I'm not taking it in, because maybe I'm too nervous or I can't visualize it.

> . . . at this stage I've sort of lost it too because I think I should have gone back and spoken to the Station Master and got everyone evacuated through the emergency evacuation system and started smoke ventilation straight away. I wasn't thinking clearly. I'm focusing on things in general and I'm not clearly identifying tasks and carrying them out. Then confusion reigns because in the short time span I've let things build up and I haven't been able to prioritize things. I've just let it get away a bit.

There were no such negative self-evaluations by the six more skillful ICs; rather, there was a general picture of feeling in control:

> So at this stage I thought "Right, that's the next thing I have to do is I have to give him some manpower for a start so he can start operations." I wanted to establish early on that he's going to be in charge over there, so that's why I said to him "You're the Operations Officer." So I could just send him resources and he would delegate the tasks because he had the big picture and he could see what was going on.

In relation to our goal of testing two hypotheses that effective decision making by incident commanders was associated with (a) more effective emotional self-regulation and monitoring, and (b) more rapid situation assessment, we concluded that there was strong evidence in support of the first and suggestive, but not conclusive, evidence in support of the second. Interestingly, there was no difference between the more and less effective groups of incident commanders in mean years of experience.

CONCLUDING DISCUSSION

The aim of our chapter was to present a methodology that can be used to study rigorously the routines of decision making in complex, real-world settings. We argued that conventional concurrent and retrospective data-gathering procedures are susceptible to dangers of both reactivity and lack of comprehensiveness. To demonstrate the utility of the head-mounted video cued-recall procedure, we described two studies investigating emergency management decision making by emergency Incident Commanders (ICs). Although the focus was on the methodology and its capabilities, the studies suggest several aspects of dynamic real-world decision processes that have not perhaps been given the attention they deserve because conventional research methodologies obscure such processes.

The first is that decision-making processes in a given task domain are not necessarily homogeneous. Decision processes are likely to be determined by characteristics of the specific decision task environment. We found that in task environments characterized by low levels of uncertainty (i.e., transparency, familiarity, resource adequacy), fast, recognitional, decision processes predominate, as proposed by Klein's RPD model (Ross, Lussier, & Klein, chap. 18, this volume). However, in task environments characterized by high levels of uncertainty (opacity, novelty, resource poverty), we found that slower, more complex, analytical problem-solving and choice processes were likely to dominate, as proposed by cognitive engineering theorists such as Rasmussen (1983) and Wickens (Wickens, Gordon, & Liu, 1998).

Second, we suggest that the experience of emergency management decision making involved more dynamic processes than suggested by posttask structured retrospective interview procedures such as the Klein et al. (1989) Critical Decision Method (CDM) interview. Because such retrospective interview procedures typically require subjects to break up the incident in question into critical decision points, the procedure may well result in an artifactual representation of the decision process as a sequence of discrete, chained, mental events. What emerged from our research with emergency incident managers was a representation of their decision making as more akin to engineering process control: The decision maker takes actions aimed at imposing increasing control over the task environment by progressively incorporating and adapting to feedback from that environment (Omodei & Wearing, 1995).

Third, we found that the most important single aspect of feedback from emergency incident management task environments was change in the demands/resources balance. Real-world decision making is about taking actions to change aspects of a task environment. The effectiveness of a given action is tightly coupled to the adequacy of the resources available to implement the intended action. However, some theoretical accounts of real-world decision making fail to explicitly incorporate constructs related to task demands in relation to available resources. Such accounts run the risk of implying that real-world decision making is "all in the mind" and infinite resources are available to implement the correct decision. Sadly, this is rarely, if ever, the case in real-world situations.

Fourth, we found the role of emotional and cognitive self-monitoring and self-regulation to be crucial to effective decision performance. Because conventional data-gathering procedures are likely to engender defensive self-consciousness, such processes have been largely ignored in theoretical accounts of real-world decision-making processes. Our research demonstrates clearly that in decision situations where the individual has a personal stake in the outcome, effective decision making resides in an ability to not only control cognitive and attentional resources, but also to monitor and regulate emotional states and motivated cognitive effort. Failure in such self-regulation will allow intrusion of irrelevant and disruptive emotions and self-referent cognitions, which may seriously degrade the effectiveness of the routines of decision making (Brehmer, 1992; Doerner & Schaub, 1994; Omodei & Wearing, 1995).

By way of concluding comment, the methodology we have described was developed for use in field settings. However, we have also used cued-recall procedures in our laboratory research with the *Networked Fire Chief* computer-generated microworld-simulation program. Subjects have watched replays of their simulation trials, and these replays have been used to cue recall of their decision processes so as to provide additional insights into their decision-making processes.

ACKNOWLEDGMENTS

The research for this chapter was supported by the Australian Research Council and the Melbourne Metropolitan Fire and Emergency Services Board.

REFERENCES

Bartl, C., & Doerner, D. (1998). Speechless when thinking: About the role of speech for problem solving. *Sprache und Kognition, 17*, 224–238.

Brehmer, B. (1992). Dynamic decision making: Human control of complex systems. *Acta Psychologica, 81*, 211–241.

Dickson, J., McLennan, J., & Omodei, M. M. (2000). Effects of concurrent verbalisation on a time-critical, dynamic decision-making task. *Journal of General Psychology, 127*, 217–228.

Doerner, D., & Schaub, H. (1994). Errors in planning and decision making and the nature of human information processing. *Applied Psychology: An International Review, 43*, 433–453.

Duval, S., & Wicklund, R. A. (1972). *A theory of objective self awareness.* New York: Academic Press.

Ericsson, K. A., & Simon, H. A. (1993). *Protocol analysis: Verbal reports as data* (rev. ed.). Cambridge, MA: MIT Press.

Klein, G., Calderwood, R., & Clinton-Sirocco, A. (1986). Rapid decision making on the fireground. *Proceedings of the Human Factors Research Society, 30th Annual Meeting, 1*, 576–580.

Klein, G., Calderwood, R., & MacGregor, D. (1989). Critical decision method for eliciting knowledge. *IEEE Transactions on Systems, Man, and Cybernetics, 19*, 462–472.

Kleinmuntz, D. N., & Thomas, J. B. (1987). The value of action and inference in dynamic decision making. *Organisational Behaviour and Human Decision Processes, 39*, 341–364.

McLennan, J., & Omodei, M. M. (1996). The role of pre-priming in recognition primed decision making. *Perceptual and Motor Skills, 82*, 1059–1069.

McLennan, J., Omodei, M. M., & Wearing, A. J. (2001). Cognitive processes of first-on-scene fire officers in command at emergency incidents as an analogue of small-unit command in peace operations. In P. Essens, A. Vogelaar, E. Tanercan, & D. Winslow (Eds.), *The human in command: Peace support operations* (pp. 312–332). Mets & Schilt, Amsterdam; KMA Royal Netherlands Military Academy, Breda.

McLennan, J., Pavlou, O., & Omodei, M. M. (in press). Cognitive control processes discriminate between better versus poorer performance by fire ground commanders. In H. Montgomery, R. Lipshitz, & B. Brehmer (Eds.), *How professionals make decisions.* Mahwah, NJ: Lawrence Erlbaum Associates.

Newell, A., & Simon, H. A. (1972). *Human problem solving.* Englewood Cliffs, NJ: Prentice-Hall.

Omodei, M. M., McLennan, J., & Whitford, P. (1998). Using a head-mounted video camera and two-stage replay to enhance orienteering performance. *International Journal of Sport Psychology, 29*, 115–131.

Omodei, M. M., & Wearing, A. J. (1995). Decision making in complex dynamic settings: A theoretical model incorporating motivation, intention, affect, and cognitive performance. *Sprache und Kognition, 14*, 75–90.

Omodei, M. M., Wearing, A. J., & McLennan, J. (1998). Head-mounted video recording: A methodology for studying naturalistic decision making. In R. Flin, M. Strub, E. Salas, & L. Martin (Eds.), *Decision making under stress: Emerging themes and applications* (pp. 137–146). Aldershot: Ashgate.

Omodei, M. M., Wearing, A. J., & McLennan, J. (2002). Head-mounted video and cued recall: A minimally reactive methodology for understanding, detecting, and preventing accidents in the control of complex systems. In C. W. Johnson (Ed.), *Proceedings of the 21st European Annual Conference of Human Decision Making and Control* (pp. 72–80). GIST Technical Report G2002.1, Department of Computer Science, University of Glasgow, Scotland.

Omodei, M. M., Wearing, A. J., McLennan, J., Elliott, G., & Clancy, J. (in press). "More is better?" Problems of self-regulation in naturalistic decision making situations. In H. Montgomery, R. Lipshitz, & B. Brehmer (Eds.), *How professionals make decisions.* Mahwah, NJ: Lawrence Erlbaum Associates.

Rasmussen, J. (1983). Skills, rules and knowledge: Signals, signs, and symbols, and other distinctions in human performance models. *IEEE Transactions on Systems, Man, and Cybernetics, 13,* 257–266.

Swann, W. B., Jr., Griffin, J. J., Jr., Predmore, S. C., & Gaines, B. (1987). The cognitive-affective crossfire: When self-consistency confronts self-enhancement. *Journal of Personality and Social Psychology, 52,* 881–889.

Wickens, C. D., Gordon, S. E., & Liu, Y. (1998). *An introduction to human factors engineering.* New York: Longman.

Woods, D. D., & Cook, R. I. (1999). Perspectives on human error: Hindsight bias and local rationality. In F. Durso (Ed.), *Handbook of applied cognitive psychology* (pp. 141–191). New York: Wiley.

Yates, J. F. (1998, May). *Observations on naturalistic decision making: The phenomenon and the framework.* Paper presented at the 4th Naturalistic Decision Making Conference, Warrenton, VA.

16

The Role of Experience in Consumer Decisions: The Case of Brand Loyalty

Michaela Wänke
Universität Basel

Malte Friese
Universität Heidelberg

This book is about decision making. Most of our daily decisions are made in the consumer domain, which makes consumer behavior a particularly worthwhile object for research on decision making. At least in industrialized and affluent societies, consumers are faced with an abundance of possible product choices. Any visit to the mall, any glance at a mail order catalogue, or any search on the Web will document the enormous amount and variety of alternatives in most product categories. Given the multitude of choices, marketers need to understand how consumers make their product and purchase decisions. Research in consumer behavior has proposed various models, which may differ in details but, by and large, share the same steps in the decision process (e.g., Engel, Blackwell, & Miniard, 1990). Not surprisingly, these models, although specific to consumer choice, are also quite similar to the more general models of decision making referred to throughout this book.

However, consumer choices are special in several aspects. First, whereas with many other decisions the decision maker faces a rather neutral environment, consumers are subject to quite massive attempts by marketers to influence their choices. Second, maybe more so than most other decisions, consumer choices quite often involve repeated choices. This latter aspect in particular points to the relevance of previous experience in consumer choices, which is, in the realm of this book, the focus of the present chapter.

The importance of previous experience to consumer behavior is by no means trivial, but a complex domain of scientific research as this chapter tries to illustrate. To give just one example of experience as a possible determinant of many consumer purchases, have a look at the study by Cobb and Hoyer (1986). They observed shoppers in a store and found that they spent less than 15 seconds on average when choosing a brand of tissues and looked at only two or three different brands. At least for a large range of product categories, like coffee or tissues, elaborate processes seem the exception rather than the rule. Of course consumers may simply go by price or the most appealing package, but clearly relying on experience may be one strategy to shorten the process.

After a brief outline of the steps involved in consumer decision making, the present chapter discusses the role of experience in each step of the choice process. Finally, we look in more detail at one particular aspect of experience and consumer choice—namely, brand loyalty. It becomes clear that brand loyalty as a phenomenon may be the result of different processes. We twist apart different processes underlying repeat purchases, and we discuss different impacts on these processes and, accordingly, on the resulting brand loyalty.

CONSUMER DECISION MAKING

In a first step of the decision process, consumers have to identify their needs or goals. Once they know what they need or desire, they can set out to search for potential alternatives to fulfill those needs. Subsequently, they need to evaluate the different alternatives. Based on this evaluation, they choose one alternative following different choice strategies. For most goods, the process does not end here. There are hardly any once-in-a-lifetime purchases, and the vast majority of consumer decisions are about product categories, in which one has chosen repeatedly before. In other words, consumers usually have built some experience. To what extent does this previously acquired experience influence current consumer decisions? What are the conditions modifying its impact? Before we turn to the role of experience, we outline the steps involved in consumer decision in more detail.

Need or Goal Recognition

The essential precondition for any customer's purchase decision is the observation of a discrepancy between the actual state and a desired target state. Without this discrepancy, there is no benefit of starting a decision process (for an overview of research on goal setting, see Bagozzi & Dholakia, chap. 2, this volume). One may define a need as the drive to eliminate that discrepancy and a goal as the desired ideal state. Textbooks on consumer behavior stress that goals do not equal products or brands, but rather claim that products are tools by which a goal can be fulfilled (e.g., Wells & Prensky, 1996). For example, the goal to have transportation can be fulfilled by several product categories (cars, motor cycles, bikes) and within each product category by several brands. This, in turn, involves choosing the product category and brand that best meets the goal requirements, as is outlined in the following steps. However, different from textbook wisdom, this does not preclude that product categories or brands may in fact constitute goals. To own a Porsche before one turns 30 is an example of the brand representing the goal. Obviously, whenever possible, marketers strive for their brands representing the goal, rather than representing one tool among others that fulfills a more general consumption goal.

Search for Product Alternatives

Search for possible alternatives and relevant information may be done internally, recalling alternatives from memory (memory based), or externally, stimulated by the environment such as advertising or consumer reports (stimulus based; Lynch & Srull, 1982). The retrieved alternatives constitute the *awareness set*. Only a subset of these alternatives is usually considered for purchase. This portion comprises the evoked set or *consideration set*. Naturally this portion is much smaller than the awareness set and rarely exceeds the magical number of seven plus or minus two.

To select goods from the awareness set to the considered set, however, some superficial evaluation process is necessary. The sequence of the steps in the decision making is not as linear as we list it here but involves several loops. Much like when selecting the final choice from the consideration set, selecting for the consideration set requires consumers to establish a set of evaluative criteria, engage in evaluating the alternatives by these criteria, and set a decision rule that translates the evaluations into choices.

Evaluation of Product Alternatives

Product information obtainable prior to consumption is usually made available by the marketer—for example, in advertising, on packaging, or through other forms of product communication. To some extent, consumers may acquire information from other sources, such as consumer reports or word of mouth. In addition to this externally acquired information, consumers self-generate information by making inferences from the information given or not given (for a review, see Kardes, 1993; Kardes, Muthukrishnan, & Pashkevich, chap. 8, this volume). For example, the reputation of the brand, the warranty, or the price may signal the quality of the product.

Choice Strategies

There are various decision rules that consumers may use to arrive at a choice. In a market segment with only few alternatives to choose from, customers may carefully examine each alternative and all of its attributes to pick the most appropriate one for their needs (attribute-based choice). However, most product categories offer a great variety of brands and products, differing on all kinds of attributes such as price or number of features. In those cases, consumers typically use some kind of heuristic to come to a conclusion. If consumers already hold attitudes about the brands of their considered set, they may just select the one they evaluate most positively overall (attitude heuristic). In case previously formed attitudes are not available and consumers must rely on the product attributes, they may nevertheless shortcut the effortful comparison process. For example, they may simply choose one attribute as the most important and choose the alternative, which is evaluated best on this attribute (lexicographic heuristic; Payne, Bettman, & Johnson, 1993a). Alternatively, they may allow for compensations of attributes or set minimum criteria for all attributes to be met. Of course to come to a conclusion, consumers may use attitude-based as well as attribute-based choice strategies or a mixture of them at different stages of the decision-making process (for a summary of consumer choice heuristics, see Kardes, 2001).

Postconsumption (and Repurchase)

Not all the information necessary to evaluate a product is available before actual consumption. Consumer researchers distinguish among *search attributes*, *experience attributes*, and *credence attributes* (Darby & Karni, 1973; Nelson, 1974). Before consumption the choice was based on *search attributes*, such as price, brand, or product design; *experience attributes*, such as taste or comfort, are available only after product trial; and *credence attributes*, such as reliability, require long-term usage. In contrast to search attributes, which are, at least in principle, objectively verifiable, experience attributes by definition cannot be verified before consumption because they are subjective. Interestingly, the ease with which search attributes can be verified would also predict that claims about search attributes tend to be true because the market would punish untruthful marketers. Accordingly, consumers tend to be more skeptical of claims regarding experience attributes such as taste, compared with claims about search attributes (Ford, Smith, & Swasy, 1990). Consumption experience thus plays a crucial role in the processing of product attributes. With this in mind, one can easily understand the vast amount of coupons consumers receive and the distribution of product samples and trial versions as a marketing strategy. These tactics convince consumers by letting them live through the unique experience of consumption, rather than convincing them on theoretical grounds with more or less compelling arguments. On this note, we now turn to discussing the role of experience in consumer decision making.

THE ROLE OF EXPERIENCE IN CONSUMER DECISION MAKING

Before we set out on our discussion, we should clarify what we mean by experience. Experience in consumer choice behavior may imply that consumers rely on previously performed behavior and will merely repeat previous choices in a sort of more or less established routine behavior. In a broader sense, *experience* could be defined as the sum of implicit or explicit semantic and procedural knowledge or simply as familiarity due to previous encounters. For example, in the literature of consumer behavior, experience is often used synonymously with product knowledge (e.g., Bettman & Park, 1980). This broader concept of experience has a very different implication than a mere conceptualization as routine behavior. In fact relying on experience may also imply that one has learned from previous experiences, which may lead to deliberately choosing to perform a different behavior than before. Our discussion in the following includes both types of experience effects: using previously stored information and relying on previously established routines.

Getting consumers to choose the same brand at repeat purchases is a marketing goal and is one aspect of brand loyalty—a topic to which we return later. Yet the influence of experience is not limited to the final choice, but may come to play at each stage of the decision-making process as outlined in the following paragraphs.

The Role of Experience in Need or Goal Recognition

Obviously, a conscious recognition of one's needs requires some experience. How else would we recognize that this unpleasant feeling in our stomach will be quenched by food rather than an aspirin? Particularly so-called *acquired* (as opposed to internal) needs may be learned. Who would ever crave a sugar-free latte mochachino with cherry taste if they had never tried one before?

Moreover, the mere exposure to previously tried goods may provoke the need of repurchasing this product again. For example, we all can picture ourselves wandering through a supermarket loading the cart with lots of goods we initially did not intend to buy. Simply encountering certain well-known products and brands brings about the desire to purchase them. For the domain of food products, this effect is particularly pronounced in a state of hunger, as any dieter on a shopping spree knows.

Recently, a big U.S. fast-food chain applied this logic to its new advertisement policy. While cutting the total advertising budget by a reasonable percentage, the company is trying to spot their remaining TV commercials more efficiently. As part of its new strategy, the company decided to place commercials primarily at lunch- and dinnertime. Obviously, the company's reasoning is to trigger a need for hamburgers and other famous items on their product line at the moment when people are most likely to attend to their needs concerning food.

However, note that this policy will only be successful as long as consumers experience this company's hamburgers as positively distinct in some respect from the competitors' products. If the latter one is viewed as superior in taste or price, the commercial of our first company may have triggered the need to have a burger for lunch, but consumers may decide on meeting this need with the preferred competitor's products.

The Role of Experience in Search for Product Alternatives

In a memory-based choice, only brands that are retrieved from memory are further considered; thus, more accessible brands have an advantage (Hoyer & Brown, 1990; Macdonald & Sharp, 2000; Nedungadi, 1990). Clearly previous experience is crucial here because previously purchased brands, in particular those purchased repeatedly or most recently, would be particularly accessible (Wyer & Srull, 1989). In the ideal world of the marketer, the brand would be chronically and automatically accessible when the product category or consumption goal is primed. Goals are known to activate habitual behavior (Aarts & Dijksterhuis, 2000), and thus we may assume that if a frequent brand choice behavior has been established, this behavior will be automatically activated in respective situations when the goals are present. Interestingly, in consumer behavior, the same goal may be linked to different brands or even product categories depending on the situation. For example, when ordering a beverage, a consumer may automatically think of Coke in a fast-food restaurant (and order it), but of Perrier when having lunch in a more fancy restaurant and of beer when in a bar. It is easy to imagine such long-established habits in consumer choices. However, although the literature on automatic routine activation (see Betsch, chap. 3, this volume; Johnson & Busemeyer, chap. 1, this volume) focuses on automatic links between a goal and a behavior due to frequent previous behavior, we cannot help noticing that in the consumer domain links between goals and brand choices may be established without any prior personally experienced behavior, but merely by advertising. Advertising slogans such as "Have a break, have a KitKat" aim to establish an automatic link between a situation and a brand.

The Role of Experience in Search for Information to Evaluate Alternatives

Experience may impinge on the evaluation process in several manners. First, experience plays a role in deciding which attributes are deemed relevant for the decision (Ross, Lussier, & Klein, chap. 18, this volume). Second, experience may influence the extent and outcome of the search process. Finally, experience may affect how the information is processed.

Experience Affecting the Selection of Evaluative Criteria. Suppose you had never been on a beach vacation, but now for the first time in your life you want to spend 2 weeks by the sea. Your travel agent has generously equipped you with an abundance of travel catalogues and brochures. How would you know which of the many features listed for each resort is relevant for your enjoyment? You may try to simulate your experience, and clearly you will arrive at some criteria. Yet during your vacation, you may discover that the features you considered important beforehand do much less to determine your satisfaction than you had thought and vice versa. For example, you may consider a room with sea view absolutely necessary before your vacation, but while you are there you discover that you hardly spend time in that room anyhow. In fact research shows that people are not overly adept to forecasting their affective reactions to stimuli (Gilbert & Wilson, 2000). The next time you face a choice of a beach resort, you may be more likely to take your experience into account when evaluating different options.

Experience Affecting the Extent and Outcome of Information Search. Most obviously, having experienced consumption will change the available information. Only after consumption can experience attributes be fully evaluated. Experiencing consumption improved the accessibility of experience attributes compared with communication of these attributes via advertising. Vice versa search attributes were more accessible and more confidently held after exposure to advertising compared with experience (Wright & Lynch, 1995).

Experience with a product category also affects the extent of external information search. One may expect that external information search is highest among inexperienced consumers and decreases with existing knowledge. Evidence suggests, however, that external search is most extensive in moderately experienced consumers (e.g., Alba & Hutchinson, 1987; Johnson & Russo, 1984). Consumers with high objective knowledge about a product seem to rely more on internal search (Raju, Lonial, & Mangold, 1995) or they even refrain from any substantial search at all. Consumers who are completely unfamiliar with the product category also engage less in information search presumably because they could not use the acquired information and find it more confusing than helpful. Furthermore, the lack of expertise to evaluate the information available leads to a deficit of motivation to find the best alternative and focus on an easy solution instead (Bettman & Park, 1980; Johnson & Russo, 1984).

When consumers habitually choose one specific brand or product, they may lack the motivation to search for information about alternatives, even internally, as long as the habitually chosen alternative meets their demands (Verplanken, Aarts, & van Knippenberg, 1997; Verplanken, Myrbakk, & Rudi, chap. 13, this volume). However, with increasing routine strength, the tendency of confirmatory search for the preferred brand also increased (Betsch, Haberstroh, Glöckner, Haar, & Fiedler, 2001; see also Haberstroh, Betsch, Glöckner, Haar, & Stiller, chap. 12, this volume).

Experience Affecting the Processing of Information. As mentioned earlier, consumers do not merely rely on the product information provided by the marketer. Rather they make their own inferences about attributes based on the available information. Quite often these inferences take the form of heuristics. Although some heuristic inferences may be acquired from external sources or mere logic (e.g., that a long warranty indicates high quality), inference rules are also likely to be acquired by own experience. For example, a history of high failure rates in foreign cars may lead one to conclude that foreign cars are unreliable. Moreover, knowledgeable consumers are more likely to notice when advertisers withhold crucial information (Kardes, Sanbonmatsu, & Herr, 1990) and to infer understated conclusions about specific product benefits from the attributes (Kardes, Kim, & Lim, 1994).

Finally, research suggests that the familiarity and ease of retrieval of the information, which are clearly a function of previous purchases, affect how the information is evaluated. Most prominently, research on the mere exposure effect (Bornstein, 1989) showed that previously encountered stimuli were evaluated more favorably. Other research suggested that easily retrieved information is deemed more diagnostic for a judgment (Wänke & Bless, 2000). Given that previous product experience, as mentioned earlier, increases the accessibility of experience attributes, it is not surprising that, after product consumption, experience attributes are thought to be more important for product judgment (Wright & Lynch, 1995).

The Role of Experience in Choice Strategies

Whether consumers engage in attitude-based or attribute-based choice primarily depends on whether they have previously formed brand attitudes on which they can rely, provided they are accessible. Although actual consumption experience is not a prerequisite to attitude formation, consumers will more likely have formed attitudes of previously consumed brands. Moreover, as we outline in more detail later, attitudes built on direct experience are more accessible (Regan & Fazio, 1977). Consequently, one may expect the tendency for attitude-based choices to increase with prior brand experience.

Clearly, consumers are likely to rely on once established decision rules. If one has fared well with always choosing the brand on sale, why should one switch to other strategies? A possible deviation from well-established routines may be introduced, however, if the situation is perceived as different from before (see also Betsch, Fiedler, & Brinkmann, 1998).

The Role of Experience in Postconsumption (and Repurchase)

As described previously, a consumption experience will increase the accessibility and relevance of experience attributes (Wright & Lynch, 1995). Compared with an initial consumption, the repurchase decision involves more or other attributes. One may easily conclude that once a consumer has sampled a brand, and thus verified or falsified the hypotheses he or she had held before, which were based on the search attributes, this experience will determine future behavior toward the brand. As marketing guru, Philip Kotler, put it: "Sampling is the most effective and most expensive way to introduce a new product" (1988, p. 648). This reasoning is well in line with research from social and consumer psychology. Attitudes based on direct, behavioral experience are held with greater clarity, confidence, and stability compared with attitudes formed via indirect information about the attitude object (Marks & Kamins, 1988; Regan & Fazio, 1977; Smith & Swinyard, 1982, 1988). Therefore, experience-based attitudes are more accessible and, ultimately, more powerful determinants of future behavior toward the attitude object (Fazio & Zanna, 1981; Smith & Swinyard, 1982).

However, although experience may certainly increase the impact of experience attributes *relative* to search attributes, we may easily think of instances where search attributes nevertheless predominated in the decision. Whereas common logic would predict that we do not buy brands that proved unsatisfactory previously, we all know of counterexamples. How often have we sworn never to fly a particular airline again in the moment of despair over delay and rude service, but the next time we book a flight these awful experiences are forgotten and we feel attracted by the low price, the bonus miles, or the convenient connections.[1] This example illustrates that previously acquired knowledge or previously built judgments only play a role if this information is accessible and deemed relevant for the current judgment (Bohner & Wänke, 2002; Kim & Shavitt, 1993). At the repurchase situation, whether experience or search attributes predominate will depend on their relative accessibility in the situation.

Of course repeat purchases within a product category are particularly prone to experience in yet another manner. In principle, consumers may restart an elaborated evaluation and choice process at every purchase. More likely, however, they may simplify their life and stay with their previous choices, provided they have sufficient satisfaction. After all who would want to go through all the information on cereal boxes every other week. In case of exceedingly low involvement, a person might not even complete the decision process described earlier, but rather choose a highly accessible alternative at an early stage. Although such repeat purchase behavior serves the consumer in possibly truncating the choice process at an early stage, it is still a somewhat deliberate act of picking one option and not the other. With growing frequency and consistency, repeat purchase behavior may become habitual—that is, the behavior is better described as an automatic process rather than a conscious selection (Aarts & Dijksterhuis, 2000; Verplanken, Myrbakk, & Rudi, chap. 13, this volume). Verplanken, Aarts, and van Knippenberg (1994) gave an example of such habitual behavior in the domain of travel mode choice. The habit to choose a specific means of transportation explained a significant portion of variance of subjects' behavior independently of other predictors. Moreover, habit moderated the attitude–behavior relationship in this study, such that the attitude–behavior relation was weak when the habit was strong and vice versa.

The routine saving a maximum of capacity is a habit, which allows consumers to not even consider alternatives, but choose a repeat-purchase product with a minimum of energy and information processing. Thus, we can think about the cognitive processes underlying the decision process as a continuum, with the poles of accurately gathering and weighing attributes of each alternative on the one side time and again and habitually (i.e., automatically) choosing the same option on the other side. From this perspective, one may conceive of brand loyalty as a form of laziness, which would imply that brand loyalty should be highest for low-involvement products such as toothpaste, cereals, or pencils. However, we all know of faithful customers who would not even consider buying any other car than a BMW or

---

[1]Of course the opposite is also possible. Unfavorable search attributes may overshadow a positive consumption experience. Good service or delicious taste are discounted when facing a high price, whereas competitors offer the same product category for considerably less money.

spending their vacation anywhere else but the quaint little village in Tuscany. This would suggest that brand loyalty is not merely an energy-saving device in low-involvement or low-capacity situations, but may also come to bear when involvement is high. Let us have a closer look at the processes and conditions that elicit repeat purchases.

BRAND LOYALTY AND ITS MODERATING CONDITIONS

Repurchasing a brand is indeed effort saving as should be clear from the earlier description of the decision process. Repurchasing a brand allows a consumer to ignore all other brands—to forget about information search and comparison processes. Consumers are saved from determining which attribute is most important. All they have to do is search for their brand and pay at the cashier. As Cobb and Hoyer (1986) observed, consumers with positive brand attitudes and a history of frequently buying this brand took significantly less time in their decision process than other consumers. Accordingly, one may expect brand loyalty to be positively related to processing constraints (see Bless & Igou, chap. 11, this volume): The less consumers are able or willing to engage in processing, the higher the brand loyalty. As we elaborate, this relationship depends on how we define brand loyalty. Most commonly, *brand loyalty* is defined as a series of repeat purchases of the same brand (e.g., Antonides & van Raaij, 1998), although of course more complex definitions have been proposed (e.g., Jacoby & Kyner, 1973), and one review counts more than 50 different definitions (see Wilkie, 1994). Most definitions add that brand loyalty is often accompanied by a positive attitude toward the brand.

One may easily imagine that a favorable brand attitude leads to purchasing and repurchasing the brand (Fazio, 1990; Fishbein & Ajzen, 1975), which over time may develop into a routine behavior. Vice versa, theories in social psychology hold that behavior often results in consistent attitudes (Bem, 1972; Festinger, 1957). Despite this multitude of theoretical grounding, favorable brand attitudes and respective repeat choices do not necessarily go hand in hand. Repeat purchase despite unfavorable attitudes (Dick & Basu [1994] referred to this as *spurious loyalty*) and, vice versa, low brand patronage despite favorable attitudes (latent loyalty) are also possible. For example, consumers' attitudes may have deteriorated only after they established a routine behavior, and now consumers may shy from high psychological costs of a thorough review and evaluation of other alternatives. Rather than going through this load of cognitive work, one may refrain from penalizing the familiar brand and stick to it instead. Repeat purchase without favorable attitudes may also be due to the (perceived) absence of adequate alternative products. In case of spurious loyalty, consumers may abandon the brand rather easily once they are offered an alternative. Low brand patronage despite favorable attitudes, in contrast, may be due to external factors that keep consumers from buying the brand, such as distribution problems or high price. If these external barriers are removed, purchase is likely. These examples illustrate the need to distinguish more clearly between attitudinal and behavioral aspects of brand loyalty. Moreover, the definition of brand loyalty as repeat purchase does not necessarily imply routine behavior because, although the decision process repeatedly arrives at the same outcome, in principle, this may also be due to quite elaborate decision making. In fact a highly thoughtful attribute-based decision process is likely to arrive at the same choices if neither the evaluative criteria nor the available options have changed. In the following, we discuss the implications of routine purchase behavior, favorable brand attitudes, and elaborate decision making on repeat purchases. We suggest that routine behavior has quite different implications from positive brand attitudes for repeat purchases.[2]

The Impact of Motivation for Elaborate Processing on Brand Loyalty

In the domain of consumer choices, motivation to engage in effortful processing should be low when there is little risk in making a suboptimal decision. Risks are mainly defined financially, socially, sanitary, or hedonically.[3] One would expect that consumers rely more on their routines the lesser the perceived risk because, in a low-risk situation, consumers may safely stick to their routines. Indeed there is evidence that habitual repeat purchases increase under low compared to high involvement (Beatty, Kahle, & Homer, 1988). Conceptualizing brand loyalty as resulting from favorable brand attitudes would also imply brand loyalty under low risk.[4] If risk is low, consumers are not motivated to engage in an attribute-based comparison. Rather they rely on their attitude toward the brand (attitude heuristic; Sanbonmatsu & Fazio, 1990). So far low involvement would imply higher repurchase rates either because of higher reliance on habits or on favorable attitudes.

---

[2]Other researchers have already pointed to different implications of both conceptualizations. For example, positive affect toward the brand may be a more important predictor of repurchase compared with previous behavior as a predictor (Baldinger & Rubinson, 1986). We limit our discussion to different implications with regard to processing constraints.

[3]Of course other ways in which purchases may be perceived as bad bargains are possible as well.

[4]If brand attitudes and behavioral routines have opposite implications, the choice depends on the relative accessibility.

However, if risk is low, one may equally expect that consumers take the brand most prominent on display in the shelf or the one that is otherwise most salient in the situation. This reasoning may imply a switch from the previously purchased brand. To sum it up, when the perceived risk is low, and thus motivation to process brand information to arrive at a brand choice is low, we may or may not find repeat purchases. The choice is determined by what is most accessible in the situation, which may be a routinized behavior, a favorable brand attitude, or salient external cues. Both favorable brand attitudes and established routines would imply repeat purchases, but their strength needs to be considerably high to override salient external cues.

What would high risk imply for whether consumers go back to their previously chosen brand? The prior hypothesis of decreasing brand loyalty with increasing involvement would predict that consumers are more likely to switch to another brand of coffee rather than their usual brand when they are expecting important guests—that they would abandon their usual brand of chocolate if it is a gift for someone special. Does this sound likely? First of all, if risk is high, consumers should be more likely to engage in a more meticulous evaluation and choice process rather than relying on routines. They should gather all relevant attributes and compare them thoroughly to arrive at a well-based decision.[5] Alternatively, those who have already formed an attitude toward the brand may simply rely on their previous attitude provided they do not perceive a need to form a new attitude (Bohner & Wänke, 2002; Kim & Shavitt, 1993). One aspect that may determine whether the previously built attitude is used is the involvement in the previous situation. Research on attitude–behavior consistency has shown that attitudes built under conditions of high personal relevance were more predictive of behavior than those built under low personal relevance (Haugvedt & Priester, 1997; Leippe & Elkin, 1987). Thus, if we assume that previously a consumer has elaborately thought about a brand and consequently built an attitude, this attitude is rather likely to predict behavior in another situation. In general, attitude strength has been known to moderate the attitude–behavior consistency. The stronger a favorable attitude, the more likely it will guide respective behavior (Fazio & Roskos-Ewoldson, 1994; for a review of attitude strength, see Petty & Krosnick, 1995). Consequently, consumers who rate their usual brand quite favorably and with considerable strength should be even more likely to buy it for important occasions. For less important occasions or when risk is low, they may be

---

[5]In the absence of strong attitudes and if the risk of a suboptimal decision is high, consumers should be likely to thoroughly elaborate their decision and undergo an attribute-based choice. Given that neither their criteria nor the environment changed, the likelihood of repurchase is high. Note, however, that it is unlikely that in these instances consumers would not rather store their summary evaluation as an attitude.

tempted to go for sales or buy another brand if the preferred one is out of stock. However, consumers who hold less favorable attitudes are more likely to make the effort and search for a better brand.

All this predicts rather high brand loyalty under high involvement, although for different reasons. We suggest that spurious loyalty—brand loyalty based on routine behavior, which is not linked to a particularly positive attitude—will decrease with higher involvement, whereas brand loyalty based on a positive attitude toward the brand will show no difference or even increase with higher involvement depending on the accessibility. Automatically activated favorable brand attitudes may also be effective under low involvement (Fazio & Towles-Schwen, 1999) and, unless other factors are interfering, can also affect choices under high involvement. Less accessible attitudes, however, may only be used when thinking about the brands at choice. Figure 16.1 gives a graphical illustration of this hypothesis.

There is partial evidence for this hypothesis in the literature on high-involvement purchases. Huber and Herrmann (2001) reported a positive correlation between brand loyalty (as measured by "intention to make repeat purchase of brand" and "prepared to recommend brand," both rather attitudinal measures) and involvement for car buyers. The authors explained this positive correlation as mediated by the choice process: "Once an involved buyer has made his choice of brand, this appears to suit his particular style and he is more likely to remain loyal to it" (p. 112). Other studies also identified more extensive information search in high-involvement situations, which consequently led to brand loyalty (Beatty et al., 1988).

Unfortunately, few studies measured, let alone manipulated, involvement. In the marketing world, *involvement* is often defined as a product characteristic rather than a consumer characteristic. A study conducted by the Gesellschaft für Konsumforschung (GfK; Hupp, 2000a, 2000b) investi-

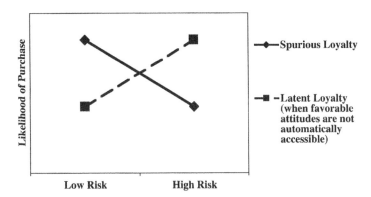

FIG. 16.1. Proposed interaction of attitude toward the regularly chosen product and involvement/risk on brand loyalty.

gated brand loyalty in different product categories that one can assume to involve more or less risk. This study found low brand loyalty for toothpaste and detergent, but high brand loyalty for mineral water and yogurt. Although we can only guess, because only repurchases were measured but no other data were collected, this pattern is in line with higher loyalty for higher risk. Despite the equally low financial risk, choices of mineral water and yogurt may involve more of a risk because differences in these categories are quite noticeable. If one has found a brand of yogurt one likes, chances are that a switch in brands may entail a disappointment. Detergent and toothpaste, in contrast, do not differ much for consumers. Moreover, whether attitudes guide behavior also depend on the accessibility of the attitude. If a brand automatically activates a favorable attitude, purchase is more likely compared to when the equally favorable attitude is less accessible (Herr & Fazio, 1993). It is reasonable to assume that hedonic products, in particular food, are more likely to activate attitudes automatically simply because taste is such a strong cue (see also Hsee, 1996). Somewhat similar, one may also argue that a hedonic product category such as yogurt is more likely to evoke affect-based choices compared with detergent, leaving more room for variance in product choice for the latter (see also Slovic, Finucane, Peters, & MacGregor, 2002).

In summary, we suggest that the perspective that low risk implies routine decision rules and (therefore) more brand loyalty is too simple. On the one hand, high risk should elicit more processing and comparing because of the costs involved in a wrong choice. Thus, we would expect less routine behavior and more brand switching. Yet this depends on consumers' confidence to do better with an extended search and a switch of products. For favorably evaluated brands, the confidence to find more acceptable brands is probably rather low. In case of favorable brand attitudes, we would expect high brand loyalty even in high-risk choices. In contrast, low risk will imply more routine behavior and thus more brand loyalty. This tendency may be challenged by other equally effortless processes. For example, when risk is perceived as low, consumers may be more likely to switch to special offers or buy the one that is in stock at that outlet.

The Impact of Capacity Constraints on Brand Loyalty

Under time pressure (e.g., shopping 5 minutes before closing time), consumers should rely more on their routines (Betsch et al., 1998). They should be more likely to buy what they always buy. They should also rely more on their overall attitude, rather than engage in an attribute-based comparison (Sanbonmatsu & Fazio, 1990; Sanbonmatsu, Prince, Vanous, & Posavac, chap. 6, this volume). To that extent, we would predict higher repurchase rates under capacity constraints, provided consumers have either a routine or favorable brand attitude accessible.

There is one caveat, however. Capacity constraints should only increase brand loyalty when the brand is easy to acquire. When its acquisition is involved with difficulty, constraints should promote switching rather than searching for one's usual brand.

Given the recent developments in attitude research (Fazio & Olson, 2003; Wilson, Lindsey, & Schooler, 2000), a further refinement is needed. Recent theorizing assumes that individuals may hold multiple attitudes. Under capacity constraints, behavior is guided by the most easily accessible or automatically activated attitudes (Fazio & Towles-Schwen, 1999). Within this realm, we have shown elsewhere (Wänke, Plessner, & Friese, 2002) that when consumers held conflicting brand attitudes, their product choices were much more in line with their most accessible attitudes when they had to make their choice under time pressure. Consumers who stated a preference for no-name versus well-established brands on a rating scale, but vice versa on the implicit association test (IAT), chose the no-name brands when the could select products to take home. However, when the choice was made under time pressure, they were more likely to select well-established brands. In other words, under time pressure, the choices of consumers who held conflicting implicit and explicit attitudes corresponded with their implicit attitudes, but conflicted with their explicit attitudes. When no time pressure was experienced, their behavior corresponded with the explicit attitudes and conflicted with the implicit ones.

If consumers cannot rely on previous routines or attitudes, they will have to engage in some steps of decision making or choose at random. As mentioned earlier, a thorough decision elaboration is quite likely to arrive at the same conclusions the second time it is made. Thus, when no routines or attitudes are available, one might expect higher repurchase rates the higher the processing capacity.

The Impact of Age on Brand Loyalty

Routine behavior with or without positive attitudes would predict that older consumers are more likely to show brand loyalty because by and large older people exhibit constrained processing (Cole & Balasubramanian, 1993; Hess & Slaughter, 1990; Reder, Wible, & Martin, 1986; for a more differentiated view, see John & Cole, 1986; Yoon, 1997). Moreover, one would also expect that brand preferences are more stable in older compared with younger consumers because older people should have established their tastes and are less susceptible to peer influences—in summary, they have had a life to find out what they like.

Despite these rather plausible hypotheses, the evidence is not supportive. A study by the GfK examined age effects on brand loyalty for 10 fast-moving consumer goods and found basically no systematic relationship between age and brand loyalty (Hupp, 2000a, 2000b). Other studies are also inconclusive. Note that brand loyalty is just one of many routines, and older consumers may shortcut the decision process by buying the cheapest brand or use any other heuristic. Note that in the GfK study, all 10 product categories were rather uninvolving and risk was rather low. Based on the prior reasoning that brand loyalty may provide a good strategy to minimize risk as well as processing effort, we might in fact find more brand loyalty for expensive goods under older than younger consumers. Although both age groups would want to minimize risk, younger consumers may be more likely to engage in effortful processing, whereas older consumers may be more likely to rely on their experience.

The Impact of Mood on Brand Loyalty

As elaborated by Bless and Igou (chap. 11, this volume), there is ample evidence that good mood should foster reliance on general knowledge structures. For brand loyalty as a routine behavior, we would thus expect a positive effect of good mood. Indeed good mood causes consumers to shorten complexity of a decision process (Gardner, 1985). Likewise, we would expect that consumers are more likely to rely on their preexisting attitudes in a good mood rather than processing anew (Bless, Mackie, & Schwarz, 1992). We are not aware of any study that investigated brand loyalty as a function of mood. However, there is evidence that consumers in a happy rather than sad mood rely more on their attitude toward the mother brand than on product specific attributes when evaluating brand extensions (Bless & Igou, chap. 11, this volume). We would also predict that happy mood would make consumers more prone to rely on simple, well-learned inferences. Consumers may be more likely to infer the quality from the price or the country of origin, rather than from processing attribute information in a happy rather than a sad mood.

CONCLUSION

Clearly, previous experiences play a role in consumer decision making. Previously stored attitudes, previously stored knowledge, and previous behavior may influence every step in the brand choice: the considered alternatives, the information used in the evaluation process, the choice strategies, and the actual purchase. We focused on brand loyalty, the most prominent case of experience-based behavior. Routinely choosing a particular brand is not only a highly efficient shopping behavior, but building brand loyalty is also the achieved goal of marketers. Routine repurchases may be independent of positive brand attitudes. Whereas marketers have little power to influence consumer routines and habits, they do everything they can to influence consumer attitudes. For marketing purposes, a conceptualization of brand loyalty as a favorable brand attitude seems a more fruitful approach. We argued that attitudinal aspects of brand loyalty imply different predictions about the impact of variables on repurchases as compared with routines or mere habits without involving favorable attitudes. Admittedly, so far there is only spurious evidence for many of our assumptions. Research on brand loyalty has been descriptive rather than theory based. In this respect, we would be gratified if our proposed hypotheses stimulate future research. Alas, we have no doubt that—as always—empirical evidence will detect more complexities, but these in turn will allow us to understand consumer behavior in more depth.

REFERENCES

Aarts, H., & Dijksterhuis, A. (2000). Habits as knowledge structures: Automaticity in goal-directed behavior. *Journal of Personality and Social Psychology, 78*, 53–63.

Alba, J. W., & Hutchinson, J. W. (1987). Dimensions of consumer expertise. *Journal of Consumer Research, 13*, 411–454.

Antonides, G., & van Raaij, W. F. (1998). *Consumer behaviour: A European perspective.* Chichester, England: Wiley.

Baldinger, A. L., & Rubinson, J. (1996). Brand loyalty: The link between attitude and behavior. *Journal of Advertising Research, 36*, 22–34.

Beatty, S. E., Kahle, L. R., & Homer, P. (1988). The involvement-commitment model: Theory and implications. *Journal of Business Research, 16*, 149–167.

Bem, D. J. (1972). Self-perception theory. *Advances in Experimental Social Psychology, 6*, 1–62.

Betsch, T., Fiedler, K., & Brinkmann, J. (1998). Behavioral routines in decision making: The effects of novelty in task presentation and time pressure on routine maintenance and deviation. *European Journal of Social Psychology, 28*, 861–878.

Betsch, T., Haberstroh, S., Glöckner, A., Haar, T., & Fiedler, K. (2001). The effects of routine strength on information acquisition and adaptation in recurrent decision making. *Organizational Behavior and Human Decision Processes, 84*, 23–53.

Bettman, J. R., & Park, C. W. (1980). Effects of prior knowledge and experience and phase of the choice process on consumer decision processes: A protocol analysis. *Journal of Consumer Research, 7*, 234–248.

Bless, H., Mackie, D. M., & Schwarz, N. (1992). Mood effects on attitude judgments: Independent effects of mood before and after message elaboration. *Journal of Personality and Social Psychology, 63*, 585–595.

Bohner, G., & Wänke, M. (2002). *Attitudes and attitude change.* Hove, England: Psychology Press.

Bornstein, R. F. (1989). Exposure and affect: Overview and meta-analysis of research, 1968–1987. *Psychological Bulletin, 106*, 265–289.

Cobb, C. J., & Hoyer, W. D. (1986). Planned versus impulse purchase behavior. *Journal of Retailing, 62*, 384–409.

Cole, C. A., & Balasubramanian, S. K. (1993). Age differences in consumers' search for information: Public policy implications. *Journal of Consumer Research, 20,* 157–169.

Darby, M., & Karni, E. (1973). Free competition and the optimal amount of fraud. *Journal of Law and Economics, 16,* 67–86.

Dick, A. S., & Basu, K. (1994). Customer loyalty: Toward an integrated conceptual framework. *Journal of the Academy of Marketing Science, 22,* 99–113.

Engel, J. F., Blackwell, R. D., & Miniard, P. W. (1990). *Consumer behavior* (6th ed.). Chicago, IL: Dryden.

Fazio, R. H. (1990). Multiple processes by which attitudes guide behavior: The MODE model as an integrative framework. *Advances in Experimental Social Psychology, 23,* 75–109.

Fazio, R. H., & Olson, M. A. (2003). Implicit measures in social cognition research: Their meaning and uses. *Annual Review of Psychology, 54,* 297–327.

Fazio, R. H., & Roskos-Ewoldson, D. R. (1994). Acting as we feel: When and how attitudes guide behavior. In S. Shavitt & T. C. Brock (Eds.), *Persuasion: Psychological insights and perspectives* (pp. 71–93). Boston, MA: Allyn & Bacon.

Fazio, R. H., & Towles-Schwen, T. (1999). The MODE model of attitude-behavior processes. In S. Chaiken & Y. Trope (Eds.), *Dual-process theories in social psychology* (pp. 97–116). New York: Guilford.

Fazio, R. H., & Zanna, M. P. (1981). Direct experience and attitude-behavior consistency. In L. Berkowitz (Ed.), *Advances in experimental social psychology* (Vol. 14, pp. 161–202). New York: Academic Press.

Festinger, L. (1957). *A theory of cognitive dissonance.* Stanford, CA: Stanford University Press.

Fishbein, M., & Ajzen, I. (1975). *Belief, attitude, intention, and behavior.* Reading, MA: Addison-Wesley.

Ford, G. T., Smith, D. B., & Swasy, J. L. (1990). Consumer skepticism of advertising claims: Testing hypotheses from economics of information. *Journal of Consumer Research, 16,* 433–441.

Gardner, M. P. (1985). Mood states and consumer behavior: A critical review. *Journal of Consumer Research, 12,* 281–300.

Gilbert, D. T., & Wilson, T. D. (2000). Miswanting: Some problems in the forecasting of future affective states. In J. Forgas (Ed.), *Thinking and feeling: The role of affect in social cognition* (pp. 178–197). Cambridge, England: Cambridge University Press.

Haugvedt, C. P., & Priester, J. R. (1997). Conceptual and methodological issues in advertising effectiveness: An attitude strength perspective. In D. Wells (Ed.), *Measuring advertising effectiveness: Advertising and consumer psychology* (pp. 79–93). Mahwah, NJ: Lawrence Erlbaum Associates.

Herr, P. M., & Fazio, R. H. (1993). The attitude-to-behavior process: Implications for consumer behavior. In A. A. Mitchell (Ed.), *Advertising exposure, memory, and choice* (pp. 119–140). Hillsdale, NJ: Lawrence Erlbaum Associates.

Hess, T. M., & Slaughter, S. J. (1990). Schematic knowledge influences on memory for scene information in young and older adults. *Developmental Psychology, 26,* 855–865.

Hoyer, W. D., & Brown, S. P. (1990). Effects of brand awareness on choice for a common, repeat-purchase product. *Journal of Consumer Research, 17,* 141–148.

Hsee, C. K. (1996). The evaluability hypothesis: An explanation for preference reversals between joint and separate evaluations of alternatives. *Organizational Behavior & Human Decision Processes, 67,* 247–257.

Huber, F., & Herrmann, A. (2001). Achieving brand and dealer loyalty: The case of the automotive industry. *International Review of Retail, Distribution and Consumer Research, 11,* 97–122.

Hupp, O. (2000a). Informationssuche und Kaufentscheidung—eine Frage des Alters? [Information search and purchase decision—A question of age?]. *Markenartikel, 6/2000,* 36–40.

Hupp, O. (2000b). Markentreue—eine Frage des Alters? [Brand loyalty—A question of age?]. *Markenartikel, 5/2000,* 32–33.

Jacoby, J., & Kyner, D. B. (1973). Brand loyalty vs. repeat purchase behavior. *Journal of Marketing Research, 10,* 1–9.

John, D. R., & Cole, C. A. (1986). Age differences in information processing: Understanding deficits in young and elderly consumers. *Journal of Consumer Research, 13,* 297–315.

Johnson, E., & Russo, J. (1984). Product familiarity and learning new information. *Journal of Consumer Research, 11,* 542–550.

Kardes, F. R. (1993). Consumer inference: Determinants, consequences, and implications for advertising. In A. A. Mitchell (Ed.), *Advertising exposure, memory and choice* (pp. 163–191). Hillsdale, NJ: Lawrence Erlbaum Associates.

Kardes, F. R. (2001). *Consumer behavior and managerial decision making* (2nd ed.). Upper Saddle River, NJ: Prentice-Hall.

Kardes, F. R., Sanbonmatsu, D. M., & Herr, P. M. (1990). Consumer expertise and the feature-positive effect: Implications for judgment and inference. In M. E. Goldberg, G. Gorn, & R. W. Pollay (Eds.), *Advances in consumer research* (Vol. 17, pp. 351–354). Provo, UT: Association for Consumer Research.

Kardes, F. R., Kim, J., & Lim, J.-S. (1994). Moderating effects of prior knowledge on the perceived diagnosticity of beliefs derived from implicit versus explicit product claims. *Journal of Business Research, 29,* 219–224.

Kim, K., & Shavitt, S. (1993). Toward a model of attitude reuse versus recomputation. In K. Finlay, A. A. Mitchell, & F. C. Cummuns (Eds.), *Proceedings of the Society of Consumer Psychology* (pp. 105–110). Clemson, SC: CtC Press.

Kotler, P. (1988). *Marketing management: Analysis, planning, implementation, and control* (6th ed.). Englewood Cliffs, NJ: Prentice-Hall.

Leippe, M. R., & Elkin, R. A. (1987). When motives clash: Issue involvement and response involvement as determinants of persuasion. *Journal of Personality and Social Psychology, 52,* 269–278.

Lynch, J. G., & Srull, T. K. (1982). Memory and attentional factors in consumer choice: Concepts and research methods. *Journal of Consumer Research, 9,* 18–37.

Macdonald, E. K., & Sharp, B. M. (2000). Brand awareness effects on consumer decision making for a common, repeat purchase product: A replication. *Journal of Business Research, 48,* 5–15.

Marks, L. J., & Kamins, M. A. (1988). The use of product sampling and advertising: Effects of sequence of exposure and degree of advertising claim exaggeration on consumers' belief strength, belief confidence, and attitudes. *Journal of Marketing Research, 25,* 266–281.

Nedungadi, P. (1990). Recall and consumer consideration sets: Influencing choice without altering brand evaluations. *Journal of Consumer Research, 17,* 263–276.

Nelson, P. (1974). Advertising as information. *Journal of Political Economy, 82,* 729–754.

Payne, J. W., Bettman, J. R., & Johnson, E. J. (1993a). The use of multiple strategies in judgment and choice. In N. J. Castellan, Jr. (Ed.), *Individual and group decision making: Current issues* (pp. 19–39). Hillsdale, NJ: Lawrence Erlbaum Associates.

Petty, R. E., & Krosnick, J. A. (Eds.). (1995). *Attitude strengths: Causes and consequences.* Hillsdale, NJ: Lawrence Erlbaum Associates.

Raju, P. S., Lonial, S. C., & Mangold, W. G. (1995). Differential effects of subjective knowledge, objective knowledge, and usage experience on decision making: An exploratory investigation. *Journal of Consumer Psychology, 4,* 153–180.

Reder, L. M., Wible, C., & Martin, J. (1986). Differential memory changes with age: Exact retrieval versus plausible inference. *Journal of Experimental Psychology: Learning, Memory, and Cognition, 12,* 72–81.

Regan, D. T., & Fazio, R. H. (1977). On the consistency between attitudes and behavior: Look to the method of attitude formation. *Journal of Experimental Social Psychology, 13,* 28–45.

Sanbonmatsu, D. M., & Fazio, R. H. (1990). The role of attitudes in memory-based decision making. *Journal of Personality and Social Psychology, 59,* 614–622.

Slovic, P., Finucane, M., Peters, E., & MacGregor, D. G. (2002). The affect heuristic. In T. Gilovich, D. Griffin, & D. Kahnemann (Eds.), *Intuitive judgment: Heuristics and biases* (pp. 397–420). Cambridge: Cambridge University Press.

Smith, R. E., & Swinyard, W. R. (1982). Information response models: An integrated approach. *Journal of Marketing, 46,* 81–93.

Smith, R. E., & Swinyard, W. R. (1988). Cognitive response to advertising and trial: Belief strength, belief confidence and product curiosity. *Journal of Advertising, 17,* 3–14.

Verplanken, B., Aarts, H., & van Knippenberg, A. (1994). Attitude versus general habit: Antecedents of travel mode choice. *Journal of Applied Social Psychology, 24,* 285–300.

Verplanken, B., Aarts, H., & van Knippenberg, A. (1997). Habit, information acquisition, and the process of making travel mode choices. *European Journal of Social Psychology, 27,* 539–560.

Wänke, M., & Bless, H. (2000). The effects of subjective ease of retrieval on attitudinal judgments: The moderating role of processing motivation. In H. Bless & J. P. Forgas (Eds.), *The message within: The role of subjective experience in social cognition and behavior* (pp. 143–161). Philadelphia, PA: Psychology Press.

Wänke, M., Plessner, H., & Friese, M. (2002, May). *When do implicit attitudes guide behavior—and when don't they.* Paper presented at the Association of Consumer Research Asia Pacific Conference, Beijing.

Wells, W. D., & Prensky, D. (1996). *Consumer behavior.* New York: Wiley.

Wilkie, W. L. (1994). *Consumer behavior* (3rd ed.). New York: Wiley.

Wilson, T. D., Lindsey, S., & Schooler, T. Y. (2000). A model of dual attitudes. *Psychological Review, 107,* 101–126.

Wright, A. A., & Lynch, J. G. (1995). Communication effects of advertising versus direct experience when both search and experience attributes are present. *Journal of Consumer Research, 21,* 708–718.

Wyer, R. S., Jr., & Srull, T. K. (1989). *Memory and cognition in its social context.* Hillsdale, NJ: Lawrence Erlbaum Associates.

Yoon, C. (1997). Age differences in consumers' processing strategies: An investigation of moderating influences. *Journal of Consumer Research, 24,* 329–342.

17

Positive and Negative Effects of Prior Knowledge on Referee Decisions in Sports

Henning Plessner
University of Heidelberg

Referees[1] are involved in most competitive sports; moreover, in some sports, the assessment of athletes' performance depends exclusively on human judgments. The tasks of referees vary from simple judgments to complex decisions. Many of these tasks surpass the limited human capacity to process information (e.g., Salmela, 1978). For example, given the speed of the modern tennis game, the human perceptual system does not allow for differentiating between a ball that is on the line and one close to it (Jendrusch, 2002). It lacks the appropriate temporal resolution. However, decisions have to be made by referees even when situations are ambiguous or unclear, or when important information is missing due to personal or situational factors. Such situations seem to occur quite often in sport competitions. For example, in a recent study on the influence of crowd noise on referee decision in soccer, Nevill, Balmer, and Williams (2002) asked referees to make assessments for 47 typical incidents taken from an English Premier League match. One of the findings was that none of these challenges resulted in a unanimous decision by all qualified referees participating in the study (see also Rainey, Larsen, Stephenson, & Coursey, 1989). Additionally, referees not only have to make decisions about situations, but also have to evaluate the performance of other people, and there is always some inter-

---

[1]Depending on sports and specific tasks, referees are also called umpires, officials, linesmen, judges, and others. In this chapter, the term *referee* refers to the general category of people who monitor and control the application of the rules in a sporting competition.

action between referees and the athletes involved. Consequently, it has been argued that refereeing in sports follows general principles of social judgment, and therefore referees tend to make systematic judgment biases based on cognitive processing like all people in social judgment situations (Plessner & Raab, 1999).

This assumption—that referee decisions can be considered as social judgments—has recently been outlined in more detail in a theoretical framework for the study of judgment and decision making in sports (Plessner, 2003). It is called A Social Cognition Approach to Refereeing in Sports (see Fig. 17.1). The basic assumption of this framework is that decisions of referees in sports can be understood as a product of social information processing. On a basic level, this means that it is useful, at least for pragmatic reasons, to differentiate between several stages of information processing (i.e., perception, categorization, memory processes, and judging; cf. Fiedler & Bless, 2001). These processes lead from the actual performance (e.g., a tackling in soccer) to a decision (e.g., sending a player off the field). An erroneous decision can stem from different processing stages—for example, from the misperception that a player hit his opponent's leg instead of the ball or from the false memory that the player has persistently infringed the rules of the game before this situation and is now due for a strong punishment. To take adequate measures to prevent decisions errors, it is therefore important to identify their sources on the corresponding processing stage.

Several factors have been identified in the literature as having an important influence on one or several information-processing stages of referees. These are at first the written rules. They constitute the main difference between judgments in sports and judgments studied usually in social cognition

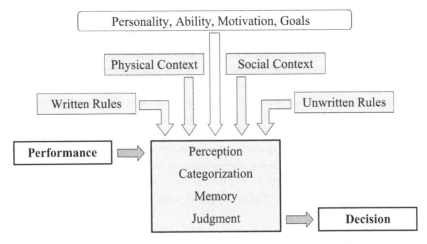

FIG. 17.1. A Social Cognition Approach to Refereeing in Sports (Plessner, 2003).

research. One must become familiar with the rules of a sport before studying the processes of referee decisions. Another important factor is the physical context—for example, the visual angle from which a referee perceives a situation. This factor also plays a minor role in ordinary social cognition research, but can be a major determinant in referee decisions. For example, Oudejans et al. (2000) found that the high percentage of errors in offside decisions in football mainly reflects the viewing position of the assistant referee. Although they should stand in line with the last defender, they are positioned too far behind on average. By considering the retinal images of referees, Oudejans et al. (2000) predicted a specific relation of frequencies in different types of errors (wrongly indicating offside vs. not indicating an actual offside) depending on the area of attack (near vs. far from the assistant referee and inside or outside the defender). In an analysis of 200 videotaped matches, this prediction could be confirmed, thus demonstrating that assistant referees' decisions directly reflect the situations as they are projected on their retinas. In a similar vein, Ford, Goodwin, and Richardson (1995) found umpires' ball-strike judgments in baseball to be influenced by their viewing position (see also Ford, Gallagher, Lacy, Bridwell, & Goodwin, 1997).

The other factors found to exert a specific influence on referees' information processing are personal factors, such as the ability, motivation, and goals of a referee; the social context of a decision (e.g., the presence and reactions of spectators), and the so-called unwritten rules. Experiences and prior knowledge, the topic of this volume, are involved in all of these last three factors. I refer to them as the effects of expertise, inappropriate knowledge, and social norms.

EXPERTISE OF REFEREES

In many decision contexts, a decision maker's years of experience are a good indicator of the quality of his or her decision making (e.g., Omodei, McLennan, & Wearing, chap. 15, this volume; Shanteau, Friel, Thomas, & Raacke, chap. 14, this volume). Experienced decision makers are, therefore, considered experts in these contexts. Yet the expert status of referees as decision makers is debatable at least. Mascarenhas, Collins, and Mortimer (2002) pointed to referees' expertise as a crucial determinant of decision accuracy, and Plessner and Betsch (2002) stressed that, in contrast to experts in other areas, referees' abilities are mostly acquired in a learning environment that provides little useful feedback for the improvement of their decision skills. For example, a German survey in most Olympic sports recovered that specific decision training is the exception rather than the rule in referees' education programs (Plessner, Schork, & Roch, 2002). Additionally, there is evidence that systematic judgment errors occur even with experienced referees in their naturalistic environments (e.g., Oudejans et al., 2000; Scheer, 1973; Stallings & Gillmore, 1972; Wilson, 1976). That means many years of experience as a referee do not automatically lead to more accurate decisions.

In contrast, referees' knowledge that stems from a friendly learning environment (cf. Harvey & Fischer, chap. 7, this volume; Hogarth, chap. 4, this volume; Sedlmeier, chap. 5, this volume) could nevertheless help to improve their decision making. How this can work already on a perceptual level has been demonstrated in a study on in/out decisions in tennis (Jendrusch, 2002). As said before, in tennis it is objectively impossible to *see* whether the ball is in or out when it is close to the line. It is just too fast for the human eye. However, for a training study, electronic devices were installed on a tennis court so that it was possible to objectively assess the point where the ball hits the floor and, therefore, to provide immediately linesmen with an accurate feedback about their corresponding decisions. Linesmen of a training group received this kind of feedback during several sessions a week. As a result of this treatment, their decision making improved markedly in comparison with a control group (Jendrusch, 2002). What is most interesting about this study is that, according to all kinds of physical measures, there was no improvement in the perceptual abilities of the training group's linesmen. Rather linesmen learned to use relatively valid perceptual cues in the assessment of the hitting point—for example, the shape of the flying curve. Accordingly, creating learning environments that help referees to use multiple valid cues seems to be one important aspect that would increase the expert status of referees.

As noted earlier, some research has shown that the position of a referee on a field has an important influence on his or her decisions (Ford, Gallagher, Lacy, Bridwell, & Goodwin, 1997; Ford, Goodwin, & Richardson, 1995; Oudejans et al., 2000). Plessner and Schallies (2003) recently studied referees' expertise as a potential correcting factor in this context. They examined the influence of judges' viewing position on the evaluation of exercise presentation in men's gymnastics. This is also of practical interest because the position from where judges have to evaluate exercises is only loosely prescribed in the rules of gymnastics. In an experiment, experienced gymnastic judges and laypeople were presented with a series of photographs that show athletes holding a cross on rings (see Fig. 17.2). They were simultaneously taken from different viewpoints (0, 30, or 60 degrees from frontal view). Participants had to judge how many degrees the arms deviated from horizontal for each picture. This is a natural judgment task for gymnastic judges that is prescribed by the rules. It has been expected to be the more difficult the more the viewpoint differs from frontal view. One half of the judges had a secondary task, which is to judge the duration of the picture presentation, which also varied. This task again resembled one that judges have to fulfill under natural conditions.

FIG. 17.2. An example of an athlete holding the cross on rings.

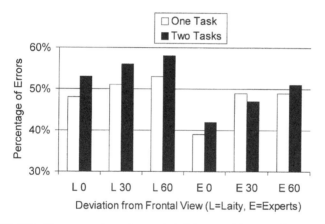

FIG. 17.3. Mean percentage of errors in judging arms' deviation from horizontal by viewing position, task number, and expertise (Plessner & Schallies, 2003).

The main results of this study are depicted in Fig. 17.3. Participants had to respond on five answer keys representing 0 degrees, 1 to 15 degrees, 16 to 30 degrees, 31 to 45 degrees, and more than 45 degrees. Therefore, answering by pure chance would have resulted in an error rate of 80%. As can be seen, the overall performance of the referees was much better than that of the laypeople; in contrast to the lay judgments, they were not influenced by the secondary task. However, the expert judgments were still significantly influenced by the viewing position—that is, the error rate increased with an increase in deviation from a frontal view. Although expertise led to more accurate judgments and helped overcome capacity limitations, it did not prevent judges from being influenced by basic perceptual limitations (cf. Oudejans et al., 2000).

In accordance with these results and those of other studies (e.g., Bard, Fleury, Carrière, & Hallé, 1980; MacMahon & Ste-Marie, 2002; Ste-Marie, 1999, 2000), Ste-Marie (2001) drew this conclusion: If in some sports judgments of experienced referees are indeed found to be more accurate than judgments of laypeople or novices, it is so because experienced referees in general do not encounter the same processing limitations as novices. Based on a problem-solving approach, she argued that experienced referees have some specific knowledge that helps them save processing capacities. They know what information is relevant, what to expect, and what are the typical interrelations among variables. This may be of even more concern in the sports domain than in other areas of expertise research because sport evaluation occurs under time-pressured situations with continuously incoming information. This kind of knowledge seems not to be attained as an automatic consequence of mere experience in a sport—for example as an athlete (Allard, Deakin, Parker, & Rodgers, 1993)—but would also need at best some specific, structured, and effortful training. As said before, however, decision training with adequate feedback that would facilitate the acquisition of such expert knowledge is rare in referees' education (Plessner, Schork, & Roch, 2002).

Focusing on expertise, research shows that knowledge could help referees make more accurate decisions and, therefore, could have a positive effect. It has been shown that, although quite a few starting points for the improvement of referees' expertise have been identified in the literature, there is much left to do. Currently, there are as many studies demonstrating an expert advantage of experienced referees above less experienced as not. Now I turn from studies on potential "good" knowledge to studies on "bad" or inappropriate knowledge—that is, knowledge that has a distorting or biasing influence on referees' cognitive processes and subsequent decisions.

INAPPROPRIATE KNOWLEDGE

To begin with, some evidence is presented to illustrate that referees' perceptual judgments may be biased by experiences that should be irrelevant with regard to the decision. Ste-Marie and her colleagues (Ste-Marie, 2003; Ste-Marie & Lee, 1991; Ste-Marie & Valiquette, 1996) conducted a series of experiments designed to mirror the warmup/competition setting in gymnastics. In the first phase of the experiment, judges watched a series of gymnasts perform a simple element and decided whether the performance was perfect or flawed. The judges' task was the same in the second phase that followed, except that the gymnastic elements shared a relationship with the items shown in the first phase. Some of the gymnasts were shown during the second phase with the identical performance as in the first phase (e.g., both times perfect), and others were shown with the opposite performance (e.g., first perfect and then flawed). Findings show that the accuracy of perceptual judgments during the second phase varied dependent on this experimental manipulation. In the condition where the performance in the first and second phases differed, perceptual judgments were less accurate than in the conditions where performances were the same for both phases (Ste-Marie & Lee, 1991). For example, when the gymnast presented a perfect performance in the second phase, it was more likely to be recognized by the judges if they had also seen the athlete with a perfect performance in the first phase. These memory-influenced biases occurred even with a 1-week break between the first and second phases (Ste-Marie & Valiquette, 1996) and irrespectively of the cognitive task the judges had to perform during the first phase (Ste-Marie, 2003). Together these experiments provide strong evidence that referees' perceptual judgments are strongly influenced by the prior experiences they might have had with the athletes under consideration.

In a similar vein, basketball referees were found to be influenced in their decisions by the star status of a player (Lehman & Reifman, 1987). Rainey, Larsen, and Stephenson (1989) found that in baseball there were effects of pitcher reputation on umpires' ball-strike judgments. Jones, Paull, and Erskine (2002), as well as Strauss and Pier (2002), found soccer referees to be influenced in their decisions by prior information about the aggressiveness of players.

Prior knowledge about an athlete is not the only source for distorting influences on referees' judgments and decisions. Frank and Gilovich (1988) were able to show that even culturally shared knowledge that was totally irrelevant to the task at hand can have an influence on sport decisions. They assumed that in most cultures there was a strong association between the color black and aggression. A black dress of a sports team could, therefore, serve as a prime that automatically activates in the referee the concept of aggression. In one of their experiments, referees watched videotaped segments of a football game in which the defensive team was wearing either black or white uniforms. It was actually the same event in both cases; the uniforms' color was controlled technically. The referees made judgments about the defensive team's action after each play. The results show that referees were more likely to penalize the team wearing a black uniform than the team wearing a white uniform. Although this effect appears somewhat impressive on a first view, it is questionable whether this effect can be of significance in a real competition. For example, Frank and Gilovich (1988) exclusively investigated judgments concerning the team wearing either a black or white uniform. If the color black would indeed serve as a conceptual prime, it would be quite likely that the opposite team is in a disadvantage as well, such that the effect would be equalized for both teams. However, this is a research question that still needs some clarification.

Other information that was found to exert an influence on referee decisions are the responses of other people involved in a competition—for example, the decisions of other referees (e.g., Scheer, Ansorge, & Howard, 1983; Wanderer, 1987) and the reactions of coaches (e.g., Levitt & Tockman, 1991). In a recent study, Nevill, Balmer, and Williams (2002) showed that even the well-confirmed phenomenon of a home advantage in team sports (cf. Courneya & Carron, 1992) can be explained by the influence of such information on refereeing decisions. Specifically, they investigated whether crowd noise has an influence on soccer referees' decisions concerning potential foul situations. They assumed that referees have learned to use crowd noise as a decision cue because in general it would serve as a useful indicator for the seriousness of the foul. However, because the reaction of a crowd is usually biased against the away team, the use of this knowledge would be inappropriate. In an experiment, referees had to assess various challenges videotaped from a match in the English Premier League. Half of them observed the video with the original crowd noise audible, whereas the other half viewed the video in silence. This presence or absence of crowd noise had a strong effect on decisions made by the referees. Most important, referees who viewed challenges in the noise condition awarded significantly fewer fouls against the home team than those observing the video in silence, thus constituting the effect of a home advantage (see also Sutter & Kocher, 2004). The authors concluded that this effect might be partly due to heuristic judgment processes in which the salient, yet potentially biased, judgment of the crowd served as a decision cue.

The various experiments point to cumulative evidence that referees sometimes rely on knowledge that should have no influence on their decisions given that they primarily have to judge the actual performance presented by the athletes. However, Strauss and Pier (2002) recently reported that they could find an influence of soccer players' aggressive reputation on referee decision only in ambiguous situations, but not when a scene has been prerated clearly as either a foul or as no incident. That means the influence of inappropriate knowledge on referee decisions may be confined to ambiguous situations. Nevertheless, as I pointed out in the beginning, ambiguous situations seem to occur quite frequently in sport competitions.

The effects of inappropriate knowledge on referee decisions are extremely unwelcome, and most referees in sports would argue that it should have no influence on their decisions. It is not that clear if this evaluation also holds for the last type of knowledge that will be presented in this review. This is the knowledge about unwritten rules.

SOCIAL NORMS

Similarly to the behavior of people in other kinds of social groups, people who practice a specific sport together tend to form social norms. The norms are rules of behavior shared by members of that group. They can be explicit or implicit. In sports this can lead to the phenomenon that some unwritten rules exist alongside the official rules. An example of such an unwritten rule is the fact that gymnastics coaches typically place the gymnasts in rank order from poorest at the beginning to best at the end in a team competition. They are not required to do it; there is no explicit rule stating that they have to do so. However, it has been found that this unwritten rule leads to different performance expectancies if an athlete starts as the first of his team than if he starts as the last, and that these expectancies exert a biasing influence on the evaluation of gymnastic exercises (Ansorge, Scheer, Laub, & Howard, 1978; Scheer, 1973; Scheer & Ansorge, 1975, 1979). In an experiment following this line of research, Plessner (1999) investigated the cognitive processes underlying this expectancy effect. Therefore, different performance related expectancies have been induced in gymnastic judges by the manipulation of athletes' order of appearance in a videotaped competition. Half of the judges were presented with routines[2] in the last position of a team order—that is, when they expected a high performance and the other half of the judges saw these routines in the first position, that is when they expected a low performance. The use of judges' protocol sheets as the dependent variable enabled the researcher to determine the processing stages that were influenced by judges' performance-related expectancies and provided a rare opportunity for an online measurement of cognitive processes. For example, Plessner (1999) found the categorization of perceived value parts (i.e., the attributed difficulty to single gymnastic elements) to be biased by judges' expectancies. Gymnastic elements increase in their value from A to E parts, with E parts being the most difficult parts. Table 17.1 shows how a routine on horizontal bar has been categorized as much more difficult when the judges expected a high performance than when they expected a rather low performance, although both experimental groups perceived the same amount of value parts. Thus, the judges categorized the perceived value parts in accordance with their performance-related expectancies, which stemmed from an unwritten rule.

The unwritten rule of rank order in gymnastic teams is of general concern for people involved in this sport (e.g., it also exerts an influence on coaches' strategic considerations during a competition). There is also evidence for other unwritten rules that evolved directly among referees (e.g.,

---

[2]In the context of gymnastics, the exercise presentation of an athlete that has to be evaluated by the judges is called a *routine*.

TABLE 17.1
Median Number of Recognized Value Parts on Horizontal Bar
as a Function of Performance Expectancy (Plessner, 1999)

Expected Performance	Content of the Target Routine		
	B Parts	C Parts	D Parts
Low	3	3.5	0.5
High	2	3	2

Rainey & Larsen, 1988; Rainey, Larsen, Stephenson, & Olson, 1993). Such an unwritten rule may also lie at the heart of an effect that has recently been demonstrated in a study on penalty decisions in soccer (Plessner & Betsch, 2001). According to the rules in soccer, a penalty should be awarded against a team that commits one of several offenses inside its own penalty area—for example, tripping an opponent. It is important to note that earlier decisions within the match should have no influence on a penalty decision. However, it has been frequently alleged that referees tend to make so-called concession decisions. Most intriguing is the claim that the probability of awarding a penalty to a team in an ambiguous foul situation increases if no penalty has been awarded to the same team in a similar situation before. In our experiment, referees made decisions for each of 20 videotaped scenes from an actual match in the Spanish Primera Division. The tapes were manipulated as follows. In three scenes of one video, defenders in their penalty areas committed potential fouls. The first two scenes involved the same team, and the third scene occurred in the penalty area of the opposite team. For about one third of the participants, the videotape was edited in a way that, instead of the first foul scene inside the penalty area, a ball-out situation appeared on the screen. We expected and found the remaining participants to divide into two groups based on their decisions: (a) those who award a penalty in the first scene, and (b) those who do not. Therefore, we were able to compare the probability of awarding a penalty in the second scene under three conditions (no prior penalty decision, penalty awarded in a prior situation, and no penalty awarded in a prior situation). The main results of this experiment can be seen in Table 17.2. Compared with those participants who saw a ball-out situation, instead of the first foul scene in the penalty area (no prior penalty decision), the probability of awarding a penalty in the second scene decreased when they had awarded a penalty before (penalty awarded in a prior situation) and increased when they had not (no penalty awarded in a prior situation). This can also be described as a negative contingency between successive penalty decisions concerning the same team. Additionally, we found a positive contingency between successive penalty decisions concerning first one and

TABLE 17.2
Percentage of Penalties Awarded by Prior Penalty Decision
Concerning the Same Team (Plessner & Betsch, 2001)

No Prior Penalty Decision	Prior Penalty Decision	
	Penalty Awarded	No Penalty Awarded
n = 43	n = 13	n = 59
18.6%	0%	33.9%

then the other team. No such effects could be found for similar sequences of free-kick decisions. An obvious difference between penalty and free-kick decisions is the fact that the latter are much more frequent within a match than penalty decisions. Furthermore, the consequences of penalty decisions are much more significant because they can determine the winner and loser of a game.

Therefore, it is quite likely that referees perceive the possibility of awarding a penalty as a limited option that one should not take too frequently. This unwritten rule could at least partly explain the contrast effect in successive penalty decisions concerning the same team. That is, once participants awarded a penalty to a team, they are assumed to shift their criterion for awarding a penalty to the same team to a higher level in subsequent situations. Moreover, penalty situations may activate decision strategies that are somewhat equality oriented. This orientation could lead to a concession decision, as a kind of summary response to repeated offenses, as well as to the assimilation effect that we found when both teams were involved.

CONCLUSIONS

The reported studies demonstrated effects of prior knowledge on decisions of referees in sports. The reason that these effects are so strong and persistent lies in the fact that referee decisions can be considered as social judgments. Besides others, they have to be made under time-pressured circumstances in which at least sometimes important information is missing and cognitive capacities are constrained. Some of the knowledge-based influences on decisions that have been reported are welcome, whereas others are rather not. It is important to tell the positive and negative effects of prior knowledge apart to develop measures for the education of referees that support the acquisition of good knowledge (e.g., knowledge that helps circumvent capacity limitations, and measures that help avoid influences of bad or inappropriate knowledge, which leads to biased judgments and faulty decisions). The Social Cognition Approach to Refereeing in Sports

(Plessner, 2003) covers most of the reported effects and provides a helpful framework for the understanding of systematic errors in sport decisions and their formation on different stages of information processing. Therefore, it can serve as a solid basis for the development of specific training modules and decision aids to prevent biases and improve decision making. However, in the development of these measures, one has to take care that their application does not interfere with referees' other functions—for example, game management (e.g., Brand, 2002; Mascarenhas, Collins, & Mortimer, 2002).

Most of the studies cited in this chapter begin with the assumption that referees are in principle motivated to make accurate decisions. Yet this is not always the case, and sometimes politics and the intention to put some athletes at an advantage and others at a disadvantage exert an even stronger distorting influence on referees' decisions than their prior knowledge (e.g., Ansorge & Scheer, 1988; Mohr & Larsen, 1998; Seltzer & Glass, 1991; Ste-Marie, 1996; Sumner & Mobley, 1981; Whissel, Lyons, Wilkinson, & Whissel, 1993). However, intended biases and politics in referee decisions are beyond the scope of the present chapter.

REFERENCES

Allard, F., Deakin, J., Parker, S., & Rodgers, W. (1993). Declarative knowledge in skilled motor performance: Byproduct or constituent? In J. L. Starkes & F. Allard (Eds.), *Cognitive issues in motor expertise* (pp. 95–107). North Holland: Elsevier Science.

Ansorge, C. J., & Scheer, J. K. (1988). International bias detected in judging gymnastic competition at the 1984 Olympic Games. *Research Quarterly for Exercise and Sport, 59*, 103–107.

Ansorge, C. J., Scheer, J. K., Laub, J., & Howard, J. (1978). Bias in judging women's gymnastics induced by expectations of within-team order. *Research Quarterly, 49*, 399–405.

Bard, C., Fleury, M., Carrière, L., & Hallé, M. (1980). Analysis of gymnastics judges visual search. *Research Quarterly for Exercise and Sport, 51*, 267–273.

Brand, R. (2002). Wie präsentieren Schiedsrichter umstrittene Entscheidungen? Eine gegenstandsverankerte Analyse von Videodaten [How do referees present contentious decisions? An analysis of videotapes based on grounded theory]. *Psychologie & Sport, 9*, 110–119.

Courneya, K. S., & Carron, A. V. (1992). The home advantage in sport competitions: A literature review. *Journal of Sport and Exercise Psychology, 14*, 13–27.

Fiedler, K., & Bless, H. (2001). Social cognition: The construction of social reality. In W. Stroebe, M. Hewstone, & G. Stephenson (Eds.), *Introduction to social psychology* (4th ed., pp. 115–149). New York: Springer.

Ford, G. G., Gallagher, S. H., Lacy, B. A., Bridwell, A. M., & Goodwin, F. (1997). Repositioning the home plate umpire to provide enhanced perceptual cues and more accurate ball-strike judgments. *Journal of Sport Behavior, 22*, 28–44.

Ford, G. G., Goodwin, F., & Richardson, J. W. (1995). Perceptual factors affecting the accuracy of ball and strike judgments from traditional American League and National League umpire perspectives. *International Journal of Sport Psychology, 27*, 50–58.

Frank, M. G., & Gilovich, T. (1988). The dark side of self- and social perception: Black uniforms and aggression in professional sports. *Journal of Personality and Social Psychology, 54*, 74–85.

Jendrusch, G. (2002). Probleme bei der Bewegungsbeobachtung und beurteilung durch Kampf-, Schieds- und Linienrichter [Judges', referees', and linesmen's difficulties in the perception and evaluation of movements]. *Psychologie & Sport, 9,* 133–144.

Jones, M. V., Paull, G. C., & Erskine, J. (2002). The impact of a team's reputation on the decisions of association football referees. *Journal of Sports Sciences, 20,* 991–1000.

Lehman, D. R., & Reifman, A. (1987). Spectator influence on basketball officiating. *The Journal of Social Psychology, 127,* 673–675.

Levitt, E. E., & Tockman, R. S. (1991). Impact of the sideline behavior of coaches on the decisions of game officials. In W. K. Simpson, A. D. LeUnes, & J. S. Picou (Eds.), *Applied research in coaching and athletics* (pp. 185–194). Boston: American Press.

MacMahon, C., & Ste-Marie, D. M. (2002). Decision-making by experienced rugby referees: Use of perceptual information and episodic memory. *Perceptual & Motor Skills, 95,* 570–572.

Mascarenhas, D. R. D., Collins, D., & Mortimer, P. (2002). The art of reason versus the exactness of science in elite refereeing: Comments on Plessner and Betsch (2001). *Journal of Sport and Exercise Psychology, 24,* 328–333.

Mohr, P. B., & Larsen, K. (1998). Ingroup favoritism in umpiring decisions in Australian Football. *The Journal of Social Psychology, 138,* 495–504.

Nevill, A. M., Balmer, N. J., & Williams, A. M. (2002). The influence of crowd noise and experience upon refereeing decisions in football. *Psychology of Sport & Exercise, 3,* 261–272.

Oudejans, R. R. D., Verheijen, R., Bakker, F. C., Gerrits, J. C., Steinbrückner, M., & Beek, P. J. (2000). Errors in judging "offside" in football. *Nature, 404,* 33.

Plessner, H. (1999). Expectation biases in gymnastics judging. *Journal of Sport and Exercise Psychology, 21,* 131–144.

Plessner, H. (2003). *A social cognition approach to refereeing in sports.* Paper submitted for publication.

Plessner, H., & Betsch, T. (2001). Sequential effects in important referee decisions: The case of penalties in soccer. *Journal of Sport & Exercise Psychology, 23,* 200–205.

Plessner, H., & Betsch, T. (2002). Refereeing in sports is supposed to be a craft, not an art: Response to Mascarenhas, Collins, & Mortimer (2002). *Journal of Sport & Exercise Psychology, 24,* 334–337.

Plessner, H., & Raab, M. (1999). Kampf- und Schiedsrichterurteile als Produkte sozialer Informationsverarbeitung [Judgments by officials in sports as products of social information processing]. *Psychologie & Sport, 6,* 130–145.

Plessner, H., & Schallies, E. (2003). *Judging the cross on rings: A matter of achieving shape constancy.* Paper submitted for publication.

Plessner, H., Schork, P., & Roch, K. (2002). *Der Stand der Schiedsrichterausbildung und -auswahl in den olympischen Sportarten in Deutschland* [The state of referee education and selection in Olympic sports in Germany]. Heidelberg: Unpublished manuscript.

Rainey, D. W., & Larsen, J. D. (1988). Balls, strikes, and norms: Rule violations and normative rules among baseball umpires. *Journal of Sport & Exercise Psychology, 10,* 75–80.

Rainey, D. W., Larsen, J. D., & Stephenson, A. (1989). The effects of a pitcher's reputation on umpires' calls of balls and strikes. *Journal of Sport Behavior, 12,* 139–150.

Rainey, D. W., Larsen, J. D., Stephenson, A., & Coursey, S. (1989). Accuracy and certainty judgments of umpires and nonumpires. *Journal of Sport Behavior, 12,* 12–22.

Rainey, D. W., Larsen, J. D., Stephenson, A., & Olson, T. (1993). Normative rules among umpires: The "Phantom Tag" at second base. *Journal of Sport Behavior, 16,* 147–155.

Salmela, J. H. (1978). Gymnastics judging: A complex information processing task, or (who's putting one over on who?) Part 1 & 2. *International Gymnast, 20,* 54–56 & 62–63.

Scheer, J. K. (1973). Effect of placement in the order of competition on scores of Nebraska high school students. *Research Quarterly, 44,* 79–85.

Scheer, J. K., & Ansorge, C. J. (1975). Effects of naturally induced judges' expectations on the ratings of physical performances. *Research Quarterly, 46,* 463–470.

Scheer, J. K., & Ansorge, C. J. (1979). Influence due to expectations of judges: A function of internal-external locus of control. *Journal of Sport Psychology, 1,* 53–58.

Scheer, J. K., Ansorge, C. J., & Howard, J. (1983). Judging bias induced by viewing contrived videotapes: A function of selected psychological variables. *Journal of Sport Psychology, 5,* 427–437.

Seltzer, R., & Glass, W. (1991). International politics and judging in Olympic skating events. *Journal of Sport Behavior, 14,* 189–200.

Stallings, W. M., & Gillmore, G. M. (1972). Estimating the interjudge reliability of the Ali-Frazier fight. *Journal of Applied Psychology, 56,* 435–436.

Ste-Marie, D. (1996). International bias in gymnastic judging: Conscious or unconscious influences? *Perceptual and Motor Skills, 83,* 963–975.

Ste-Marie, D. (1999). Expert-novice differences in gymnastic judging: An information processing perspective. *Applied Cognitive Psychology, 13,* 269–281.

Ste-Marie, D. (2000). Expertise in women's gymnastic judging: An observational approach. *Perceptual and Motor Skills, 90,* 543–546.

Ste-Marie, D. (2001). *Expertise in the context of sport evaluation: Circumventing information processing limitations.* Paper presented at the 10th World Congress of Sport Psychology, Skiathos.

Ste-Marie, D. (2003). Memory biases in gymnastic judging: Differential effects of surface feature changes. *Applied Cognitive Psychology, 17,* 733–751.

Ste-Marie, D., & Lee, T. D. (1991). Prior processing effect on gymnastic judging. *Journal of Experimental Psychology: Learning, Memory, and Cognition, 17,* 126–136.

Ste-Marie, D., & Valiquette, S. M. (1996). Enduring memory-influenced biases in gymnastic judging. *Journal of Experimental Psychology: Learning, Memory, and Cognition, 22,* 1498–1502.

Strauss, B., & Pier, M. (2002). *Urteilsverzerrungen von Fußballschiedsrichtern* [Judgment biases of referees in football]. Paper presented at the 43rd Congress of the German Psychological Society, Berlin.

Sumner, J., & Mobley, M. (1981). Are cricket umpires biased? *New Scientist, 91,* 29–31.

Sutter, M., & Kocher, M. G. (2004). Favoritism of agents—The case of referees' home bias. *Journal of Economic Psychology, 25,* 461–469.

Wanderer, J. J. (1987). Social factors in judges rankings of competitors in figure skating championships. *Journal of Sport Behavior, 10,* 93–102.

Whissel, R., Lyons, S., Wilkinson, D., & Whissel, C. (1993). National bias in judgements of Olympic-level skating. *Perceptual and Motor Skills, 77,* 355–358.

Wilson, V. E. (1976). Objectivity, validity, and reliability of gymnastic judging. *Research Quarterly, 47,* 169–174.

EDUCATING THE ROUTINES OF DECISION MAKING

18

From the Recognition Primed Decision Model to Training

Karol G. Ross
Klein Associates Inc.

James W. Lussier
U.S. Army Research Institute for the Behavioral and Social Sciences

Gary Klein
Klein Associates Inc.

Routines of expert decision making are largely unconscious and require a rich store of experiences to operate successfully (Klein, 1989). This understanding seems to leave us with little opportunity to develop training interventions. How do we teach someone to do something that is unconscious? How do we give novices the requisite experience that it takes years for experts to acquire? In this chapter, we answer those questions by first describing the nature of expert decision making in terms of the Recognition Primed Decision (RPD) model, which consists of two processes—recognition and mental simulation. We then discuss the two processes of gaining expertise—acquisition of contextualized knowledge in the form of mental models, and practice applying these mental models in context to develop richness in one's recognition and mental simulation abilities. Finally, we describe two training programs to illustrate how training can support the improvement of decision-making routines and the development and use of mental models.

THE ROUTINES OF RECOGNITIONAL DECISION MAKING

The cognitive processes in the RPD model are intuitive (i.e., largely unconscious and based on a "gut-level feeling" about the current situation). Experts are usually unaware of their underlying cognitive routines or that they are even making decisions (Klein, 1998). The keen intuitive ability that we credit to experts is in fact the process of rapidly integrating information from a large array of accumulated experiences to size up a situation and select a course of action through recognition, and then assessing that course of action through mental simulation. Interaction with the environment "calls forth" the cognitive processes that cause one's experience to come to bear on a current situation. The RPD model is in contrast to classic models of decision making (see Hogarth, chap. 4, this volume, for further discussion of this contrast), which postulate that decision making requires deliberate analysis and comparison of a number of alternative courses of action prior to a decision being made.

The first process in the RPD model is recognition. It consists of four routines—cue recognition, generation of expectancies, identification of relevant goals, and recognition of typical actions. These routines integrate mental models that have been created through experience with features of the current situation. Each time a decision maker confronts a situation, he or she rapidly and unconsciously tailors the recognition activity. (For more information about automatic cognitive processes in decision making, see Johnson & Busemeyer, chap. 1, this volume.) Recognition is rarely a one-for-one pattern matching process. If this were true, expertise could be developed by learning a "playbook" for a definitive set of situations encountered in practice. Instead of using a pattern-matching process, the decision maker recognizes features or cues in a situation from a number of previous experiences. A cue is an aspect of the immediate situation—the color of smoke from a fire, the color of a patient's skin, the presence of an enemy scout vehicle. The decision maker knows from experience what other elements are typically found in a situation when a particular cue is present (i.e., a typical pattern for the type of situation being encountered). This sense of typicality is associated with typical goals (it is important to lower this patient's temperature), typical actions (this fire involves chemicals so we need help to handle hazardous materials), and typical sequences of activity (a larger unit is probably following that scout vehicle and will be here within the hour). The decision maker monitors those cues to ensure that the expected activities and interactions unfold (i.e., that the situation has been understood correctly). (For more discussion on how expertise is applied in dynamic environments, see Omodei, McLennan, & Wearing, chap. 15, this volume.)

Because recognition is rarely simple one-for-one pattern recognition, the expert must bring together features from different experiences to understand a novel or complex situation. The expert does this by creating a story. Storybuilding integrates a number of patterns to account for various features in the situation. The story paints a picture of how the situation got to its current state and elaborates on what else is about to unfold. If any aspects of the situation do not fit the story (i.e., expectations of how things will work in the situation are violated), then the expectations and features of the situation have to be examined and the story amended as needed.

Once the expert has assessed the situation to a satisfactory degree, he or she recognizes a typically successful action that needs to be taken. To ensure that the action is satisfactory, he or she uses the process of mental simulation to evaluate how well that action fits the current situation. Mental simulation is like a film playing out in one's mind—the course of action unfolds over time interacting with salient features of the situation. If undesirable consequences are encountered in the "film," the expert adjusts the "script" and replays the film. Once a satisfactory mental simulation of the course of action is achieved, a decision is made to implement it. The mental simulation need not be perfect, but it must be satisfactory in terms of risks and uncertainty. Experts almost always decide to go with the first satisfactory course of action they recognize—perhaps refining some elements of it during mental simulation (Klein, Wolf, Militello, & Zsambok, 1995). Figure 18.1 illustrates these two fused processes of recognition and mental simulation.

Without recognition of salient situational cues, expectancies, typical goals, and typically successful actions, the novice has no anchors to help him understand a situation and quickly generate a basic idea of what will work. The novice often spends too much time generating courses of action and compar-

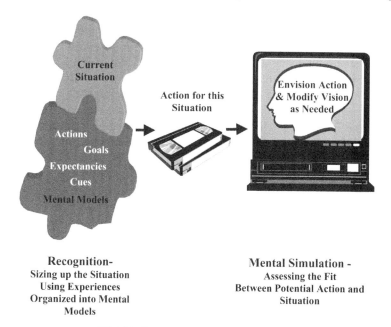

Recognition-
Sizing up the Situation
Using Experiences
Organized into Mental
Models

Mental Simulation -
Assessing the Fit
Between Potential Action and
Situation

FIG. 18.1. Two processes of the RPD model.

ing them against each other instead of mentally simulating and deepening on a basically satisfactory course of action vis-à-vis features of the situation. Good recognitional abilities leave time to study the situation deliberately, if needed, once an action has been decided on to fine tune execution.

HOW RECOGNITIONAL DECISION-MAKING SKILLS DEVELOP

Expert performance is based on extensive knowledge that is "indexed." Indexing consists of facts and causal relationships being linked in terms of:

- Cues—If I see this, it means this larger pattern probably exists in the situation.
- Expectancies—In that pattern, I've usually seen things unfold in this way.
- Goals—It's important in this type of situation to do this.
- Typical actions—I've see this goal achieved by doing the following.

The resulting patterns of cues, expectancies, goals, and typical actions are mental models. Mental models include both contextualized technical knowledge and cause-and-effect relationships, which vary from domain to domain. Developing an expert's knowledge base is not just a simple process of memorizing large amounts of decontextualized factual information, principles, knowledge schemata, or of being exposed to a variety of circumstances. Simply knowing a lot of information or rules about situations will not meet the two conditions for a novice to gain expertise. First, the novice must acquire information in a manner that makes it mentally accessible in the appropriate situations (i.e., the information must be indexed as it occurs in real situations). When information is appropriately indexed, a cue is recognized immediately, and it calls forth the associated information appropriate for conditions of similar situations. The same piece of information may or may not be a cue in situations with different conditions. Indexing of information during experiences allows the expert to quickly see through large amounts of information and spot cues in new experiences. Second, the novice must practice recognizing cues, expectancies, goals, and action and performing mental simulation in context. Knowing about patterns and using patterns are two different types of knowledge. Because the routines of expert decision making are not verbally encoded, one cannot "learn about" decision making to increase expertise. One must practice making decisions. Tailoring this practice is what creates expertise. (For more information on the development of expertise, see Shanteau, Friel, Thomas, & Raacke, chap. 14, this volume.)

Experts in any domain must, of course, learn large amounts of technical information, and a certain acquaintance with a field's knowledge is needed for the novice to enter into more advanced learning leading to expertise. However, factual knowledge that is not acquired through experience—real or surrogate—is often not accessible during later performance, and therefore may not contribute to expert performance. As soon as possible, technical knowledge must be integrated into realistic contexts. Learning of decontextualized facts leads to "inert knowledge"—in other words, "knowledge that can usually be recalled when people are explicitly asked to do so but is not used spontaneously in problem solving even though it is relevant" (Cognition and Technology Group, 1990, p. 2). When people learn new information in the context of meaningful activities, the knowledge is indexed and automatically accessed during performance as a tool to make a decision or solve a problem, rather than as an abstract set of facts.

Bransford, Sherwood, Hasselbring, Kinzer, and Williams (1990) described the alternative to memorizing and recalling facts and figures out of context as "conditionalizing" knowledge (i.e., acquiring knowledge "in the form of condition-action pairs mediated by appropriate goal-oriented hierarchies rather than as isolated facts"; p. 120). When a learner perceives new information as trite or old, as is often the case when information is given out of context, the knowledge will not necessarily be remembered and cannot be applied appropriately. We have seen this many times in the area of military expertise. In our work to engage practitioners in advanced learning, we often describe mental models associated with tactical decision making. Students assert that they already know this information as if the mental models are somewhat trite. However, knowing about the mental models and applying them to realistic problems are two different kinds of knowledge as we discover in training sessions. In general, the way in which knowledge is learned determines how knowledge will be used. Brown, Collins, and Duguid (1989) argued that inert knowledge is avoided only when learning is embedded in the social and physical contexts within which it is to be used.

The development of contextualized mental models allows experts to access a wide range of information quickly to see a situation in great depth. Novices use hastily formed, concrete, and superficial problem representations, whereas experts use deep structures to represent what they are seeing (Larkin, 1981). Experts form fast (but not hasty), deep, rich assessments of what they are seeing. This ability to use mental models to form rich assessments is not just a function of experience. A person can work in a domain for many years and have a variety of experiences and still not be an expert decision maker. (For further discussion of learning from experience, see Sedlmeier, chap. 5, this volume.) Whether the performer's knowledge base supports expert performance depends on how the performer has "exercised" the decision-making routines during previous experience.

Training interventions can bring the unconscious routines to a conscious level to expand and focus them. Some people are able to construct this kind of learning implicitly without training interventions through their own unstructured observation, reflection, and discussion with others. (For a discussion of implicit learning from experience, see Sedlmeier, chap. 5, this volume.) The development of expertise for them is not really a conscious process, but a natural result of reflecting on experience. Most people need specific coaching to learn to "see" what an expert is seeing in a situation. This type of training boosts development toward expertise. Without reflection and/or coaching, many people experience a variety of situations without "putting together the pieces" in a way that allows deep insight into cues, expectancies, and typical goals and actions. We have all heard of the proverbial person who claims to have 10 years of experience, but who actually seems to have experienced the first year 10 times over, never deepening in their understanding. Without practice that challenges assumptions and encourages reflection, the learner may continue to develop shallow interpretations, fixate on early solutions, and develop inaccurate or inadequate mental models.

In the next sections, we describe two different training programs developed to move the learner along the path toward expertise by helping them elaborate their mental models and making the results of the recognitional decision-making routines explicit so that they can be refined. Both training programs recognize the intuitive nature of expert decision making and the need to provide experiences to enhance the developmental process. The first training program is Decision Skills Training (Pliske, McCloskey, & Klein, 2001), which has been used in a variety of domains. Decision Skills Training uses cognitive task analysis to structure scenarios, and it supports the participant in accelerating his or her learning curve by providing surrogate decision-making experiences. The second training effort is the "Think Like A Commander" program, which is used specifically to train tactical thinking skills. This program was developed by the U.S. Army Research Institute for the Behavioral and Social Sciences and has been applied to training U.S. Army commanders at the brigade, battalion, and company levels (Lussier, Shadrick, & Prevou, 2003). The Think Like A Commander program structures deliberate practice of military thinking to train habits consistent with those of expert tacticians.

THE DECISION SKILLS TRAINING PROGRAM

Decision Skills Training is a program developed by Klein Associates and applied across many domains of practice. It is based on our understanding of how expertise develops and functions in dynamic settings. The training uses carefully constructed surrogate experiences so novices can:

- Explore and reveal the limits of their mental models, including factual information and cause-and-effect relationships
- Practice seeing and assessing cues and their associated patterns, generating expectancies, and identifying goals and typical actions
- Envision the situation-specific mental model they have developed in the training context as it is plays out
- Receive feedback on what they are not recognizing or accounting for in their mental model and course of action
- Compare their perceptions and decisions with others when the training is done in a small-group setting

The training is based on the premise that we cannot tell someone how to perform largely unconscious processes. There is no lecture component on how to make decisions or what strategies to employ. Instead we provide a carefully structured context in which students perform and reflect on their performance. We give the students a situation that is realistic enough that they can recognize cues in the context of specific boundary conditions of that situation and assess how possible decisions will unfold. We then provide them with structured discussion and reflection on their recognition and mental simulation processes.

The Decision Skills Training program consists first of methods to "unpack" the knowledge base of experts in a field so that the knowledge is available to training developers. Second, stories (vignettes) are carefully constructed to include realistic cues in context. Third, we use a variety of tools to help the students practice decision making and reflect on their surrogate experiences.

Step 1: Training Development—Unpacking Expertise

Much expert knowledge is tacitly held and involves recognitional routines so well learned and familiar that the expert may be unaware of drawing on that knowledge or going through the process of making an intuitive decision (Crandall, Zsambok, & Pliske, 1997). The automatic nature of expertise is a limitation to domain experts sharing their knowledge. Domain experts generally need help to describe how they do such things as recognizing patterns and anomalies, building stories to account for how situations have developed, recognizing leverage points for action, and mentally simulating solutions in the course of performance.

We use Decision Skills Training in a variety of domains. In each domain, we must come to an understanding of the way expertise works to construct training. We leverage stories told by experts to unpack that domain-specific expertise. Using cognitive task analysis methods, primarily the Critical Decision Method (Crandall & Getchell-Reiter, 1993; Hoffman, Crandall, & Shadbolt, 1998), we hone in on critical events from experts' experiences. We prompt an expert to recount critical events while we help the expert focus on key decisions that took place and deepen on the cognitive processes that occurred. Probing questions help the expert remember cues, expectancies, goals, and actions that he or she recognized and the mental model(s) that the expert built in the recounted situation. The interviews are conducted in a language that experts use, not in cognitive research technical terms. The experts are really just telling a story from their point of view. Inevitably, the experts report that they also learn a great deal as they recount their experiences to expert listeners. We capture the results of interviews into tables and other representations that separate out the cues, things a novice might not notice or do, and typical goals and actions. These form the basis for training development.

Step 2: Constructing the Vignette

Training development centers on authoring the context-rich training vignettes—low-fidelity simulations of incidents that might occur in real operational environments. The vignettes have low physical fidelity, but high cognitive authenticity. By cognitive authenticity, we mean that the vignettes contain all the types of information an expert would attend to in that situation to solve the problem posed, and that the problems presented are those with which experts have grappled. There is also information that is not relevant, as one would find in a real situation. We are able to adjust the difficulty of the vignette while maintaining cognitive authenticity by increasing the amount of uncertainty, adding more extraneous information to be sifted out by the student, using patterns that require a number of cues to be recognized and put together, increasing the number of interactions to account for by increasing the number of organizations or players in the scenario, adding complicating factors such as difficult terrain to traverse, providing limited resources in the vignette, or creating more than one task to be addressed at a time.

Incidents collected from experts are not used intact. Instead elements are emphasized and tailored to sharpen the focus on desired features, but elements are never added that we did not gather directly from expert interviews. Decision Skills Training vignettes have been implemented in both paper-and-pencil and electronic form, including a Web-based distributed format. A vignette presents a dilemma with some level of uncertainty and a requirement that forces the student to make a decision. Each participant has a limited amount of time to consider how he or she would react, which adds time pressure to the exercise. Facilitation ensures that the participants do not just have an experience, but that they focus on the cognitive aspects of that experience, consider the depth of their understanding, and view the likely consequences of their decisions. Facilitation exercises cause reflection on the cognitive processes without trying to teach the participants to be cognitive psychologists.

Step 3: Facilitating Decision Skills Development

Given the learning points we want to emphasize in a vignette, we select from existing facilitation techniques that we have developed. Learning points might include recognition of certain types of cues and the patterns they infer, emphasis on building a story of how the existing situation developed, highlighting one or more mental models associated with the domain, and using mental simulation to anticipate how a decision will look in implementation. The existing facilitation tools are integrated with findings from the cognitive task analysis to help us give feedback that illustrates what an expert might do in the specific vignette situation, how an expert views the situation, and places where a novice might have trouble in a situation.

The facilitation tools are based on strategies that experts use to learn more effectively and rapidly (Chi, Glaser, & Farr, 1988; Ericsson, 1996; Ericsson & Charness, 1994; Klein & Hoffman, 1993). The strategies include: (a) engaging in deliberate practice so that each opportunity for practice has a goal and evaluation criteria, (b) obtaining feedback that is accurate and diagnostic, (c) building mental models, (d) developing metacognitive skills, and (e) becoming more mindful of opportunities for learning. (For more information on the role of feedback in the development of expertise, see Harvey & Fischer, chap. 7, this volume.)

Some techniques are used before the vignette exercise to prepare for it, some during the exercise, and some after. Two of the facilitation techniques we use for improving individual decision making are the Decision Making Critique and the Uncertainty Management Exercise.

The Decision Making Critique is used after the vignette exercise and is intended to facilitate thinking about what went well and not so well during an exercise. It consists of a series of questions designed to identify the critical judgments and decisions made during the exercise. These questions explore important cues that might have been seen earlier, assessments that were mistaken, types of uncertainties encountered, and how uncertainty was handled. The Decision Making Critique starts with the facilitator helping students identify the difficult decisions they had to make during the vignette exercise. Each decision is discussed to bring the cognitive challenges to the forefront and examine ways they could have been dealt with. Discussion questions include, "Why was the decision difficult?" "Why did you choose that course of action?" "What one piece of information would have helped you the most?"

The Uncertainty Management Exercise introduces students to different aspects of uncertainty and tactics for managing it. It can be used in the middle of a vignette exercise to increase the power of recognitional strategies. Dynamic, real-world situations always include uncertainty, and this can stop the decision maker from reaching a satisfactory conclusion to the recognition processes. The goal is to help students learn how to get uncertainty down to an acceptable level so they can reach a satisfactory assessment and course of action, not to eliminate uncertainty because this is rarely possible. The facilitator gives students examples of the types of things that can cause uncertainty in the workplace, then asks the student to list up to five things they are uncertain about in the current situation.

The student then assigns each item listed to a "type of uncertainty" category, including such things as missing or incomplete information, distrust of the information, conflicting information, information that is too complex to interpret, and ambiguous information. Next the student lists what he or she is doing to deal with the uncertainty using a list of typical coping strategies, such as seeking information, waiting to see how the situation evolves, making assumptions to fill information gaps, or "shaking the tree." (Shaking the tree is the strategy of taking a bold action to actively shape the environment instead of waiting to see how it evolves.) The facilitator then leads a discussion to talk about what types of uncertainty are most commonly holding people up from assessing the situation or making a decision and what uncertainty management tactics the students should use more.

Decision Skills Training is relevant to individuals and teams in a variety of organizations and domains where practitioners are expected to rely on their own judgments in making decisions, but are not given the structure to strengthen their judgment skills.

THE "THINK LIKE A COMMANDER" (TLAC) TRAINING PROGRAM

The TLAC training program supports the development of tactical expertise in military environments. It is based on an understanding of how expertise is developed and embodies the concept of deliberate practice of thinking skills (Ross & Lussier, 1999). The RPD model provides a particularly apt description of the conditions under which expert battlefield leaders must perform. The thinking that underlies battlefield decisions does not occur in isolation or in a calm reflective environment; it occurs in a very challenging environment. Commanders must think while performing—assessing the situation, scanning for new information, dealing with individuals under stress, and monitoring progress of multiple activities of a complex plan. A plethora of events compete for their attention. In a complex activity like battle command, expert performance levels cannot be attained without relying on the automaticity resulting from past performance. *Automaticity* refers to the appropriate activation of cognitive activities in response to situations, without reference to procedures, without monitoring one's own cognition to see whether one is making the "right" response, and with effective and efficient "form." The training methodology is based on an understanding of the following stages of development:

- Experts typically develop a good conceptual understanding of the elements of their domain. Yet knowledge alone is not sufficient for expert-level performance.
- Repetitive performance causes thinking processes to become automatic so that they can be performed quickly and accurately with less mental effort.
- As more and more basic elements become automatic, more complex models can be manipulated without a proportionate increase in mental effort. This enables experts to use their knowledge flexibly and creatively in complex situations.
- The concomitant rise in automaticity and cognitive flexibility is characteristic of expert performance.

Advanced military leaders typically achieve the first stage (a deep conceptual understanding of the elements of tactical decision making) through years of study, reading, and consideration of tactical problems. However, progress through the successive stages is rare because opportunities for performance that is both realistic and valuable are limited. The TLAC program provides structured practice for military leaders to progress in their ability to apply tactical thinking routines rapidly and without conscious thought to compensate for stress and highly complex conditions.

The cornerstone of developing expertise is the use of deliberate practice. A main tenet of the deliberate practice framework is that expert performance is the result of extended periods of intense training and preparation (Charness, Krampe, & Mayr, 1996; Ericsson, Krampe, & Tesch-Römer, 1993). Repetitive performance causes behavior to become automatic. However, it is important that the behaviors which become ingrained conform to those of an expert—that they are the right behaviors. It is a well-known phenomenon that novices, through performance alone, will improve rapidly for a short time, but then may continue performing for decades without further improvement. Practice alone does not make perfect; it must be structured to ensure that performance—in this case, thinking—is done in a correct manner.

The TLAC model consists of a set of eight "themes" that have been determined to be common elements in the thinking framework of successful tactical thinkers (Deckert, Entin, Entin, MacMillan, & Serfaty, 1994). These are the habitual thinking patterns of the expert tactician that automatically surface when he or she is confronted with a tactical situation. It is not sufficient to simply memorize the eight common themes and learn the questions that commanders must ask. In fact, the eight themes are already very well known to officers who have achieved the first stage described earlier. Despite that familiarity, the themes—and their associated behaviors—are rarely exhibited during tactical field exercises. Thus, the problem is one of performance, not knowledge. It cannot be cured by gaining more knowledge, only by ingraining the habits of thought to such an extent that they are displayed under battlefield conditions, when attention must be directed to the issues at hand rather than to metacognitive concerns. The eight themes with brief descriptions are:

- *Keep a Focus on the Mission and Higher's Intent:* Commanders must never lose sight of the purpose and results they are directed to achieve—even when unusual and critical events may draw them in a different direction.
- *Model a Thinking Enemy:* Commanders must not forget that the adversaries are reasoning human beings intent on defeating them. It is tempting to simplify the battlefield by treating the enemy as static or simply reactive.
- *Consider Effects of Terrain:* Commanders must not lose sight of the operational effects of the terrain on which they must fight. Every combination of terrain and weather has a significant effect on what can and should be done to accomplish the mission.
- *Use All Assets Available:* Commanders must not lose sight of the synergistic effects of fighting their command as a combined arms team. They consider not only assets under their command, but also those that higher headquarters might bring to bear to assist them.
- *Consider Timing:* Commanders must not lose sight of the time they have available to get things done. Experts have a good sense of how much time it takes to accomplish various battlefield tasks. The proper use of that sense is a vital combat multiplier.
- *See the Big Picture:* Commanders must remain aware of what is happening around them, how it might affect their operations, and how they can affect others' operations. A narrow focus on your own fight can get you or your higher headquarters blind-sided.
- *Visualize the Battlefield:* Commanders must be able to visualize a fluid and dynamic battlefield with some accuracy and use the visualization to their advantage. A commander who develops this difficult skill can reason proactively like no other. "Seeing the battlefield" allows the commander to anticipate and adapt quickly to changing situations.

- *Consider Contingencies and Remain Flexible:* Commanders must never lose sight of the old maxim that "no plan survives the first shot." Flexible plans and well-thought-out contingencies result in rapid, effective responses under fire.

The central component of the TLAC program is the vignette based on tactical situations drawn from a single overarching scenario. A short—typically 2 to 4 minutes in duration—audiovideo file presents the tactical situation. Although each vignette has no officially sanctioned solution, each does have a set of unique "indicators" that represent important considerations of expert battlefield commanders. These are the elements of the situation—the key features—that should play a role in the decision maker's thinking. For each vignette, 10 to 16 such indicators were determined.

Once the presentation is completed, the student is asked to think about the situation presented and to list items that should be considered before making a decision. Over time, the instructor decreases the amount of time students are allowed, forcing them to adapt to increased time pressure.

After each student completes his or her list, the instructor leads a class discussion. Class members discuss the second- and third-order effects related to actions students suggest. Students are encouraged or required to discuss and/or defend considerations relevant to the vignette. Such coaching by a subject-matter expert is a key part of the learning process to enable the student to develop expert habits.

In the final phase of each vignette, the students see the list of considerations that experts believed were important, along with the list they initially made, and they mark the indicators they have in common with the experts. Students are also asked to make the same evaluation on the class as a whole. The purpose in this step is to allow the student to get a true representation of their individual performance. For example, a student may only get 50% of the important considerations for a given vignette. During the class discussion, however, 90% to 100% of the key considerations may be discussed. Students may inappropriately believe that their performance was directly linked to the performance of the class as a whole. Once the students rate their performance, they are given feedback linking it to the general themes (e.g., 25% for the "Model a Thinking Enemy" theme). This individual feedback supplements and complements the feedback given by the instructor during the class discussion phase of the training. The students are then able to focus their future thinking processes.

Recent research (Shadrick & Lussier, 2002) examined the effectiveness of Think Like A Commander training. The results reveal a significant effect $[F(1, 23) = 19.62, p < .05]$, indicating that participants identified significantly more critical information as they continued training. On average, the percent of the expert indicators identified by the students rose from about one third to about two thirds across seven vignettes despite that time for performance was decreased from 15 minutes to 3 minutes over those trials. It has not yet been determined whether the increase will transfer to more challenging battlefield environments, and, if so, what amounts of repetition are required to achieve the necessary level of automatization.

SUMMARY

The training programs described earlier are somewhat different in execution, but they both support the development of mental models, the acquisition of knowledge in context, and the practice of high-level cognitive activities with coaching. Both take the learner further along the path to "expert intuition," the unconscious or automatic application of mental models and mental simulation when the performer is confronted with new situations.

At the heart of both of these training programs is the carefully crafted story. What is to be learned and practiced has been made explicit and incorporated by the training developers. Stories represent our most powerful means to transfer expertise and allow the learner to activate that expertise in new situations. The story is a package for describing the important causes and effects to which we want to draw attention. It is through constructing and understanding stories that we make sense of the world.

Training automatic, high-level thought processes may seem difficult or impossible at first given that the mental models that experts use are not verbally encoded, that the models are unique to each expert, and experts develop the models and the way in which they use them through active engagement with the world over years of practice in their domain. Yet careful research into the natural decision-making processes of experts and the types of mental models they use in particular domains can reveal the source and common elements of experts' intuitive routines and make them available to successfully support the growth of intuitive expertise.

REFERENCES

Bransford, J. D., Sherwood, R. D., Hasselbring, T. S., Kinzer, C. K., & Williams, S. M. (1990). Anchored instruction: Why we need it and how technology can help. In D. Nix & R. Spiro (Eds.), *Cognition, education and multimedia* (pp. 115–141). Hillsdale, NJ: Lawrence Erlbaum Associates.

Brown, J. S., Collins, A., & Duguid, P. (1989). Situated cognition and the culture of learning. *Educational Researcher, 18*(1), 32–42.

Charness, N., Krampe, R., & Mayr, U. (1996). The role of practice and coaching in entrepreneurial skill domains: An international comparison of life-span chess skill acquisition. In K. A. Ericsson (Ed.), *The road to excellence: The acquisition of expert performance in the arts and sciences, sports and games* (pp. 51–80). Mahwah, NJ: Lawrence Erlbaum Associates.

Chi, M. T. H., Glaser, R., & Farr, M. J. (Eds.). (1988). *The nature of expertise*. Hillsdale, NJ: Lawrence Erlbaum Associates.

Cognition and Technology Group. (1990). Anchored instruction and its relationship to situated cognition. *Educational Researcher-Vanderbilt University (CTGV), 19*(6), 2–10.

Crandall, B., & Getchell-Reiter, K. (1993). Critical decision method: A technique for eliciting concrete assessment indicators from the "intuition" of NICU nurses. *Advances in Nursing Sciences, 16*(1), 42–51.

Crandall, B. W., Zsambok, C. E., & Pliske, R. (1997). *Sharing job-specific expertise via on-the-job training: A review of the literature and recommendations for future research* (Contract N61339-97-M-0888 for the Naval Air Warfare Center TSD). Fairborn, OH: Klein Associates Inc.

Deckert, J. C., Entin, E. B., Entin, E. E., MacMillan, J., & Serfaty, D. (1994). *Military decision-making expertise* (Final report). Fort Leavenworth, KS: Army Research Institute.

Ericsson, K. A. (1996). The acquisition of expert performance: An introduction to some of the issues. In K. A. Ericsson (Ed.), *The road to excellence: The acquisition of expert performance in the arts and sciences, sports, and games* (pp. 1–50). Mahwah, NJ: Lawrence Erlbaum Associates.

Ericsson, K. A., & Charness, N. (1994). Expert performance: Its structure and acquisition. *American Psychologist, 49*(8), 725–747.

Ericsson, K. A., Krampe, R., & Tesch-Römer, C. (1993). The role of deliberate practice in the acquisition of expert performance. *Psychological Review, 100*(3), 363–406.

Hoffman, R. R., Crandall, B. W., & Shadbolt, N. R. (1998). Use of the critical decision method to elicit expert knowledge: A case study in cognitive task analysis methodology. *Human Factors, 40*(2), 254–276.

Klein, G. (1998). *Sources of power: How people make decisions*. Cambridge, MA: MIT Press.

Klein, G., Wolf, S., Militello, L., & Zsambok, C. (1995). Characteristics of skilled option generation in chess. *Organizational Behavior and Human Decision Processes, 62*(1), 63–69.

Klein, G. A. (1989). Recognition-primed decisions. In W. B. Rouse (Ed.), *Advances in man-machine systems research* (Vol. 5, pp. 47–92). Greenwich, CT: JAI Press.

Klein, G. A., & Hoffman, R. (1993). Seeing the invisible: Perceptual/cognitive aspects of expertise. In M. Rabinowitz (Ed.), *Cognitive science foundations of instruction* (pp. 203–226). Hillsdale, NJ: Lawrence Erlbaum Associates.

Larkin, J. L. (1981). Enriching formal knowledge: A model for learning to solve textbook physics problems. In J. R. Anderson (Ed.), *Cognitive skills and their acquisition* (pp. 311–334). Hillsdale, NJ: Lawrence Erlbaum Associates.

Lussier, J. W., Shadrick, S. B., & Prevou, M. I. (2003). *Think like a commander prototype: Instructor's guide to adaptive thinking* (ARI Research Product 2003-01). Alexandria, VA: U.S. Army Research Institute for the Behavioral and Social Sciences.

Pliske, R. M., McCloskey, M. J., & Klein, G. (2001). Decision skills training: Facilitating learning from experience. In E. Salas & G. Klein (Eds.), *Linking expertise and naturalistic decision making* (pp. 37–53). Mahwah, NJ: Lawrence Erlbaum Associates.

Ross, K. G., & Lussier, J. W. (1999, December). *A training solution for adaptive battlefield performance*. Paper presented at the Interservice/Industry Training, Simulation, and Education Conference, Orlando, FL.

Shadrick, S. B., & Lussier, J. W. (2002). *Think like a commander at the armor captain's career course*. Proceedings from Interservice/Industry Training, Simulation, and Education Conference. Retrieved from the World Wide Web: http://www.iitsec.org.

19

Knowledge, Argument, and Meta-Cognition in Routine Decision Making

David W. Glasspool
John Fox
Cancer Research UK

What type of processes are involved in making everyday decisions? How is our knowledge brought to bear on the decisions we must make? How are we able to reflect on and manipulate our own decision processes? In this chapter, we take a view of routine decision making that is informed by our work in medical decision support, within which these are important questions. We view routine decisions as those that are taken frequently, employing forms of evidence or argument that are "normal" for those who make the decisions. Routine decisions depend on shared knowledge that is uncontroversial and may well be explicitly documented.

Until relatively recently, the most influential theories of reasoning and decision making were developed by mathematicians and logicians, often informed by problems in some practical domain such as medicine or economics. Their work led to theoretical concepts with great intellectual depth and formal rigor, such as statistical decision theory (SDT), but that have little to say about the prior questions.

Dennis Lindley (1985) summarized the basic tenets of SDT as follows:

> ... there is essentially only one way to reach a decision sensibly. First, the uncertainties present in the situation must be quantified in terms of values called probabilities. Second, the consequences of the courses of action must be similarly described in terms of utilities. Third, that decision must be taken which is expected, on the basis of the calculated probabilities, to give the greatest utility. The force of "must" used in three places there is simply that

any deviation from the precepts is liable to lead the decision maker in procedures which are demonstrably absurd. (p. vii)

The mathematical arguments for this claim are well known and need not be
repeated here (Lindley provides an excellent source). However, despite the
force of Lindley's assertion, there are difficulties with expected-utility and
other mathematical techniques for decision making. First, there are difficulties with actually determining probabilities and utilities in many real-world
situations. Second, there is growing evidence that people do not naturally
make decisions as outlined earlier, although people are nonetheless surprisingly good at making decisions in difficult situations, under time pressure, or with incomplete information. Third, the SDT approach ignores
some of the most important aspects of decision making—knowing when to
make a decision, how to frame it, and how good a decision it is. In the next
section, we expand on these issues, examining the contribution of cognitive
science to the study of judgment and decision making. From this discussion, we develop four desiderata for understanding (routine) decision making, which we set out at the end of the section.

We then present a cognitive framework that attempts to address our desiderata through two novel features. First, it explicitly includes a set of important processes surrounding the decision process, including issues such
as framing the problem, selecting appropriate alternatives for a decision,
acting on the decision, and taking account of any resulting feedback. Second, it emphasizes the role of knowledge in decision making. The framework addresses the issue of bringing different (possibly conflicting) bodies
of knowledge to bear on a decision by defining a representational scheme
for knowledge based on logical argumentation. Finally, we show how this
framework can be applied to practical decisions in a health care setting,
and we finish by discussing how well the framework meets our desiderata.

COGNITIVE PROCESSES IN REASONING
AND DECISION MAKING

Despite the apparent clarity and lack of ambiguity of mathematical approaches to thinking about problems like judgment and decision making,
the whole field of reasoning under uncertainty has been dogged by philosophical as well as technical disputes for many years. For example, Kyburg
(1990) observed that "Many proponents of many [different] views have argued that their interpretation of probability is the correct (or the most useful, or the only useful) interpretation." In recent years, a new group—the
cognitive scientists—has entered the debate about rational judgment. Among
their important contributions was the demonstration that normative frame-

works for decision making have surprisingly little to say about how people actually make decisions or reason under uncertainty. A massive body of empirical work, and theoretical ideas ranging from Herbert Simon's (1982) concept of bounded rationality to Kahneman and Tversky's program of research into the "heuristics and biases" that underpin human reasoning under uncertainty (Kahneman, Slovic, & Tversky, 1982) attest to the now generally accepted conclusion that human reasoning and decision making are based on rather different principles from those that have preoccupied mathematicians and logicians. We see four specific challenges from this perspective to traditional mathematical decision procedures:

1. *The assessment of decision options in the absence of quantitative probabilities and utilities.*

Few researchers now believe that normative probability and decision theory are the best basis for understanding human decision making, and many doubt that they even represent gold standards against which human cognitive processes should be assessed. The program of Gigerenzer and his colleagues (Gigerenzer & Todd, 1999) indeed sought to extend the Heuristics and Biases perspective by suggesting that human judgment is not a degenerate form of mathematical thinking, but has its own rationality. It now seems likely that biological, environmental, and other demands on mammalian cognitive function created a far wider range of needs and constraints than those addressed by the abstract norms of expected-utility and other mathematical theories. Animals must operate in a world in which information and knowledge are limited, time is of the essence, and environments are unpredictable and even capricious.

Traditional mathematical decision procedures, by contrast, depend on the ability to estimate the required parameters—typically probabilities and utilities—associated with the application domain. This is often problematic in real-world applications. In clinical settings, for example, even highly routine ones, these data are not easily obtained. The cost of obtaining good probability estimates frequently outweighs the perceived benefits, and there are deep philosophical and technical difficulties in trying to capture human values and preferences as quantitative utilities.

2. *The nature and role of "knowledge" within decision processes.*

The challenge from the cognitive sciences to the whole mathematical paradigm of uncertain reasoning and decision making goes even deeper than this, however. It questions the adequacy of quantitative formalisms to represent the kinds of knowledge and forms of reasoning that are routinely employed in decision making. A mathematical characterization of any process necessarily involves creating an abstraction of that process, removing extraneous detail to facilitate formal analysis and development. Thus, traditional decision-making theories abstract away from all forms of knowledge other than statistical relationships in their pursuit of more precise and quantitative methods. However, if abstraction goes too far, there is a danger of oversimplifying the problem, "decontextualizing" the process we are trying to understand. Therefore, it is not surprising that, in medicine, although some routine decision making may rely on subjective probabilities, clinicians also appear to solve problems by reasoning, rather than calculation, using more domain-specific knowledge.

For example, one might predict the probability that a particular set of symptoms will occur as a result of a particular disease by either (a) collecting information about disease–symptom correspondence in a large number of patients, or (b) working out the likely effects of the disease using a knowledge of the biological processes and systems involved. To diagnose a patient, a clinician might use this second type of knowledge to make deductions from a knowledge of disease processes and their effects on the appearance and morphology of abnormal features. However, once knowledge is abstracted to the level of statistical correspondences, all information about the processes underlying the data is lost, and there is no way to incorporate it into decision making. Reasoning, however, can generalize to new areas where no statistical information is available. For a concrete example of this distinction, Tonnelier et al. (1997) discussed a decision support system that constructs arguments using domain knowledge of this type in an area where it is not possible to determine statistical probabilities—the possible carcinogenicity of new chemical compounds.

3. *A description of the "complete" decision cycle, from the framing of a decision to the final choice.*
Human decision makers have other strengths that are not acknowledged within the classical decision theory perspective. For example, Shanteau (1987) observed that expert decision makers know what is relevant to specific decisions and what to give priority to in a busy environment. By contrast, classical decision theory focuses on only a small part of the decision process: making the choice. Lindley (1985) followed his prescription for rational decision making (quoted earlier) with this advice:

> The first task in any decision problem is to draw up a list of the possible actions that are available. Considerable attention should be paid to the compilation of this list [though] we can provide no scientific advice as to how this should be done. (p. vii)

His unwillingness to give "scientific advice" on how to determine the possible decision options highlights the problem: This is an important part of the business of making a decision—there is arguably no point in even attempting to take a decision at all until this step has been carried out. In medicine, for example, the determination of these things is at the heart of clinical work. Even in routine medicine, practitioners need to be able to structure their decisions: They need to decide what hypotheses to consider and which sources of evidence are relevant.

4. *The basis of meta-cognitive skills.*
Finally, as Shanteau (1987) pointed out, human decision makers can also make decisions about their own decision processes: which decisions to make and when, and when to make exceptions to general rules. For example, medical decision makers need to be able to decide the type of decision that is required: "Should I attempt a diagnosis? Or just make a risk assessment? Is it sufficiently urgent that I should go straight for a treatment? Or should I refer the patient to a colleague who is more experienced?" These questions go beyond even Lindley's step of listing decision candidates. They point to meta-cognitive processes of reasoning about the decision process, determining goals and framing decisions that are not touched on by SDT approaches.

The development of an alternative framework, which is formally sound but avoids the shortcomings of standard quantitative decision procedures, is the major theme of this chapter. In the next section, we introduce a general framework for understanding cognition that has emerged from consideration of the issues outlined earlier within the field of medical cognition. In the discussion, we review the extent to which the model meets the prior challenges.

A GENERAL MODEL OF COGNITION AND DECISION

Figure 19.1 is a model of a general cognitive agent that has emerged from a variety of lines of research on medical reasoning, decision-making, planning and other tasks (Fox & Das, 2000). We refer to it as the *domino* agent because of its shape. The left-hand side of the domino deals primarily with decision making, whereas the right deals primarily with the organization and enactment of plans.

The nodes of the domino can be viewed as state variables, whereas the arrows are inference functions. Inference mechanisms derive data of the type at the head of the arrow based on data of the type at the tail together with general and domain-independent knowledge. The outer labels on the nodes (in italic) show the kinds of information involved in particular classes of decision in the medical domain, whereas the inner labels (in bold) refer to equivalent, but more general, concepts that are independent of any specific domain of decision making.

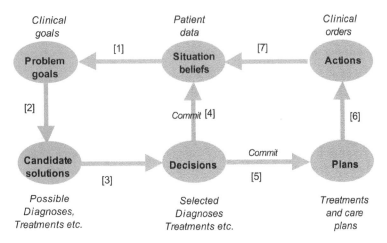

FIG. 19.1. The domino model of decision making in cognition.

The domino model was developed as a parsimonious description of the processes involved in a wide range of medical decisions and medical care plans. There are two areas where our account of decision making differs strongly from traditional normative accounts like expected-utility theory. First, the domino is intended to provide a framework for understanding and formalizing the context within which decision making is carried out. The account is thus widened to cover areas traditionally excluded from mathematical approaches, including the motivation for a decision (the agent's goal) and its framing (identifying the candidate solutions for solving the problem or achieving the goal). Second, the reasoning that is at the heart of decision making in this model is not some form of expected utility calculation, but a versatile form of logic reasoning called *argumentation*. Argumentation is the pivot around which our account of decision making turns. We introduce the concept in more detail in the next section.

The domino incorporates a number of steps that are required for general cognition, including decision making. To illustrate this, consider a clinical situation in which we are presented with a patient who has inexplicably lost a great deal of weight. This could indicate a possible disease, so the first step is to establish a clinical goal to diagnose the cause of the weight loss (the inference process required to establish the goal is represented by arrow [1]). According to the model, the goal gives rise to a set of inferences about the possible explanations of the weight loss (arrow [2]). Taken together, these two steps represent the "framing" of the diagnosis decision. Once the frame of diagnostic alternatives has been created, we need to formulate a set of arguments for and against the competing explanations (arrow [3]). The argumentation process may take into account various types of knowledge, including known causes of weight loss, statistical associations between this symptom and alternative diagnoses, and so on. The final step in this decision process is to assess the arguments to arrive at a specific diagnosis decision (arrow [4]) such as cancer.

Whatever the chosen diagnosis, it becomes a new piece of data or a belief. Any belief can give rise to a new goal, and in this example, it is to choose the best treatment of the condition. Once again several treatment options may be identified (arrow [2]), such as chemotherapy, surgery, and radiotherapy, and there are varied arguments for and against these options (arrow [3]). Arguments may take into account a variety of knowledge about the treatments, including their expected efficacy, undesirable side effects, interactions with other treatments, and possibly safety.

Once the arguments for each alternative have been formulated, we need to assess their overall "force" to arrive at the choice of an appropriate therapy plan (arrow [5]). The plan that implements a medical treatment decision typically consists of a number of component actions. The domino model extends to cover the implementation phase, in which actions of the plan are scheduled to meet various constraints on time, data, and other resources (arrow [6]). Some actions can lead to new information about the agent's environment, such as new beliefs about the patient's state, response to treatment, and so on (arrow [7]). This may result in additional goals being raised (e.g., to manage unexpected side effects or failures to achieve original goals). These initiate further cycles of decision making and planning.

The Role of Knowledge in Decision Making

Regardless of what procedure an agent uses to make decisions, it is clear that it must be able to apply its knowledge to those decisions. In general, an agent may have many different sources of knowledge that apply to a particular decision, and these may provide uncertain or conflicting support for different options. As well as establishing the possible options open to it in making a decision (arrow [2] in Fig. 19.1), an effective decision maker must marshal the arguments for and against each option on the basis of its knowledge and combine these (possibly inconsistent) arguments to arrive at a considered decision (arrows [3], [4], and [5]). The logical argumentation approach we adopt in the domino framework formalizes the use of knowledge in decision making.

Informally, arguments are reasons to believe in possible states of the world (e.g., reasons to believe a patient has a disease) and reasons to act in particular ways to bring about or prevent anticipated states of affairs (e.g., reasons to select one particular medical treatment rather than another). From a formal point of view, arguments can be seen as lines of reasoning that support or oppose claims. The idea has much in common with Keynes'

(1921) notion of logical probability. The distinction between informal argument and formal reasoning was first recognized by the philosopher Toulmin (1957).

We adopt the neutral term *agent* to refer to any entity that has goals it wishes to achieve and a body of knowledge it can apply to achieve these goals; the agent might be a person, an artificial intelligence, or some abstract theoretical entity. The agent's knowledge base may include general knowledge about the world (dealing with time, space, properties of physical objects, etc.) and may include formal or technical knowledge like medical knowledge (e.g., knowledge of anatomy, biochemistry, physiology, immunology, epidemiology, etc.). The knowledge base is partitioned into a number of different segments that reflect these ontological distinctions; we call these *theories*. Theories can be thought of as collections of assertions. Some assert general facts about the world (e.g., "all cancers are diseases"), whereas others represent assertions about a specific situation (e.g., "this patient may be suffering from breast cancer"). Others represent rules like "if there is an abnormality we should establish the cause."

Suppose that an agent of this kind acquires some information about a particular situation, such as a patient complaining of unexplained weight loss. In such circumstances, the agent adopts the goal of finding the most likely explanation of this abnormal situation. According to the domino model, the first step is to identify candidate explanations, such as the loss of weight is caused by a gastric ulcer or cancer. Formally we refer to these alternative explanations as *claims*. The agent applies its knowledge to construct arguments for and against the competing claims.

To give an example of the way in which different theories may lead to conflicting arguments, the agent could argue for the hypothesis of gastric ulcer (a claim) on the grounds that the patient has pain after meals, using a causal theory that gastric acids irritate pain receptors in the lining of the stomach that are exposed by the ulceration process. On the other hand it may argue using a statistical theory that a peptic ulcer is unlikely on the grounds that the patient is only 20, and a peptic ulcer in a patient under 50 is very rare. In fact we can develop any number of arguments for and against the alternative claims, drawing on different theories. Generally, each theory will have one or more lines of backing that justify its use. For example, the backing for a theory might be the body of scientific literature supporting its use.

To make a decision between competing claims, we have to assess the arguments for and against each claim, combining them into a case for each claim and then deciding which case is the strongest. For example, we might use a simple but effective method famously described by Ben Franklin, in which the more positive arguments for a claim the greater our confidence in it, the more negative ones the greater our doubt. Such linear models with uniform weights have proved to be highly effective in a range of applications (Fox & Das, 2000). It is also possible to attach different weights to arguments. For example, Emery et al. (2000) described a decision support system using arguments with only "low" or "high" strength. Many simple arithmetical functions can be used to aggregate the weighted arguments into some overall measure of confidence. We can take this further by attaching real numbers to the arguments, and it is possible to capture the "strength of argument" as a conventional probability or expected value (Fox & Parsons, 1998). This is important because it shows that argumentation may encompass expected-utility theory as a special case. However, an attraction of the argumentation approach is that it can accommodate a wide range of other decision procedures that may be more appropriate when probabilities and utilities cannot be determined.

The aggregation process brings together collections of arguments to define a preference order over the set of competing claims. The complete decision cycle requires one last step—to commit to one or other of the competing claims, adopt a plan of action, or accept a hypothesis about the present situation (arrows [4] and [5]).

APPLYING THE DOMINO MODEL: SUPPORTING ROUTINE MEDICAL DECISIONS

The domino model and its argumentation representation of knowledge can be used in several ways:

- It can be used as the basis of a model to understand the cognitive processes a decision maker must go through to frame, apply knowledge to, and take a decision.
- It can be used as the basis of a model of executive functions in human cognitive psychology (Glasspool, 2000; Glasspool & Cooper, 2002; Shallice, 2002).
- It can be used as the basis of a computational system for automatic decision framing and decision making (Black, 2003).
- It can be used as the basis for computerized decision-support systems, which guide the user through framing a decision, collecting the relevant data, applying appropriate domain knowledge, taking the decision, and acting on the results.

Much of our work has involved the last of these approaches, so we conclude with an example illustrating the use of the domino/argumentation model as a framework for decision support.

The UK Department of Health (DoH) requires that patients who show any signs of early cancer should be seen and assessed by a cancer specialist within 2 weeks of their family doctor deciding they need to be investigated. The DoH has developed and published criteria to assist doctors in deciding whether a particular patient needs to be referred under the 2-week standard (Department of Health, 1999). These criteria can be straightforwardly expressed as arguments using the approach outlined earlier. A formal example of one such argument for making the decision to refer the patient urgently is shown next. This example is taken from the breast cancer section of the guidelines:

Claim: Patient should be referred to a breast specialist.

Grounds: (The situation in which this argument is valid) Abscess or breast inflammation that does not settle after one course of antibiotics.

Qualifier: (Whether the argument supports or opposes the claim, and by how much) This argument "supports" the claim.

Theory: Specialist medical knowledge and general knowledge about time and urgency.

Backing: Authorized by UK Department of Health.

The Early Referrals Application (ERA) project (Bury, Humber, & Fox, 2001) implements these guidelines as arguments within a domino framework using the PROforma language (Fox et al., 1997). PROforma breaks such guidelines down into tasks that correspond to sections of the domino model. The ERA project has been deployed in two evaluation trials by the UK National Health Service. Figure 19.2 shows the process required to apply the breast cancer guideline represented in PROforma.

The shapes in Fig. 19.2 represent tasks of different types, and the arrows linking them specify their ordering (the task at the tail of an arrow must be completed before the task at the head of the arrow can begin). The diamond shape is an enquiry—this task gathers data and corresponds to process [7] on the domino framework of Fig. 19.1. The circle represents a decision and corresponds to processes [1] through [5] in Fig. 19.1, and the squares represent actions corresponding to process [6]. The PROforma language treats the domino framework as an execution engine (Black, 2003). For the guideline we are considering, this operates as follows.

The first task in Fig. 19.2 that can be executed is the enquiry (corresponding to domino process [7] in Fig. 19.1). This can be viewed as bringing data into the "beliefs" node of the domino. The data that are required correspond to the grounds of the various arguments, which are used in making the referral decision. In PROforma, these must be specified in advance (however, in general, the domino model allows for a more dynamic approach; e.g., inquir-

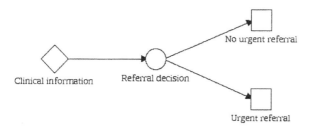

FIG. 19.2. The breast cancer early referral guideline implemented in PRO-forma, a language that abstracts sections of the domino framework and can be represented graphically. See text for details.

ing about data only as particular arguments are brought into play). In this example, a set of arguments like the one earlier are present, so this step results in a new set of beliefs about the symptoms of the patient.

Next, the decision task can be executed. This corresponds to processes [1] to [5] of Fig. 19.1. Process [1] involves raising a new goal—in this example, a goal to decide on urgent or nonurgent referral is raised as soon as sufficient data have been gathered on which to base the decision. Process [2] involves determining the candidates (a set of alternative claims). The PROforma language allows these to be predefined for each decision. In this simple case, the candidate claims "urgent referral" and "nonurgent referral" are specified in advance.

A number of argument schemas for each claim are defined within the decision task, corresponding to the DoH guideline. These are instantiated with actual data values from the Beliefs node, and any arguments that are invalid (i.e., for which grounds do not exist) are rejected (process [3]). Now a decision can be made between the candidate claims. According to the DoH guidelines, the claim "urgent referral" is accepted if any argument is valid (i.e., if its grounds are met). The claim "nonurgent referral" is accepted otherwise. This results in updated beliefs (process [4]).

Finally, Fig. 19.2 shows two actions. Which of these is able to proceed depends on the outcome of the decision (process [5]). In this simple example, single actions are specified rather than extended plans, and the execution of one of these corresponds to process [6]. In the ERA application, the execution of one of these actions results in a recommendation (to refer or not) being presented to the user along with the arguments for and against that course of action.

The domino framework can thus be seen as providing the context within which data are gathered, a decision is framed and taken, and the decision is acted on. The argumentation knowledge representation fits into this framework to inform appropriate framing and data gathering as well as informing the decision.

DISCUSSION

We share with others (e.g., Gigerenzer & Todd, 1999) the view that human decision making is optimized to meet a wider range of requirements and performance constraints than are considered in classical accounts of rational decision making and, further, question the idea that existing prescriptive models offer a gold standard against which human decision making may be judged. In fact we argue that such theories are rather weak because they do not provide a complete account of decision making. We set out earlier four general issues that exemplify this weakness and that we see as important desiderata for an alternative account. The domino framework and the argumentation knowledge representation are our concrete proposal for such an account. We now consider how well it fares in addressing our desiderata.

1. *The assessment of decision options in the absence of quantitative probabilities and utilities.*
The argumentation approach allows a generalized account of decision making that can encompass traditional approaches (such as Bayesian probability and expected utility) as a special case. However, such approaches can be seen as one end of a spectrum, where probability and utility information is available and applicable. At the other end of the spectrum, one has to deal with cases where these measures are inappropriate or estimates are impractical to obtain. The argumentation approach allows a range of less quantitative decision procedures to be used in such cases, from using simpler (e.g., integer) weights on arguments right down to simply comparing the number of arguments for and against the decision regardless of type. We have shown in a number of experimental studies that argumentation is a robust mechanism for establishing preferences and making decisions even in the absence of quantitative data (Fox & Das, 2000).

This is not to imply that decision making at the more qualitative end of this spectrum is necessarily impoverished. On the contrary, we believe that sophisticated reasoning is often used to generate arguments using other types of knowledge than statistical. For example, knowledge of chemical and biological processes are used by Tonnelier et al. (1997) to reason causally about the likely carcinogenicity of newly synthesized compounds, for which no statistical information exists.

2. *The nature and role of "knowledge" within decision processes.*
Human decision makers are able to bring large bodies of knowledge, in the form of diverse theories about the world, to bear in making decisions. Argumentation provides an account of the way in which different bodies of knowledge can generate different and possibly conflicting arguments, and

of how decisions can be made even when very different types of evidence must be reconciled. However, the process by which arguments are aggregated to arrive at a consistent preference ordering over competing claims is critical to this account.

To date only a few procedures for aggregating arguments have been investigated (Fox & Das, 2000). We have found that surprisingly simple approaches, such as counting arguments for and against a claim, can often allow practical decisions to be made when no more principled method for combining arguments is available. However, more work is required to fully understand the different ways in which heterogeneous sets of arguments can be combined and the circumstances under which they lead to appropriate decisions.

3. *A description of the "complete" decision cycle, from the framing of a decision to the final choice.*
The domino model encompasses processes of goal selection, candidate listing, preference ordering of candidates, decision commitment, and plan execution, and it provides a framework for understanding how they interact. This set of processes was arrived at based on psychological experiments and experience developing a number of clinical decision support systems (Fox & Das, 2000).

An interesting line of support for this set of processes comes from neuropsychological theory. Norman and Shallice (1986) proposed a dual system for the control of thought and action based on psychological findings. One system, Contention Scheduling (CS), is responsible for the control of routine behavior. This can be modulated by a second system, Supervisory Attention (SAS), when deliberate control of behavior is exercised. Shallice and Burgess (1996) proposed a decomposition of SAS based on neuropsychological findings. Glasspool (2000), Glasspool and Cooper (2002), and Shallice (2002) showed that this decomposition maps cleanly to the domino framework, and they used this mapping to develop an outline computational model of SAS. This mapping suggests a concrete neurological basis for the existence of the types of processes we proposed in the domino model and their general interrelationship.

However, although setting out this general relationship is an important first step, as yet we have an incomplete understanding of the internal operation of these processes. Two important examples are the processes ([1] and [2] in Fig. 19.1), which determine appropriate goals given a particular set of beliefs and list appropriate candidate solutions. For limited domains, it is straightforward to implement such processes, but general solutions are more difficult to specify. Some preliminary work has been carried out within the domino framework by Glasspool and Cooper (2002), and Shallice and Burgess (1996) considered these issues in more detail. A number of theoretical accounts exists in the AI and neuropsychological literature, and we consider reconciling these with the domino approach to be the most important area for further work.

4. *The basis of meta-cognitive skills.*
We believe that an account of meta-cognitive functions in decision making is an important theoretical and practical challenge for decision theorists. Experts frequently "know a lot about what they know" and often have good communication skills and the ability to articulate their decisions and how they arrived at them. They can adapt to changing task conditions and are able to find novel solutions to problems. How can an agent "explain" the reasons for its beliefs or actions? How can it reflect on its assumptions and knowledge and decide whether a decision is no longer needed? We rely on such capabilities every time we seek the advice of a physician, and training in the cognitive and social skills required to satisfy these demands is a normal part of modern medical education.

The processes specified by the domino framework ([1] to [7] in Fig. 19.1) need not be explicit. For example, process [1], determining the goal of a decision, may be served by a tacit recognition process (Ross, Lussier, & Klein, chap. 18, this volume), and process [2], determining the set of candidate options between which to decide, may involve tacit processes of recognition (Ross et al., chap. 18, this volume; Shallice & Burgess, 1996) or learned rules (Johnson & Busemeyer, chap. 1, this volume), rather than explicit analytic problem solving (Shallice & Burgess, 1996). In fact we expect that multiple alternative processes are often available to implement any of the domino arrows. Shallice and Burgess (1996) argued that both tacit and explicit procedures are available for process [2], for example.

However, to the extent that reasoning or communication about the decision process is to be successful, the end products of these processes—the goals and options generated—must be explicitly available (as beliefs) as input for further reasoning and decision-making cycles. The domino assumes that all beliefs are explicitly represented. This is not surprising given its origins in decision support systems, where an important goal is to be explicit about the decision process. In developing the domino as a cognitive model, we expect it will be necessary to also allow tacit beliefs (which affect behavior, but which are not available for reasoning).

Explaining the reasons for decisions is particularly important for an artificial decision maker. An attraction of the argumentation approach is the natural way in which it allows decisions to be explained by reference to the argument structures constructed to make them. We have found this approach to be valuable in implementing decision-support software, which is able to explain the rationale for a recommended decision by giving the valid arguments for and against it and the alternatives. Emery et al. (2000) demonstrated that this approach was appreciated by physicians, who found the explanations easy to understand and reassuring.

The domino framework along with the argumentation approach to knowledge representation allow flexible, robust, and easy to understand artificial decision-making or decision-support systems to be built. Our goal is to improve the performance of computer systems on each of these criteria. In our view, an appreciation of the full range of processes involved in framing and making a decision, and the way in which knowledge is brought to bear by these processes, is vital to both understanding human decision making and building computer systems that genuinely aid decision making.

ACKNOWLEDGMENTS

This work was supported in part by award L328253015 from the UK Economic and Social Research Council and Engineering and Physical Sciences Research Council.

REFERENCES

Black, E. (2003, April). Using agent technology to model complex medical organisations. *Agent-Link News, 12.*

Bury, J., Humber, M., & Fox, J. (2001). Integrating decision support with electronic referrals. In R. Rogers, R. Haux, & V. Patel (Eds.), *Medinfo. 2001.* Amsterdam: IOS Press.

Department of Health. (1999). *Referral guidelines for suspected cancer.* London: UK Department of Health.

Emery, J., Walton, R., Murphy, M., Austoker, J., Yudkin, P., Chapman, C., Coulson, A., Glasspool, D., & Fox, J. (2000). Computer support for interpreting family histories of breast and ovarian cancer in primary care: Comparative study with simulated cases. *British Medical Journal, 321,* 28–32.

Fox, J., & Das, S. (2000). *Safe and sound: Artificial intelligence in hazardous applications.* Cambridge, MA: MIT Press.

Fox, J., Johns, N., Lyons, C., Rahmanzadeh, A., Thomson, R., & Wilson, P. (1997). PROforma: A general technology for clinical decision support systems. *Computer Methods and Programs in Biomedicine, 54,* 59–67.

Fox, J., & Parsons, S. (1998). Arguing about beliefs and actions. In A. Hunter & S. Parsons (Eds.), *Applications of uncertainty formalisms* (Lecture Notes in Artificial Intelligence). New York: Springer.

Gigerenzer, G., & Todd, P. M. (1999). *Simple heuristics that make us smart.* Oxford: Oxford University Press.

Glasspool, D. W. (2000). *The integration and control of behaviour: Insights from neuroscience and AI.* Technical Report 360, Advanced Computation Lab, Cancer Research UK.

Glasspool, D. W., & Cooper, R. (2002). Executive processes. In R. Cooper (Ed.), *Modelling high level cognitive processes* (pp. 313–362). Mahwah, NJ: Lawrence Erlbaum Associates.

Kahneman, D., Slovic, P., & Tversky, A. (Eds.). (1982). *Heuristics and biases.* Cambridge: Cambridge University Press.

Keynes, J. M. (1921). *Treatise on probability.* London: Macmillan.

Kyburg, H. (1990). *Science and reason.* Oxford: Oxford University Press.

Lindley, D. V. (1985). *Making decisions* (2nd ed.). Chichester, England: Wiley.

Norman, D. A., & Shallice, T. (1986). Attention to action: Willed and automatic control of behaviour. In R. J. Davidson, G. E. Schwartz, & D. Shapiro (Eds.), *Consciousness and self-regulation* (Vol. 4, pp. 1–18). New York: Plenum.

Shallice, T. (2002). Fractionation of the supervisory system. In D. T. Stuss & R. T. Knight (Eds.), *Principles of frontal lobe function* (pp. 261–277). Oxford University Press.

Shallice, T., & Burgess, P. (1996). The domain of supervisory processes and temporal organization of behaviour. *Philosophical Transactions of the Royal Society of London B, 351,* 1405–1412.

Shanteau, J. (1987). Psychological characteristics of expert decision makers. In J. Mumpower (Ed.), *Expert judgement and expert systems* (Vol. F35). NATO ASI Series.

Simon, H. (1982). *Models of bounded rationality.* Cambridge, MA: MIT Press.

Tonnelier, C. A. G., Fox, J., Judson, P., Krause, P., Pappas, N., & Patel, M. (1997). Representation of chemical structures in knowledge-based systems. *Journal of Chemical Information and Computer Sciences, 37,* 117–123.

Toulmin, S. (1957). *The uses of argument.* Cambridge: Cambridge University Press.

20

Current Research on Routine Decision Making: Advances and Prospects

Tilmann Betsch
Susanne Haberstroh
University of Erfurt

In this final chapter, we summarize the 19 chapters in the present volume. Our discussion is arranged in seven parts. First, we attempt to provide the overall picture by sketching out a new perspective on decision making that shines through all of the chapters. Second, we discuss theoretical advances. Third, we summarize essential findings that extend the list of routine effects we discussed in the introduction. Fourth, we consider methodological advances in decision research in the field and in the lab. Fifth, we focus on applied research and give some examples of how expert decision makers can be trained to improve their decision routines. After discussing emerging themes in decision research, we close with outlining possible directions for future research.

A NEW LOOK AT DECISION MAKING

The breadth of a scientific perspective is jointly bound by meta-theoretical conceptions and research methodology. Immersed in the spirit of rationalism and using the gambling paradigm as a silver-bullet method of research, cognitive psychologists have been studying humans from a rather narrow perspective over the past decades. In gambling studies, individuals are presented with a small set of alternatives and well-defined outcomes in terms of stated values and probabilities (e.g., $100 guaranteed or a 1/10 chance of winning $1,000). This paradigm allows the researcher to investigate selectional processes involving evaluation, information integration, and application of a choice rule. Such a restricted approach, however, ignores pre- and postselectional processes such as goal setting, behavior generation, search for information, and implementation of the chosen behavior.

Decision research has witnessed several departures from this narrow perspective. With the advent of multiple-strategy models (e.g., Beach & Mitchell, 1978) and process-tracing methodology (e.g., Payne, Bettman, & Johnson, 1993), information search was seen as a genuine part of a decision. In recent years, researchers from different areas of psychology also began to consider the very early stage of a decision, involving recognition of the situation and identification of goals and behavioral alternatives (e.g., Aarts & Dijksterhuis, 2000; Goldstein & Gigerenzer, 2002; Klein, 1989). Additionally, in attitude research, scholars investigated the relation between intentions and behavior implementation (e.g., Fishbein & Ajzen, 1974; Gollwitzer, 1999; Verplanken & Aarts, 1999).

Taken together, the first deviations away from the "narrow view" resulted in a process orientation. Accordingly, decision making consists of at least three phases (see Fig. 20.1). The preselectional phase involves the identification of the problem, behavior generation, and information search. The selectional phase involves appraisal or evaluation processes, information integration, and application of a choice rule. The postselectional phase is directed by volitional processes heading for the implementation of the chosen behavior (for a discussion of phase models, see Betsch, Haberstroh,

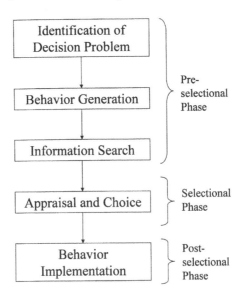

FIG. 20.1. A process perspective that overcomes the narrow look of early utility theory.

& Höhle, 2002). Unfortunately, however, the various departures from the narrow view did not merge into an integrative conception shared by the different subdisciplines of decision research.

The contributors to this book represent different or even rival camps of decision research (e.g., Naturalistic Decision Making: Ross, Lussier, & Klein; Judgment and Decision Making: Hogarth, Johnson, & Busemeyer; Social Psychology: Bagozzi & Dholakia; Consumer Psychology: Kardes, Muthukrishnan, & Pashkevich). Nevertheless, the similarities within their conceptions of decision making are striking. In virtually all of the chapters, an integrative perspective becomes apparent. This new look is not characterized by the exclusion of processes. Accordingly, decisions are no longer viewed as singular or isolated events in time, but as being embedded into the stream of the individual's experience. Hence, decisions have a past and a future. Past experiences are stored in memory and have an impact on all phases of the decision process (preselectional, selectional, postselectional). Further, future events inform the individual about the consequences of a chosen behavior. These experiences, in turn, influence subsequent decisions.

Such an approach is obliged to acknowledge the importance of two faculties that are intimately tied to each other: feedback learning and memory. Both have been largely ignored by the vast majority of decision researchers in psychology and were not systematically included by previous extensions of the narrow approach. Subsequently, feedback learning and memory are the central themes in this book. Throughout the chapters, we find ample evidence indicating the need to consider these processes to understand how individuals make decisions. The "new look" is depicted in Fig. 20.2.

THEORETICAL ADVANCES

Transfer of Theories

The role of learning in choice has been addressed by many theories outside the field of decision making. The narrow scope of utility theory and the dominance of the gambling paradigm led the majority of decision researchers to ignore theoretical progress in neighbor fields. A straightforward method to advance decision theory is to increase transfer of knowledge between fields. A couple of contributors to the present volume discuss how this could be achieved.

Sedlmeier (chap. 5, this volume) shows how principles of associative learning can be applied to judgment and decision making. With reference to the PASS model, a computational model of associative frequency learning and judgment, he outlines how knowledge is acquired and represented in memory. He argues that associative learning of frequencies (e.g., rates of

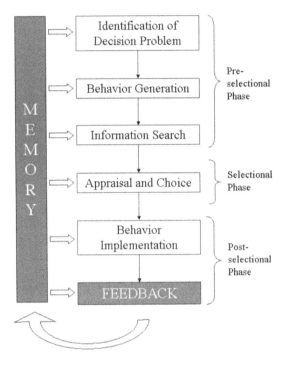

FIG. 20.2. An integrative perspective: Decision making involves feedback learning and memory processes.

success and failure) provides the basis for behavioral intuitions that guide routine decision making.

Another aspect of learning and memory is considered by Sanbonmatsu and colleagues (chap. 6, this volume). Assume you evaluate a behavior for the first time. You might arrive at a summary evaluation expressing how much you like or dislike the behavior. Once such a summary evaluation or attitude has been formed, it can be stored in memory and used in later judgments and decisions. Sanbonmatsu and colleagues discuss the multiple roles of attitudes in information search, appraisal, and choice. In line with attitude-behavior models, they argue that the extent to which attitudes co-determine decision making depends on the strength of association between a stored attitude and a behavior. This contribution again underlines the importance of associative learning processes in preference formation and decision making.

In a similar vein, Harvey and Fischer (chap. 7, this volume) elaborate on a mental model approach to account for feedback effects in probabilistic judgment and decision making. Plessner (chap. 17, this volume) gives another example of theoretical transfer. He borrows from the general information-processing framework from social cognition to explain the influence of categories, schemas, and expectations on experts' decisions.

General Frameworks

How can prior experience and behavioral knowledge be integrated into general frameworks of decision making? Several contributions in this volume address this topic. Bagozzi and Dholakia (chap. 2, this volume) introduce a broad framework of goal setting and goal striving. It captures decision making (goal setting), choice implementation (goal striving), and feedback learning. Within this framework, the stream of action is conceptualized as a dynamic self-regulation of imperatives or goals. The behavioral alternative represents a goal that serves higher order goals. Decision making involves the motivational processes of assessing the desirability and feasibility of behavior. Behavioral implementation involves volitional processes such as control, enactment, and modification of the chosen behavior ("When, where, how, and how long should I act?"). Feedback learning is triggered by the affective reactions, which arise vis-à-vis the goal-relevant outcomes of the behavior ("How do I feel about achieving/not achieving my goals?"). In turn, the feedback affects future goal setting and attainment. This framework allows for a process-oriented assessment of the role of prior experience in decision making. Bagozzi and Dholakia discuss a number of mechanisms by which prior experiences influence memory, evaluation, and motivation in goal setting and striving. As such their approach extends paramorphic models of routine decision making (e.g., Bentler & Speckart, 1979), which treat prior behavior merely as a predictor variable without considering psychological processes.

A second integrative framework is provided by Hogarth (chap. 4, this volume). He distinguishes two systems of thought: the tacit and the deliberate. The deliberate system involves explicit and analytic reasoning. The tacit system operates automatically. It produces intuitive responses that are reached "with little apparent effort and typically without conscious awareness." Hogarth integrates both systems in a process model of decision making. It comprises tacit and deliberative processes of perception, memory, behavior generation, and feedback learning. Routine decision making is assumed to capitalize on the tacit system. Building on this framework, Hogarth delineates assumptions about the relative validity of analytic and intuitive judgments and decisions. His dual-process model overcomes the emphasis of deliberative processes in decision theory. According to his view, decision making always involves an interaction of the two processes of analysis and intuition.

Glasspool and Fox (chap. 19, this volume) put forward a third comprehensive framework of decision making. Their domino model also mirrors the new broad perspective unifying the contributions to this volume. The authors place a special emphasis on the processes "surrounding the decision process." They address issues such as framing of the problem, generation of alternatives, role of knowledge, meta-cognition, and, last but not least, feedback processing. Their conception of decision making radically differs from traditional utility theory. They assume that explicit decision making is not a form of expected-utility calculation, but rather a form of argumentation. Arguments are reasons to believe in possible states of the world. Evidently, reasons rest on knowledge such as stored experiences, theories, or any other sort of world knowledge. In their chapter, Glasspool and Fox use the domino model as a basis for aiding expert decision making.

Theories of Routine Decision Making

Theories allow the researcher to make predictions about the world. The book contains two novel theories of routine decision making—rule-based decision field theory (RDFT; Johnson & Busemeyer, chap. 1, this volume) and preference theory (Betsch, chap. 3, this volume). Both theories embrace learning processes and account for automatic and deliberative forms of decision making. Additionally, both theories assume that a single mechanism of choice underlies all forms of decision making. However, aside from these two similarities, the two models make a number of distinct assumptions.

RDFT belongs to the broad class of criterion-dependent choice models. It advances decision field theory put forward earlier by Busemeyer and Townsend (1993). Information search involves sequential sampling of information in memory and the environment. Each piece of input information can be used to update the preference for a behavioral alternative. If the preference exceeds a threshold, the behavior is chosen and processing of information is terminated. A number of factors contribute to setting the threshold, such as time, importance of the task, or personality variables. Two classes of information can be considered for updating of an alternative's preference—attribute values or advice from learned rules. Including the latter possibility allows the theory to capture a variety of phenomena. A learned rule might represent a policy or script, a formal choice rule, or even the advice from an expert or decision support system. Moreover, RDFT assumes that rules are evaluated taking feedback information into account. In summary, the authors sketch out a formal model of decision making and feedback learning. They apply their theory to a number of routine effects documented in the literature. For example, RDFT accounts for recognition-primed routine choice and the influence of routine strength on information search and appraisal.

Preference theory (Betsch, chap. 3, this volume) merges assumptions from the literature on learning, memory, behavior regulation, and decision making. It assumes that choice is primarily a function of the affective reactions evoked by the behaviors under consideration. A behavior is chosen if its overall affective reactions exceed a particular threshold (in such, this theory also belongs to the class of criterion-dependent choice models). Affect toward a behavior mirrors the person's experiences of goal promotion (or obstruction) and new evidence.

Both autonomous and deliberative processes direct decision making. Preference theory uses a connectionist metaphor to describe these processes. The autonomous system involves parallel processing of information (goals, behaviors, affective responses, etc.) in a hypothetical working network. By changing activation, the system seeks to find a behavioral solution that sufficiently dominates competitors with regard to its overall affect. Autonomous processes do not change the structure of the network (links between constituents), which primarily reflects prior learning. Therefore, autonomous processing leads to conservatism in choice. Structural changes require deliberative processes. Under deliberative control, new information can be added to the network, and relations between elements can be changed in accordance with new evidence or contextual changes. Thus, deliberation can produce base-rate neglect and exaggeration of new evidence. The relative influence of autonomous and deliberative processing is determined by personal and contextual factors. Preference theory accounts for biases in information search and attenuation effects in appraisal of evidence, and it predicts conditions under which individuals are likely to maintain or abandon their routine.

ESSENTIAL FINDINGS IN BASIC AND APPLIED RESEARCH

In the introduction, we briefly reviewed empirical evidence illustrating the multiple influences of routines on decision making. The list of findings is extended by contemporary research reported in the present volume. The subsequent sections summarize the advances achieved in basic and applied research.

Feedback Learning, Memory, and Routine Decisions

Decision makers learn from enactment of their choices. A chosen behavior can produce changes in the external environment and the organism, which represent feedback to the decision maker. The impact of feedback on subsequent decisions depends on the learning environment, the processing system, and the characteristics of the feedback sample. The structure of the learning environment is of essential importance for learning (Harvey & Fischer, chap. 7, this volume). Robin Hogarth (chap. 4, this volume) introduced the illuminative distinction between "kind" and "wicked" learning environments. In a wicked environment, feedback is unreliable, invalid, highly complex, or ambiguous. Each of these factors inhibits adaptive feedback learning (Harvey & Fischer, chap. 7, this volume; Kardes et al., chap. 8, this volume) and decreases the quality of subsequent intuitions in decision making (Hogarth, chap. 4, this volume).

Whether feedback helps or hurts in improving decision quality also depends on how the individual processes feedback information. The role of motivation has been repeatedly addressed throughout the book. Empirical evidence, however, is mixed. Clearly, motivation does not generally improve feedback learning (Harvey & Fischer, chap. 7, this volume); even high motivation can have detrimental effects on decision making (Kardes et al., chap. 8, this volume; Wänke & Friese, chap. 16, this volume). For example, if a routine is learned under high motivation (careful elaboration of feedback), individuals are subsequently more reluctant to abandon the routine even if it has become inadequate (Wänke & Friese, chap. 16, this volume). Moreover, processing of feedback information in routinized decision making is often biased by prior knowledge. For instance, consumers tend to misinterpret neutral evidence as confirmation of their behavioral expectations, thus revealing a pseudodiagnosticity effect (Kardes et al., chap. 8, this volume). Routine decision makers are also susceptible to ignore disconfirming evidence if the context resembles routine learning conditions (Haberstroh et al., chap. 12, this volume).

Storage and retrieval of routines from memory are influenced by characteristics of the feedback sample. Not surprisingly, chronic accessibility and the tendency to choose a routine increase with enactment and reinforcement frequency (Bagozzi & Dholakia, chap. 2, this volume; Betsch, chap. 3, this volume). As such the predictive value of past experience is contingent on its frequency (Verplanken, Myrbakk, & Rudi, chap. 13, this volume).

There is also evidence for a sample size effect. If the relative success rate of a routine is experimentally held constant, the impact of routines on subsequent decisions increases with a higher total frequency of feedback experiences (Haberstroh et al., chap. 12, this volume). There are mixed results concerning the relation between sample size and confidence. Increase in sample size can increase confidence in judgments and decisions (Sedlmeier, chap. 5, this volume). However, there is also evidence that increases in (reliable) feedback samples can decrease overconfidence (Harvey & Fischer, chap. 7, this volume).

Routines and the Generation of Behavioral Alternatives

As stated in the introduction, automatic processes, such as recognition of the situation, play a key role in routine activation and choice. There is increasing support for the notion that the generation of behaviors is a goal-directed process regardless of whether one considers automatic or deliberative decisions (Bagozzi & Dholakia, chap. 2, this volume; Omodei, McLennan, & Wearing, chap. 15, this volume; Verplanken et al., chap. 13, this volume). Accordingly, behavior generation is not solely guided by external cues. Goals, motives, and needs seem to function as a search device or filter mechanism for behavior activation. Another point addressed in this book concerns the number of alternatives generated at the beginning of a decision process. Ross, Lussier, and Klein (chap. 18, this volume) obtained evidence that experts generate fewer and better behavioral options than novices. Hence, routine decision makers are able to reduce the complexity of decisions by focusing on a subset of promising alternatives. Again this observation indicates that generation of alternatives is a selective and criterion-dependent process, which involves implicit assessment of the behaviors' applicability. In other words, behavior generation seems to involve some sort of decision making, yet we still know little about the underlying mechanisms.

Routines and the Search for Information

Previous research has indicated that routine decision makers tend to take less information into consideration than novices (e.g., Verplanken, Aarts, & van Knippenberg, 1997) and reveal a tendency to confirm biases in familiar contexts (Betsch, Haberstroh, Glöckner, Haar, & Fiedler, 2001). Recent evidence compiled in this volume provides a more complex picture. Routine decision makers seem to be more efficient in muddling through the problem space compared with novices. Similar to behavior generation, experts tend to primarily focus only on the relevant pieces of information (Plessner, chap. 17, this volume; Wänke & Friese, chap. 16, this volume). Especially when confronted with high-stake decisions, experts devote a large amount of cognitive capacity to assess relevant information (Omodei et al., chap. 15, this volume). Note that focusing on relevant information allows routine decision makers to increase efficiency; they need less time and fewer cognitive resources to process information than novices. Therefore, the finding that routine decision makers consider less information should not be misinterpreted as a decrease in accuracy.

Nevertheless, routines may still yield systematic biases in information search. Routines may serve as expectations that shift the individual's attention away from evidence supporting alternative courses of action (Kardes et al., chap. 8, this volume). This tendency might become attenuated when individuals are in a good mood because it has been shown that good mood fosters reliance on learned concepts (Bless & Igou, chap. 11, this volume). Moreover, routine decision makers might be prone to focus on desirability and neglect feasibility information because they already know that the routine is viable (Bagozzi & Dholakia, chap. 2, this volume).

Routines and the Appraisal of Evidence

In the introduction, we reviewed findings indicating that new information often looms less than prior knowledge in routine decision making. We concluded that the processes underlying these attenuation effects are not yet well understood. A few contributors to this volume pinpoint possible causes for the attenuation of new evidence. Routine decision makers might employ strategies based on prior attitudes (Sanbonmatsu et al., chap. 6, this volume), expectations (Plessner, chap. 17, this volume), or schematic behavioral knowledge, such as scripts and behavioral rules (Bless & Igou, chap. 11, this volume). Appraisal of new information might be biased in the direction of prior knowledge. Accordingly, information consistent with prior knowledge is augmented relative to inconsistent information.

Similarly, Jungermann and Fischer (chap. 9, this volume) found that prior information (advice given by an expert) changes the relative importance of information later encountered by clients. If prior information is based on a huge sample of experiences and strongly embedded in long-term memory, decision makers might ignore new evidence even if has been encoded. Thus, routine deciders might employ attitude-based strategies for evaluation more frequently than attribute-based strategies (Sanbonmatsu et al., chap. 6, this volume; Wänke & Friese, chap. 16, this volume). Yet research on the dynamics of appraisal processes in routine decision making is still developing. In other areas of psychology, researchers have devoted much more effort to understand the interplay of prior knowledge and new information. Social cognition, for example, has accumulated a huge number of theories and data on this issue, especially in the areas of stereotyping and person perception research (e.g., Nisbett & Ross, 1980; Srull & Wyer, 1989). Certainly, future research in decision making would benefit from recognizing the advances achieved in these neighboring fields.

Routines and the Implementation of Behavior

The problem of behavior implementation resonates in all chapters that report choice measures (e.g., Haberstroh et al., chap. 12, this volume; Kardes et al., chap. 8, this volume; Omodei et al., chap. 15, this volume; Reimer,

Bornstein, & Opwis, chap. 10, this volume; Sanbonmatsu et al., chap. 6, this volume; Shanteau, Friel, Thomas, & Raacke, chap. 14, this volume; Verplanken et al., chap. 13, this volume). Choice implementation is intertwined with all of the processes discussed so far. Accordingly, factors influencing memory, information search, and appraisal also impact on choice. There are some interesting findings, however, that mainly apply to the behavioral level. Reimer and colleagues (chap. 10, this volume) review their research on group decision making. They induced problem-solving routines in their participants. They found strong evidence for maladaptive transfer effects of these routines when groups of participants were to figure out new strategies for similar problems. Groups seem to amplify routine maintenance effects indicating a genuine process-loss effect. These studies pave the way for an emerging field in routine decision research—the role of routines in group decision making.

Haberstroh and colleagues (chap. 12, this volume) report evidence suggesting that flexibility in choice may increase under good mood. The finding that happy participants were more likely than sad participants to abandon inadequate routines merges with other research addressing the impact of mood on information processing (Bless & Igou, chap. 11, this volume). The role of motivation, in contrast, is less clear. To be sure motivation in general does not encourage individuals to deviate from their routines (Wänke & Friese, chap. 16, this volume). The multiple influences that different sources of motivation have on behavior implementation are still not well understood.

ADVANCES IN RESEARCH METHODOLOGY

The research reported in this book utilizes a remarkable variety of different methods including laboratory experiments (e.g., Jungermann & Fischer, chap. 9, this volume; Reimer et al., chap. 10, this volume), field experiments (e.g., Plessner, chap. 17, this volume), and observations in natural contexts (e.g., Omodei et al., chap. 15, this volume). Sophisticated computer tools are used to evaluate theories in mathematical simulations (Johnson & Busemeyer, chap. 1, this volume; Sedlmeier, chap. 5, this volume) and dynamic microworld-simulation (Haberstroh et al., chap. 12, this volume; Shanteau, Friel, Thomas, & Raacke, chap. 14, this volume). Computer tools are also used to educate routine decision makers (Glasspool & Fox, chap. 19, this volume; Ross et al., chap. 18, this volume). Researchers attempt to access the mental processes underlying decision making by recording sequences of information acquisition (Haberstroh et al., chap. 12, this volume; Shanteau et al., chap. 14, this volume) by means of verbal protocol analysis (Haberstroh et al., chap. 12, this volume) or by assessing self-reports and recall data (Omodei et al., chap. 15, this volume; Verplanken et al., chap. 13, this volume).

Routine strength (prior repetition of a choice) is commonly measured and still rarely manipulated under strictly controlled conditions (but see the contributions by Haberstroh et al., Reimer et al., and Shanteau et al.). We should highlight two advances in the measurement of routines. Verplanken and colleagues (chap. 13, this volume) outline two techniques to measure the strength of automatized routines (habits)—the response frequency measure (RF) and the Self-Reported Habit Index (SRHI). Both measures incorporate aspects of automaticity, such as the ease of behavior generation (RF) or lack of awareness and control (SRHI). Shanteau and colleagues (chap. 14, this volume) introduce a content-independent measure of expertise—the Cochran-Weiss-Shanteau (CWS) index. This index does not require external or domain-specific standards of performance, but instead solely relies on an assessment of consistency and discrimination of the individuals' responses to changing decision situations.

Granted the plethora of methods documented in this volume, it struck us to observe that virtually none of the reported studies employed the gambling paradigm. Barron and Erev (2003) recently showed that the gambling paradigm could be easily advanced and employed to study decision making based on feedback. One can simply have participants play the same lottery several times, give them feedback after each game, and observe their subsequent choices. The majority of authors, however, prefer more complex settings involving multiple goals, information search, changing payoffs, or changing context conditions. Moreover, they also consider types of problems that are more representative of decision making in applied domains, such as medicine (Glasspool & Fox, chap. 19, this volume; Jungermann & Fischer, chap. 9, this volume), consumer behavior (Kardes et al., chap. 8, this volume; Wänke & Friese, chap. 16, this volume), aviation (Shanteau et al., chap. 14, this volume), sports (Plessner, chap. 17, this volume), military (Ross et al., chap. 18, this volume), and fire fighting (Omodei et al., chap. 15, this volume).

Notably, the departure from the gambling paradigm is not accompanied by a decrease of experimental rigor. For instance, computer-controlled microworld-simulations create complex and dynamic decision environments and, at the time, allow the researcher to impose a high degree of experimental control over the independent variables (see Betsch et al., 2001, for a discussion). We can only speculate as to whether the multimethod approach in this volume indicates an emerging trend in general decision research. Within the new holistic conception of decision making we described earlier, however, such a development is indispensable and can only be applauded.

EDUCATING ROUTINE DECISION MAKING

Two chapters in this book give examples of how routine decision makers can be trained to improve the quality of their decisions.[1] Glasspool and Fox (chap. 19, this volume) sketch out a computerized approach to aiding medical decision making that is based on their domino model. According to the model, decision making can be described in terms of logical argumentation. The computerized support system is built along the lines of the argumentation process outlined in the model. It structures the problem and helps the decision maker to navigate through the problem space, consisting of grounds, qualifiers, and theoretical backups for decisions. Basically the support system helps experts update their beliefs to arrive at informed decisions by taking a multitude of relevant information into account.

Ross and colleagues (chap. 18, this volume) present two training programs for battlefield decision making developed in front of Klein's recognition primed decision (RPD) model (Klein, 1999). The RPD model assumes that decision making involves two essential processes: recognition (evaluating the situation based on mental models) and mental simulation (assessing the fit between a potential action and the situation). These processes are automatized and difficult to access via introspection. Ross and colleagues describe techniques that help decision makers elaborate their mental models and make the results of decision-making routines (recognition, simulation) explicit so that these processes can be refined. As such the authors train automatic processes in experts by elaborating the backup knowledge explicitly.

Although the trainings outlined in the two chapters capitalize on different theories and involve different techniques, they have some important points in common. Both approaches dwell on the same broad meta-perspective described in the beginning. Learning and memory processes are seen as essential parts of real-world decision making. In accordance with this conviction, all trainings aim to improve the individuals' knowledge, either via aiding the process of updating beliefs (Glasspool & Fox, chap. 19, this volume) or developing mental models (Ross et al., chap. 18, this volume). Moreover, both approaches use explicit procedures to control learning. Finally, the decision-support systems described by the authors are closely tied to theory. Glasspool and Fox use the domino model, and Ross and colleagues use the RPD model to derive their technologies. These contributions underline Kurt Lewin's dictum that there is nothing more practical than a good theory.

---

[1]For a comprehensive overview on the recent advances in this area, consult Salas and Klein (2001).

EMERGING THEMES

Overcoming Delimitation in Decision Research

We started this summary with an outline of an integrative perspective shared by virtually all of the contributors to this volume (see Fig. 20.2). Accordingly, feedback learning and memory processes are seen as integral parts of human decision making, which continues even after a choice is made and implemented. The organism is sensitive to the consequences of the decision. Feedback experiences, inferences drawn from them, policies, scripts, and rules are stored in memory. Adult decision makers possess a huge arsenal of decision-relevant knowledge. Consequently, memory processes help them routinize identification of a decision problem, generation of behavioral alternatives, search for relevant information, appraisal of information, and, finally, selection and implementation of a behavior. This broad perspective has considerable implications for research and theory formation.

In the introductory chapter, we described the unfortunate separation between different research camps in the field, which concentrated on either routine or deliberative decisions. We are pleased to note that the contributions to this book are not plagued by this problem. Obviously, a focus on either type of decision making would not make much sense within a broad meta-theoretical framework emphasizing processes of learning and memory. An essential part of these processes are directed and performed by the automatic system, such as associative learning, recognition of routine decision problems, and affect-based choice. However, deliberative or controlled processes can also influence routines of choice, learning, and memory. For instance, humans can use formalized procedures to assess new or routine behaviors. They may deliberatively interpret feedback information or use explicit strategies to control prospective memory when they eventually wish to eliminate a bad habit. Therefore, it is necessary to consider both types of processes. This conviction is shining through the vast majority of the contributions to this volume.

Emphasizing the Role of Intuition and Affect in Decision Making

Utility theory pinpoints two fundamental determinants of decision making: value and probability. Regardless of whether one agrees with the particular axioms of utility theory, one can hardly deny that these variables are of crucial importance. An organism insensitive to the success or failure rate of behaviors is not capable of differentiating good from bad choices and, hence, will fail to satisfy its needs and goals in the long run. The lesson to be learned from the literature on conditioning is that animals and humans are remarkably sensitive to both the value and relative frequency (probability) of the outcomes of their choices.

Classical decision research has been focusing on deliberative assessment of values and probabilities. Deliberation, however, represents just one possible route through which values and probabilities might impact decisions. Several contributors to this volume suggest another pathway: intuition. The new emerging notion of intuition seems to differ from previous ones, such as the concept of intuitive judgment in the "heuristics and biases" literature (Kahneman, Slovic, & Tversky, 1982). According to this view, intuitive decisions are made by using shortcut strategies, or heuristics. These strategies often circumvent the direct assessment of quantity and quality by using other types of information such as availability or representativeness as predictors of the target to be judged.

In contrast, the alternative concept of intuition holds that the memory system can process and communicate essential information without conscious control within the organism. Especially in recurrent decision making, affect provides a powerful means to communicate prior experiences. Affective reactions are quick and immediate and do not require deliberative inferences (Zajonc, 1968). Affect provides a direct trajectory to past experience because the disposition to affective reactions can reflect the rates of prior success and failure. This notion mimics the memory and learning perspective discussed at the outset. Several scholars from the field of decision research have begun to consider the role of affect in intuitive decision making (e.g., Slovic, Finucane, Peters, & MacGregor, 2003). The contributions to this book indicate that it is worthwhile to further pursue this line of research. To borrow Herbert Simon's terminology, intuition and affect provide important mechanisms of bounded rationality, and thus can be conceived as the key determinants of routine decisions.

FUTURE RESEARCH DIRECTIONS

Studies investigating routine effects in decision making will continue to be important additions to the literature. We still know little about the psychological mechanisms underlying the generation of behavioral alternatives, search and appraisal of new information, and choice implementation in routine decision makers. There are only a few studies that systematically consider the role of personal and contextual factors in routine maintenance and deviation. Thus, the question of "under which conditions do individuals quit with their routines" will potentially be a significant one to be addressed by future research. This issue has important implications, especially for application. Improving decision performance requires the decision maker to adapt to changing contexts. Maladaptive routines have to be replaced by better ones. Professional decision makers who solidify their routine repertoire will fail to benefit from feedback in the future and, in turn, will fail to improve their level of expertise in the future.

Another issue concerns testing theories. The emerging field of routine decision research has devoted comparatively little effort to theory testing so far. Not surprisingly, any emerging field will be initially busy with the identification of nontrivial phenomena or "effects" that justify its existence. Moreover, theories of routine decision making were scarce in the beginning. Since then a few theories have become available that allow us to make testable predictions (Betsch et al., 2002, for an overview). Theoretical progress requires, as a prerequisite, to pinpoint competing predictions on the conceptual level and test them against each other under strictly controlled (laboratory) conditions. Otherwise the field would soon suffer from an accumulation of theories and models that peacefully coexist with each other.

The aim of theoretical integration is incompatible with leniency on the theoretical level. Accepting coexistence of theories (which share the same subject) implies acceptance of separation between fields. An example of such division is the current relation between the naturalistic decision making (NDM) approach and classical decision research. Despite some visible productions of rapprochement (e.g., inviting an out-group speaker to a conference; cf. Yates, 2001), both communities still mostly ignore, neglect, or attenuate the theoretical advances of the other. As a consequence, each field is busy nursing its own theories and apparently discredits competitive theory testing (or may even deny it as a possibility).

The final point is related to the former. The interplay between prior knowledge and new information (the key issue in routine decision making) has been addressed in different areas outside the field of judgment and decision making (e.g., in learning theory, behavioral economics, or social cognition). Many achievements, both on the theoretical and empirical levels, have been made in these fields, but remain almost unnoticed by decision researchers. Naturally, we are aware of the routines of research. As a matter of habit, scholars primarily read those contributions that appear in the journals of their own field. Such habits are hard to break especially because they are reinforced by publication policies (it is unlikely to get an article published that ignores the literature from the home field, but one is rarely punished for ignoring results from other fields). Nevertheless, integrative theoretical work in decision making would strongly benefit from exchange. It is our firm conviction that understanding the routines of decision making necessitates integrative theories. This requires theorists to be conceptually open and receive the advances made in neighboring fields. The broad meta-conception of decision making (Fig. 20.2) behind the contributions to this book provides a useful framework for integration. We are confident that such a framework can serve as a starting point for further integrative endeavors in the field of decision research.

REFERENCES

Aarts, H., & Dijksterhuis, A. (2000). Habits as knowledge structures: Automaticity in goal-directed behavior. *Journal of Personality and Social Psychology, 78,* 53–63.

Barron, G., & Erev, I. (2003). Small feedback-based decisions and their limited correspondence to description-based decisions. *Journal of Behavioral Decision Making, 16,* 215–233.

Beach, L. R., & Mitchell, T. R. (1978). A contingency model for the selection of decision strategies. *Academy Management Review, 3,* 439–449.

Bentler, P. M., & Speckart, G. (1979). Models of attitude-behavior relations. *Psychological Review, 86,* 452–464.

Betsch, T., Haberstroh, S., Glöckner, A., Haar, T., & Fiedler, K. (2001). The effects of routine strength on adaptation and information search in recurrent decision making. *Organizational Behavior and Human Decision Processes, 84,* 23–53.

Betsch, T., Haberstroh, S., & Höhle, C. (2002). Explaining routinized decision making—a review of theories and models. *Theory and Psychology, 12,* 453–488.

Busemeyer, J. R., & Townsend, J. T. (1993). Decision field theory: A dynamic-cognitive approach to decision making in an uncertain environment. *Psychological Review, 100,* 432–459.

Fishbein, M., & Ajzen, I. (1974). Attitudes towards objects as predictors of single and multiple behavioral criteria. *Psychological Review, 81,* 59–74.

Goldstein, D. G., & Gigerenzer, G. (2002). Models of ecological rationality: The recognition heuristic. *Psychological Review, 109,* 75–90.

Gollwitzer, P. M. (1999). Implementation intentions: Strong effects of simple plans. *American Psychologist, 54,* 493–503.

Kahneman, D., Slovic, P., & Tversky, A. (Eds.). (1982). *Judgment under uncertainty: Heuristics and biases.* Cambridge: Cambridge University Press.

Klein, G. A. (1989). Recognition-primed decisions. *Advances in Man-Machine System Research, 5,* 47–92.

Klein, G. A. (1999). *Sources of power. How people make decisions.* Cambridge, MA: MIT Press.

Nisbett, R., & Ross, L. (1980). *Human inference: Strategies and shortcomings of social judgment.* Englewood Cliffs, NJ: Prentice-Hall.

Payne, J. W., Bettman, J. R., & Johnson, E. J. (1993). *The adaptive decision maker.* Cambridge: Cambridge University Press.

Salas, E., & Klein, G. (Eds.). (2001). *Linking expertise and naturalistic decision making.* Mahwah, NJ: Lawrence Erlbaum Associates.

Slovic, P., Finucane, M., Peters, E., & MacGregor, D. G. (2003). The affect heuristic. In T. Gilovich, D. Griffin, & D. Kahneman (Eds.), *Intuitive judgment: Heuristics and biases* (pp.). Cambridge: Cambridge University Press.

Srull, T. K., & Wyer, R. S., Jr. (1989). Person memory and judgment. *Psychological Review, 96,* 58–83.

Verplanken, B., & Aarts, H. (1999). Habit, attitude, and planned behavior: Is habit an empty construct or an interesting case of goal-directed automaticity? In W. Stroebe & M. Hewstone (Eds.), *European review of social psychology* (Vol. 10, pp. 101–134). Chichester: Wiley.

Verplanken, B., Aarts, H., & van Knippenberg, A. (1997). Habit, information acquisition, and the process of making travel mode choice. *European Journal of Social Psychology, 27,* 539–560.

Yates, J. F. (2001). "Outsider": Impressions of naturalistic decision making. In E. Salas & G. Klein (Eds.), *Linking expertise and naturalistic decision making* (pp. 9–33). Mahwah, NJ: Lawrence Erlbaum Associates.

Zajonc, R. B. (1968). Attitudinal effects of mere exposure. *Journal of Personality and Social Psychology, 9*(2).

Author Index

Subject Index

For Product Safety Concerns and Information please contact our EU
representative GPSR@taylorandfrancis.com Taylor & Francis Verlag GmbH,
Kaufingerstraße 24, 80331 München, Germany

Printed and bound by CPI Group (UK) Ltd, Croydon, CR0 4YY

08/05/2025

01864505-0001